To All World Wide Web Publishers

I've known Greg Holden for a long time. He was a quick convert to the Macintosh from the inflexible and kludgy NBI word processors that were the norm for his office at the University of Chicago in 1984. Greg was an early and enthusiastic convert to the Web in early 1994. He explored, he fiddled, he connected, and he pushed his knowledge of the Internet and the Web so that he could see its enormous potential, and its serious pitfalls.

In the space of a year, Greg's become a Webmeister, but he's also leveraged his knowledge about publishing and what constitutes a successful publication into a reflective critique of what's wrong with most WWW publishing today, and how to fix it.

Publishing on the World Wide Web takes even the rawest of Web novices and immerses them into all the issues defining successful versus failed Web publishing. Everything from the technical gimcrackery to the ethical positioning is covered, with stops among various Web publishing techno-continental signposts, including Web servers and browsers, home pages, HTML, CGIs, Adobe Acrobat, No Hands Common Ground, and QuickDraw GX PDDs.

Greg will teach you why, when, and how to publish on the WWW. He'll give you all the details and, more importantly, the contextual clues to make your WWW publishing efforts worthy of praise. Greg puts all of this into a book that, quite frankly, is as easy to grasp as any I've read.

That, of course, is the reason this book is part of the Don Crabb Macintosh Library for Hayden Books. Greg and I worked on its first outlines, on its developing chapters, and its finished product. Greg Holden, my friends, is one of those up-and-coming computer book authors that you'll look back on a few years from now and ask, "hmm, how'd this guy get his start?, he's good." Well, read *Publishing on the World Wide Web* and you'll know the answer. Greg knows how to cover his topics completely, without detouring into baloneyville (a land from which all writers need rescuing occasionally!).

This book captures the essence of the incredible power of hypertext, graphics, sounds, and video clips that can make up a successful WWW home page. But don't take my word for it. Read the book and tell me what you think. *Publishing on the World Wide Web* lives in the Don Crabb Macintosh Library because it delivers the inside goods on WWW publishing from one of its newest experts. Let it be your companion for finding and delivering the WWW pages now percolating in your noggins.

See you on the ether,

Don Crabb
July 1995
Chicago, IL

decc@cs.uchicago.edu
URL: http://cs-www.uchicago.edu/~decc

P.S. Once you get your home pages written, send me the URLs so I can check 'em out and write about them!

Publishing on the World Wide Web

for Macintosh

Greg Holden

Hayden
Books

Publishing on the World Wide Web for Macintosh

©1995 Hayden Books, a division of Macmillan Computer Publishing

Library of Congress Catalog Number: 95-077736
ISBN: 1-56830-228-2

97   96   95   4   3   2   1

Interpretation of the printing code: the rightmost double-digit number is the year of the book's printing; the rightmost single-digit number is the number of the book's printing. For example, a printing code of 95-1 shows that the first printing of the book occurred in 1995.

Dedication

To my wife and partner in crime, Mary, Mrs. Polish-America of 1995, a great writer and editor in her own right, who assumed all the housework and childcare so I could get this book done, and who will, one day, get the attention she deserves. With all my love.

The Hayden Books Team

Publisher

David Rogelberg

Managing Editor

Pat Gibbons

Acquisitions Editor

Stacy Kaplan

Development Editor

Kezia E. Endsley

Technical Editors

Geoff Duncan, Michael Bishop

Interior Designer

Fred Bower

Cover Designer

Sandra Stevenson Schroeder

Production

**Angela Calvert, Jennifer Eberhardt,
Kevin Foltz, Joe Millay,
Erika Millen, Beth Rago,
Gina Rexrode, Erich J. Richter,
Christine Tyner, Karen Walsh,
Robert Wolf**

Indexer

Chris Cleveland

Manufacturing Coordinator

Paul Gilchrist

Production Manager

Kelly Dobbs

Production Team Supervisor

Laurie Casey

Graphic Image Specialists

Becky Beheler, Todd Wendt

Production Analysts

Angela Bannon, Bobbi Satterfield

Composed in

Times and Franklin Gothic

About the Author

A former newspaper reporter, **Greg Holden** is assistant director of publications at the University of Chicago, where he has worked since 1983. He created his first publications for the university using the Macintosh and Apple LaserWriter in 1985. He has a master's degree in English, and when he is not fooling with a Mac he likes to write poetry, listen to music, and play with his two daughters, Zosia, age 2-1/2, and Lucy, age 1.

He and his family live in an old house in Chicago that he has been rehabbing for—well, for many years now. He is also a co-coordinator for the Chicago branch of Jewel Heart, a Tibetan Buddhist meditation and study group.

Acknowledgments

Although publishing on the Web does allow a degree of independence, no publisher should work in isolation. It's always best to assemble a team of professionals to provide input, feedback, and support.

I could not have produced this book without the assistance of my own *ad hoc* team:

My wife, Mary, who not only tolerated my frequent absences but who contributed to the chapter on copyright and copyedited the entire text.

Don Crabb, my tech editor, who forwarded my initial proposal to Hayden, and then encouraged me every step of the way (decc@cs.uchicago.edu).

Roberta Baranowski (my boss), who granted my requests for "just one more day off," and under whose guidance I developed many of the publications skills shared in this book.

Ann Lindner, who helped in ways too numerous to mention.

Tim Webster, who helped make scans, did a lot of research, provided technical input, and never complained when I asked for one more favor.

John "The Usurper" Casler, Hypertext guru, who introduced me to the Web in the first place and who wrote the HyperCard, AppleScript, and FileMaker scripts (John_Casler@paranet.com).

CyberFeminist Susan Soric, champion Web surfer, who had a knack for discovering just the right detail exactly when I needed it, and who uses the Web especially to help women survivors of the war in Croatia and Bosnia-Herzegovina (CyberSue@aol.com).

To the team at Hayden Books, who turned out to be just as nice to work with as Don said they would be: publisher David Rogelberg, managing editor Pat Gibbons, and especially my cheerleader/acquisitions editor Stacy Kaplan, and my patient and vigilant development editor Kezia Endsley, who turned this into an even better book than I originally envisioned.

My two tech editors, Geoff Duncan and Mike Bishop; they not only kept me from looking bad, but I benefited immensely from their experience. Geoff, in particular, provided tons of useful advice and cautionary statements that enriched the text considerably.

Last but not least, thanks to my parents, and to my two gurus—my spiritual teacher, Gelek Rinpoche, and my writing teacher, Molly Daniels.

Contents at a Glance

Table of Contents

Foreword

Well, look: I'm going to write this foreword, readers, but I'm not going to pretend that I'm all that happy about it. Don't get me wrong, here. I know you're probably all excited about the possibilities of the World Wide Web, and that just from flipping through this volume here in the bookstore you've confirmed for yourself that in terms of universal coolness, the Web is better than sliced bread which has been dressed in the cat's pajamas. And I want to tell you you're *right* to think that way, really, even though the very thought of the Web causes the bile to well up from whatever part of whichever bodily system bile is supposed to well up from. I can't remember what it is, because as I'm sure you've gathered by now, the Web has me rather rattled.

I mean, try to see this thing from my point of view. In 1984, with trembling hands and a sketchy list of instructions that an acquaintance had dictated to me over the phone a few hours earlier, I turned on my clunky Corona PC, manually established a 1200 baud connection to a UNIX dialup host, launched a then-alien UNIX program known as Telnet, and after feeding the thing a bewildering sequence of numbers and periods, I was welcomed as a guest into a high-energy physics lab located in Colorado.

At that point, a gauzy apparition shimmered into physical presence right there next to me, accompanied by a fanfare of poorly synthesized electronic horns. It congratulated me on having joined the small-but-growing Net community and promised that though becoming a NetGeek meant never demonstrating an iota of fashion sense ever again, I'd be in for many, many years of incredibly cool online adventures. The apparition then presented me with a list of pizza joints in my area which delivered after 2AM and shimmered away.

And the spectre was 100% correct. Though the tools for navigating the Internet were arcane and poorly documented, I learned them all, amassing knowledge of UNIX, Telnet, Kermit, NNTP, FTP, uucp, and other complex acronyms which I list in the hopes that I'll confuse you enough that you'll be a little impressed. And though learning all of those tools was not unlike falling down and landing on the pocket I keep my keys and Swiss Army Knife in, it wasn't nearly as difficult as meticulously filling log book after log book with electronic addresses, passwords, account names, names of human contacts and dialup numbers…a bewildering array of profane incantations which were required to gain access to Internet sites and information.

But it was all worth it, not the least because to the casual observer, I was some sort of minor deity. I would demonstrate the variety of sources of information available on the Internet, and after ten minutes of fluttering my hands over the keyboard, moving through system after system, flitting through governments, countries, universities, and megalithic corporations, the effect upon my audience was so profound that immediately after switching off my modem, people would pass me babies to bless. Yes, the impact was *that* dramatic. In later years, I began to assemble my own online services, and after a half-hour tour of *those* they'd meekly ask me if there wasn't something I could do about irregular plate tectonics. At the beach, children's beach balls would be carried out by the undertow and their owner's parents would ask me if I wouldn't mind just trotting out there and retrieving it for them. Never underestimate the power of a really good demo.

Then, along comes this hotsy-totsy World Wide Web, and where does it leave me? Now there's no need to know a dozen different Internet tools inside and out. No meticulously maintained logbooks of addresses and passwords, either. Today, any eight-year-old child can, after spending ten or twelve hours installing and configuring software, fire up Netscape or Mosaic or MacWeb, click three buttons, and within moments be counting missile silos in the Ural Mountains, courtesy of a KH-14 spy satellite gatewayed to a CU-CME server. "But look!" I used to pathetically offer, before I rediscovered my pride, "I've just written a macro, which in just a half an hour gives you the weather in Norway!" Then the kids would kick me in the shins and make fun of my clothes before continuing to load up full-motion video clips onto their own personal Web pages.

So you can understand why I'm a little bitter about all of this. I mean, sure, I've still got my Hardware and Science Fiction Geekdoms to fall back on, but nonetheless it'll take me a while to accept the fact that now the doors of the NetGeek club have been thrown open to every Tom, Dick, and Harriet. I'll just sort of soldier on, and occasionally cuddle up with my nine-volume AT&T System V documentation every so often, just for old times' sake.

Still, as a card-carrying member of the human species, I'm dashed proud that a society which dilly-dallied for 30,000 years before developing a combination shampoo and conditioner managed to create something as wonderful as the Web so quickly. It took many years for us to understand the impact that the automobile could have on our society, to see the role it would serve beyond its initial function. Ditto for television. With the advent of the Web, electronic communications is finally beginning to take its rightful place as an integrated component of human society. Unlike all other forms of public communication, which either limit you to a piddling handful of listeners or require you to become dwarfed by the rules and rates of a much larger organization, the Web allows you to put information in the hands of tens of thousands of people cheaply and easily, whether you're a proud member of the proletariat or a cowering part of the industrial bourgeoi…er, I mean, one of those Stalwart Captains of Industry which make our society great.

So read on and learn. Someday you'll tell your great-grandkids about this period of history. And then they'll probably kick you in the shins and go back to their 4-D holoencephalographic trispatial navigators. When they do, listen carefully because you can be sure that wherever I am, I'll be laughing.

Sincerely,

Andy Ihnatko

July, 1995

MacUser magazine

Introduction

Life is full of paradoxes. What seems simple on the surface can turn out to be incredibly complex. What might appear at first glance to be impossible to comprehend can in fact be easy to do.

Publishing, for instance, is deceptively simple. In the same vein, publishing with HTML on the World Wide Web might seem intimidating, but once you understand the basic commands and other organizing principles, it becomes easier than you imagined.

My goal in writing this book is to decode what seems at first glance like incomprehensible computerspeak. I set out to provide only the important information, to explain concepts clearly, and to provide examples that teach you, step-by-step, how to acquire the skills you need to publish effectively on the Web.

Maybe you are a computer person who is always eager to ride the crest of all new waves. This book contains information about traditional publishing that will allow you to consolidate your electronic expertise with communications fundamentals. Maybe you are by trade a public relations writer, graphic designer, poet, printer, or other member of what we now think of as traditional publishing. You will be able to follow my instructions and implement your skills in exciting new ways. Maybe you have a business or hobby that you want to market. This book helps you do so.

The Internet and the World Wide Web are so newsworthy right now that you can hardly go through a day without hearing a reference to one or the other.

For example, in an article in the May 1995 issue of the *Atlantic Monthly,* James Fallows complained about the slowness of files accessed via a modem and then concluded: "You're not missing that much."

I found the article oddly reassuring. If someone in the mainstream media couldn't see the excitement, usefulness, and tradition-shattering impact of this new communications medium, it must still be full of opportunities. It's not yet passé. Now is the time for you and me to take advantage of the electronic publishing revolution.

Fallows' viewpoint is rapidly becoming a single cry in the wilderness. Publishers big and small are jumping enthusiastically onto the Internet. Now the criticism lies in how commercialized the Web is becoming and how it is losing its early innocent charm.

There is some truth to this. But I believe there is no use worrying about it. The best thing to do is to learn how to play the game smart and stake one's claim. The Web allows equal access to small business as well as multinational conglomerates.

Goals of Online Publishing

Everything on the Web cannot and should not look the same as it does in print. But many of the problems and issues facing publishers in both worlds are similar. So are the solutions. It's easy to get so caught up in new technology that it seems everything is new. In fact, the basic goals and objectives are the same as they've always been; only the means of conveying your message have changed.

One fundamental goal of this book is to apply the time-tested principles of print publication—writing, editing, and design—to publishing on the Web. Again and again you'll read references to professionals from whom you can learn. Make use of the knowledge of people who have been at this for a while, whether they are librarians, marketers, or journalists.

It might take only a week or even less to learn basic HTML. But it would take years to master every nuance of publishing. You have to learn these nuances from people who have been doing it for a while. This book places those years of experience in the palm of your hand.

The content published on the Web has to be conceived differently from words printed on a page. Words and headings are skimmed much more quickly onscreen, because they are harder to read and not portable (at least not yet). They're also nonlinear: text and images can be linked to one another in any order, and thus, they have to be arranged neatly and clearly in easy-to-digest chunks rather than huge chapters.

I have tried to balance my own enthusiasm for the Web (which often borders on addiction) with the sort of skepticism that comes from years of making mistakes and enjoying hard-won successes in writing and publishing. There is a lot to consider when you begin to think about putting your stuff before the world. When it's done right, though, it's one of the best things you can do. My aim is to give you the skills to publish your material easily and effectively.

Assumptions

In this book, I am assuming that:

- You aren't an absolute beginner, but already have some knowledge of what the Internet is. If you do need some background on the Internet, see Appendix A.

- You have done some surfing for information on the Web and have some basic experience with navigating in a hypertextual environment.

- You may even have a connection to the Internet and use a browser program regularly.

On the other hand, you should assume that:

- Just because I use Netscape for all the examples in this book and believe it is the best Web browser available, you don't have to use Netscape yourself. You'll also benefit if you use Mosaic, MacWeb, or other software.

- Although the book concentrates on the Macintosh, that doesn't mean it can't be used by someone who works in a Windows or UNIX environment. It's the basic principles of publishing that are important, no matter what tools you use to implement them. And HTML is basically a cross-platform language.

About the Web Site

You'll find a number of useful resources on the Web site for *Publishing on the World Wide Web for Macintosh* that are intended to supplement and update what's presented in the printed book.

The exercises in the HTML Tutorial in Chapter 3 are there so you can do the work on the Web and follow along with the book if you want. The additions to your word processor's spellchecker (Chapter 9) can be found there. So is the HyperCard stack that generates HTML (Chapter 5), as are the current leaders in the "Worst Web Typo" and "Slowest Page to Load" contests.

Because the Web is a great place to update information that's changed since a publication went to press, the Web site also includes updated links to many of the sites listed in the book, as well as corrections and additions that didn't make it as this book went to press.

The URL for the Web site is http://www.mcp.com/hayden/webmacpublishing. Please visit me there!

Book Conventions

The following typographic conventions help to clearly identify various elements in the text so you can more easily understand what's going on:

- HTML code within code lines appears in Franklin Gothic typeface.

- HTML tags within the text appear in all caps and with brackets, such as the <ISINDEX> tag.

- Placeholders for actual values within URLs and tags appear in italic to indicate that they need to be replaced with actual values. In this example:

  <BODY BGCOLOR = "*RRGGBB*">

  RR, GG, and BB would be replaced with the amount of red, green, and blue for your body color, respectively.

- **Bold text** denotes new terms or accentuated words.

- Commands from Netscape and other browsers appear in **bold typeface**.

- HTML Character-entity tags (i.e. ** **) appear in bold to ensure that they stand out from other punctuation.

- URL addresses appear in special typeface to set them off from the rest of the text, such as http://www.mcp.com/hayden/webmacpublishing.

The following graphical elements also denote special text.

Note: Notes provide you with extra information on the topic at hand or provide definitions and background information for new terms.

Tip: Tips suggest new or better ways to accomplish the goal at hand.

Greg's Soapbox

Greg's Soapbox is an aside relating my own experience, suggestions, or preferences when dealing with the Web. These are valuable in that they provide you with suggestions from someone who has surfed the Net.

Warning: Warnings do just that; they warn you of pitfalls, potential disasters, or other blockades to getting your message across.

Where to Find It

The Where-to-Find-It sidebar provides the URL address (for example, http://www.hotwired.com/) of the site mentioned in the particular section. With this address in hand, you can visit the site yourself. If the address doesn't seem to work, check the Web site for this book (http://www.mcp.com/hayden/webmacpublishing) for an updated URL.

Now that I've set the groundwork, read on to find out some of the Who-What-and-Whys of Web publishing: why you should consider becoming an information provider on the Web; what it means to go online; who some of the new electronic publishers are; where you can find examples to help you plan your own publishing efforts; and how to get started with publishing on the Web.

A Note about Accuracy

This book intended to serve as a bridge between the old and the new. Based on my years of experience as a journalist and publications manager, I did my best to convey to you the principles of print media that could be applied to the World Wide Web. They are ideas and skills that have stood the test of time and will be relevant as long as words are used to communicate.

However, having a compulsion for perfection, I experienced moments of panic that parts of my book would become obsolete between the time I sent it to the publisher and the time it hit the streets.

For instance, Netscape Navigator, the browser software I was using to write the book, came out with several new versions of its program while I was in the middle of it. That is why some of the examples use version 1.0N screens and others use 1.1N. At the same time, HTML 2.0 was rapidly evolving into version 3.0. Both versions are discussed in this book.

Home pages whose images I captured one day might have changed appearances or Uniform Resource Locator (URL) addresses the next. In an effort to make the book as useful as possible, I have included exact URLs for many sites. You may, however, try to access some and find that they're not there, or that the appearance of the page has changed.

In other words, my editors and I have made every effort to be as accurate as possible, but we can't ensure all accuracy for locations on the Internet that have changed since the book went to press. Strangely enough, if the Web being constantly in a state of flux creates a problem, that very characteristic of it creates a solution. All you have to do to find the latest information is to check the home page for this book on the Web for updates. And, most important, I have every confidence that the tips and exercises I have included in this book will be helpful for years to come.

A Note about URLs

In the sidebars, you'll find a number of items entitled "Where to Find It" that point to URLs for resources you can find on the Web. A URL is a Uniform Resource Locator. It's the standard address for anything on the Internet.

A URL has three parts:

1. The name of the Internet protocol used (FTP, gopher, HTTP).

2. The name of the Internet host (www.mcp.com, or ftp.apple.com).

3. The folders (if any) your browser has to go through to find the file you're looking for (/hayden/webmacpublishing).

Some URLs can get pretty long and involved if a file is in a folder in a folder in a folder, and so on.

Because this book is about the Web, most of the URLs listed here begin with "HTTP," which stands for HyperText Transfer Protocol. This is the system by which information is transmitted on the Web.

Please disregard any periods at the end of URLs in this book. URLs never have periods at the end. I've only included periods to make them part of a complete sentence. For instance, the URL for this book is http://www.mcp.com/hayden/webmacpublishing, without an ending period (or comma).

Part I

Why You Should Publish
on the World Wide Web

Why You Should Be Publishing on the World Wide Web

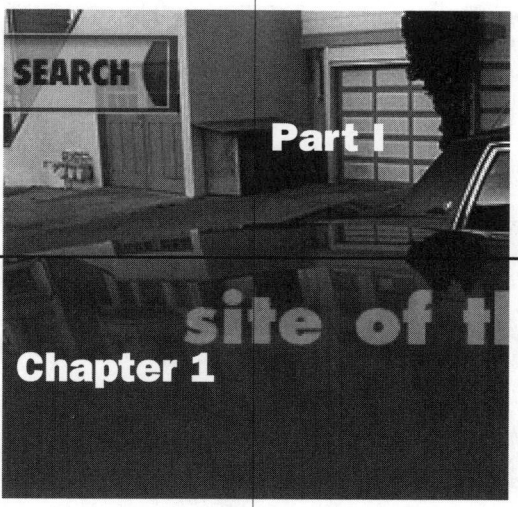

Part I

Chapter 1

Those of us who have been communicating with ink and paper know our limitations. We are accustomed to the constraints of an 8-1/2" × 11" or 4" × 9" world, the size of the paper on which we arrange our words, pictures, and graphics. Printing presses restrain us to two or four colors of ink or, if we are lucky or feeling extravagant, six colors and a coat of varnish. We then spend vast sums of money and psychic energy on the imperfect science of getting our publication into the hands of those who want to see it.

Those constraints begin to vanish when both amateur and professional publishers take their messages to the World Wide Web, the graphical and user-friendly part of the Internet that most closely resembles the look and feel of traditional advertising and print communication.

If you have information to provide or something to communicate, you should be putting your material on the World Wide Web now. A potential gold mine in readership and advertising income awaits you online. Publishing on the Web not only expands your audience, but it puts your words and images before the world instantly (and often, inexpensively), provides you with interactive feedback, and allows you to do a number of things you cannot do in print.

> **Note:** What exactly does it mean to "publish" something electronically? It means that you are making documents, images, or sound files available by posting them on a computer connected to the Internet. This computer is a *server* that serves your files to users. Either you own and operate the server, or you pay an Internet service provider to include your files on their server. Your documents can then be seen on the Web by anyone who is using a Web browser program such as Mosaic or Netscape and who has the URL address for the file or files you want them to see. Usually, publishing suggests words and images printed on paper. On the Web, it can mean a number of different things such as text, graphics, sound, animation, color, and video. Case studies of articles on the Web are presented in Chapter 2.

The Audience

What's the rush? For one thing, the potential market is enormous. Although no one knows exactly how many people are on the Internet, conservative estimates have quoted the figure of 20 million users worldwide. (Lately, people have been estimating 40 million Internet users.)

The Web has been the fastest growing part of the Net, swelling from a few thousand users just a few years ago to more than 13 million today. Some sites with particularly "hot" or new information get as many as 100,000 visitors a day, or even a million per week.

A survey conducted in April–May 1995 by the Georgia Institute of Technology indicated that the typical Web user is 35 years old. More than 80 percent are educated white males. Most work with computers. In other words, there is a huge audience of young professionals and avid consumers currently surfing the Net, just looking for people who have information to convey.

Ten Advantages of Going Online

Here are ten reasons why you should be publishing on the Web right now:

1. *Instead of a local audience, you reach the whole world.* For a poet or artist, the implications are exciting: instant readers, without having to face rejection from publishers. For any organization, going on the Web is a way to get immediate, worldwide attention. Publishing on the Web can be a boon to a local magazine or newspaper as well (see item 3).

2. *The start-up investment in both time and personnel is low*, considering the audience that can result. One commercial service provider in my area charges only $30 per month for unlimited access to the Internet. A good Web site can be set up by only one, two, or three talented people.

3. *You get a huge new audience* for your advertisers that can be identified and packaged. If you wish, you can compile marketing information to get a snapshot of your audience.

4. *You aren't limited by what you can print on paper*. You can go beyond words and photos to include sound and video. If you are adapting an existing publication for the Web, you can include material that wasn't in the original booklet or brochure—add some notes or hypertext links to other related publications.

5. *What you publish is not the "last word."* Most sites on the Web are continually "under construction." While it's important to clearly define what you want to say and how you want to present yourself, the Web allows you to build your online publication in stages, and to revise it on an ongoing basis.

6. *You can publish much more on the Web than on paper.* Because what you're publishing resides on electronic media and not on paper, you don't have to

worry about your publication fitting in an eight-, sixteen-, or forty-eight page format. You are limited only by the storage capacity of your server.

7. *Immediacy* is one of the Web's greatest advantages. On the Web, time is no longer a limitation. Information contained in a paper publication that is printed monthly or bi-monthly, for instance, can be updated more frequently online. A meeting or seminar that is suddenly scheduled won't make it into your periodical, but you can put the announcement on the Web.

8. *Publishing on the Web evens the playing field among information providers.* The Web is a true democracy. Small organizations or individuals have a voice as loud as a large multinational corporation's. On the Web, customers can't tell if you have $20 million or $20 in assets, 10,000 or ten employees. The one who gets the most attention is the one who presents the best content and has the most attractive Web site.

9. In some cases, putting your booklet, catalog, or brochure on the Web *can allow you to eliminate a print publication altogether,* thus saving the cost (financial and environmental) of printing.

10. *Reading in a hypertext environment is fun.* It allows the reader to navigate easily in a nonlinear way, and if you haven't had the time or person-power to create an index for your catalog, that's not a problem on the Web, because the reader can do textual searches.

The Web versus Commercial Services

The millions of people who already have accounts with commercial online services such as Prodigy, CompuServe, or America Online may be wondering what all the fuss is about. Why should they go through the trouble of downloading a browser and making the first tentative "surfing" runs across the Web? What can they get on the Web that they don't have already?

The commercial services have no doubt of the Web's importance: they all provide access to the Web one way or another, thus giving their subscribers a gateway to a whole new world of information. One significant difference is that, on the Web, you can publish information about yourself or your organization in a much more attractive, organized, and extensive way than on a commercial bulletin board service.

When you connect to CompuServe, Prodigy, or America Online, you only have access to what that particular commercial provider has arranged for you to see. You can get on "chat" lines, download software, send and receive email, and read newspapers and magazines. You can't put out much news about yourself, unless you want to pay a fee to that commercial provider and start "Your Own News Service, Inc.," for example.

Note: Some large-scale news operations whose contracts with commercial online services were expiring in spring 1995 were opting not to renew those contracts and start up their own operations on the Web, to save money and have greater control over content. America Online announced in June 1995 that it would offer a standalone Internet service along with its commercial online operation.

The Web, in contrast, lets most people with a dedicated Internet connection or access to a server put out at least a "home page" of information that can include words, images, audio, or anything the user/designer wants the online world to see.

Users who have not only a connection but also a computer designated as a server and the right server software can set up their own Web site to publish substantial amounts of information and to market their goods or services.

The Web gives you the ability to connect to a far wider range of sites than any one commercial service can provide. The contents are not limited to one central location but originate in offices, homes, and businesses all around the globe. The selection of Web services hasn't been predetermined or edited by anyone, which has both good and bad points.

On the downside, the Web is short on organization, and puts a premium on the user's ability to search, explore, and randomly encounter information. Sites are often amateurish. Information changes constantly and without warning. (All of these can be advantages for potential publishers because if their home pages are attractive and well-organized, they are likely to be way ahead of the competition.)

The Web is an unordered, loosely regulated, unpredictable, personal, and immediate mass of information that you can explore for hours and that can lead you down any number of paths to things you never expected to discover. If, like me, you consider all of these characteristics to be potential assets, the very things that make it an exciting medium for communication, read on.

Some Disadvantages

There are, of course, some *real* disadvantages that Web publishers have to accept. For instance, in most cases, unless you use specialized software such as Acrobat or Common Ground (see Chapter 8, "Preserving Your Publication with Portable Document Software"), you don't have control over how your product looks on the reader's computer screen. Type sizes and styles depend on how the users have configured their Web browsers; theoretically, your document might appear ten different ways on ten different computers. (In truth, though, most people stick to a common typeface like Times as their default, so your document's appearance is *somewhat* predictable.)

You can spend hours designing complex graphics in, for example, Adobe Photoshop, but they will appear no sharper than the resolution (usually 72 dots per inch) of the screen on which they appear. In fact, designers for the Web are faced with the unusual challenge of having to scale down a publication's graphics—making them simple and small so that they appear quickly on the computer accessing them over the Internet.

It's great to have the ability to update and correct your home page after it's on the Web, but you have to make sure someone is going to assume responsibility for doing updating and maintenance. (See the section entitled "Staff Considerations: What's a Webmaster?" that follows.)

How to Become an Information Provider

If these considerations haven't dulled your eagerness to begin Web publishing, you may be asking yourself how to get online. Here is a quick rundown of some basic steps:

- Assess your goals (see the section "Why Do You Want to Do This?" that follows).

- Decide how much money you want to spend or save (see the section called "The Money Question" that follows). Your bank account has a bearing on the next step.

- Decide if you are going to set up your Web server yourself, or if you are going to buy space on one of the many Internet providers around the country. Going with an Internet provider is fine if you want to publish a home page or related pages, or even a publication like a magazine. It saves you from having to buy and maintain hardware and software, for instance, but you will pay a monthly fee (see Appendix C for more information on providers).

- On the other hand, you should set up your own Web server if you work at an educational or government institution, for instance, and are lucky enough to have a direct connection to the Internet already, or if you are setting up an extensive corporate Web site and have the time, money, and personnel to devote to the project.

If you have decided to set up your own Macintosh-based Web server, you need:

- A direct connection to the Internet (see the following section for more information).

- A dedicated computer to act as the server (explained next).

- Someone to maintain the site (see the section "Staff Considerations" that follows).

- Server software such as WebSTAR or MacHTTP.

- An IP address and domain name servers for your site.

- CGI-type scripts to capture data, process email, allow searches, or provide other functions (explained in Chapter 5).

- A home page for the server (in addition to home pages for the various operations, departments, or individuals who will be providing information on the server) (explained in Chapter 3).

Why Do You Want to Do This?

If you have purchased this book, you are probably committed to publishing on the Web. The place to start is to assess your goals and ask yourself why you want to go online.

There are plenty of pages on the Web that serve as what one marketing expert calls "information dumps"—repositories of useless or outdated material. Many home pages seem to be created for no other reason than personal vanity.

To avoid falling into this category, always ask yourself: What is the impact or effect I want to have? How will my Web publication further me or my business? What will it do for my strategic message? How does it fit into my overall communications plan?

The right answer is this: Publishing on the Web is the best way to accomplish your long-term goals. The next chapter talks more about goals and objectives, but keep that in mind for now.

The Money Question

You also have to decide if your Web publishing effort is intended as a money-making or money-saving venture. If you're hoping for substantial income from going on the Web, be realistic about it.

The World Wide Web is literally an open market. There's almost no control over what goes out on the Web or who has access to it. Because the Web is so loosely organized, there are no pointers to assure that viewers will get to your site by name recognition alone. That puts the burden on you to make your content as interesting and attention-getting as possible.

Some publishers (particularly news services) are beginning to charge subscription fees for full access to some of their content. But it's uncertain how much money can be made from this. If you can attract advertisers (like the jewelry store mentioned in Chapter 2), your site could turn out to be lucrative.

The prospect of saving money by going online is a more likely one. You may be able to eliminate some "throwaway" publications by publishing them online.

If paper and postage costs continue to rise the way they have in recent years, some publishers, particularly newspapers, may *have* to publish online just to stay in business.

Staff Considerations: What's a Webmaster?

No, it's not a new comic book superhero. It's the person you may have to hire to help you get on the Web and to maintain your site once you get there.

Again, there's a substantial difference between a simple personal publishing operation and a large-scale one. If you are putting a home page or pages on a site operated
by an Internet provider, the provider's staff is likely to act as the Webmasters.

A company or large organization with its own Web server will need to designate
someone to perform the following Webmasterish functions, none of which requires
superhero strength, but mostly takes time and technical ingenuity:

- Make sure the correct HTTP server software is on the server.

- Create the actual HTML documents for the site.

- Organize and keep track of the files so they don't change location suddenly,
  thus breaking everyone in the organization's existing links to them.

- Write or find Common Gateway Interface scripts or other tools for processing
  forms, performing searches, and providing other functions such as counting
  how many people have visited a site.

Where to Find It

Where do you find a Webmaster?
The best place is on the Internet.
If you see a home page or site that
displays some technical expertise
and common sense, approach the
author. Also try posting a message
on a Usenet newsgroup in your
area that lists job openings.

- Answer questions and educate
  others in the organization about the
  Web, the Internet, and going online.

- Troubleshoot when something goes
  wrong.

- Process email inquires about the
  site and forward them to appropriate staff members.

- Update what's been published to
  avoid having a "cobweb site" (a site
  whose contents aren't current).

The Importance of Maintenance

That last point in the previous section deserves some elaboration. Updating is
essential: it's embarrassing to have someone type in your URL address and discover
information that's already out of date, or plainly inaccurate. In the Web, as in life,
increased opportunities bring increased responsibilities, and you should take them
into consideration before you begin to write your first HTML document.

You have to decide how often you're going to update—if another office or department sends you revised information for your catalog, for instance, are you going to drop all other projects and put the information online immediately? You may want to decide to let the revisions pile up and have the Webmaster put them on your server only once a week, or once a month.

Getting Connected

Note: Web server software is available not only for Macs but also for Windows, VMS, and UNIX. You can also run UNIX software on a Mac. Because this book focuses on publishing on the Web for Macintosh users, however, I concentrate on Macintosh computers and server software.

First, you need a connection to the Internet. Then, you need a Macintosh computer dedicated solely to the task of acting as a Web server. The bandwidth of your connection is essential—without a connection good enough to handle a large number of simultaneous connections, it doesn't matter how fast your computer's processor is. Those are the two most important pieces of hardware you need to become an information provider.

The Computer

The general perception persists that Macs are inferior to UNIX servers because, for instance, the Mac operating system does not support multiple threads. Also, servers running MacHTTP software can only handle a limited number of connections at once (although the new commercial version of MacHTTP, called WebSTAR, extends MacHTTP's functionality considerably).

On the other hand, Mac servers are generally less expensive than UNIX equipment, and are a good option if you are just starting out in Web publishing and don't want to make a big investment at first. Mac servers are also more difficult to "hack" into than UNIX machines.

So, how powerful a Macintosh computer do you need? Very simple servers have been set up on computers as humble as a Macintosh Plus (although I wouldn't recommend it). As a general rule, the faster the better. The important thing is that it is a dedicated server that isn't used for any other purpose. That's what will be required to accommodate all the visitors you'll receive when you create a professional-looking Web publication using the techniques described in this book.

The Connection

To be an information provider, you have to have a direct connection to the Internet, whether you are fortunate enough to work in an educational or governmental institution that has one, or whether you buy space on an Internet provider.

The number of Web readers who can access your site at one time is determined by the bandwidth of your connection to the Internet. A relatively simple connection, such as that afforded by a 28.8kbps modem, won't allow many simultaneous users. (You shouldn't be running a Web server with a dialup connection, anyway, if you can avoid it.) I recommend faster ones, such as a 56K frame relay or even a more expensive T1 or ISDN line. (See Appendix C for more information.)

The Software

You have to have a piece of Apple Computer software called MacTCP installed on your server. This is the software that allows the computer to exchange data with other computers on the Internet. Use version 2.0.4 or higher.

Next, you need to install the software that will allow your computer to use HyperTalk Transfer Protocol (HTTP), the language of the Web. The Mac

---

Where to Find It

MacTCP 2.0.4 can be downloaded at ftp:/ftp.info.apple.com/Apple.Support.Area/Apple.Software.Updates/US/Macintosh/Networking.and.Communications/Other_N&C. For information on setting up a Web server, go to http://web66.coled.umn.edu/Cookbook/contents.html.

Where to Find It

WebSTAR is available for purchase at http://www.starnine.com/. However, MacHTTP 2.2 can still be downloaded for free from the Web. One location is ftp://ftp.uwtc.washington.edu/pub/Mac/Network/WWW/MacHTTP2.2.sit.bin. You can find out about another server product for the Mac, NetWings, at http://netwings.com.

---

environment uses WebSTAR, formerly called MacHTTP. You simply download
MacHTTP on your server and you're on your way.

There are a number of server software options for the Macintosh, but the most
popular is MacHTTP, written by Chuck Shotton of BIAP Systems. It is currently
being sold by StarNine Technologies as WebSTAR. WebSTAR runs faster than
MacHTTP and comes with AppleEvents scripts, Adobe Acrobat reader software,
and other tools.

Where to Find It

Some good instructions on setting
up a Web server on a Macintosh
computer can be found at the
Web66 site: http://
web66.coled.umn.edu/. A
sample list of some MacHTTP
servers arranged by type of
computer is at http://
www.ape.com/machttp_talk/
machttpservers.by.mac.html.

The Address

You will also need to get an IP (Internet
Protocol) address for your server from
your Internet service provider or network
administrator. This will be a formidable-
looking series of numbers, such as
195.99.89.00.

An IP address should, however, be aliased
to one or more recognizably human
domain names. This is called Domain
Name Server (DNS) service. This is
usually your host's name with periods
separating the various components, such
as www.mysite.org. DNS can also be
handled by your Internet provider, who is responsible for registering such names
with a group called InterNIC.

Implications for Publishing

How did all this come about? Did the Web's creators have publishing in mind when
they conceived it? Some aspects of the publishing revolution were anticipated by
one of the principal architects of the Web, Tim Berners-Lee, in a 1992 article in
which he envisioned the "market economy in information" that we are now beginning to see. The elimination of the conventional publishing industry was not one of
the outcomes he foresaw, however—just the opposite:

" . . . publishing houses, far from being unnecessary, will be in for exciting
times. Their jobs and those of librarians seem to have merged into one as
classifiers and reviewers of the world's knowledge."[1]

These are certainly "exciting times" for people who have something to communicate. It's long been a theory of mine that everyone has something to say, whether
they know it or not. But not everyone has a place to speak or a means to be heard.
The Web gives you that. The writer of fiction, poetry, or drama who has been
working in isolation can find a place to get his or her stories or poems read, or to
connect to other writers.

Does this mean that would-be novelists will no longer submit their work to publishers, and that fewer and fewer novels will be printed? Will the Web make books and
magazines obsolete? What does the Web mean for those of us who are still involved
in conventional print publishing?

One likely answer is that publishing on the Web can work together with conventional
publishing: the Web can act as a tool to help authors produce books much more
quickly and efficiently for those publishers.

With the World Wide Web, the landscape of publishing has changed dramatically, in
a way that can make production easier and quicker. One of the original goals of the
Web was *centralized publishing:* easy access via the Internet to source material,
instruction manuals, reference books, and the content of your work (your notes,
drafts, images, and sounds).

You also have access to people who are important to your project—your collaborators, your proofreaders or editors, and your readers or customers. The means of
production may be far flung, but as long as they are connected by the Net, they are
all accessible from a computer. What makes the Web unique, however, is that it
provides the means of *distribution* as well.

Experience the Web

No book, CD, disk, video, or television show about the Internet or the World Wide
Web can convey the excitement of centralized publishing on the Web because that
depends on your own individual interests and how you absorb information. You have
to *experience* it to truly appreciate it.

I, personally, have done the following things on the Web: researched my family tree and discovered where my great-grandfather lived in 1905; discovered a "virtual" outlet for antique fountain pens, which I collect; put out some of my prose and poetry; and completed most of the research for this book.

When I was trying to learn how to draw a clickable imagemap in the shape of a mandala, a Tibetan tool for meditation, I was able to look up some photos of real Tibetan mandalas for inspiration. To solve a problem using Mac-ImageMap, a program for creating imagemaps, I emailed the author of the program, Lutz Weimann, in Germany. I was happily surprised to find Herr Weimann's answer waiting for me the following morning. In Cyberspace, nothing is two thousand miles away, and almost no one is unreachable. It's all right there, waiting for you to make the connection.

In the next chapter, you see how other people are making the connection so you can get some ideas for yourself.

[1] Tim Berners-Lee, "Electronic Publishing and Visions of Hypertext," *Physics World* 5 (June 1992), 14-16.

Strategies for Publishing on the Web: Case Studies

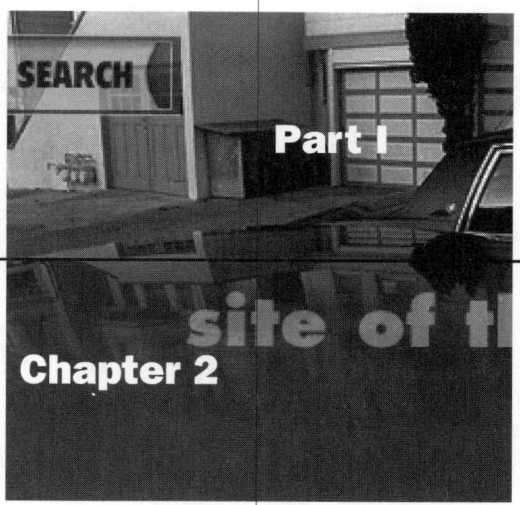

SEARCH

Part I

Chapter 2

site of t

If you have purchased this book, you have already decided that you want to publish on the World Wide Web. The next step is to ask yourself the all-important question: Why?

Assessing Your Goals

You're going to be reading the word "goals" a lot in the pages that follow. To my mind, you can never think about goals too often, no matter what you're trying to accomplish.

Begin by asking yourself: What are my goals in going on the Web? Think before you leap. There are plenty of "information dumps" on the Web whose contents are useless or outdated. And it's becoming alarmingly easy to get lost in the burgeoning crowd of electronic information providers.

If you plan ahead, learn from what others are doing and map out a strategy; your site will be a valuable part of your communications effort. By learning the skills taught in this book, you'll reap the benefits of going on the Web and you'll stand out from your competitors.

Evaluating Publications Strategies

Oooh, there's a pompous heading. This isn't as intimidating as it sounds. It means that instead of simply presenting a long and not-very-useful list of "cool Web sites," I've selected some sites that illustrate practical aspects of providing information on the Web. This chapter examines how some publishers have confronted particular problems or issues so you can develop strategies for your publishing effort. I'll leave the surfing for "cool sites" up to you.

> **Note**: A number of URLs are given in this chapter (and throughout this book) for information about software or other resources. At the end of each address, I've typed a period to avoid being cited by the grammar police. Be aware, though, that the period is not part of the address. For instance, a correct address would be "http://www.sgi.com" and not "http://www.sgi.com."

Case Studies

Because you are probably wondering who I am and what kinds of publishing I've done throughout my former lives, I'll start by sharing some examples I've worked on. Then I'll give a quick overview of how some traditional publishers (such as newspapers) and some nontraditional ones (businesses both large and small, but mostly small) are jumping on the Web and becoming more successful because of it.

Greg's Soapbox

You'll notice that most of the examples in this chapter come from individuals or comparatively small organizations who are publishing on the Web. Why aren't any multinational conglomerates mentioned? Because this is a list of sites that I like for one reason or another or that illustrate a particular aspect of Web publishing. My intention is not to provide a comprehensive list. I'd have to fill a CD-ROM with an encyclopedia of Web publishing to accomplish that goal. (Hey, not a bad idea, actually. Where did I put the telephone number of my editor at Hayden?)

Catalogs and Databases: Two Options

My first case study is the College Research Opportunities Program (CROP) Directory, which is used to match professors at the University of Chicago with student assistants. The listings it contains describe the work, tell whether a position is paid or unpaid, indicate qualification requirements, and so on. It has a small but enthusiastic audience, but is useful only for a short period.

Where to Find It

The University of Chicago CROP Directory is at http://www-college.uchicago.edu/crop/crop.html. For more information on converting a FileMaker database to HTML, see Chapter 5.

For many years, the CROP Directory booklet was printed twice a year, just before the beginning of a quarter. Students then picked it up from various distribution points around campus and contacted professors that were doing research that interested them. It cost about $1,500 to produce each issue—which contained about 56 pages, stapled together, and printed as cheaply as possible.

Last year, the directory went on the Web for the first time, and this year, the printed version was eliminated. (All students at the U of C, as at many universities, have access to the Internet and Web and can ask for help in getting connected if they need it.)

The data processing process was streamlined, and the university saved money. Having the information online (see Figure 2.1) means students can examine it faster and easier than they could before. The shelf life of the printed booklet was only a week or two, but the information is now useful longer because it can be updated frequently.

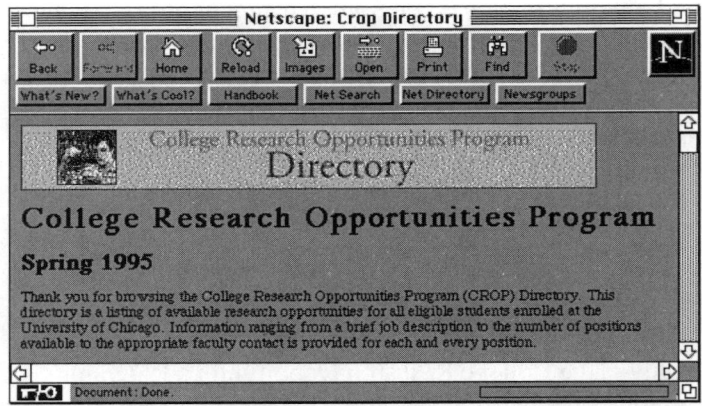

Figure 2.1 Online CROP directory home page.

How was it done? Creating the home page was the easy part. Gathering the data and formatting it so that it would appear on the home page in just the right way was not quite as simple, but let me describe the process because you might adapt it for your own projects.

Let's begin at the beginning.

> **Note:** What's a home page, anyway? A home page is like the "front door" to your Web publication. (Tim Berners-Lee, the person primarily responsible for creating the World Wide Web, prefers to call it a "welcome page," which pretty much describes its function.) This is the page that you want visitors to see when they first come to your Web site. It is the place where you introduce the site and give visitors some idea of what its purpose is, what they might find in it, and how they can get to specific documents in your site or to other, related sites or resources on the Internet.

How was this home page created? Many of the basic steps are covered in more detail in subsequent chapters, but here is a quick summary:

1. They defined the plan and the goals: allow faculty to input data directly into the database rather than having to retype all submissions; put the contents of the database online; make the database automatically generate reports such as indexes; and eliminate the printed booklet.

2. They wrote the text, organized the contents, and selected an image for the logo.

3. They scanned and saved the image and the logo in Graphics Interchange Format (GIF).

4. They created the actual home page document by typing the commands that are part of Hypertext Markup Language (HTML) into a word-processing document, the text-only markup format used to mark up text and images so they can be correctly interpreted and displayed by a Web browser such as Netscape, Mosaic, or MacWeb.

5. They put the home page document on a Web server—a computer connected to the Internet and equipped with special software such as MacHTTP. MacHTTP (once shareware, now a commercial program called WebSTAR) that allows that computer to *serve* documents to a Web browser that connect to it from elsewhere on the Internet.

    You can look inside any home page to see the source HTML used to create it. This is a great way to learn how to create your own Web documents. Figure 2.2 shows the source HTML for the CROP home page shown in Figure 2.1.

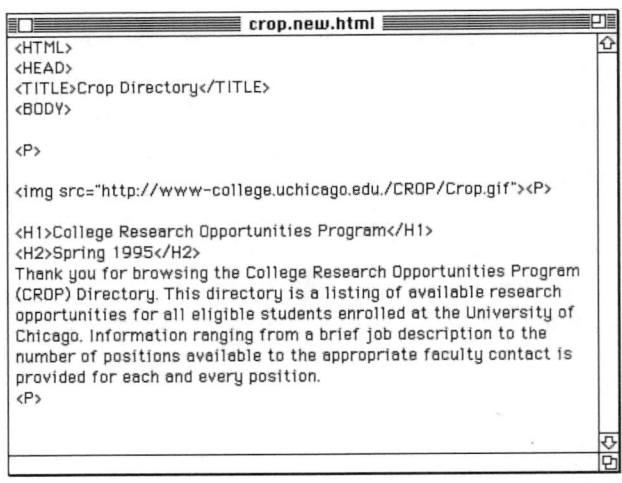

```
crop.new.html
<HTML>
<HEAD>
<TITLE>Crop Directory</TITLE>
<BODY>

<P>

<img src="http://www-college.uchicago.edu./CROP/Crop.gif"><P>

<H1>College Research Opportunities Program</H1>
<H2>Spring 1995</H2>
Thank you for browsing the College Research Opportunities Program
(CROP) Directory. This directory is a listing of available research
opportunities for all eligible students enrolled at the University of
Chicago. Information ranging from a brief job description to the
number of positions available to the appropriate faculty contact is
provided for each and every position.
<P>
```

Figure 2.2 HTML commands.

As you can see, the HTML commands are enclosed by the less-than (<) and greater-than (>) symbols. The actual text that appears onscreen is not enclosed. The words <IMG SRC> stand for "image source" and specify what GIF image is to appear in the document (in this case, the logo). H1 and H2 are heading styles. <P> specifies a paragraph. That's about it. As you can see, HTML is amazingly easy to learn. By the time you get to Chapter 7, you'll be an expert.

To gather the data from the faculty, a clever programmer and friend of mine, John Casler, created a data entry form in Word, and then created a script in a program called HyperCard to translate the Word data into FileMaker.

For the next step, that is, to take the FileMaker Pro database and put its data online, John created "scripts" (a series of commands or routines that tells a computer program to perform some function). These scripts convert the data in each of the FileMaker fields to HTML commands so that they can be displayed on the Web (see Figure 2.3).

I'll grant you that this publication isn't going to win awards for its design, but the important thing is that it accomplishes its purpose well.

On the positive side, the University pared $3,000 a year from its publications budget and has a more useful publication. On the negative side, considerable work was involved in doing the conversion, and someone has to perform additional work updating and preparing the HTML files. As a result, the College made a commitment

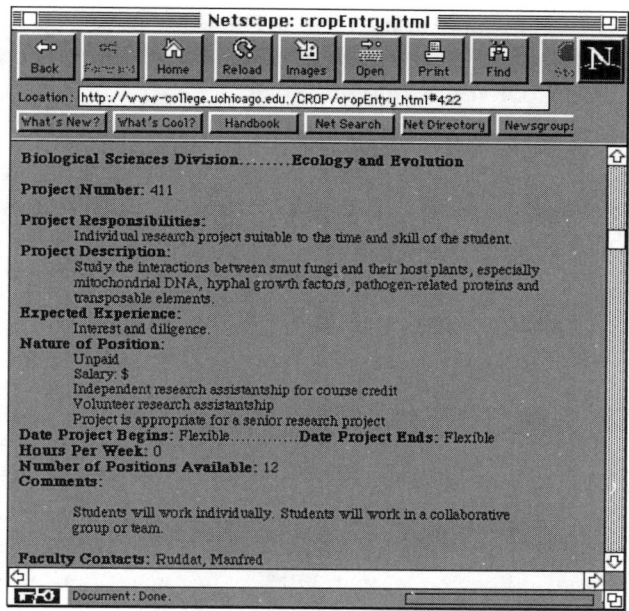

Figure 2.3 A CROP directory listing.

to communicate with students on the Web by hiring a part-time computer expert to act as Webmaster and maintain its Web server.

Michael Jones, assistant dean of the College of the University of Chicago, is pleased with the results: "We are able to keep the document more current," he says. "It is a more valuable resource for students. We can make changes to it instantly, if we want to."

A Not-So-Successful Story

I found out the hard way that if you don't have the staff available to do the work, a Web publication that seems good in theory won't actually come together in reality. The College hopes one day to streamline production by going on the Web with its massive (496 pages) course catalog, which costs about one dollar per copy to print.

The catalog consists of 50 sections, each one a separate Word document. The idea was that all of those Word files could be converted to HTML documents and put on the Web in the time (three weeks) that elapsed between submitting camera ready art to the printer and delivery of the books.

But the book's production came at the most hectic time of the year, and all available hands were busy meeting other deadlines. A student was hired to do the conversion of files, but that alone took her a solid three days. The work required to edit the HTML documents and create navigational links had to be spread out over several weeks.

The moral: converting long word-processing documents to HTML and publishing them on the Web doesn't happen by magic. Make sure you are able to find the extra money and staff time it takes to go online before you make promises you won't be able to keep.

Newspapers on the Web

Newspapers are used to putting out substantial amounts of information in a short amount of time. They ought to be well suited to going on the Web. The question is how to make it a lucrative operation, and how to do it right by making the commitment up front in time and personnel that will produce benefits later. Several examples follow that demonstrate different strategies for how newspapers can use the Web to supplement their paper publications.

Where to Find It

TimesFax, the Internet edition of *The New York Times*, is at http://nytimesfax.com/. In early 1996 a new version of the *Times,* including images and searchable ASCII (unformatted digital) text, is scheduled to be available on UMI, a Michigan-based information provider opening its own Internet service. UMI is at http://www.umi.com/.

Strategy One: Provide a Condensed News Summary

The New York Times sends an eight-page fax version of the first edition of each day's newspaper to 150,000 readers around the world. It's a radically condensed version of the paper that includes front page, business, foreign, national, and sports stories, as well as a recent (not current) TNYT crossword puzzle (see Figure 2.4).

The strategy with the *TimesFax* is to quickly and easily take an existing

34

Figure 2.4 Web version of *TimesFax*. (Property of *The New York Times*.)

summary of a newspaper and make it available on the Web in a format that preserves the look of a newspaper, with the official logo and newspaper-style columns.

To accomplish these goals, *TimesFax* is published on the Web using a program called Adobe Acrobat. Acrobat and other similar software programs preserve the layout of a document, including original typefaces and photos, by taking a computer "snapshot" of it. (See Chapter 8 for more information on this "portable document software.")

35

You'll notice that at the bottom of the page there are two display ads. Clicking them takes you out of the *TimesFax* home page and onto the home page of the respective advertisers, Advil and AT&T.

For a publisher, the merits of online advertising are obvious: it can help pay the costs of going online, buying a server, paying a Webmaster, and acquiring software.

For the advertisers, the benefits are less clear; the pros and cons are discussed further in Chapter 13, "Advertising on the Web." The company can put out a lot of information about itself on its own site. But an obvious problem for the original site is that a reader who clicks an advertiser's hypertext link will be taken away from the original site and may or may not return.

Note: Hypertext is defined more fully at the end of Chapter 4, but basically, it allows you to navigate through information or between computers by clicking text or images that serve as a clickable link. The link then takes you to another location in a matter of seconds. You may have seen this in action in the Help files offered by many word-processing programs. Click one item in a list of topics, and an explanation appears instantly onscreen. Hypertext is one of the features of the World Wide Web that make it such a user-friendly way of navigating the Internet. Virtually all sites and documents on the Web can be accessed by such links.

Strategy Two: Be More Comprehensive/More Immediate than a Newspaper

Sometimes a news story is so compelling that you just can't read enough about it. A news story in a paper, or even a television documentary, leaves you hungry for more. You don't even want to wait for the paper to come out or the paper isn't available in your area. You want to see a story as soon as it hits the wire. For you, the Web is a dream come true.

The *Tacoma News-Tribune's* online publications provide several options for news junkies who want more news faster than they might get in a paper. And, of course, the implications for citizens of countries where the government has tried to censor the dissemination of news and opinions are astounding.

Where to Find It

You can find a list of online newspapers at Yahoo, an excellent index of information that attempts to bring order to the information on the Web. Go to http://www.yahoo.com. A list of links to commercial news services and other journalism resources on the Internet can be found at http://www.jou.ufl.edu/commres/.

The *News-Tribune's* Internet newspaper, Trib.com, allows you to search headlines and live AP wire feeds. The site requires you to register before giving you full access to the news content.

The *News-Tribune* is also using *TRIBweb* to branch out beyond the confines of traditional journalism (see Figure 2.5). It has offered books for sale, trout fishing tips (remember, it's located in Washington state), and selections from the *Vladivostok News,* as well as a searchable index of movie reviews.

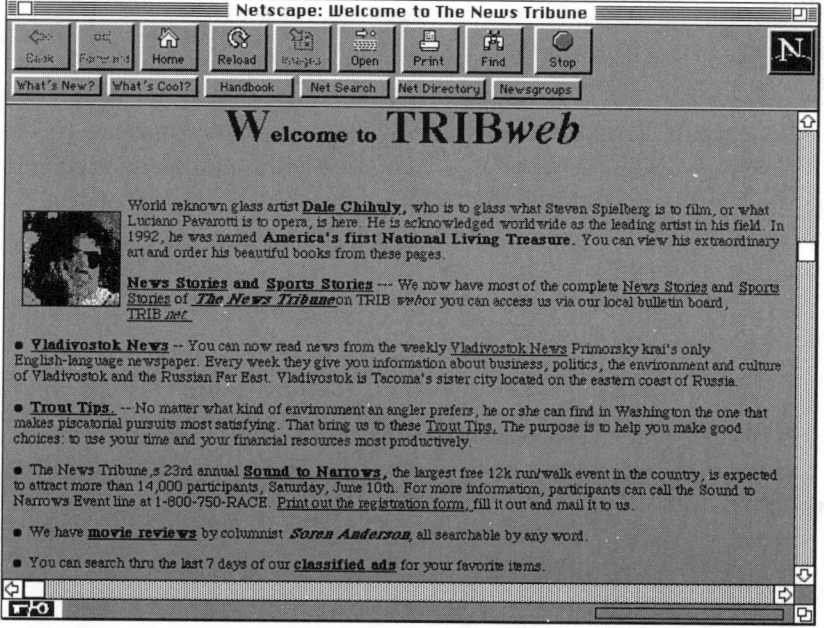

Figure 2.5 *TRIBweb* online news service.

Where to Find It

The *Tacoma News-Tribune's* Web site, *TRIBweb,* is at http://www.tribnet.com/.

Where to Find It

NandO.Net, the online service of the *News & Observer* of Raleigh, North Carolina, was the first major newspaper on the Web. It allows you to search the Reuters wire service as well as some AP wire stories. The address for NandO.Net is http://www.nando.net/.

Where to Find It

The Mercury Center server is at http://www.sjmercury.com/.

How does the paper get so much news onto the Web so fast? It uses Common Gateway Interface (CGI) tools that take the newspaper's stories and format them three different ways:

- In Microsoft Word format for a fax version of the paper.

- As unformatted ASCII text to go on a bulletin board service.

- As HTML documents for the Web.

Strategy Three: Design a News Service for the Web

The site that most people in the Bay area refer to when they think of a newspaper on the Web is the Mercury Center server of the *San Jose Mercury-Tribune.*

What makes Mercury Center such a good Web publication? It isn't just an attempt to transfer some of a newspaper's content to the Web; it's a publication designed specifically for the Web.

It uses the basic elements of a Web home page rather than a newspaper page—there's a consistent logo at the top of each section; buttons used to organize stories; and short summaries of stories that lead to full versions.

Searchable Ads

Mercury Center allows free access to headlines and summaries but charges a monthly fee for access to full stories. Access is free, however, to one of its best resources: a searchable database of more than 10,000 classified ads.

Personalized News

One of Mercury Center's features, Newshound, personifies the wave of the future in the business of news gathering: personalized newspapers (see Figure 2.6). Automated searches from papers is among the services offered, which is something you can't do with the paper that is thrown on your doorstep each morning. (Figure 2.6 is reprinted with permission of Mercury Center, http://www.sjmercury.com.)

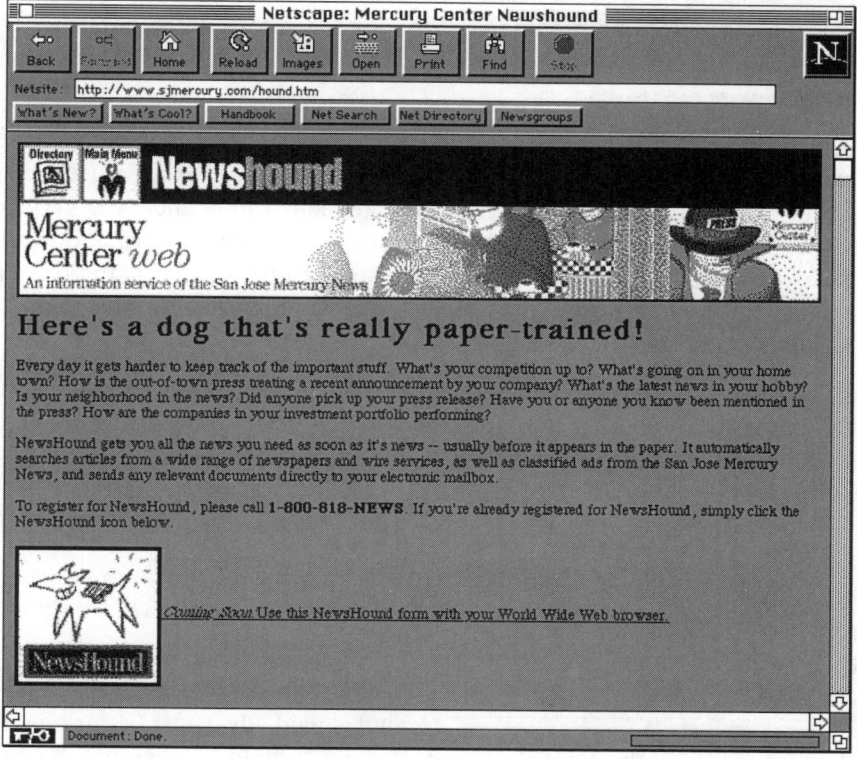

Figure 2.6 Newshound page.

Online Options for Magazines

Immediacy is a problem for magazines that are published weekly, or monthly—but a Web version of a magazine can get the word out faster than in print, and often, in even greater depth.

Option One: Complement Your Other Publications

A Web site can be an effective complement to a printed publication or other non-digital media (such as radio and TV stations). A printed magazine, for instance, can refer readers to its Web site, and the Web site can serve to promote the printed publication, as well as to enhance the kinds of information it delivers.

Mac/Chicago magazine, a regional magazine for Macintosh users, publishes bi-monthly in print, but its Web site allows it to bring more timely information on local and national events to its readers.

The Web site (Figure 2.7) has also enabled the magazine to reach a broader spectrum of readers than it formerly could with a small marketing budget. Because the site is included in various Web indexes such as InfoSeek and Yahoo under the very common words "Macintosh" and "Chicago," Web readers seeking information about the city of Chicago or the Macintosh see the Web site's address listed in the search results, and some have followed the link and discovered Mac/Chicago. In this way its Web site helps bring new readers to the print magazine.

Says Editor & Publisher Jennifer Dees, "Our Web site lets us do things we couldn't do in the magazine alone. For example, if we review a CD-ROM in the magazine, we can include a video clip from it on the Web site."

Where to Find It

Mac/Chicago's Web site is at http://www.macchicago.com/.

Mac/Chicago's print edition also refers readers to the Web site for links they can follow to contact companies whose software or hardware products are reviewed in the magazine.

The Mac/Chicago Trade Directory, which includes paid advertiser listings, is included in each issue of the print magazine. But the digital version on Mac/Chicago's Web site is searchable. It also has hyperlinks built-in, so the user can just click to contact an advertiser via email for more information. In some cases, the user can also click a graphic that takes them to the advertiser's own Web site.

The Mac/Chicago site also includes links to the sites of local user groups and related professional associations.

Figure 2.7 Mac/Chicago home page.

Option Two: Provide Exciting Content and Design

Any survey of publishing ventures on the Web has to include *HotWired*, the online vehicle of *Wired* magazine, which has been on the Web since October 1994.

HotWired tries hard to be outrageous, shocking, and fascinating and, for the most part, it succeeds.

No matter what you think of *HotWired*'s design, you have to acknowledge that it is successful. As of summer 1995, *HotWired* had 215,000 registered users, with between 1,000 and 1,500 new registrants per week. Reportedly the publication has more advertisers than it has advertising space. *HotWired* wouldn't confirm this to me, but did say that its current "open rate" for advertising is $7,500 for a two-week run.

In contrast to Mac/Chicago's tiny staff, *HotWired* has more than 40 people working on its amazing, eye-catching design (the screen shot in Figure 2.8 doesn't do it justice; you have to see the site in color). The large staff is able to generate content that (with the exception of one section, "Fetish,") is totally different than *Wired* magazine's.

Like a growing number of Web publishers, *HotWired* requires its readers to register before they are allowed access to the entire publication. The registration form includes all-important ZIP codes used to compile marketing data.

The publication also provides other ways for members of its audience to interact with it: they can download movie or audio clips and they can discuss whatever is on their minds in the "Rants and Raves" section.

HotWired requires users to enter an extra security feature—a verification number—to get its full range of user services, including the ability to create a custom home page containing user-selected contents. And every time you reload a page, the graphics change!

Ross Van Woert of *HotWired* provided this description of what it's like to work there:

> "*HotWired* and *Wired* are both great places to work. Both operations are in the same building south of Market in San Francisco; in fact, we are across the hall from each other. There is always music playing on the respective sound systems; people staring intently, and intensely, into computer screens (mostly Macs, plus a few Silicon Graphics workstations at *HotWired*). People are constantly cruising through and between the two work spaces, holding animated discussions....This place has a lot of energy coursing through it."

Where to Find It

You can get connected to *HotWired* at http://www.hotwired.com/.

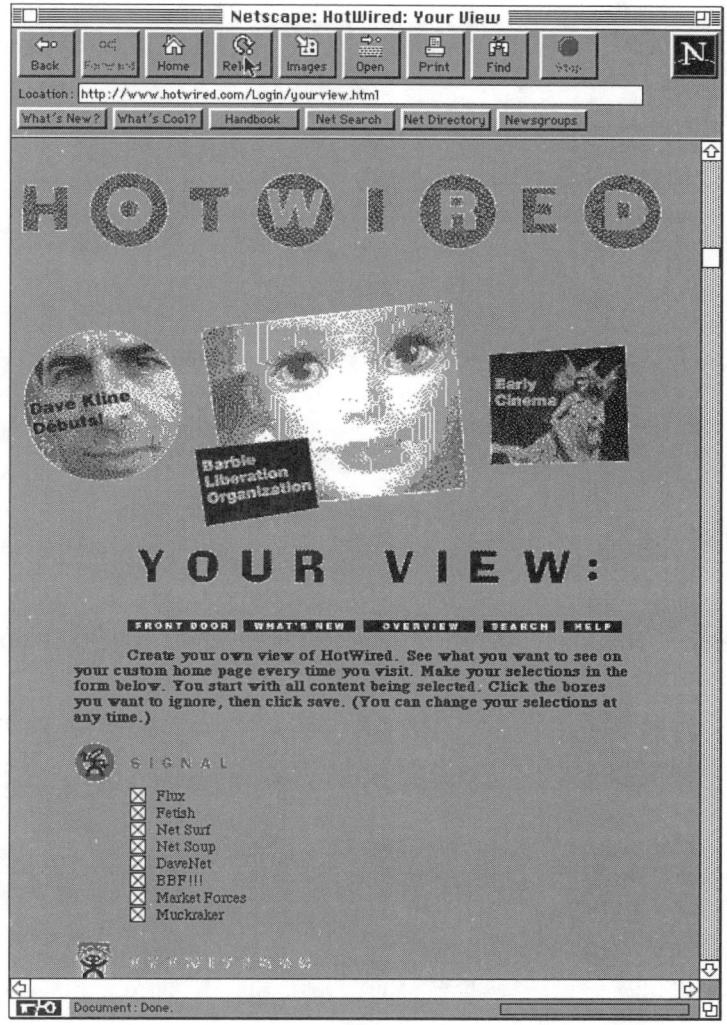

Figure 2.8 *HotWired*'s "Your View" page.

Online Strategies for Colleges and Universities

The Web will become an essential medium for promotion and communication for institutions of higher education as more prospective students, alumni, and high school guidance offices get connected to the Information Superhighway or whatever the Internet is called in years to come.

Right now, though, the Web is useful for a relatively small but growing audience, and increasingly indispensable for current college students and faculty. Many universities now offer free access to the Internet to students and staff. The Web is used to publish class schedules, reading lists and assignments, course descriptions, and any number of student newspapers, magazines, and manifestos.

The Problem: Coordination

The problem with putting a large university on the Web is the coordination effort. Universities consist of many different departments, each one populated by individuals who are clever enough to set up a Web server and a home page.

Where to Find It

A list of college and university Web sites is at http://www.mit.edu:8001/people/cdemello/univ.html. The University of Michigan Home Page is at http://www.umich.edu/.

Unlike a large corporation, a university that isn't very centralized can't always make those departments do things the same way. Does a university attempt to get all of its departments to work together to create a consistent and coordinated presentation? Are the various academic units left to their own devices? Or is there a middle ground: an official university home page, and independently designed departmental Web servers?

There is no simple answer. Each institution has to reach its own solution. I provide examples of how some are approaching the issue to help you identify your needs and wishes.

The Coordinated Approach

The University of Michigan took an approach that would be good for any large institution to follow. A committee that included the university's communications office and various campus librarians undertook the Information Gateway Project to organize U of M's online presence. Their goals were *information* and *access*. Their policy statement reads, in part:

> "The Digital Library program was established to create a comprehensive, well coordinated, and cohesive environment for the information resources of the university and to create for users the means to locate, organize, and use information. To that end, the digital library should provide both a unified view of UM resources as well as the flexibility for alternative portals to information systems and services."

Take away "university" and "UM," and substitute your own organization's name. Whatever the group, this is a good model for a mission statement.

Where to Find It

A description of how Carnegie Mellon came up with its logo and how it is intended to be used can be found at http://www.cmu.edu/cmufront/style-guide/style.guide.html. The university's home page is http:/www.cmu.edu/. Another impressive university Web site is operated by Carleton University in Ottawa, Canada: http://www.carleton.ca/.

Carnegie Mellon University

Carnegie Mellon, through its Front Door project, is attempting to come up with a visual identity on the Web (see Figure 2.9). The university created a series of standard mastheads used on home pages published by any of its departments. It can't force offices to use the logo; it can only recommend its use.

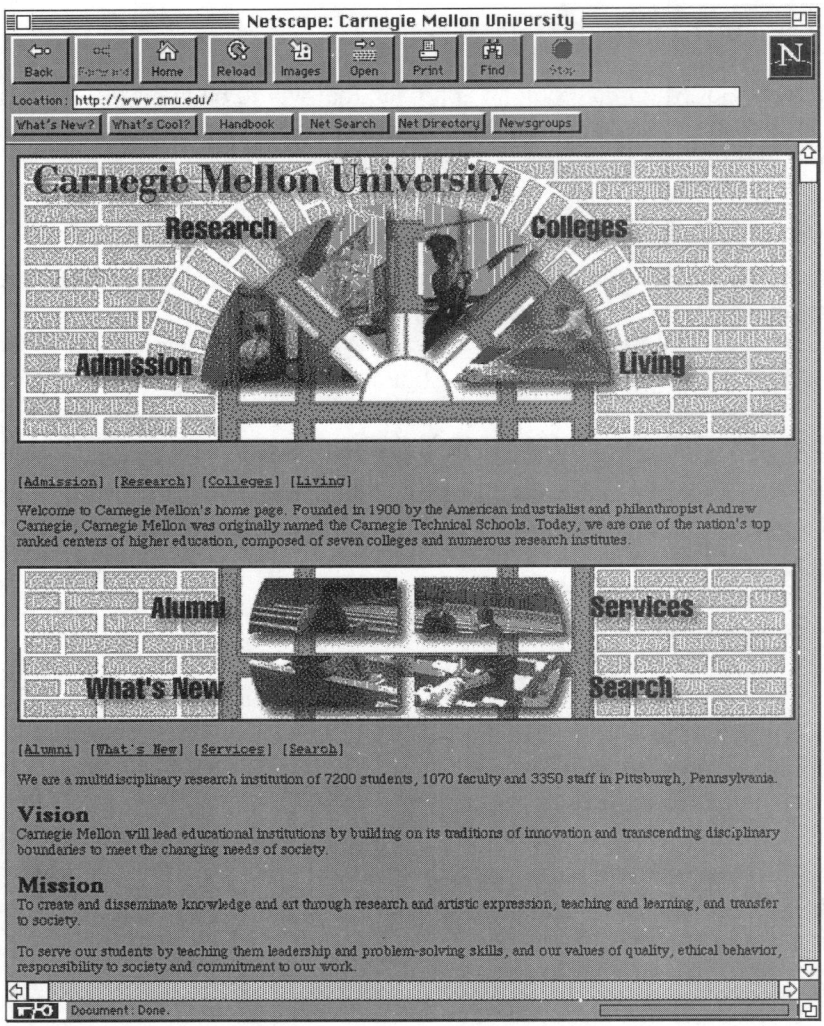

Figure 2.9 Carnegie Mellon University logo and home page.

The Phoenix Project, the University of Chicago

The Biological Sciences Division of the University of Chicago has an extensive and complex Web site that will soon be used to provide coordinated class information for much of the campus: room locations, class assignments, and so on.

Where to Find It

The gateway to Phoenicia, the Phoenix Project of the University of Chicago's Biological Sciences Division, is at http://www.bsd.uchicago.edu/.

Phoenicia allows users to navigate by means of objects. Clicking one of the objects doesn't just take you to a link; each button activates a CGI script on a Phoenicia server that calls up the requested information. Its Virtual Campus employs an elaborate series of campus maps; clicking a building takes you to various photographic views of that building (see Figure 2.10).

A Student Magazine: the Online Bucknellian

Where to Find It

The Online Bucknellian, as well as a link to "Dave," can be found at http://www.bucknell.edu/bucknellian/. Jeff Boulter is also well known on the Web for his CRAYON software: http://www.eg.bucknell.edu/~boulter/crayon/.

What do you do if you have a printed magazine and you need a fast, easy method of converting its contents to the Web? If you're Jeff Boulter, a student at Bucknell University, you use your initiative and write your own conversion program, and then put the program on the Web for others to try.

Jeff puts out a student magazine called *The Bucknellian* using the PageMaker page composition program (see Figure 2.11). When Jeff first wanted to publish an online version of the magazine on the Web, no utility was available to translate PageMaker documents to HTML.

So, Jeff wrote Dave (that's the name of the program), a PageMaker to HTML conversion utility. He reports that alumni particularly appreciate receiving the Web version of the magazine. (Adobe has since announced that a future version of PageMaker will export files directly to HTML.)

Jeff reports that the online and printed *Bucknellians* differ in that there are no ads on the Web version, and only a few photos and graphics.

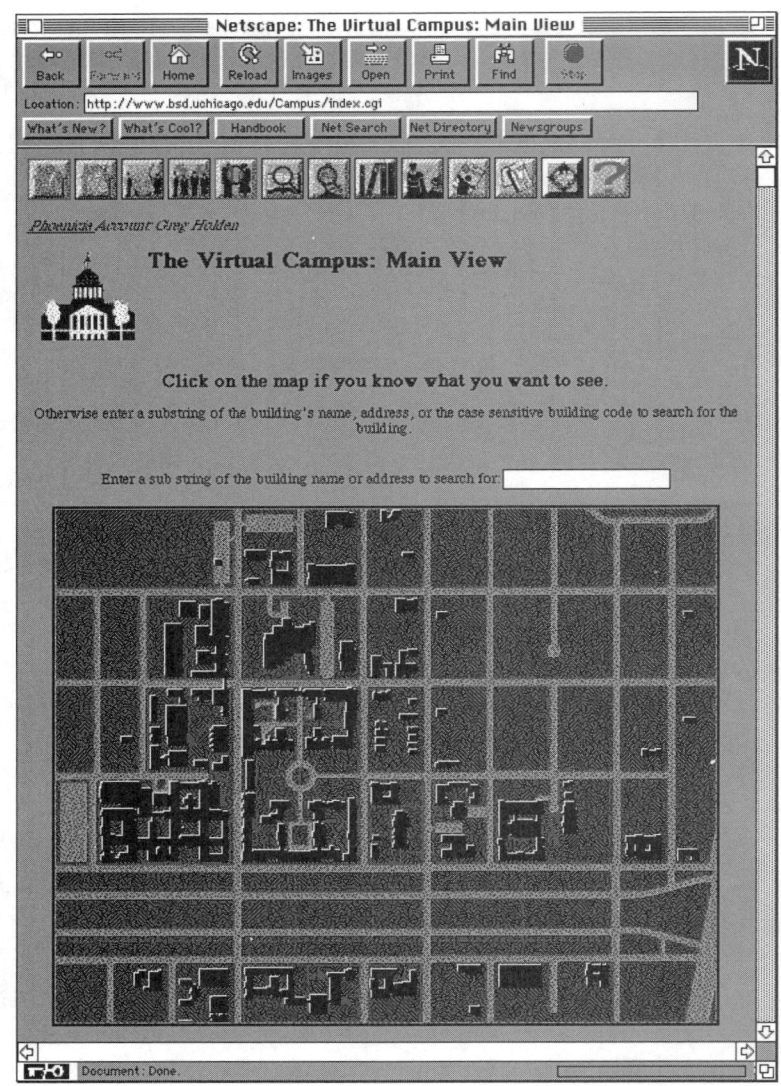

Figure 2.10 The Virtual Campus, part of the Phoenicia server.

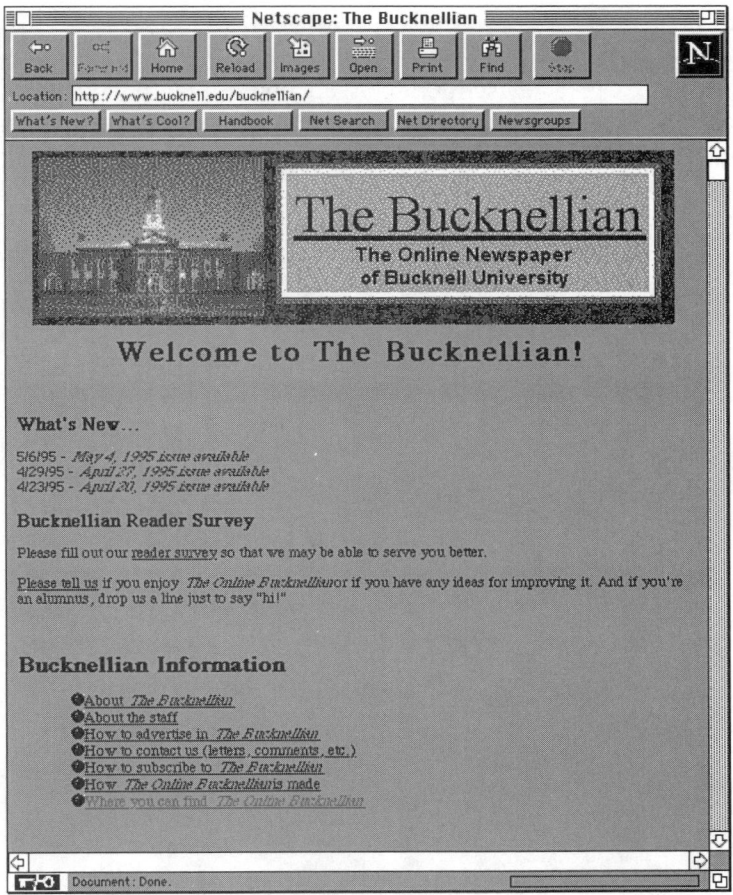

Figure 2.11 Online Bucknellian.

The printed publication comes out about 25 times per year, and work on the Web version begins as soon as the printed *Bucknellian* goes to the printer. Occasionally, while the *Bucknellian* was at the printer, the Web version was being converted to HTML and came out before the printed publication. "This makes a big difference to people who are far from Bucknell and who wouldn't get their paper until next week," Jeff says.

University of Chicago Magazine

You don't need a slick gateway script or conversion utility to put documents on the Web, however. The magazine published by the University of Chicago in cooperation with the Alumni Association does a pretty good job of converting its printed contents to the Web and adding the HTML instructions (see Figure 2.12).

Figure 2.12 U of C magazine.

Where to Find It

The University of Chicago
Magazine is at http://www.
uchicago.edu/alumni.mag/.
Oberlin Alumni Magazine can be
found at http://www.oberlin.
edu/alumni/alumni.html. As
this book was being written, there
was talk of the magazine's location changing, as well as the use
of Acrobat. You can also check
Oberlin's Web site for more
information: http://
www.oberlin.edu/.

After the magazine is printed, the stories
are saved in a standard ASCII format, and
then converted to HTML. Some conversion utilities are listed in Chapter 7, but
often it's easier to enter the commands
directly in a word processing program.

Oberlin Alumni Magazine

If you want to preserve the original look of
your program with its nice graphics and
color photos intact, and with the ability to
attach supplementary notes, put it out using
the Acrobat portable document program
mentioned earlier (see Chapter 8 for more
information).

Linda Grashoff of Oberlin College publishes an online version of the *Oberlin
Alumni Magazine* using Acrobat. To see the magazine in its Acrobat format, readers
first have to install an Acrobat Reader utility on their computers (which is free).
However, to reach those readers who don't want to use Acrobat, it's also necessary
to put out publications in an alternative format.

Virtual Shopping on the Web

This might not seem like publishing, but it is. You can take an existing business or
hobby and, by creating a home page and setting up your own server, you can find a
new market for your product or service on the Web.

A Web Site for a Small Business

You don't have to be in the business of providing information to publish something
about you or your organization on the Web. Even a relatively small business can see
benefits from an online presence.

Where to Find It

The URL of Steve Quick Jeweler's site was changing as this book was going to press. The original address was http://www.ECHI.com/SQJ.html. (Note that this URL is case-sensitive—you have to use capital letters.) If you can't locate the site there, do a search using the keywords "Steve Quick" or "Steve Quick Jeweler" and you should find it.

Steve Quick is president of Steve Quick Jewelers, which is located at 2426 North Clark Street in Chicago. His customer base was mostly local before he and an associate set up a home page on the Web in late 1994 (see Figure 2.13).

Since then, he's sold diamond wedding bands to Web customers from Texas, Maine, and Nebraska, and received inquiries from all over the United States and Canada. He's in the process of setting up two new diamond-related Web sites, and even received a call from an advertiser offering him $1,500 per page to provide a link to the advertiser's site on each of his home pages.

Although his regular walk-in business continues to provide him with many valued customers, the money he's made from the Web site has more than paid for itself. Web clients don't make their purchases over the Internet but, for added security, call a toll-free phone number provided online.

With a new site he's planning, Steve plans to target potential customers who, because they live outside large urban areas, often have to pay higher prices for diamonds than, say, New Yorkers or Chicagoans. The site will include information on how to buy a diamond, as well as jewelry for sale from his stock and that of two other large merchandisers.

"This has added an entirely new dimension to my business, and shown me a path to the future," Steve says.

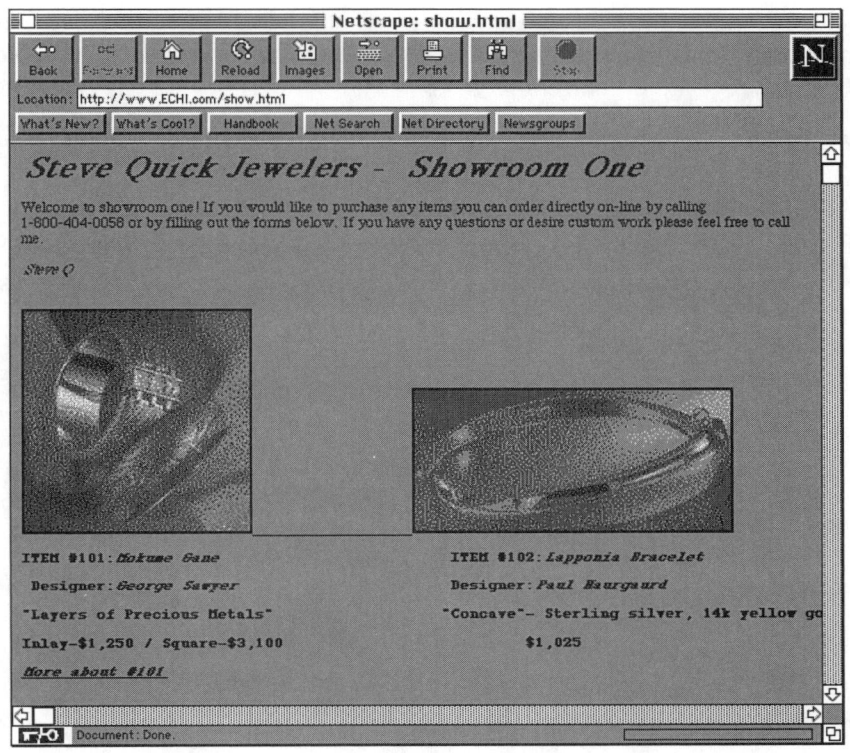

Figure 2.13 One of Steve Quick Jewelers' showroom pages.

Useful, Well-Organized Content: A Big Business's Web Site

I know I said earlier that I wasn't going to include any huge conglomerates in this chapter. But I couldn't resist mentioning Apple Computer's Web site because I visit it often to find useful documentation and software.

The main selling point for all Web sites is information, and large businesses have an advantage over smaller ones because they have plenty of content they can put on the Web. The strategy is to organize it well.

In Apple's case, they follow a good organizational practice (explained further in Chapter 11) of coming up with five or six main topic headings on their home page. Each topic can lead the reader through paths of information to find specific topics or products (see Figure 2.14).

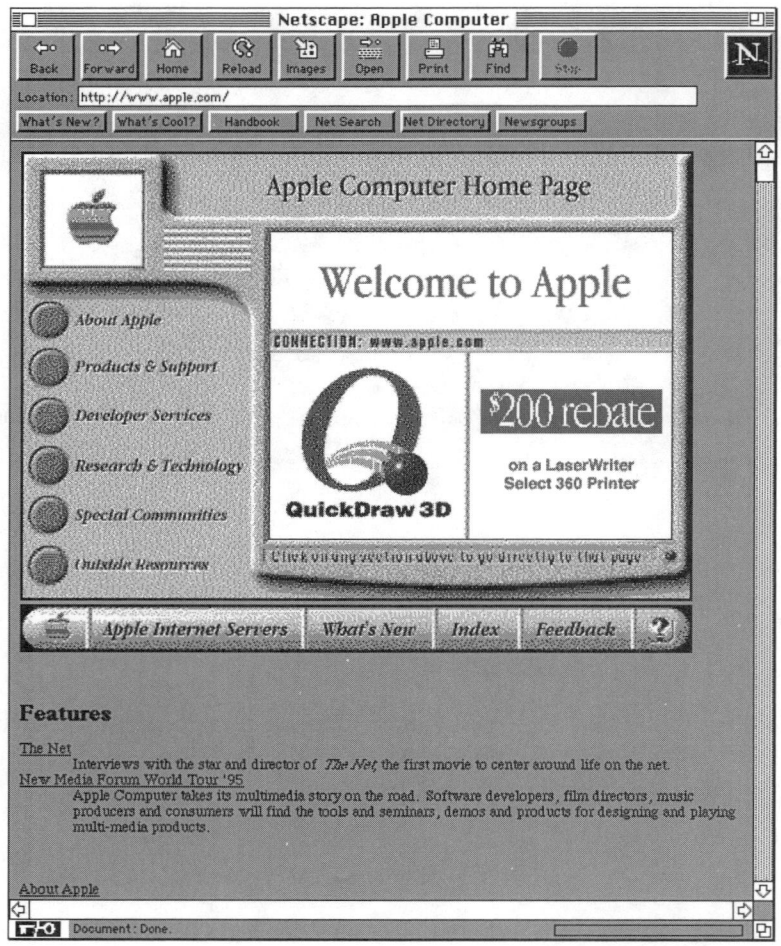

Figure 2.14 Apple computer home page. (Property of Apple Computer, Inc.)

Turn Your Hobby into a Business on the Web

Jim Monroe is a pen collector based in Pennsylvania. He sells fine vintage fountain pens in an online shopping mall called Cyteria Plaza. I'm a pen collector myself, and was happily surprised when Jim was able to fulfill an online request by turning up a cap for my Conklin Crescent Filler. In turn, I sold him an adjustable nib for an Eversharp Doric (please excuse the pen talk).

Where to Find It

Cyteria Plaza is at http://www.netaxs.com/people/labenski/plaza.html. A link to Monroe's Pen Shop is included on this page.

The thing that's impressed me about Jim's site, aside from the photos of the pens he has for sale, is the extensive form he has customers fill out. Jim pays a small monthly fee to have his home page listed in Cyteria Plaza. The server, in turn, provided some CGI scripting to process the data requested on his form. (His son Mark helped with the scripting and the setup.)

Forms make two-way communication between publishers and readers on the Web easy and immediate. A fill-out form can be created to let users interact with information providers by allowing them to make comments, request information, or tell the publisher something about who they are or where they live.

After filling out a form, a customer clicks a button that sends or "submits" the data to the host's server where it is processed by means of CGI scripts that reside on that server. If you can create a form and either write the scripts or find someone to write them for you, it's great for business (see Figure 2.15). (Some examples of CGI tools appear in Chapter 5, "Advanced HTML.")

Jim says the site has attracted only a "moderate" amount of attention, but he's sure "it's just the beginning, because the Web is in its infancy." He's sold or repaired pens for customers as far away as Korea.

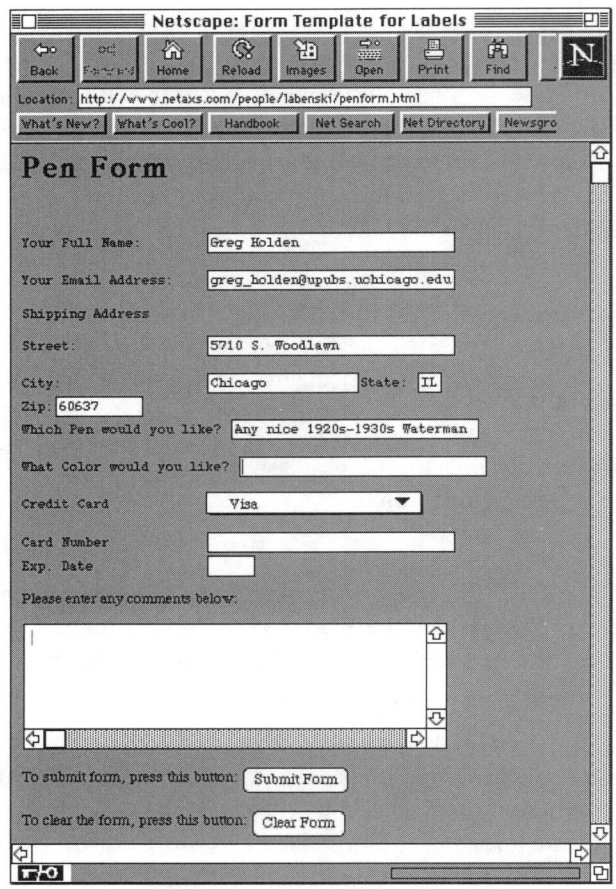

Figure 2.15 Order form.

Strategies for Book Publishers on the Web

Providing publishing order forms so customers can find and purchase books online
is just one of many techniques being tried by the rapidly growing number of book
publishers jumping on the Web.

A May 1995 article in *Publishers Weekly* estimated that 229 publishers already had a
presence on the Web. Some of the biggest ones, including Random House and
Bantam Doubleday Dell, were working on their own Web sites.

Where to Find It

Want to visit a publisher on the Web that doesn't really exist? The trials and tribulations of MCI's fictional company, Gramercy Press, are detailed at http://www.mci.com/gramercy/.

Where to Find It

A list of bookstores can be found in one of the other big Web indexing resources, the World Wide Web Virtual Library: http://www.comlab.ox.ac.uk/archive/publishers/bookstores.html. Another list is can be found on the BookWeb server: http://www.ambook.org/bookweb/sellerlist.

The Web allows book publishers not only to publicize the titles of current and forthcoming books online, but also to pursue some other marketing/sales strategies, including:

- Gathering marketing data through online book order forms.

- Including outline and sample chapters of books for review.

- Providing downloadable versions of entire books that people can purchase online and copy onto their computers without ever visiting a bookstore or waiting for their order to arrive in the mail.

- Creating an information center or discussion group related to a book or topic.

Discount Purchases

If you sell a book directly over the Internet and bypass the usual distribution and sales channels (in other words, it isn't sold through a bookstore), you can offer discounts and other advantages to customers. You can advertise all of your titles in one place, and provide a way for online bookstore customers to search for a specific title or author.

Macmillan Computer Publishing's online bookstore (see Figure 2.16) lists more than 1,100 titles and gives shipping and sales discounts to Web customers.

Figure 2.16 Macmillan Computer Publishing online bookstore.

Home Pages for Member Bookstores

Want to become a clearinghouse for information in your field? Offer as many services as possible, and give others a chance to post home pages on your site.

BookWeb, the Web site of the American Booksellers Association (ABA), allows member bookstores to create and post their own home pages. It also conducts "Internet Chats" with noted authors and provides breaking news about events such as the ABA Convention (see Figure 2.17).

Figure 2.17 BookWeb home page.

continued

Where to Find It

General information about lily can be found at http://www.lily.org/. A set of FAQs about Internet Relay Chat is at http://www.kei.com/irc.html. Homer

Chat Lines on the Web

The Web is not equipped to handle chat lines directly through browser software, but there are a couple of ways you can set up a chat line on your Web publication. Of course, you have to announce to your audience when you will be opening your group for discussion, and explain how to connect.

and IRCLE can be downloaded from the Info-Mac directory or any of its mirrors, such as ftp:// ftp.tidbits.com/pub/tidbits/ tisk/tcp/.

One option is to conduct or get involved in an Internet Relay Chat (IRC). You have to download one of two pieces of software onto your computer: Homer IRC Client or IRCLE IRC Client. You open Homer IRC and connect to a server that is set up to run an IRC.

Another way is to connect to lily, a Computer Mediated Communications (CMC) server. You have to log in to lily with telnet, or use another client. At the time I was writing this section, BookWeb was conducting chats online through lily with guest speakers at the American Booksellers Association's annual convention.

A Resource for Buyers and Small Booksellers

Besides listing books being offered by a number of smaller publishers, a bookstore (or other business) with a Web site can set up a bulletin board service where customers can exchange information and post classified ads. There's one on the BookZone home page (see Figure 2.18).

Greg's Soapbox

Web surfers are impatient. I'm no exception. If I don't remember the name of the publisher or author of a book, it's easier for me to use a search engine like InfoSeek or WebCrawler to search a specific title across the entire Web rather than to look through dozens of publishers' individual Web sites. The future for book publishers (as for other industries) may be collaboration rather than competition—the creation of a central resource or true "one-stop shopping" site containing a meta-index of searchable titles for potential Web customers.

Figure 2.18 BookZone home page.

Where to Find It

BookZone's Home Page is http://www.ttx.com/bookzone. Bookport is another good resource: http://www.bookport.com/.

Pointers to Resources: Museums and Libraries on the Web

Sometimes, the way to make a good presence for yourself on the Web is to be organized. You can set yourself up as a clearinghouse of information contained in other sources, as well as provide your own stores of information online.

Where to Find It

The Library of Congress Home Page is at http://lcweb.loc.gov/homepage/lchp.html. A link to Walt Whitman's lost notebooks can be found at http://lcweb2.loc.gov/wwhome.html. Another popular Web site, the congressional server THOMAS, is at http://thomas.loc.gov/.

Just look at the Library of Congress server. It's averaging over 40,000 visits (or in Web parlance, "hits") each day. Why? Because it offers a lot of well-organized content about this country: its governmental agencies, history, and heritage.

Among other things, the server presents special electronic versions of some of the Library's exhibits. You can find email addresses for members of Congress, excerpts of early movies, and historic photos. To give a personal example, the reproductions of the "lost" notebooks of Walt Whitman were among the most exciting things I've ever found on the Web.

The strategy Web publishers should take note of is the way the Library has organized pointers to information that it doesn't possess. In particular, when you click the link "World Wide Web" you are taken to a list of resources and guides on the Web and HTML (see Figure 2.19). To make your site useful, consider including a similar list of links to related sites and resources you've found useful on the Web.

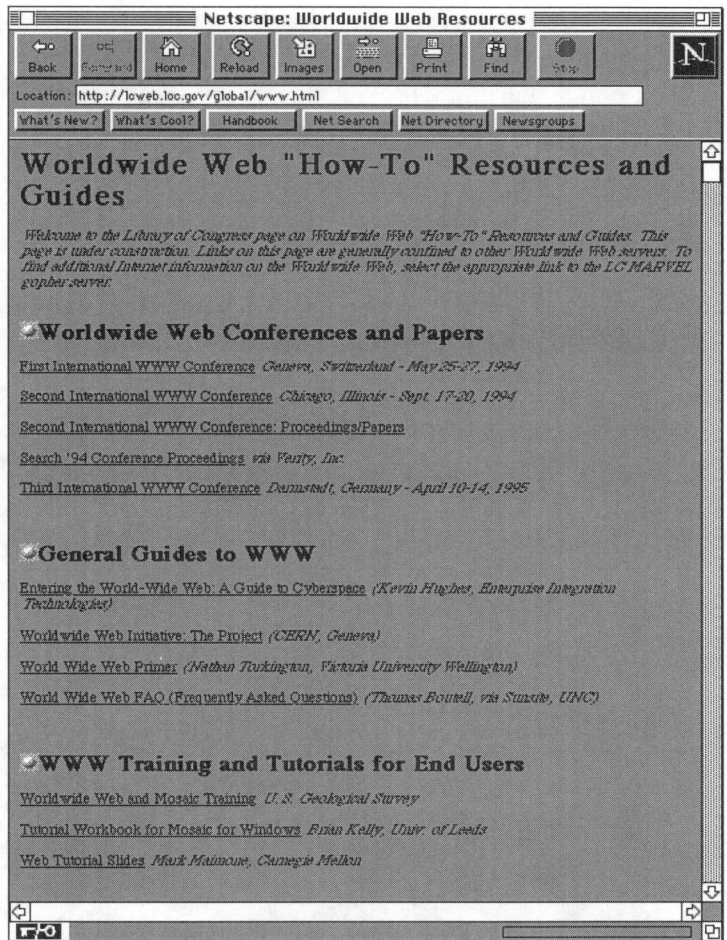

Figure 2.19 WWW resources page.

Networking with Personal Home Pages

Besides information, the Web and the Internet are about networking: establishing contacts with like-minded people who share your concern about a particular subject. That's what Usenet is all about.

Home Pages for Clubs

The strategy here is simple: have fun; provide interesting graphics and photos. One design of note is at the bottom of the page in Figure 2.20. Instead of the plain horizontal rule, you can create your own graphic image to use as a divider between sections of information. (Of course, such graphics make the page slower to load on the user's screen.)

Graphic image divides text

Figure 2.20 The Monkees home page.

Where to Find It

A medical student at the University of Michigan posted an astonishing amount of information on the Web about the musical "Miss Saigon." Go to http://www.clark.net/pub/rsjdfg/. The Monkees Home Page is at http://www.primenet.com/~flex/monkees.html.

A Personal Home Page

A personal home page can be either a profound, soul-searching means of self-expression across the emotional tendrils of Cyberspace, or a trivial, silly waste of disk space. The Web abounds with the latter. How do you create the former?

Have something to say. Ask yourself the following questions:

- Is there some special reason people would want to read about me? Do I have something important to say?

- Do I have some service or business that people might want to utilize?

- Do I belong to groups, companies, or large organizations that people might want to know about?

- Am I really busy and sometimes hard to reach, in which case I might list my office hours on the Web?

A home page that meets all of these criteria is shown in Figure 2.21. Besides being on the faculty of the Department of Computer Science at the University of Chicago, Don Crabb is a well-known computer author. (He also helped to get this book published.) And sometimes he can be hard to reach. He can announce his current whereabouts to students and other interested parties on his home page, which includes links to his latest book and a short biography.

I don't want to discourage anyone from using the Web as a means of personal expression. That's something I'd like to do, myself. Just be sure you have something to say before you hit the Net. The more useful your page is, the more goodwill you'll spread, and the contacts you make will be that much more useful.

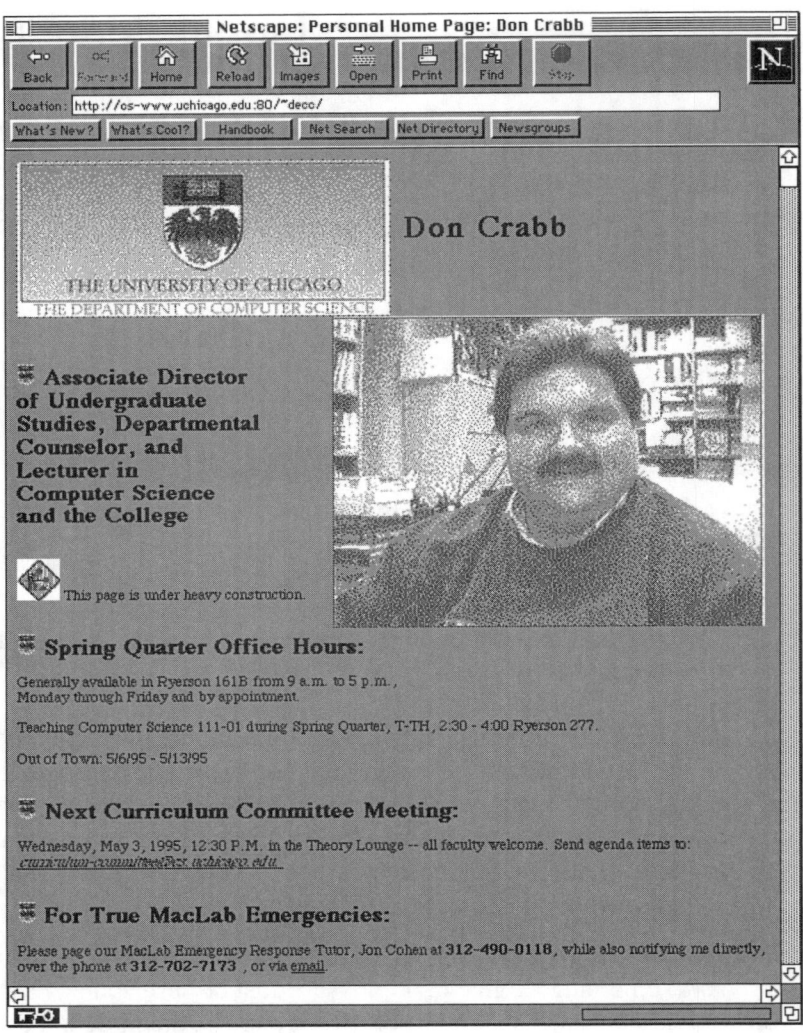

Figure 2.21 Don Crabb's home page.

Review: Greg's Top 25 Web Publications Strategies

Here's a list of the main publications strategies illustrated by the sites described in this chapter:

1. Don't be an "information dump."

2. Map out a strategy.

3. Remember that an existing database can be converted to HTML and published on the Web.

4. Consider saving money and increasing timeliness by publishing any "throw-away" booklets or brochures only on the Web.

5. Begin organizing a site by planning and designing a home page (also called a "welcome page").

6. Learn how to create Web documents by examining the HTML tags of sites you like.

7. Use scripts to automate data entry and generation of HTML.

8. Before you start, be prepared to commit the time and staff resources necessary to set up and maintain your Web publication.

9. If your business involves putting out news or information, consider publishing a condensed summary of daily news on the Web.

10. Take advantage of the fact that any information that can't be accommodated in your printed publications due to time constraints (your booklet already went to press) or space constraints (there's not enough room on the printed page) can be put on your Web site.

11. Rather than trying to convert the design of an existing publication to the Web, start from scratch; design your publication specifically for onscreen viewing.

12. Use the Web's easy interactivity by providing ways for your audience to "talk back" to you.

13. Make your home page organized and orderly. Provide buttons and short summaries of contents that lead to more complete stories or articles.

14. Consider ways to let your readers personalize the news or information they get from you.

15. Coordinate the contents of your Web publication with your other publications. Make sure they work together, and make sure your Web publishing effort fits into your overall communications plan. (Do you have one? You should.)

16. Consider releasing information on the Web well after your other for-profit publications have been sold. (If your ultimate goal is to get out of print publication altogether, you could try publishing on the Web first and see what readership you attract.)

17. Grab attention with exciting, eye-catching design and lively writing.

18. Make an effort to coordinate your Web site with others in your university, corporation, or other large organization.

19. Consider using a portable document program to preserve your original design.

20. Make a small investment in time and money and put your small business online; whenever possible, include good photos of products for sale.

21. Organize information with six or seven main topic headings.

22. Consider setting up services related to your main commercial Web site such as an information center or discussion group.

23. Make your site an information resource by providing links to related information or to software or other documentation on the Web.

24. Reach out and network, but be sure you have something to say.

25. Last but not least, have fun!

Part II

How to Publish
on the Web

How to Get Published on the World Wide Web Right Now

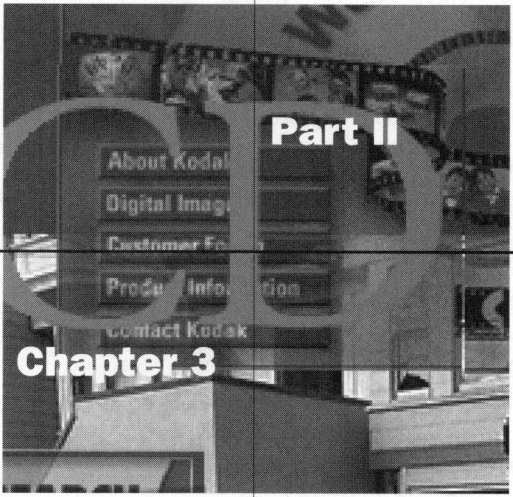

Part II

Chapter 3

By this time, you have an idea of the different kinds of material that can be published on the Web as well as the individuals and organizations who are benefiting from it. Are you ready to join in the fun yourself?

There are two vital points to keep in mind as you prepare to publish on the Web. Write them down and paste them beneath your computer screen:

- This Is Easy!

- I Can Do It!

That's all you need to keep in mind. If you don't let yourself be intimidated by computerspeak—HTTP, SGML, ISDN, or other acronyms—and by using and writing actual computer code, you'll find that publishing on the Web is remarkably free of anxiety.

A number of instructional materials already exist on how to create a home page on the Web and, particularly, on how to learn the Hypertext Markup Language (HTML) commands. Many of them can be found on the Web.

In my experience, however, the thrill of reading written material can't compare to the excitement of rolling up your sleeves, creating your own HTML documents, and instantly seeing the results onscreen. Remember, this is coming from a firm advocate of the power of the written word.

After reading a number of guides to HTML, I found that I learned more and had more fun by simply jumping in and doing it. For that reason, I have provided the following tutorial in this chapter as well as on the Web page for this book, which is part of Macmillan Computer Publishing's extensive Web site.

You will have completed your assignment in this chapter if you follow the instructions in the tutorial; however, any overachievers who want to jump to the head of the class will find more background about where HTML came from in the Frequently Asked Questions at the end of this chapter, as well as a list of HTML elements in Appendix E. Chapter 4 contains more detailed reference information about HTML.

Where to Find It

You'll find this book's home page at http://www.mcp.com/hayden/ webmacpublishing.

So go ahead, connect to the net, and call up this tutorial on your screen right now. Then you can work on the Web by following the instructions in the book, thus bringing print and visual learning together in true multimedia fashion.

So much for introduction. Let's begin!

Basic HTML: A Step-by-Step Tutorial

First, open up your browser program and connect to the Web. I am assuming that you have a browser and a connection. If you don't have a connection yet, see Appendix C, "How to Choose an Internet Provider."

If you do have a browser but can't connect just now, that's fine; you can open up your browser and follow the exercises on your computer without actually being connected to the Web.

If you don't have any of the connections or you aren't at your computer right now, take the low-tech road and just read on to the sections after this one. I won't tell anyone.

Step 1: Setting Up Your Workspace

Open your browser window (I refer only to Netscape, but you can use Mosaic or MacWeb just as well) and then follow these steps:

1. Connect to the home page for this book at the address listed previously.

2. Click HTML Tutorial.

3. Click "Preview the document you're going to make." Like the answers at the back of the math book, this shows the final result of the exercise I'm about to put you through (see Figure 3.1).

4. Go back to the Tutorial screen and make a copy of your browser window by choosing **New Window** from the **File** menu.

One screen serves as your *lesson window;* the other is a *preview window* where you can quickly see how your words and images look on a Web browser. (The windows needn't be blank. The point is to have two spaces in which to view your work.)

> **Tip:** Have you tried out all of Netscape's features, including the option of having two windows open at the same time? I was so busy surfing at first that it took me a long time to get past the basic commands like **Open Location** or **View History**. Take a few minutes to try out every one of its commands. **Reload**, for instance, lets you change the contents of a file and see the results instantly after you have saved the changes. The **Images** button loads images if you have turned off the **Auto Load Images** feature so you can see a screen without loading time-consuming graphics. Check the Preferences folder in your System Folder: Netscape creates a file called

continued

"Global History" that contains the URL for every site you've visited recently, which is great if you're trying to find the address of a site you forgot to write down the first time. And as an alternative to **Open Location,** when you choose **Show Location** in the Options menu, you type a destination in the URL address field and hit Return.

Greg's Soapbox

It's frustrating to encounter Web software without adequate documentation. Sometimes there is none at all, sometimes you have to look long and hard to find it, and sometimes it's disorganized or unwieldy (Arachnid's instructions, for instance, took up a 353K Word file, and that was only the beta version of the program.) Unfortunately, because we are in the relatively early days of the Web, this situation is not uncommon. Let the author(s) of the software know how they have met or not met your needs by sending an inquiry to them via email.

Now that you have two Netscape windows open onscreen, you have to make room for a third window. (I admit, a two-page monitor is best for this lesson. If you don't have one, resize your windows so you can flip back and forth between them. Clicking a window's title bar will make it leap to the foreground quickly when you want to look at it; double-click again and it will return to its former position.)

Open a word processing program you like, such as Microsoft Word, WordPerfect, TeachText, or SimpleText. (I prefer Word.) This serves as your text editor for entering the content and HTML tags that make up your home page.

HTML documents can be created by any word processing program—as long as you remember to save them not in your word processor's "normal" format but in plain ASCII text-only format.

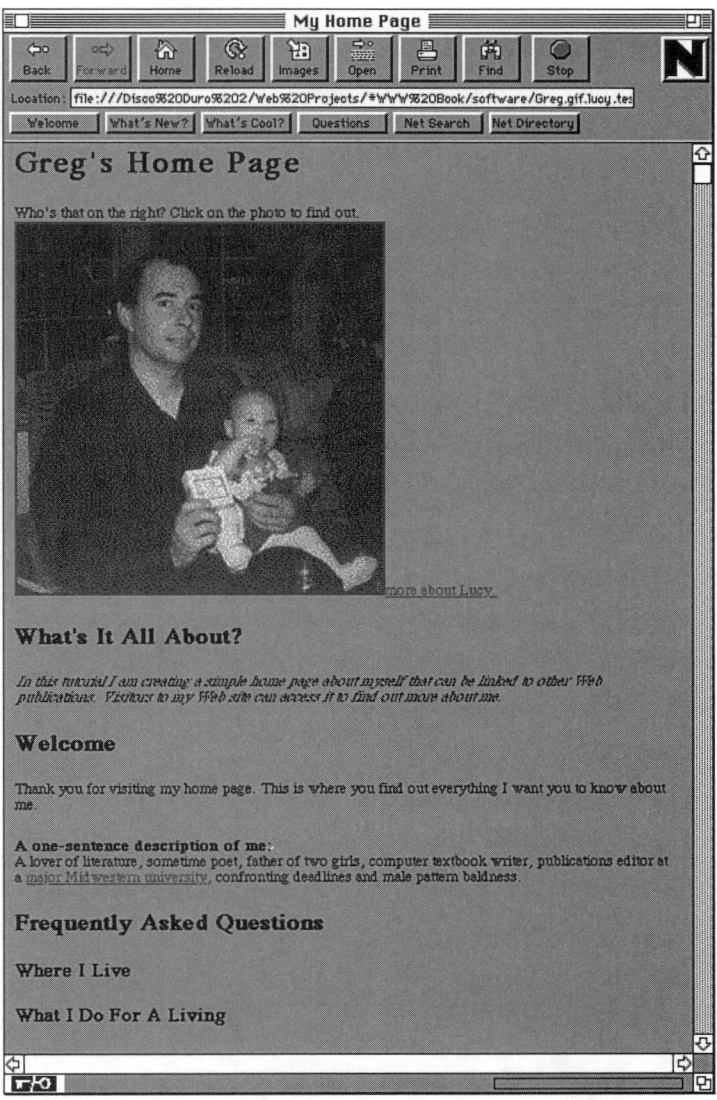

Figure 3.1 Preview of a completed personal home page.

Step 2: Creating Your HTML Document

Right now, you should be seeing (or if you are just reading along, imagining that you see) the tutorial window, the blank preview window, and the text editor window.

Enter the following text (see Figure 3.2) in the text editor window. You can duplicate my home page if you are timid. However, I'd like to challenge you to be brave enough to create your own. I won't leave you all alone because you can use mine as a model to follow. For instance, instead of "My Home Page," type "*MyName*'s Home Page."

Press Return only at the end of a paragraph, not at the end of each line; your Web browser performs the needed word wrap.

Warning: Remember to turn off "curly" or "smart" quotes in your text editor before doing this. They don't show up on Web browsers. You have to use "straight" (") quotes instead.

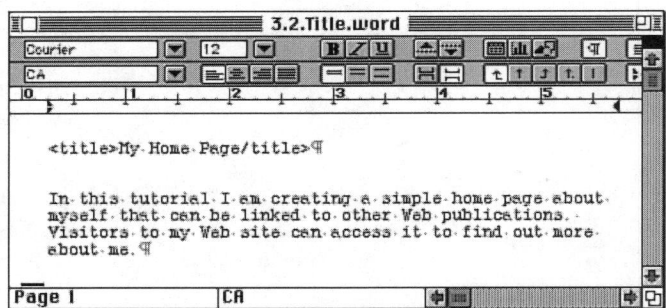

Figure 3.2 Using tags.

Congratulations: You've just entered your first HTML tag.

Note: HTML *tags* are the markup instructions that tell your Web browser how to format text. Tags are made up of the left-angle bracket (<), followed by the name of the tag, and closed by a right-angle bracket (>). Most HTML tags include a beginning tag, (<>) the ending tag (</>), and the text in between the two. All three together are known colloquially as an HTML "cookie."

The Title Tag <TITLE>. . .</TITLE>

The only code you've actually used so far is the title tag, <TITLE>My Home Page </TITLE>. All HTML documents must have this tag. This is the name your browser displays at the top of the screen.

Titles should be short but specific. Both they and tags are explained in greater detail later in this chapter.

Step 3: Naming Your HTML Document

Save your document as "Greg.html" or, if you're making your own home page, substitute your first name for mine. Be sure to save in text-only (ASCII) format.

Note: Throughout the lessons that follow I will instruct you to save any documents you create in the same folder in which your Netscape application resides. This is to keep the tutorial simple. Having all the documents in the same folder means that when you type an HTML tag that requires Netscape to look for a file or graphic, you have to type only the name of the file, for instance, "Greg.html" and not a series of folders to give Netscape a "path" it can follow to locate that file. I explain more about path names in Chapter 4.

Naming your Web document isn't particularly tricky, but there are a few things to remember:

- End your file name in "html." This tells your Web browser how to read and display the codes.

- Keep the names short but clear so you know what each one is if you are scanning a long list.

- Make sure there are no blank spaces in the name of the document. You can, however, use periods instead of spaces between words, or even characters like backslashes or the tilde (~) symbol.

- Make sure you type it here in a way that you find easy to remember. Later on, when you are making a link to this name, that link will be case-sensitive and you will have to enter it exactly.

Step 4: Previewing the Results

Follow these steps to preview your results:

1. Open your Web browser preview window.

2. Choose **Open File...** from the **File** menu.

3. Use the dialog box to find and open the file you created, "*MyName*.html."

You should now see in your Netscape preview window the words "My Home Page" in the title bar and the HTML text you created displayed underneath.

Compare your Netscape document with a sample of how your document should appear. It should look like Figure 3.3. (Don't worry if the typeface is different. You can change it in Netscape's **Preferences** window.) After viewing the sample, click the **Back** button to return to this page in the tutorial.

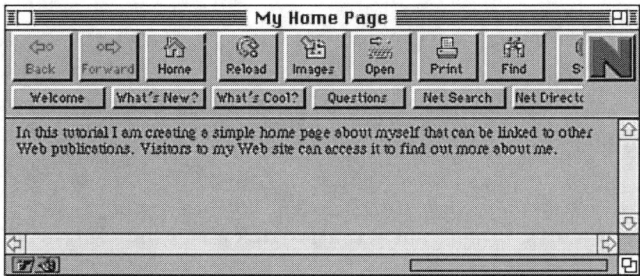

Figure 3.3 Sample text.

Is your Netscape document different than the sample? I suggest that you review the text you entered in the text editor. Make sure it matches the text instructions in this lesson.

> **Note:** In case you're wondering if everyone on the World Wide Web see
> what you've just created, the answer is no. Right now it's visible only as a
> "local" file on your computer. In order for it to be seen by the Web at large,
> it has to be put on a computer that is set up as a Web server.

Congratulations! You've just created your first HTML page. Pretty short, I admit—
but it gets better.

Step 5: Modifying Your HTML Document

If you don't have the document from the previous lesson, download it now from the
online tutorial.

If you are starting up after closing down your computer, make another copy of your
original Netscape window again to serve as your preview window, and open up your
text editor program as you did before. Once in the text editor program, open the
"*MyName*.html" file you created previously.

Below the text from the previous lesson, press Return a few times and enter the
following text. Type Return at the end of the line:

Thank you for visiting my home page. This is where you find out everything
I want you to know about me.

Select **Save** from the **File** menu to update the changes in your HTML file.

Now, return to the Netscape preview window where the previous version of your
file was displayed. Note that the new text you entered in the previous steps is not yet
visible. To see the changes, select **Reload** from the **File** menu. This tells Netscape to
read the same HTML file and display whatever changes have been made (and saved)
in it. You should now see the text you just entered.

As you can see, Netscape ignored the extra blank lines you entered. However, typing
them in your text editor was fine because it made it more readable for you to work in
that document.

Compare your document to the online sample of how it should appear (see
Figure 3.4).

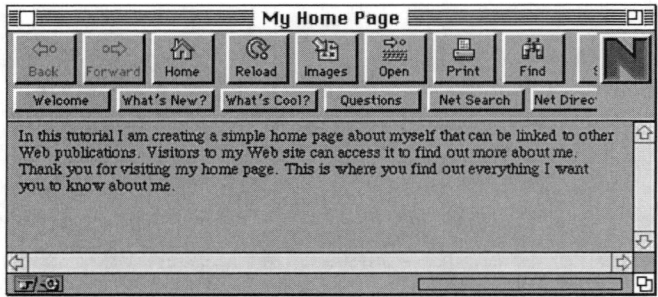

Figure 3.4 Your sample, continued.

Step 6: Inserting Paragraphs and Line Breaks

As you just discovered, Netscape (like other Web browsers) ignores any carriage returns typed in your text editor. It recognizes the paragraph tag only when you want to insert a blank line and start a new paragraph.

The Paragraph Tag <P>

The official HTML code for a paragraph break is

    <p>. . .</p>

I say "official" because only HTML 3.0 specifies paragraph tags this way. Earlier versions used only <P>. This is explained more fully in Chapter 4. In all my examples, I use <P>. . .</P>.

> **Tip:** Note that here, or at any point in this tutorial, if you do not have a copy of the working document from the previous section, you can download a copy from the home page for this book.

Here are some steps for inserting paragraph breaks:

1. Reopen your *workspace* (your Web browser and text editor program, if they aren't already open).

2. Go to the text editor window.

3. Open your working document, "*MyName*.html" (if it isn't already open).

4. Go back to the sentence you typed earlier, and then enter the paragraph tag:

    <p>Thank you for visiting my home page. This is where you find out everything I want you to know about me.</p>

5. Then press Return (not necessary but it makes the HTML more readable) and type

    <p>A one-sentence description of me:</p>

    Ever try to describe yourself in one sentence? Try it now. Remember, only you are going to see this initial draft, so don't dig too deep into your psyche. Just write anything off the top of your head. If you would rather duplicate my home page, copy my text from this Netscape page.

6. Select the text with your mouse, **Copy** it, and **Paste** it into your text editor at the end of the sentence you just typed (you may want to type another carriage return to separate the two sentences in your text editor):

    <p>A lover of literature, sometime poet, father of two girls, computer textbook writer, publications editor at major Midwestern university, confronting deadlines and male pattern baldness.</p>

7. **Save** the changes.

8. Return to your Netscape preview window and choose **Reload** to see your new text, as in Figure 3.5.

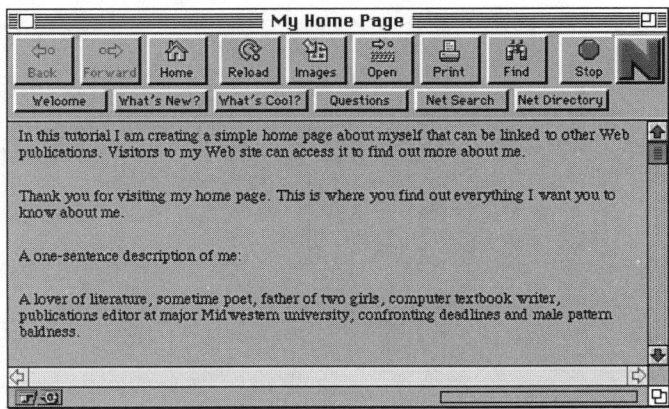

Figure 3.5 Paragraph tags in action.

As you can see, in each case, the paragraph tag inserted a blank space and starts a new paragraph. The way to start a new line or paragraph without inserting a blank space is by the line break tag, <BR>.

The Line Break Tag

The line tag <BR> never uses an accompanying </BR>. Let's try it out by going back to the text you just entered:

1. After the phrase "A one-sentence description of me," delete the colon and both parts of the paragraph tag. Replace the </P> end tag with <BR>. Again, for clarity, type a carriage return after it. Note that after I type
 I will move the </P> tag to the end of the next paragraph, as this defeats the purpose of <BR> by inserting a blank space before the paragraph:

   ```
   <p>A one-sentence description of me<br>
   A lover of literature, sometime poet, father of two girls, computer
   textbook writer, publications editor at major Midwestern university,
   confronting deadlines and male pattern baldness.</p>
   ```

2. **Save** your document. Go back to the preview window and choose **Reload**. The results are seen in Figure 3.6.

Paragraph tag inserts blank space after paragraph.

Line break tag: no blank space.

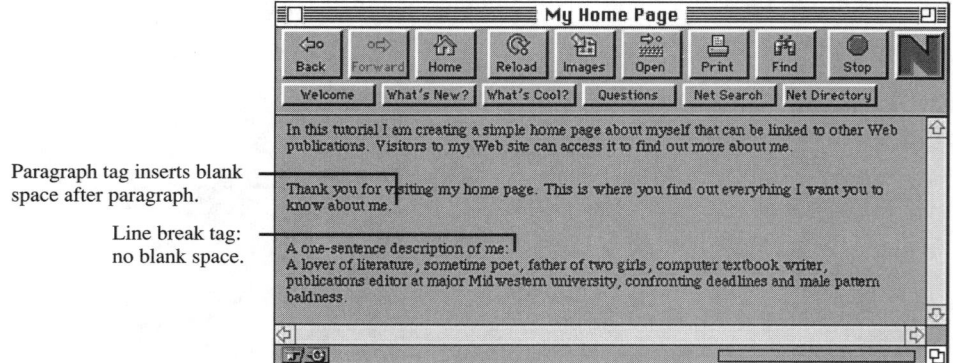

Figure 3.6 The results.

Adding some carriage returns can make your HTML document easier to read and edit. You should feel free to add them to make your HTML readable both for you and that mysterious "undercover" Web audience—the readers who will be examining and possibly emulating your Web page's source code.

Step 7: Organizing Your Document with Headings

Now that your personal home page has at least some initial content, you can add some organizing elements, beginning with headings.

HTML uses heading tags with the following format:

<h*N*>Words For Heading</h*N*>

where "*N*" is a number from 1 to 6.

The numbers correspond to the six different styles or "levels" of headings that HTML recognizes. Again a fuller explanation of headings appears after this tutorial. But just jump in and try them out in your home page document:

Go into your text editor and put your cursor or text tool just before the first words of your home page: "In this tutorial...." Type:

1. <H1>*MyName*'s Home Page</H1>

2. Press Return.

3. <H2>What's It All About?</H2>

4. Press Return.

   Note that you don't have to type a paragraph tag (<P>. . .</P>) after a heading. A blank space is inserted automatically after each heading in HTML. Also note that you didn't type a paragraph tag when you entered the first paragraph. It didn't matter, because Netscape assumed it was a paragraph. However, you should add it now for consistency.

5. Type <P> before "In this tutorial..." and </P> after "...more about me."

6. Place your cursor before the next paragraph "Thank you for visiting..." (before the <P> tag, that is) and type <H2>Welcome</H2>.

7. Press Return.

8. Below the text you've already entered, create other headings for future sections of your home page. Enter the following:

    ```
    <h2>Frequently Asked Questions</h2>
    <h3>Where I Live</h3>
    <h3>What I Do For A Living</h3>
    <h2>Sports</h2>
    <h2>Hobbies or Other Interests</h2>
    <h2>Favorite Web Sites</h2>
    ```

9. **Save** the changes in your text editor.

10. Return to Netscape, **Open**, and **Reload** the HTML file.

> **Note:** You can control the appearance of the headings you just created on your computer by changing Netscape's settings in its Preferences window. For example, you can have Netscape display H1 headings as Times bold, 36 point bold, and dark green in color; H2 headings as Times bold, 24 point, italic, and red in color; and so on. Of course, readers viewing your home page can make the changes on their computers as well. The HTML codes designate only that headers are of a certain type. How they are displayed is controlled by the user.

Check your work by comparing your page to Figure 3.7. If some of the headings do not appear correctly, make sure the start and end tags have the same level number.

If you're feeling adventurous, try this test. Open your HTML document in the text editor and delete the backslash (/) after the <H1> tag, "*MyName*'s Home page." Without the correct ending tag, Netscape interprets all of the succeeding text as part of that header (see Figure 3.8). Be sure to replace the backslash and restore your page to its original appearance.

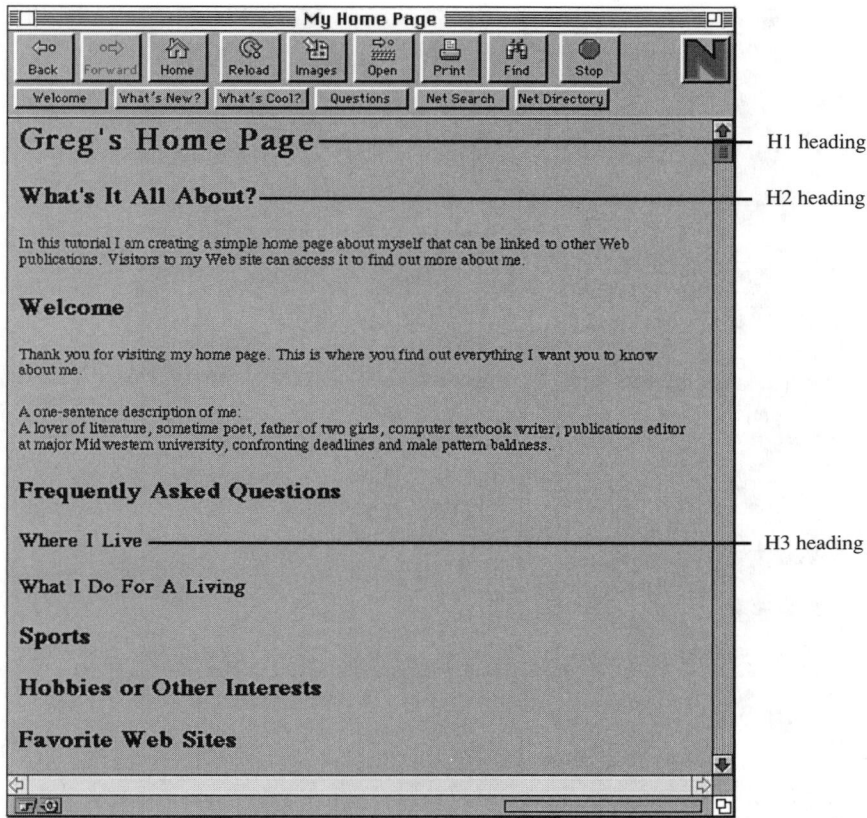

Figure 3.7 Headings in HTML.

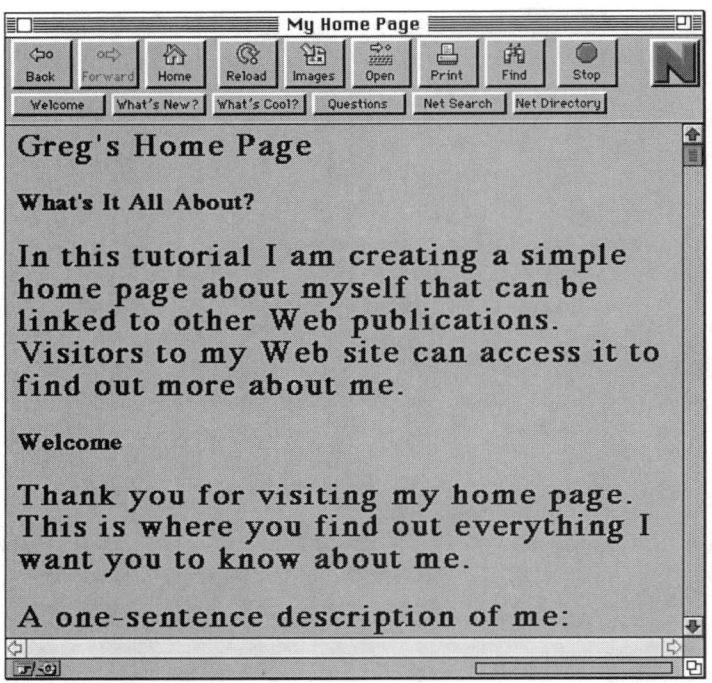

Figure 3.8 Oops! Missed a tag.

Step 8: Adding Emphasis with Styles

Another way to add emphasis to various textual elements in your document is by adding traditional formatting instructions. There are two kinds of emphasis you can add in HTML: logical styles and character styles.

For the purposes of this beginning tutorial, I just have you insert some of the character styles: bold, italic, and typewriter style.

HTML recognizes four tags for text style attributes. They should be used judiciously within a page (see Chapter 9 for how to break up a text with styles and other formatting elements).

Here are the basic tags for stylized text:

```
<b>Make this text bold...</b>
<i>Make this text italic...</i>
<tt>Make this text typewriter...</tt>
```

Typewriter text is a monospace font.

Style tags can also be combined:

```
<b><i>Make this text bold and italic...</b></i>
```

Now you can add some style to your home page. Reopen your workspace if it is not open already. Open your document "*MyName*.html" in your text editor. Let's make the entire first paragraph "In this tutorial..." italic. Before the word "In," type <I>. At the end of the paragraph, but before the paragraph tag <P>, type </I>.

Note: The underline tag, <U>. . .</U>, is a Netscape Extension to HTML and is not supported by all browsers, so we'll skip it for now.

Go to the last word of the second paragraph and add the bold tag, as follows:

```
...everything I want you to know about <b>me.</b></p>
```

Note that the end tag should go after the period at the end of the sentence. Putting the </B> between the word "me" and the period would result in a blank space before the period, a commonly seen HTML mistake:

```
...everything I want you to know about me .
```

Let's also add the bold tag around a heading, like this:

```
<b>A one-sentence description of me:<br></b>
```

Save your changes in your text editor and **Reload** your home page document in your Netscape preview window. The result should look like Figure 3.9.

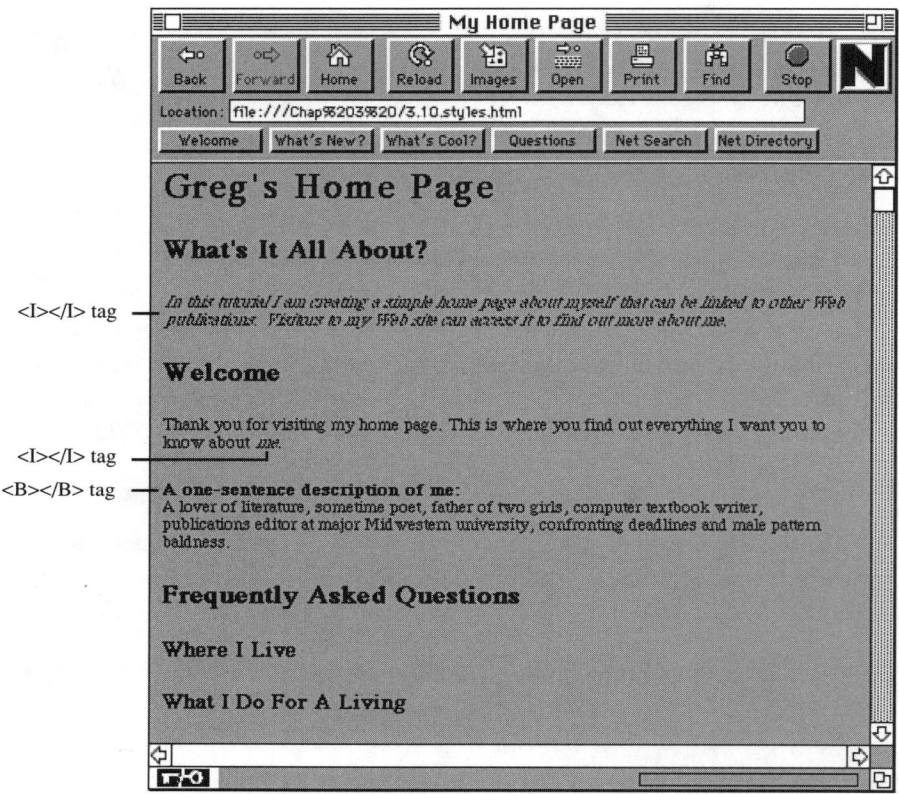

Figure 3.9 Adding character styles in HTML.

Step 9: Organizing with Lists

There's one more formatting element to discuss: lists. Lists are sometimes treated as being a step beyond "basic" HTML. However, I regard them as important tools for making a document more readable, and besides that, they're easy to create, so I am including them in "basic" HTML.

HTML can display three kinds of lists: unordered, ordered, and glossary or definition lists. Lists are useful not just for arranging a series of steps. They can also be used to produce the following:

- An outline

- An index

- A table of contents

The list you just read is called an *unordered list* in HTML. An unordered list has a "bullet" before each item. The appearance of the bullet depends on the font being used. In Times, the bullet is a small square; in Geneva, it is a large round dot.

Ordered lists have a numeral before each item.

Glossary lists indent the definition of an item in a separate paragraph beneath that item, as shown in Figure 3.10.

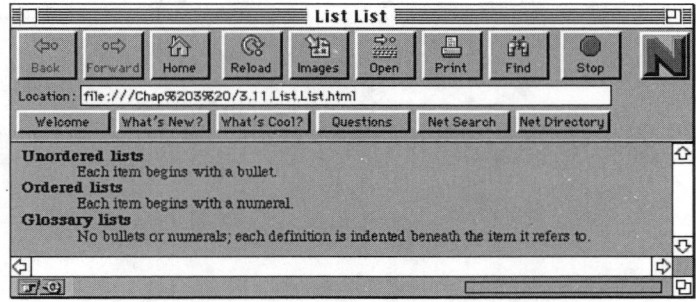

Figure 3.10 A glossary list.

A complete discussion of lists is included in Chapter 4. For now, let's insert some simple lists into our home page. After the title "Hobbies or Other Interests," type Return. (Again, this is not strictly necessary in HTML; it's only to make the code easier for you to read.) This is followed by (again, feel free to substitute your own "real" information):

```
<ul>
<li>collecting antique chewing gum wrappers
<li>ongoing comparison of Chicago-style deep-dish pizza restaurants
<li>surfing the Internet
</ul>
```

That was an unordered list. Now let's go to the heading "Favorite Web Sites." Press Return. Then type the tags for an ordered list:

```
<ol>
<li>Yahoo
<li>Virtual Tourist
<li>Best of the Web
</ol>
```

91

Note: There is a </LI> tag, but in most cases it can be omitted. For the sake of simplicity, I'm omitting it here.

The resulting lists are shown in Figure 3.11. If your lists don't look like this, check your beginning and end tags to make sure (1) they're both present, and (2) all the greater-than and less-than symbols are present.

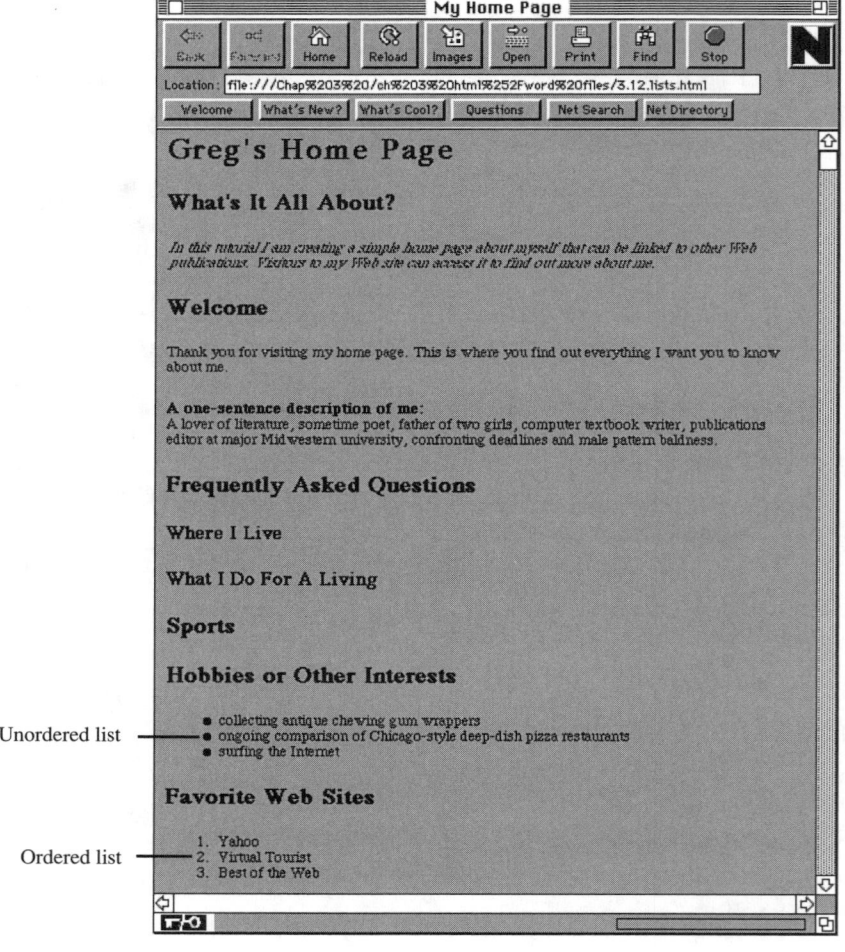

Figure 3.11 Lists in an HTML file.

Step 10: Putting Graphics on Your Home Page

So far, you've examined how you can apply tags and other HTML commands to text so that Netscape can show the text properly. Now it's time to learn one of the things that makes the Web a powerful means of communication—its capability to integrate graphics as well as text. You'll learn how to place an in-line graphic on your home page.

There are three basic ways to put a photo or other graphic on an HTML page:

- Click a link to a graphics file that has been set up to download automatically onto your computer.

- Copy a graphic you see on the Web.

- Scan or draw your own image and convert it to a file that can be named in your HTML text and displayed in your Web browser.

Where to Find It

Remember the address? I'm at http://www.mcp.com/hayden/ webmacpublishing. There are many sources of downloadable graphics on the Web. These are only a few: OTIS online art gallery (http:// sunsite.unc.edu/otis/otis.html) and the Smithsonian Institution (file://photo1.si.edu/images). An archive of "ASCII Art" is at ftp: //ftp.cs.ttu.edu/pub/asciiart/. A few public domain icons can be found at http://www.bsdi.com/ icons/tonys.html. Remember to check the copyright before you download any images.

Remember to open your workspace if it isn't open already. Open Netscape and connect to the tutorial. Make a second Netscape window to preview your work. Open your HTML document "*MyName*.html" in your text editor.

Let's start with the easiest way first: click a file I have set up for you on my Web tutorial page.

You'll see a miniature version of the image I want you to download. Click the miniature image once to download the full image to your computer. Save it in the same folder or directory as your HTML file "*MyName*.html" with the name "Greg.gif."

Graphics Formats

While it's downloading, here's a word about graphics formats. The file you are downloading is saved in a file format called GIF, for Graphics Interchange Format. This is one of the most popular of several graphics formats that can be included in HTML.

GIF images may be up to 8 bits (256 colors) in depth and are always compressed. Saving a graphic in GIF turns it into a binary format that can be read by different computers over a network.

Where to Find It

GIF Converter, a shareware utility for converting files to GIF, can be found at file://photo1.si.edu/images/ viewer.applications/mac/ GifConverter.

If you've already been working in desktop publishing, you're probably familiar with graphics formats like PICT, EPS, or TIF files. None of those can be displayed over the Web. They can, however, be converted to GIF using one of several shareware utilities.

Check in the Finder to make sure the file "Greg.gif" has been saved in the same folder as your previous HTML files. If not, move it to the correct location. Yes, there's a reason for this. You have to tell your browser in HTML exactly where to find a file so that Netscape can display it. This can get complicated when you are arranging lots of files in different folders on a server. It's not going to get complicated in this test, however, because we're going to put everything in the same location.

In-Line Graphics

An image that appears within the contents of a HTML page, such as the photo of me on the next page, is called an *in-line graphic*. The tag that specifies an in-line graphic in HTML is

```
<IMG SRC="filename.gif">
```

where *"filename.gif"* is the name of a GIF file that exists in the same directory of folder as the HTML document. Here's how to use this new tag on your home page:

1. Open your HTML document *"MyName*.html" in your text editor.

2. Under the heading "<H1>*MyName*'s Home page</H1>" type:

    ```
    <IMG SRC="Greg.gif">
    ```

Then press Return. Doing so will insert the photo you downloaded at the top of your home page.

3. **Save** your changes and **Reload** them in Netscape (or **Open** it if you haven't done so).

You should be looking at the beautiful countenance of Lucy Maud Holden and her proud father: me. If you are able to scan and insert your own photo on your own home page, you will immediately feel the thrill that "going graphic" gives the Web publisher. Exciting, isn't it?

Figure 3.12 Tutorial home page with graphics.

If your home page doesn't look like this, check the line of HTML you just typed. There should be a blank space between <IMG> and <SRC>, but no space in <SRC=">. Also make sure "Greg" is capitalized. Although tag names in HTML are not case-sensitive, when you are making a reference to a graphic or file name, you have to get that name exactly right. Computers don't guess about these things.

You don't have to put a <P> </P> tag after the graphic because the element before it is a header. Usually the way to make an in-line graphic go on a line of its own is to put the paragraph tag around it.

Copying a Graphic from the Web

The second way to enliven your home page with graphics is to copy an image you like from the Web.

Copying images from the Web, like copying text, is easy—so easy, in fact, that it alarms those who are concerned with issues of copyright protection.

Warning: Because Chapter 15 discusses the issues surrounding copyright of electronic information and how you can protect yourself from having others steal your material, I will only remind you about what you take off the Web. *All material on the Web is protected by copyright whether there is a copyright notice or not. Take only what is specified as public domain.*

There are a couple of sources for copyright-free material on the Web. Let's go to one now. In Netscape, click the **Open** button and type the address:

    ftp://ftp.brunel.ac.uk/WWW/images/

Note: Each browser has its own command for copying text or graphics. In Mosaic or MacWeb, you save a file to your hard drive by choosing **Load to Disk** or **Save As...**

Now follow these steps to copy a graphic in Netscape 1.0:

1.   Choose **Save Next Link As...** from the File menu.

2.   The cursor will change to an oversize plus sign when it is over a link. Click a link with that plus sign to copy the desired object.

3.   Pick a color—any color. (I selected "greendot" for this example.)

4. When the prompt window appears, designate a name and location for the file. Save it in the same folder as your *MyName*.html file.

   Do that now by picking an image at the archive you have chosen. If you can't open that archive, click the link Sample GIF2 in the tutorial.

5. Go into your text editor and open your home page document "*MyName*.html." Go to the following line:

   ```
   <h2>Frequently Asked Questions</h2>
   ```

   Change the line to read:

   ```
   <h2><IMG SRC="greendot.gif">Frequently Asked Questions</h2>.
   ```

6. **Save** your file and **Reload** in Netscape. The heading "Frequently Asked Questions" should now have a dot to the left of it, as shown in Figure 3.13.

Note: The process of copying has been simplified in Netscape 1.1. Clicking and holding a link or object displays a popup menu with appropriate options enabled. Clicking and holding any displayed graphic displays an option for saving the image to disk.

This is how HTML allows you to insert an in-line image into a line of text. You can insert the graphic into the middle of a line, or at the beginning or end, simply by including the <IMG SRC...> tag inside the element tags that surround the text.

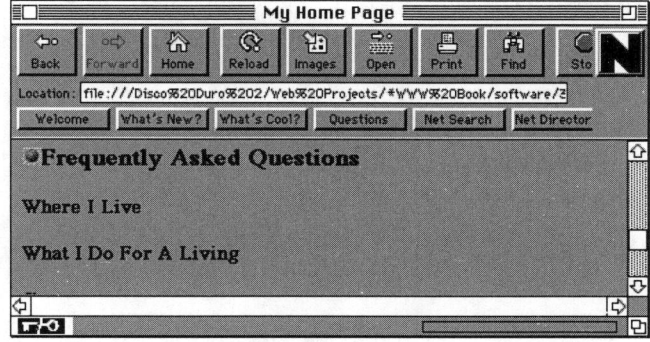

Figure 3.13 An in-line image copied from the Web.

Creating Your Own Graphic

If you are a desktop designer, you know all about creating graphics. You know that you can draw an original graphic and save it in a format like PICT or TIF to put in a program like QuarkXPress or PageMaker.

Creating or converting a file to publish on the Web won't be too difficult for you. You can:

- Save your file as a GIF.
- Convert an already-related file using a shareware utility, such as GIF Converter, or a graphics program like Photoshop.

If you're like me and don't do much scanning of photos or drawing in programs such as FreeHand, take heart. You can do one of two things:

- Call in a favor with someone you know who has a scanner and can create the file for you.
- Find yourself a scanner.

Links: An Introduction

So far, your home page has been pretty one-dimensional, a world unto itself. It's about time you began to construct some hypertextual links, the HTML tags that connect your document to other documents you've created, or to other sites around the Web, and indeed, the whole Internet. Links are the way you begin to really weave a "web" of information.

Links are sometimes called "hypertextual links," "hypertext links," or "hyperlinks." In any case, the "hyper" comes from "hypertext," a wonderful, revolutionary re-evaluation of how information is consumed and the nature of thought itself. Sound interesting?

You can find out more by jumping ahead (in a hypertextual sense) to the section "What's the 'Hypertext' Part of HTML?" later in this chapter.

HTML makes links using *anchor* tags to designate:

- A jumping-off point in your document.
- A location where you will jump to by clicking the text or object contained above as the jumping-off point.

It's a little like tying a rope to a boat and throwing the anchor on the other end of the rope out across the water to stop the boat. You "anchor" the front end and throw out the anchor to another point on the water's bottom. The term "anchor" in HTML actually comes from Ted Nelson's early work on hypertext, not from boating, but the image helps me to grasp the concept.

> **Note:** The distinction isn't always clear, but *links* and *anchors* are different things. Anchors are the two tags, the start tag <A HREF=" "> and the end tag </A>. Links are (1) the destination text contained between the anchor text, or (2) the act of making a hypertextual jump from one element to another.

Linking to a Destination within the Same Document

The simplest kind of link joins one point in a document file to another point in the same document file. This is helpful if you have a large document with many sections and you want to direct the reader to those sections easily.

The starting point is sometimes called the link; the destination is sometimes called, well, the destination. The destination specifies where you go if you click the link. The link is formed by typing:

```
<A HREF="destination">TEXT</A>
```

The following discussion explains each of the previous tags:

<A...	is the start tag. Leave a blank space after it.
<HREF>	is the attribute assigned to this tag. An attribute gives some more specific instructions to a computer command. <HREF> stands for Hypertext REFerence. In this case, you're making an anchor that serves as a hypertext reference for the clickable link text that follows.
="#"	is required for designating a named anchor in HTML.
destination	is an arbitrary name for this link; it need not correspond to actual text. See the next section to create your destination.

TEXT   is the actual text that appears onscreen as the jumping-off
                    point.

</A>   is the end tag of the anchor.

This anchor is highlighted as a link that the Web reader can click to jump to the destination. The destination is specified by typing:

```
<A NAME="destination">TEXT</A>
```

The opening section of the University of Chicago College course catalog, for instance, contains a great deal of information organized into separate subsections. At the head of the document, we placed the following links to places farther along in that same document:

- Liberal Education at Chicago

- The Curriculum

- Course Credit

- Academic Advising

- Academic Regulations and Procedures

- Special Opportunities

The first item in the list, the *link*, is formed as follows:

```
<ul>
<1i><A HREF="#Curric">The Curriculum</A>
```

"Catalog.html" is the name of the file, and "Curric" is an arbitrary name I have assigned to the link. Because this is a "same file" link, I don't have to include "Catalog.html." The destination is formed around the words "The Curriculum" as follows:

```
<H2><A NAME="Curric">The Curriculum</A><H2>
```

Note: A link can be made to a specific location (1) not only within a single file, (2) but also to another document in the same computer, or (3) even across computers, as shown:

```
(1) <A HREF="#Curric">The Curriculum</A>
(2) <A HREF="Second.Catalog.html#Curric">The Curriculum</A>
(3) <A HREF="http://www.AnotherCollege.edu/
catalog.html#Curric">The Curriculum</A>
```

Creating a "Same File" Link

Let's add a "same file" link to the home page we're creating. Open the
"*MyName*.html" file in your text editor. Go to the line in the first paragraph and
place an anchor around the words "Other Web Publications," as shown in
Figure 3.14.

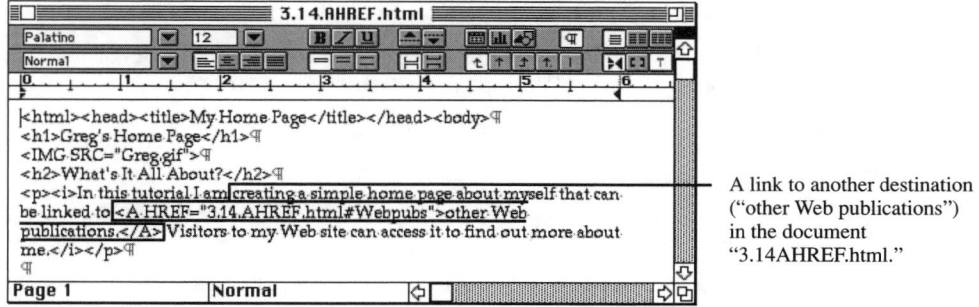

A link to another destination
("other Web publications")
in the document
"3.14AHREF.html."

Figure 3.14 Creating an anchor.

Go to the heading "Favorite Web Sites" at the bottom of your document and type:

```
<H2><A NAME="Webpubs">Favorite Web Sites</A>
```

Save your changes and **Reload** your document in the Netscape preview window.

The words <u>other Web publications</u> should be underlined. Click them and you should
jump ahead to "Favorite Web Sites." If this link doesn't work, check to make sure
the file you are working on is in the same folder as Netscape. Also check the code
to make sure you spelled everything exactly right.

Note: Be aware that the other Web publications link leads visitors right past your home page to a place where they can jump to another site on the Web, never to return. For this reason, you might want to take out the <A HREF> and <A NAME> anchors after completing this lesson.

Linking to a Local File

A second type of link is nearly the same as the first. The difference is that it takes you from the document you're viewing to a separate file located in the same directory or folder on your computer, otherwise known as a "local" file.

The form for the link is shown here:

```
<A HREF="filename.html">highlighted link text</A>
```

The file name must be an HTML file and thus should end in .html. Whatever text appears before the start and end tag will appear underlined and/or in color.

In your text editor, open your HTML home page document and go the heading "Hobbies or Other Interests." Type the following:

```
<H2><A HREF="hobbies.html">Hobbies or Other Interests</A>
```

You've created a link to a file that doesn't exist yet. Don't worry; it is about to spring to life:

- **Save** and **Close** your HTML document.

- **Open** a new document and type the following text (or copy it from the tutorial display in Netscape to save yourself some typing. Better yet, type something about one of your own hobbies):

```
<H1>Greg's Hobbies</H1>
<H3>Fountain Pens</H3>
About the only hobby I have time for these days is hunting for fountain
pens. I collect them, you see. Unfortunately, after being neglected for
many years, fountain pens are undergoing a sort of renaissance
among people who value a link to a bygone era.
<H3> Birdwatching </H3>
I'm into birdwatching, too. Over the last few years, I've seen more
than fifty-five different species of both migratory and nesting birds in
or around our little back yard in the middle of this city. The most
```

unusual was an American Woodcock I saw in our neighbor's yard early
one morning a few years ago.

Save this file with the name "hobbies. html." Make sure you save it in the same
folder as "*My Name*.html" and "Greg.gif."

Go to your browser's preview window. The heading "Hobbies or Other Interests"
should be underlined and/or in color. Click it, and you should jump to the file
"Greg's Hobbies" (see Figure 3.15). Stay in this file; you'll use it for the next lesson.

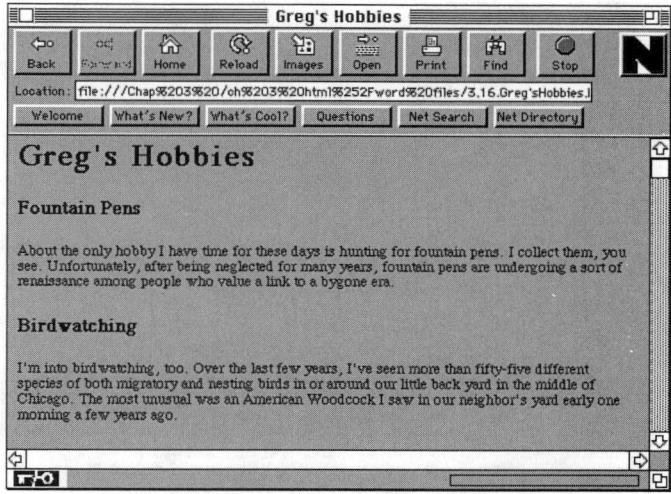

Figure 3.15 Greg's Hobbies file.

Linking to a File on Another Computer

The real power of creating a Web is realized when you make a link on your home
page to another site on the Web. If your home page is a magazine or newspaper,
you might link to an advertiser. If it's a personal home page, you might link to any
number of your favorite Web sites to give people an idea of what you're interested
in and what you've found on the Web.

Go into your text editor to the bottom of the file you just typed or copied. After the
last paragraph ("...a few years ago."), type the text seen in Figure 3.16.

Remember to type the address carefully, or you can copy and paste the text from
your tutorial screen. As I said before, although tags in HTML are not case-sensitive,

103

addresses referred to in anchors are. If an address uses a lowercase "www," don't type it as "Www" or "WWW."

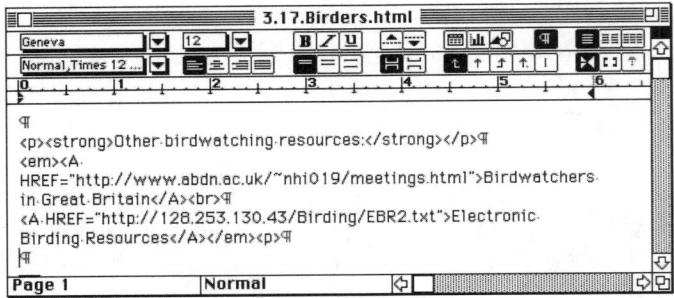

Figure 3.16 Links to birding resources.

Check the addresses you typed to make sure they are accurate.

Save "hobbies.html" and **Reload** the document in your Netscape preview window. You should see what's illustrated in Figure 3.17.

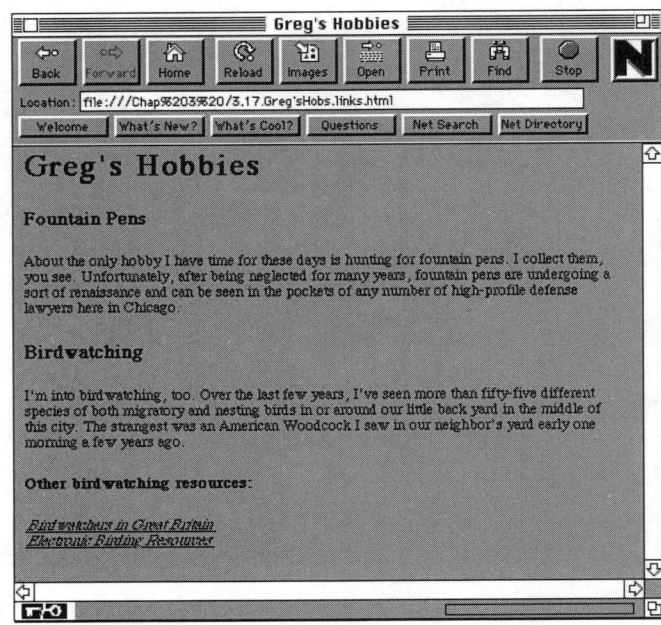

Figure 3.17 Links to birding resources viewed by the browser.

If you're already connected to the Internet, you can click one of the links and see where it takes you. If you click "Birdwatchers in Great Britain," you should see the screen illustrated in Figure 3.18.

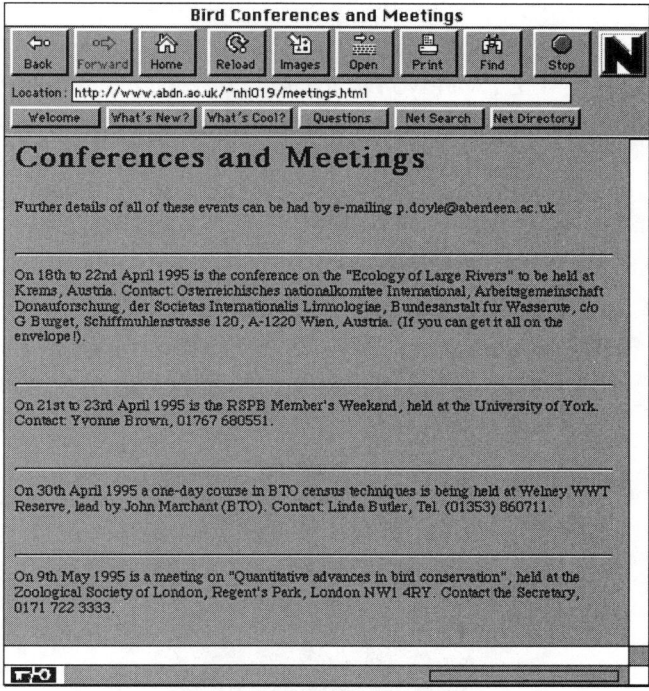

Figure 3.18 Birding news from Great Britain.

If you get a message such as "Cannot connect to remote host" or "URL not found," go back to your text editor and check to see that you've typed the address correctly.

Also, don't be alarmed if you get a message like "Connection refused by host." That probably means there is too much network traffic between your site and the UK to allow you to connect right now. Try again later.

Take a moment to celebrate: you've made your first links on the Internet, one domestic and one international.

Linking to an External Graphic

The anchor tag can also enable you to link to a graphic file that opens in an external window. When the link to the graphic is selected, the image is downloaded and Netscape launches a helper application to display it on a window separate from the home page you're visiting.

For this particular lesson, I want you to use my home page, Greg.html. Open your text editor window and **Open** your home page document. If you didn't save a copy from before, download one now from my tutorial page.

Download the GIF image "UC.gif" from this tutorial. Be sure to save it in the same file as the proverbial "*MyName*.html". If you aren't following the tutorial on a computer, Figure 3.19 shows the image.

Figure 3.19 UC.gif, otherwise known as Cobb Hall, the University of Chicago.

Find the words "major Midwestern university" in the "one-sentence description of me," and enter the following anchors around them:

    <A HREF="UC.gif">major Midwestern university,</A>

Save the [My Name].html file and **Reload** in the Netscape preview window.

Now click the link you just created, "<u>major Midwestern university,</u>" A picture of a building on the University of Chicago campus should be displayed (Figure 3.20).

Figure 3.20 UC.gif as displayed in Netscape.

Turning an Existing Graphic into a Link

A graphic image can be turned into a "hot spot" that can be turned into a link. You do this by including the <IMG> tag inside the anchors of the link tag <A HREF. . .></A>. Here's how I did this with the photo of me holding my daughter at the top of my home page:

1. In my text editor program I opened the HTML document with the source code for "My Home Page." This document includes the <IMG> tag that produces my photo:

    ```
    <IMG SRC="Greg.gif">
    ```

2. I created a simple HTML document about my daughter Lucy and saved it in ASCII format as "lucy.html" in the same folder as my home page document.

3. I added <A HREF. . .> </A> link anchors around the <IMG> tag I referred to in step 1, as follows:

    <A HREF="lucy.html"><IMG SRC="Greg.gif"></A>

This, by itself, is enough to turn the image "Greg.gif" into a clickable link. This line of HTML instructs your Web browser that an image named "Greg.gif" serves as a link to the file "lucy.html." In this case my browser, Netscape, is designating that a graphic is a link by drawing a black box around the image. (It might be hard to see the box in Figure 3.21, but you can see it as the image is appearing on the Netscape window.)

In general, though, such "hot" images might appear a number of different ways. They might have a colored border around them, and/or your cursor will turn into a pointing hand when it passes over a "hot" image.

A clickable image
outlined with a box.

Figure 3.21 A clickable image.

Because, as I said, the box around a clickable photo is sometimes hard to see (especially for those with monochrome monitors), it's usually a good idea to provide some text as an alternate clickable "hot spot" to accompany a clickable graphic. (This is also a good idea for Web readers who are using text-based browsers like Lynx, or others who turn off automatic loading of images because they have a slow modem connection.)

Therefore, I type the following:

```
<p>Who's that on the right? Click on the photo to find out.<A
HREF="lucy.html"><IMG SRC="Greg.gif">more about Lucy</A>
```

The way to add an alternate textual link to a graphic link is to add the "clickable text" between the anchors. In the previous example, "more about Lucy" shows up as a highlighted link as well as the photo "Greg.gif" (Figure 3.22).

Textual link

Figure 3.22 A clickable image with accompanying clickable text.

Connecting to Home

No matter where you are, in the world at large or the World Wide Web, it's good to maintain some kind of connection to home. There's one kind of link that's an important part of virtually any home page: a phrase or button that says "back to home page." We will create a button that serve as a link from the "hobbies.html" page created earlier back to your home page file.

1. Open the "hobbies.html" page in your text editor.

2. At the bottom of the page type:

    ```
    <HR>
    <A HREF="MyName.html">Back to My Home Page</A>
    ```

    The <HR> or "horizontal rule" tag (which you read about in greater detail in Chapter 4) creates a horizontal rule across the page.

3. **Save** and **Reload** the "hobbies.html" document in Netscape. The highlighted words <u>Back to My Home Page</u> should appear beneath a horizontal rule.

4. If you're feeling adventurous, you can implement what you just learned about clickable graphics and incorporate a button or other graphic in your link to "home." This is done by inserting a reference to the button (or other graphic) with the anchor. Here's what I typed for my link:

    ```
    <A HREF="Greg.html"><IMG SRC="right-hand.xbm">Back to My Home Page</A>
    ```

    where "right-hand.xbm" is a clipart graphic that I downloaded from the Web (Figure 3.24). You can use a photo as well as a generic icon.

Where to Find it

You can find plenty of icons, buttons, and images on the Web by clicking the **Net Search** button and doing a search for "icons" or "buttons." One good collection, WWW Icons and Images, is at http://www.lirman.fr/bib-icons/Alcons. Clipart as well as icon collections are at Yahoo: http://www.yahoo.com/Computers/Multimedia/Pictures/Clip_Art.

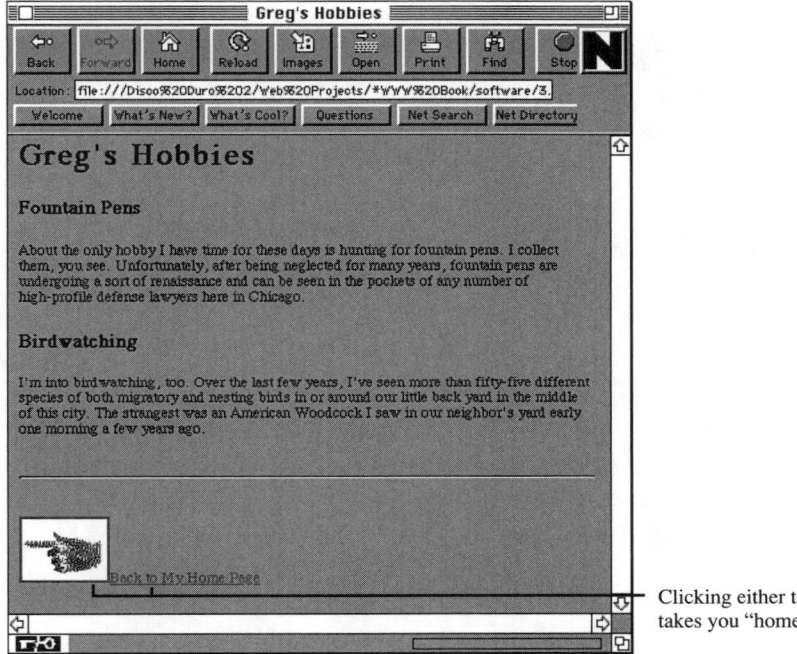

Clicking either text or graphic
takes you "home."

Figure 3.23 A graphical link to "home."

Summary

That's all there is to basic HTML. Although those of us who are used to the point and click, code-free environment of the Macintosh might not be used to working in HTML, it's remarkably easy to use.

Are you now a Web publisher? Almost! You have created a publishable document or "web" of documents that you can send to your Internet provider to be posted on the Web. (Many Internet providers publish personal home pages for their subscribers.)

Now that you actually have some hands-on experience with HTML, the reference information presented in Chapter 4 should make even more sense.

Basic HTML for Web Publishers: Reference Information

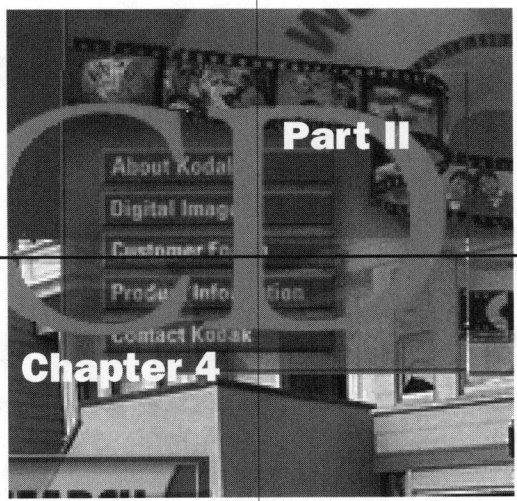

Part II

Chapter 4

Congratulations on successfully completing the hands-on tutorial and creating your first HTML document. Now it's time to back up and examine the subject in greater detail—to learn the basic commands needed to publish effectively on the Web.

Hang onto your hats, because this chapter gives you a complete and

comprehensive rundown of every possible permutation of HTML code that you will
ever need to know or that could possibly be theorized by even the wildest imagina-
tion.

Right—and if you fell for that I've got an EtherTalk bridge over the Chicago River
to sell you, cheap!

The truth of the matter is that although this chapter does give reference information
about HTML, it is by no means comprehensive. Why not? Well, there are several
reasons. For one, the medium and the language are changing constantly.

For another, you don't need to be an expert in HTML *per se*. The purpose of this
book is to help you achieve your communications goals by sensibly and effectively
publishing on the World Wide Web. That's what I intend to teach you to do.

Greg's Soapbox

One of the aspects of Web publishing that drives some people crazy is its
dynamic and fluid nature. This is a characteristic that has shaken up the
very concept of what it means to publish. Traditionally, when something
was published on paper—in a book, newspaper, or magazine—it was
preserved as if carved in stone for posterity. The notion of a "fixed" text
doesn't exist on the Internet. You don't have to wait a year to produce a
second or revised standard edition of your opus. Almost instantly, as you
get feedback from readers and expand your contacts on the Web, you can
incorporate new knowledge into your online documents. Personally, I find
this notion absolutely exciting and intriguing.

At the end of the reference section, you will find an FAQ section on HTML. You
might find it helpful to read through that section because many of your questions
about HTML will probably be answered there.

HTML Reference

Yes, sports fans. Here's the section you've been waiting for—a reference point for
Web publishers. In it you will find brief information about basic HTML structure
and commands. (For a quick reference to any tag, refer to Appendix E, "HTML
Elements.")

The contents are divided into the basic elements or tools of publishing:

- The overall plan
- The message: your text or content
- Type styles: both display type and body type
- Graphics: photos, logos, line art, and color
- Page layout
- Organization (navigation through your Web and links)
- Fulfillment (response and feedback)

These are the means by which your message is presented to your audience, thus achieving your communications goals. The process is illustrated in Figure 4.1.

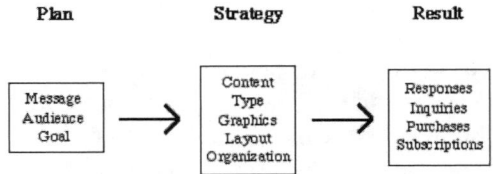

Figure 4.1 Achieving communications goals.

Planning Your HTML Publication

All too often, authors go ahead and publish something with only a vague notion of what they want to accomplish, or without even identifying their intended audience.

Before you decide to put anything online, ask yourself: Is the World Wide Web the best place for this material? Would I be better off with a brochure, a newspaper ad, a commercial, or a made-for-TV movie?

Begin by coming up with a publications *plan*. What is the goal of your publication? Decide what it is you want to say, and who you want to hear it.

Once you have a goal and a plan, map out a *strategy* for implementing it. This is where HTML comes in. Decide how you will use HTML. Will you have a flashy page with lots of graphics? Would you rather go for the sober, official look? Is your page a world unto itself, or is it a jumping-off point for other related resources to which you want to point the reader? Get your resources (your text and any photos, graphics, sound bites, or video clips) together, and combine them on a Web document using HTML.

The publisher's job doesn't end when a work goes online. You should determine the result you are looking for. Do you want people to respond to you somehow? If so, you need to have a way to process those inquiries or purchases.

An essential part of planning is understanding the guts of the software you're working with. In this case, you need to bear with me while I explain HTML's basic elements and document structure.

HTML Elements

There are two types of elements in HTML: *character entities* and *markup tags*.

Character Entities

Character entities are codes used to present special characters that HTML cannot display otherwise, such as an accent mark. Character entities are important for Web publishers, especially those in higher education who have to present foreign proper names and titles with the correct spelling and thus avoid the wrath of persnickity faculty members. (I'm not naming names.)

The thing is, you can't create the usual accented characters by simply typing keyboard commands on your Mac. You have to enter character entities, predefined substitutes for characters that:

- aren't recognized by HTML (accented foreign characters such as é, ü, or ç), or

- perform a special function within HTML (such as the greater-than (>) and less-than (<) characters, used to designate HTML tags).

If you type the greater- and less-than characters "straight" into your document, HTML may think that whatever you've typed between the brackets is some sort of bizarre new tag it doesn't recognize.

Instead, you have to type the following character entities. All character entities are case-sensitive and begin with an ampersand (&) and are followed by a semicolon (;):

- **<** for the less-than (<) sign

- **>** for the greater-than (>) sign

For example, you type the following to display the brackets around the
<BLOCKQUOTE> tag:

<p>this is an example showing how character entities can be displayed
within HTML to display the tag <BLOCKQUOTE>.</p>

Your browser displays the character entity typed previously, as shown in Figure 4.2.

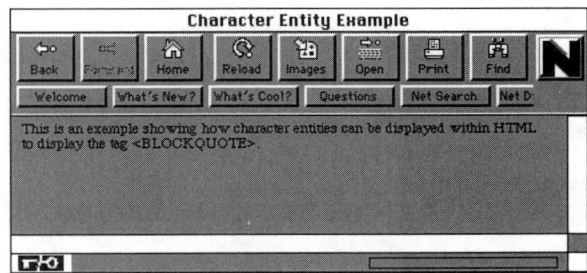

Figure 4.2 Character entities must be used to display special
characters in HTML.

Some HTML editors enter character entities automatically when you convert an
already-existing document, but if you're typing your HTML from scratch or using
something like an "ñ", it's best to look them up. A complete list is included in
Appendix F.

Tags

Markup tags are the basic building blocks of HTML. They allow you to structure
and describe the appearance of your document so that it can be displayed and
transferred from one computer to another. You do this by "tagging" or marking text
with commands that (usually) go on either side of it. The beginning tag is called the
start tag, for example, <HEAD>. The ending tag is called the *end tag,* for example,
</HEAD>.

Tags are the instructions HTML uses to tell your Web browser how your document
should look. You might think of them as an architects' instructions to builders to put
a window here and a door there in a new house. "Home," in this case, refers to a
home page, and the instructions tell the builder—Netscape, Mosaic, or another
browser—how big an element should be and where it should be positioned onscreen.

Not all tags have a start tag and end tag. Those that do are described as *nonempty* tags. Those that do not are called *empty* tags.

Nonempty Tags

Nonempty tags have text enclosed in the start and end tags that tell an HTML browser or editor to perform a certain function. Examples of nonempty tags include:

```
<b>Make this text bold</b>
<strong>Give this head strong emphasis</strong>
```

Empty Tags

Empty tags have no enclosed text and no end tag. These include:

```
<br>
```

which tells the browser to create a line break, and

```
<hr>
```

which tells the browser to insert a horizontal rule.

HTML Document Structure

Those who don't have a lot of experience in computer programming might look at an HTML document and find it a bit bewildering. Each document does have an understandable structure, however. HTML documents are divided into two parts: a "Head" and a "Body."

Head Elements

Head elements appear at the beginning of an HTML document. These elements affect the overall document. They also provide general information, such as the file's name, who wrote it, and what it is (an HTML file). The basic head elements you need to be concerned with include:

- <HTML> </HTML> (Tells the browser that this is an HTML document.)

- <HEAD> </HEAD> (Contains a tag that tells general subject of your page; usually the <TITLE> tag.)

118

A search "robot" like WebCrawler or the World Wide Web Worm scans the head of an HTML document to get information that it can use in a search, such as keywords about its subject matter.

- <TITLE> </TITLE> (Contains the text that appears within the browser window.)

Note: A robot (also known as a "worm") is a program such as InfoSeek or Aliweb that searches huge numbers of files automatically when given search criteria. A parser (or "interpreter") is a module or routine within a program that reads or "parses" computer data such as text or binary code and processes it to make it usable or readable. Netscape and Mosaic, for instance, parse or interpret the header information in an HTML document, display its title, and because of the tag <HTML>, know that the document has to be displayed as an HTML document.

It isn't strictly necessary for an HTML document to contain all three of these tags. Only <TITLE> is absolutely necessary. Your Web browser will probably display your document correctly without <HTML> or <HEAD>. But you should get in the habit of adding them because they are "good" HTML syntax and because they might be required by future versions of HTML.

Future Internet clients and servers may use standards other than HTML, so it's probably forward-looking to label your documents as HTML so that such browsers will know with certainty what to do with them.

The <HTML> </HTML> Tag

This is the opening tag in any HTML document. It defines the document for any parser or browser that reads it as being of the HTML Document Type Definition (DTD). It is considered optional by most browsers.

The start tag <HTML> goes at the beginning of the entire document. The end tag </HTML> goes at the end.

Note: When you cruise around the Web and look at the source code for Web pages you admire, you'll probably notice that many of them don't use either the <HTML> or <HEAD> tags. Yet your browser still displays the page. Technically, you don't have to use either of these tags to get your document to display on the Web. But future Internet clients and servers may use standards other than HTML, so it's probably forward-looking to label your documents as HTML so that such browsers will know with certainty what to do with them.

Also, as extensions to HTML multiply, it's possible that Web documents will contain heterogeneous elements, such as an <HTML> section, a <VRML> section, a <non-SGML-language> section, a <proprietary serving language> section, and so on. If this happens, it will be necessary to use <HTML> tags to differentiate the HTML sections.

The <HEAD> </HEAD> Tag

This is the second tag in a "correct" HTML document. Anything contained within the tag is thus designated as a "head" element that contains general information defining the properties of the entire document. Only a few tags go within the head tag. *Text should not go here!* Here's an example of an HTML document header, showing the tags that go here:

```
<html>
<head>
<title>Warbler Migration Patterns</title>
</head>
Warblers have been migrating in fewer and fewer numbers in recent years.
</html>
```

Some of the other tags that can go within the <HEAD> tag, such as <ISINDEX> or <LINK>, are explained later in this chapter.

Focusing on Your Subject: The <TITLE> </TITLE> Tag

Every document requires a short, specific title displayed at the top of your browser's window. The title should be placed within the <TITLE> </TITLE> tag, which, in turn, goes within the <HEAD> </HEAD> tag mentioned previously. Here's another example:

```
<html>
<head>
<title>A Guide to Basic HTML</title>
</head>
<body>
...the rest of your document goes here...
</body>
</html>
```

Titles are important. They must be short enough to fit on a Web browser yet specific enough to give Web readers an idea of what your document is about. (They also help *you* to remember what the subject is when you're shuffling through a list of your own files.)

Keep in mind that your title might end up on a list of "search results" on a search engine. It might also be listed as a link on someone else's page. Someone might access it randomly. Therefore, your title should be specific (Figure 4.3), not too vague and general (Figure 4.4), and not one that will send foreign readers scrambling for an English dictionary (Figure 4.5).

Figure 4.3 Keep titles short and specific.

Here is another good title found on the Web:

```
<title>Mario Cuomo Victory '94 Page</title>
```

Here are some not-so-good titles found on the Web:

```
<title>Super Home Page!</title>
<title>Chapter Nine</title>
<title>Smorgasboard</title>
```

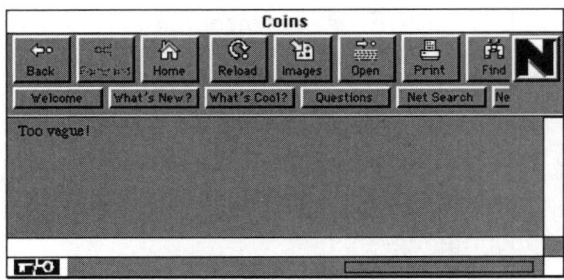

Figure 4.4 A title that's too vague.

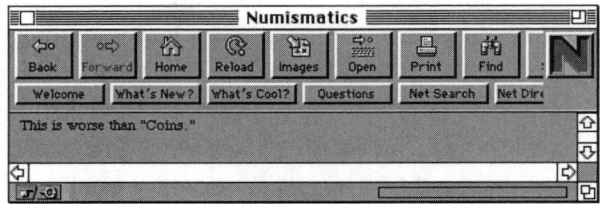

Figure 4.5 Remember, you might have foreign visitors to your Web site.

People who are paying by the minute to be connected to the Internet don't want to waste time searching through unclear or unnecessary information. A bad title just might turn them away from your Web publication.

Comments

Comments are commonly used by computer programmers, but most non-programmers are probably unfamiliar with them. These are like the little Post-It notes you might put on an artboard to give the printer instructions; they are messages that won't show up in print, but that provide useful background information about your document, such as its authorship.

Comments can go anywhere in a document, but the head is a common location for them. Each comment line begins with "**<!** " and ends with "**>**". The comment itself starts and ends with two hyphens, "**--**". Note that the exclamation mark is used only at the beginning, and there are blank spaces before and after the actual comment text, as follows:

```
<!-- This code updated by Greg Holden 4.30/95 -->
<!-- Contact me at myname@address for more info. -->
```

Warning: It's a good idea to avoid including actual HTML commands in comments. Some browsers may still pay attention to commands even if they are inside the comment tags. I haven't seen any evidence of this in Netscape, but I've heard that other browsers get confused.

Other Head Tags

The three head tags explained previously are the essential ones to know. Along with these, there are a number of other tags that might go in a head element. Some of them are rather obscure, and some are useful.

You don't need to know about the following head tags when you are a beginner, but they become useful as your documents become more sophisticated. You might also see them in someone else's code and wonder what planet they came from. Here are some brief explanations.

<ISINDEX>

This is an empty tag: there is no </ISINDEX>. This tag informs the viewer that the document is an index and can be searched by typing a keyword in a search form. When <ISINDEX> is in the head of an HTML document, it activates the Search field in Mosaic, allowing you to enter words to search, for instance.

The <ISINDEX> tag has to work with a server-side script, however. You don't just create an index by sticking this tag in your HTML document. Instead, you have to write a CGI (Common Gateway Interface) script that goes in the server that "serves" your Web documents to the Internet. You can read about this in Chapter 5.

Netscape Extension to <ISINDEX>

If your HTML document does have an <ISINDEX> tag, Netscape allows you to add the <PROMPT> tag. This lets the document's author specify something other than the default message:

"This is a searchable index. Enter search keywords:"

before the text input field of the index.

<LINK>

When you see the <LINK> tag in source code, you know the author is pretty good with HTML. <LINK> goes within the <HEAD> </HEAD> tag. It is also an empty tag; there is no </LINK>.

<LINK> is used to indicate that this document is related to documents or other objects. It might be used with attributes such as <REL>, <REV>, or <METHOD> (see Appendix E) to point to a "parent" or previous document in case the viewer has discovered it out of context and is wondering where the other documents are. It also might refer the reader to related indexes or glossaries, or give the author's email address. Here are some examples:

```
<LINK HREF="file1.html" REL="subdocument"  >
<LINK HREF="mailto:greg_holden@upubs.uchicago.edu">
```

Note that the <MAILTO> attribute is HTML's way of sending mail to people.

<BASE>

<BASE> is another tag that goes in the head of an HTML document. <BASE> is a kind of insurance policy. If your Internet provider or the person running your server misplaces your document while moving around a bunch of HTML files, doing "housekeeping," this is the place to indicate where it went in the first place. You provide the document's original URL, as in:

```
<BASE HREF="http://www.blob.dirt.edu/stuff/junk/file.html">
```

<BASE> is the URL from which relative paths are determined. If there is no <BASE>, the HTML user agent (browser) using the URL is originally used to access to the document. Think of it like a global pathname you can use to refer to documents. There are numerous practical applications for <BASE>. For example, let's say you keep all the graphics for a series of pages in one directory, and all the actual HTML in another directory a few levels removed. With <BASE>, you can refer to those graphics with relative paths without having to enter the entire path into your HTML.

<BASE> might also be useful if your site is fabulously popular in a faraway place, such as overseas, and you "mirror" your site there to improve performance and reduce Net traffic. The <BASE> reference indicates the original site of the documents.

The <BODY> Tag

The <BODY> tag subsumes basically everything in an HTML document that's not included in the <HEAD> tag. The body element is enclosed by the <BODY> </BODY> tag. The start tag <BODY> comes after </HEAD>. The end tag goes right at the end of the document, just before </HTML>.

Message (Text or Content)

Now that you have a plan and a basic understanding of the structure of HTML, let's get into the commands that affect how your message—your basic text—is presented.

Paragraph Tag <P>

Unfortunately, the most basic of the text markup tags in HTML isn't straightforward. I'll try and make it simple, though. When HTML 1.0 came out, paragraphs were empty <P> tags. There was no </P>. Paragraphs were designated as shown in Figure 4.6 (note that I've added some line break <BR> tags as well).

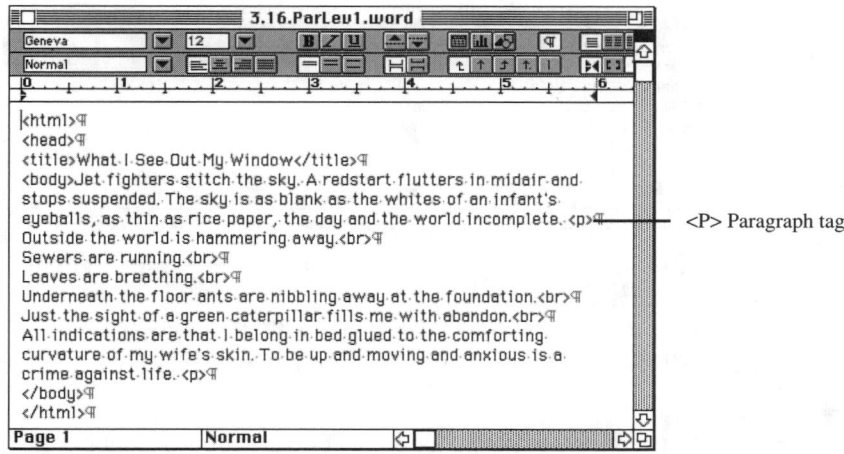

Figure 4.6 The easier way: HTML 1.0 paragraph markup.

Most browsers still assume that paragraphs will be designated like this because they were created around the time of HTML 1.0. They assume that a <P> tag denotes the end of a paragraph and inserts a blank line after it.

125

This is the easy way to specify paragraph breaks and, frankly, this is the way I and most other common folk do it. However, the current description for HTML 3.0 defines the paragraph tag as nonempty: a start tag and an end tag should enclose each paragraph. This is "encouraged but not required;" however, most browsers will still correctly display paragraphs properly delimited with <P> alone.

Another reason to use <P> and </P> (although not the most important one) is that it makes your Web pages somewhat more search-friendly. Search programs such as InfoSeek, Web "crawlers," and robots that bring back a paragraph of text for the searcher to look at work somewhat better with <P> and </P> to delimit the paragraph and thus define what the program should display.

The HTML 3.0 version of paragraph markup is shown in Figure 4.7.

<P></P> Paragraph tags →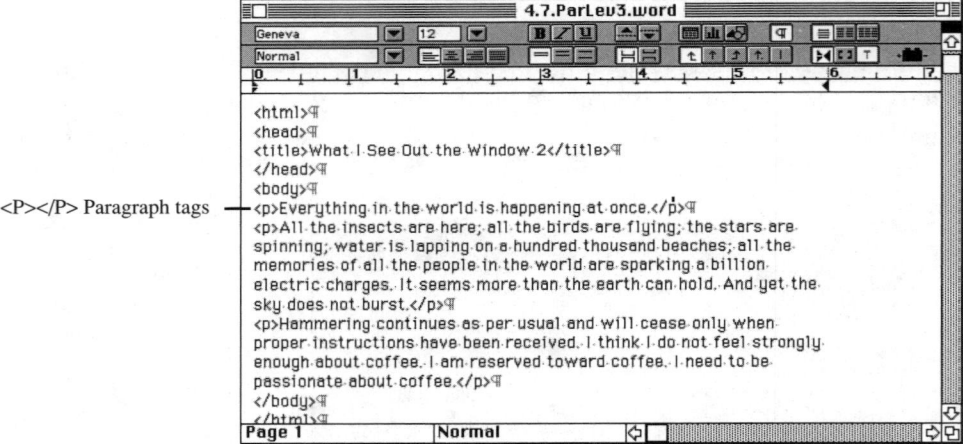

Figure 4.7 The "proper" way: HTML 3.0 paragraph markup.

 **Warning:** You don't need to use <P> after headers, or with parts of a list such as <UL>, <HR>, <DT>, or <DD>. These tags imply paragraph breaks.

Because part of my job is to teach you to write "good" HTML, I suppose I ought to promote the use of <P> </P>.

I've tried it, though, and it's a hassle. The "old" way is easier. Either system creates the same effect by ensuring that a paragraph is separated from those above and below it. Besides, whatever HTML 3.0 specifies now is bound to change in 4.0 or 5.0.

My suggestion, then, is to pick whatever alternative you're most comfortable with. If you prefer, you can simply use <P> while being aware that some future version of HTML might require you to use </P>.

You can also use <P> as a paragraph separator, rather than denoting the beginning or end of a paragraph, as shown in Figure 4.8.

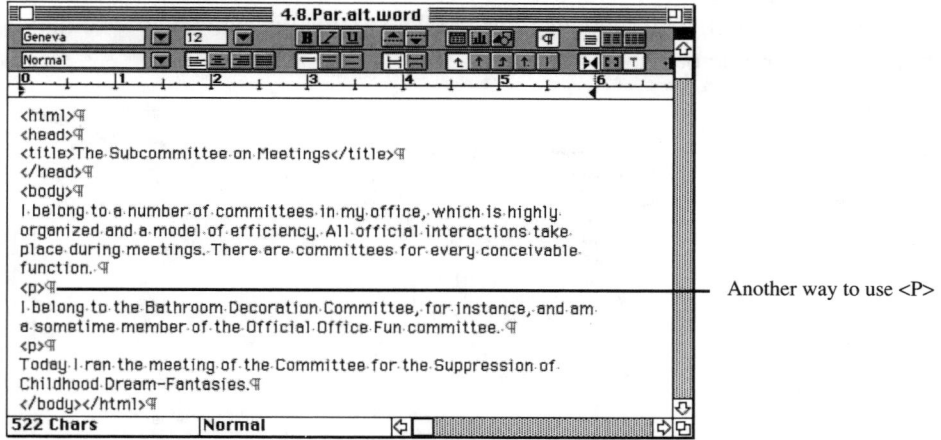

Another way to use <P>

Figure 4.8 Another alternative: using <P> as a paragraph separator.

Greg's Soapbox

No matter which method you use, what it boils down to is that Web documents are set up to have blank spaces between each paragraph, and no paragraph indents. This is not what those of us in traditional print publication are used to. On the other hand, you're not working in print; you're preparing documents that are meant to be read onscreen. They are more readable this way. Still, I eagerly await the day when publishers have such options as indented paragraphs, no space between paragraphs, or variable leading between paragraphs or between lines.

Line Break Tag

In contrast to <P> </P>, the <BR> tag is blissfully straightforward. This is an empty tag; there is no end tag </BR>. A line break is made without inserting an additional blank space. An obvious application is a poem (this is one of mine). Figure 4.9 shows a poem marked up for the Web in Word using line break tags. (You may have noticed that on occasion I put several tags on one line. That's just to keep the illustrations in this book small. Netscape displays the documents the same way whether there are three tags or one per line.)

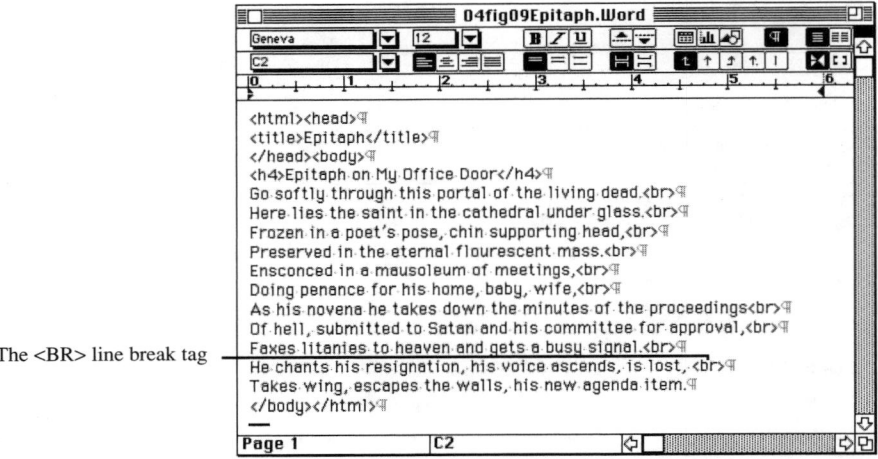

The <BR> line break tag

Figure 4.9 Text markup using line break tags.

The output in Netscape is shown in Figure 4.10.

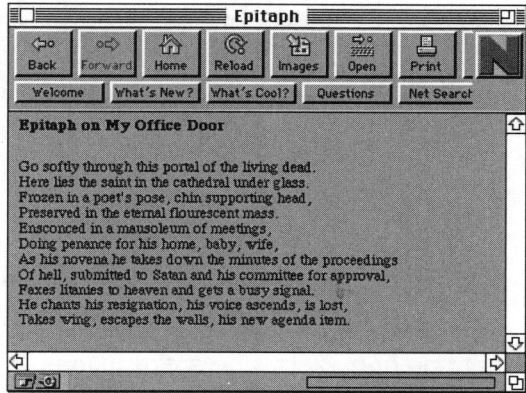

Figure 4.10 Netscape screen showing display of line break tags.

Netscape Extensions to Line Break Tags

Netscape has some nifty additions to line break tags that break text around images. Two of them, <NOBR> and <WBR>, give you more control over where lines are broken.

<NOBR> stands for "NO BReak." Text enclosed by <NOBR> </NOBR> is not broken at the end of a line. This is useful for making long HTTP addresses more readable.

<WBR> doesn't force a line break, but tells Netscape that the line can be broken where the <WBR> tag occurs. This is useful if you have a long line of text and you know exactly where you want to allow it to be broken.

Figure 4.11 shows examples of <NOBR> and <WBR>. The markup for this screen shot gave me the chance to combine character entities, definition lists, logical styles, and these new line break tags.

Note: Notice the unorthodox (some would say, improper) use of <DL><DD> to indent the fifth line of Walt Whitman's poem. It may not be

continued

the intended HTML use of the directory list, but it works. The primary purpose here is to communicate and any tool that gives more control over the appearance of a document will be favored by publishers. To those who might say, "This formatting won't be displayed by any browser other than Netscape," I'd respond, "Why don't you get Netscape, then?" Format your publication so that it looks the way you want, using the best available tools for the job.

```
<html><head><title>Netscape line breaks</title></head><body>
<dl>
<dt><strong>&lt;NOBR&gt;</strong>
<dd>More information about Netscape's extensions to HTML can be found
at: <NOBR>http://home.mcom.com/assist/net_sites/
html.extensions.html</NOBR>.
</dl>
<p>
<dl>
<dt><strong>&lt;WBR&gt;</strong>
<dd>Out of the cradle endlessly rocking,
<dd>Out of the mocking-bird's throat, the musical shuttle,
<dd>Out of the Ninth-month midnight,
<dd><NOBR>Over the sterile sands and the fields beyond where the child
leaving his bed <WBR><dl><dd>wander'd alone, bareheaded, barefoot,
</NOBR></dl>
<dd>Down from the shower'd halo...
</dl>
</body></html>
```

The output is shown in Figure 4.11.

Netscape has also come up with a number of extensions that provide control over how text breaks around "floating" images:

<BR CLEAR=LEFT> breaks the line, and moves vertically down until you have a clear left margin (no floating images).

<BR CLEAR=RIGHT> does the same for the right margin.

<BR CLEAR=ALL> moves down until both margins are clear of images.

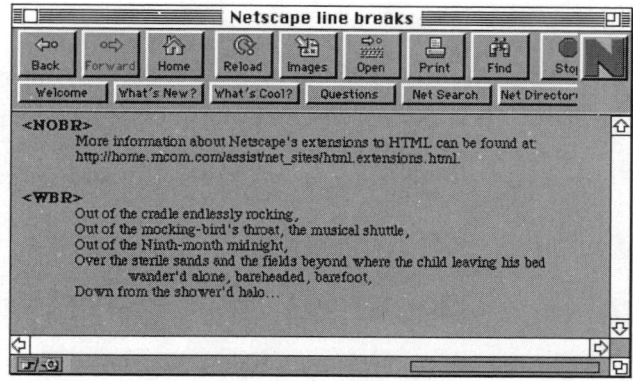

Figure 4.11 Netscape's <NOBR> and <WBR> line break extensions.

These extensions are shown in Figure 4.12.

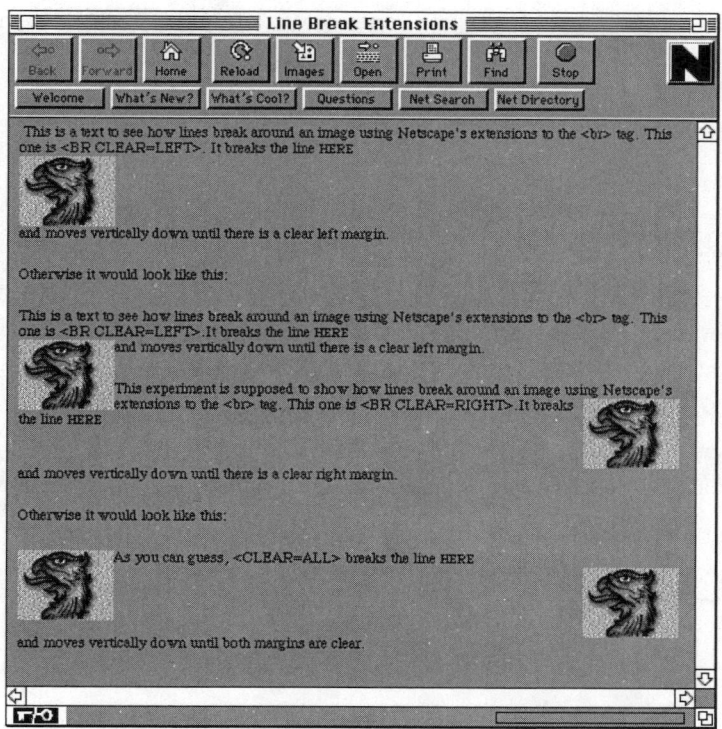

Figure 4.12 Netscape extensions allowing text wrap around images.

<BLOCKQUOTE>

The <BLOCKQUOTE> </BLOCKQUOTE> tag allows you to indent or otherwise emphasize a block of text, such as a long quotation. Typically this may be slightly indented or italicized. <BLOCKQUOTE> also causes a paragraph break, and includes a blank space both before and after the quotation. An example appears in Figure 4.13.

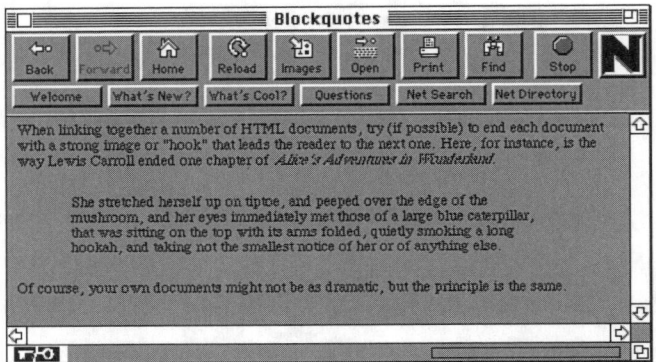

Figure 4.13 The <BLOCKQUOTE> tag in action.

The <ADDRESS> Tag

Documents on the Web don't come through the mail, so readers can actually look through a lot of information without being sure where it has come from or who wrote it.

It's important, then, to "sign" your Web page using the <ADDRESS> tag. This tells your browser to format any information contained within the start and end tags in the standard "address" format used by the program. In most cases, this will simply be italic:

```
<HR>
<ADDRESS>
Copyright 1994 Greg Holden. All rights reserved<br>
greg_holden@upubs.uchicago.edu
</ADDRESS>
```

(Be sure to separate the various parts of your address with <BR> line breaks.) The output can be seen in Figure 4.14.

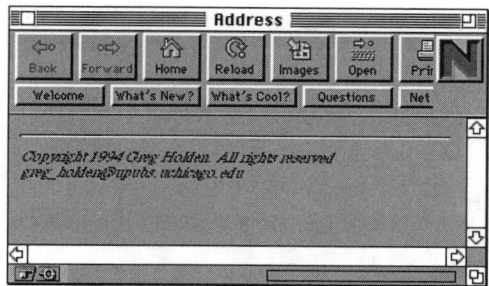

Figure 4.14 The <ADDRESS> tag.

Most addresses are preceded by a horizontal rule to separate them from the rest of the text. Near the address, but not inside the <ADDRESS> tag, you might also include some information about when a document was last updated, and an email address where the reader can get more information. An address doesn't necessarily have to include a proper name:

```
<HR>
<ADDRESS>
Webmaster@justsomenode.com
</ADDRESS>
```

Greg's Soapbox

IMHO, the best return addresses provide the most information about a document—not just when it was last updated, but some mention of the larger organization or company to which the page belongs. For instance, I might be admiring the page from the "High-Powered Imaging Lab," but I have to search through the various folders in the HTTP address for the page to discover that the lab is part of "Supertech University."

Your email address can also be a link that, when clicked, automatically sends mail to the author/Webmaster. To do this, you include a <MAILTO> URL in the link, like so:

```
<ADDRESS>
<A HREF="mailto:greg_holden@upubs.uchicago.edu">Greg
Holden@upubs.uchicago.edu</A>
</ADDRESS>
```

Does your return address have to be formatted with the <ADDRESS> tag? Can it be presented in some unusual format, such as 24 bold italic type with a blinking background? Technically, yes, but it's best to avoid this.

Putting your address at the bottom of a document in simple italic, upper- and lower-case, and separated by a horizontal rule is an informal but increasingly widespread convention on the Web. People look for your address at the bottom of your page in a predictable format. Don't make them go searching for it.

Preformatted Text

The <PRE> </PRE> or preformatted text tag is supposed to display preformatted ASCII, usually in a fixed width typewriter-like font. It allows some alignment of textual elements, but the results are uneven.

Blank spaces rather than tabs are required for alignment (just the opposite of what desktop publishers are taught). In fact, tabs are often changed to a single blank space by a browser, which is why simply enclosing a table in the <PRE> </PRE> doesn't work.

The text rarely aligns correctly the first time the text is displayed in a browser. You have to go back and forth between browser and text editor, laboriously adding blank spaces until you can get the columns to align, more or less. After all this effort, your reward is to be stuck with a misaligned table in Courier in the middle of your nice Times Roman text (see Figure 4.15).

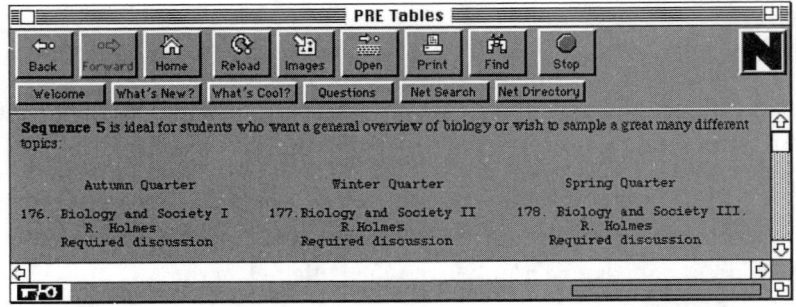

Figure 4.15 A preformatted text "table."

<PRE> works as an aligning tool only if the user has already specified a fixed-width font in the browser's Preferences menu. (Courier is the most commonly used one on the Mac.) But since HTML 3.0 now allows the creation of tables, <PRE> should probably be avoided altogether as a way to align text.

You can help your browser adjust the point side or margins of preformatted text by adding an optional attribute to the <PRE> start tag: <WIDTH>. Here's how <WIDTH> is added:

```
<PRE WIDTH=80>Put your preformatted text here</PRE>
```

This tells your browser that a maximum number of 80 characters will need to be displayed on a single line. A default value of 80 is often assumed; values of 40, 80, or 132 are recommended.

> **Note:** HTML does not allow the use of paragraph formatting elements such as <P> within preformatted text (they just won't be recognized by browsers). You *can* use character styles such as <B>, <I>, and <U>, as well as anchors.

I have seen <PRE> used to present headings in a typeface that contrasts with the rest of the body: heads will be in bold Courier, for instance, and the body text in Times Roman. So it can work.

The <PRE> tag can serve another very important purpose for Web publishers—not the purpose for which it was designed, but an essential element on any well-designed page—the all-important white space.

Using <PRE> to Insert White Space

The capability of the <PRE> tag to preserve whatever characters are within it, including blank spaces, has been exploited by some clever Webmasters as a way to insert blank space into an HTML document.

As I already mentioned, HTML doesn't recognize the carriage return character (¶) in a word processing document. Therefore, you can't create white space between textual elements by simply punching the carriage return key a couple of times—or by using multiple <P> tags.

You can, however, create white space in an HTML document when you include the normal carriage return and tab characters inside the <PRE> </PRE> tags. Figure 4.16 shows the HTML code that was used to produce white space. The white space resulting from this code is shown in Figure 4.17.

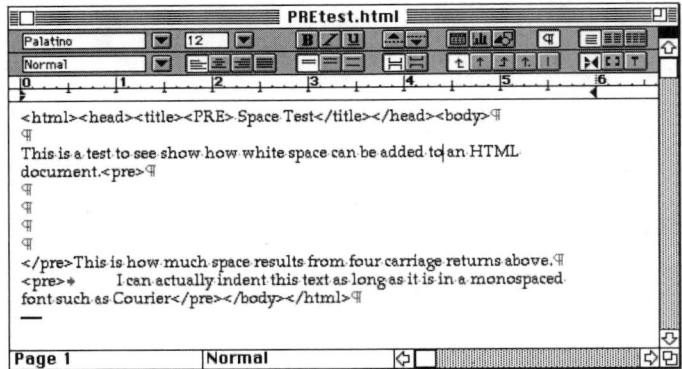

Figure 4.16 HTML code to insert white space.

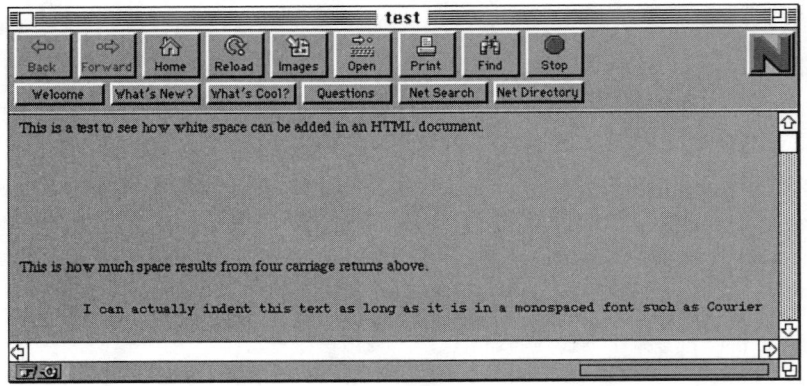

Figure 4.17 Using the <PRE> tag to insert blank space.

Emphasizing Text with Styles

Style tags are used to format words or characters in HTML. This is in contrast to using headings or list tags to format paragraphs or large blocks of text.

Anyone with experience in printing or publishing is familiar with one way of changing the look of characters through **bold,** *italic,* or <u>underlining</u>. These are classified as *character styles* in HTML.

Character styles are one of two ways to add style to text in HTML. The other is using *logical style* tags. Both are listed in Appendix E, "HTML Elements."

Note: Keep in mind that all style commands, whether they are logical or character styles, may be ignored by non-graphical browsers such as Lynx. If your first priority is to reach all possible Web readers, rather than to create a good-looking page, it's best to use some generic emphasis such as (shudder) ALL CAPS. Because this makes you look like you're SHOUTING, I suggest using one of HTML's style tags, instead.

Character Styles

One way to give emphasis to characters or words apart from the text around them is to use the italic <I> </I> tag or the bold <B> </B> tag:

```
I read about it in <i>Internet World</i>
"I'm dying to get his <b>http address!"</b>
```

The only tricky thing here is that the underline tag <U> </U> is not an "official" part of HTML but a Netscape extension, and not recognized by all browsers. This is because of the convention of underlining to indicate clickable text—and because underlining is pretty ugly and hard to read. Remember, anything you underline in an HTML document may be interpreted by your audience as "clickable."

All three character tags aren't recognized by all browsers, and for that reason, HTML authors are encouraged to use logical styles instead.

Logical Styles

Those of us who are used to bold, italic, and underline have to make an adjustment to use logical styles (called "Information Type Elements" in the current HTML 3.0 description). In other words, they're a pain. However, logical styles are recognized by many different types of computers and are the recommended means for emphasizing text in HTML.

Logical styles designate text that is to be displayed differently from the text around it. It's up to the user's individual browser program to determine how it will actually be displayed.

The most common logical styles perform roughly the same function as bold, italic, or underlining, and are easy to get used to. There are also some logical styles that specify text to be used for a special purpose. They might highlight a definition, computer code, or a sample bit of text. Table 4.1 lists the logical styles in HTML 2.0.

Table 4.1 Logical Styles

Tag	Purpose
<STRONG></STRONG>	Gives strong emphasis to selected text, usually through boldface.
<CITE></CITE>	Used for a citation to a title or other textual reference, usually making the text italic.
<EM></EM>	Gives slightly greater emphasis to text, usually through italic (or bold on Mosaic).
<TT></TT>	Turns selected text into a monospaced font such as Courier.
<SAMP></SAMP>	Text is a sample, used for examples.
<KBD></KBD>	Indicates text that the user might type at the keyboard, as in login examples.
<VAR></VAR>	Text varies; exact value is to be supplied by the user.
<CODE></CODE>	Text is to be displayed in computer code; usually rendered in a monospaced font.

Some of these last four logical styles in the table might seem to be more trouble to remember than they are worth. They often end up as whatever monospaced font your browser is set up for, such as Courier or Monaco. But <KBD> and <CODE> are useful for people creating technical documentation.

Logical versus Character Styles: The Showdown

What difference does it make, really, if you use logical or character styles? Let's take some text and mark it up both ways (with apologies to Lewis Carroll for adding even more emphasis to this passage from *Alice's Adventures in Wonderland* for this test).

Here is the character style markup:

> "But it <i>isn't</i>old!" Tweedledum cried, in a greater fury than ever. "It's new, I tell you—I bought it yesterday—my nice <i>new</i> <tt>rattle!"</tt> and his voice rose to a perfect scream.

(Yes, I know <TT> isn't a character style. I just wanted to see if there was any difference between it and <KBD>.)

The results are displayed in Figure 4.18.

Note: Italics are hard to read onscreen. When italic and roman type come together so closely, it's hard for most 72 dots-per-inch screens to separate the characters. To provide an extra space after an italic word to make it more legible onscreen, you might want to add the nonbreaking space character entity: ** **. For instance, the first italic word in the previous example would be, "But it <I>isn't** **</I>old!"

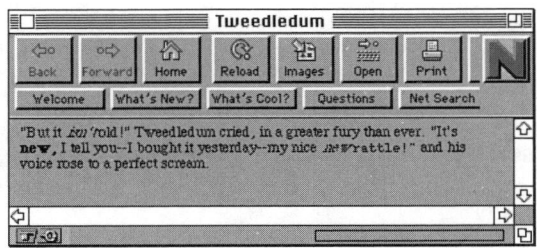

Figure 4.18 Character styles: output in Netscape.

Here is the logical style markup:

"But it <cite>isn't</cite>old!" Tweedledum cried, in a greater fury than ever. "It's new, I tell you—I bought it yesterday—my nice new <kbd>rattle!"</kbd> and his voice rose to a perfect scream.

The result is shown in Figure 4.19.

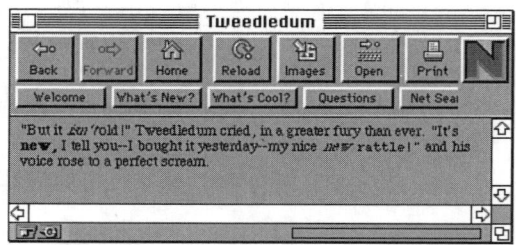

Figure 4.19 Logical styles: output in Netscape.

Looks like a tie: again, use the styles you are most comfortable with, but be aware that character styles aren't recognized by all browsers.

Lists

You can use lists to represent collections of items. There are basically six types of lists: ordered lists, unordered lists, definition lists, menu and directory lists, nested lists, and compact lists. A discussion of each of these types follows.

Unordered Lists

Here's another unordered list and the HTML code that created it. First, the code. The <UL> </UL> tag specifies the start and end of the list, and <LI> marks each *list item*:

People usually remember only three Marx brothers, but in their early vaudeville days, they included:<p>
<ul>
<li>Groucho
<li>Chico
<li>Harpo

```
<li>Zeppo
<li>Gummo
<li>Minnie, their mother.
</ul>
```

Note: First, there is no need to type a </LI> end tag. Second, make sure that you don't type the bullet (•) yourself; HTML creates it for you. If you have an already-bulleted list in a document that you are translating to HTML, delete the bullets beforehand or your Web browser will display two bullets before each item.

The result is shown in Figure 4.20.

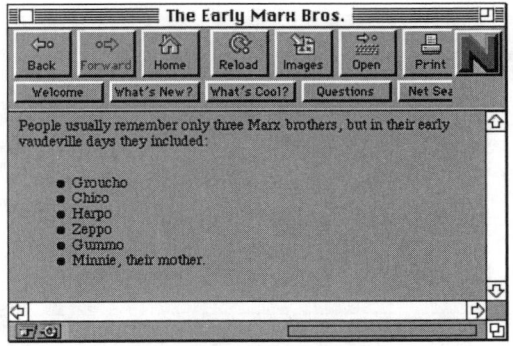

Figure 4.20 An unordered list.

Netscape Extensions to Unordered Lists <UL>

Usually, the bullets used in an unordered list change as the list moves from level to level. You move to a new level every time you "nest" a list within another list (see the section "Nested Lists" that follows). First, the bullet is a solid dot, and then a hollow circle, and then a hollow square.

A Netscape extension allows you to specify which of the three bullet forms you want to use. To indicate your bullet, you can add to the <UL> tag:

TYPE=disc, TYPE=circle, or TYPE=square

141

Ordered Lists

In an ordered list, your Web browser numbers each list item with the numerals "1, 2, 3," and so on. The only difference is that the <UL> tag is changed to <OL>. The code to create an ordered list follows. The result is shown in Figure 4.21.

```
The Marx Brothers' earliest movies are also considered to be their best.
They are, in chronological order:
<ol>
<li>The Coconuts (1929)
<li>Animal Crackers (1930)
<li>Monkey Business (1931)
<li>Horsefeathers (1932)
<li>Duck Soup (1933)
<li>A Night At the Opera (1935)
</ol>
```

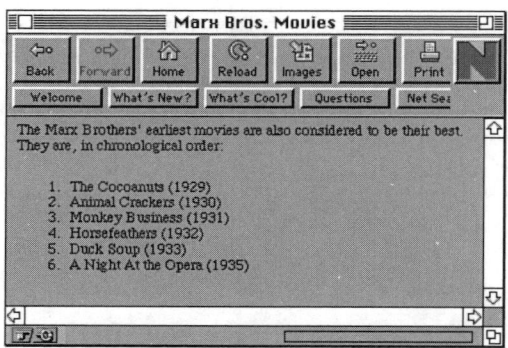

Figure 4.21 An ordered list.

Netscape Extensions to Ordered Lists <OL>

Instead of having your numbered list actually be arranged with numbers (1, 2, 3, and so on), Netscape has added a <TYPE> tag (<OL TYPE=?>) that allows you to specify whether you want list items marked with:

A. capital letters (<TYPE=A>)

a. small letters (<TYPE=a>)

I. large roman numerals (<TYPE=I>)

i. small roman numerals (<TYPE=i>)

1. the default numbers (<TYPE=1>)

In the event that you want to start an ordered list at a number other than 1, use the <START> attribute. <OL START=5>, for instance, will start the list with item number 5. <OL TYPE=? START=5 displays either an 'E', 'e', 'V', 'v', or '5' based on the <TYPE> tag.

Netscape Extensions to <LI>

Just in case you want to change the list item type from roman numbers to capital letters or numbers as you progress, Netscape lets you add the <TYPE> attribute to the <LI> tag. For example, <LI TYPE=i> places a small roman numeral before the item, <LI TYPE=A> places a capital letter before the item, and so on.

In case you need even more control over ordered lists, there's a <VALUE> attribute that allows you to change the number count for a list item and all others following it. In the following example, the numbered items proceed as follows: 1, 2, 9, 10.

```
<ol>
<li>item number 1
<li>item number 2
<li value="9">third item, numbered 9
<li>fourth item, numbered 10
</ol>
```

Definition Lists

The third kind of list in HTML is called a glossary or definition list. It can be used in presenting a list of items, each followed by an indented paragraph of definition of explanation under it. Here's an example of the resulting code, and the list it creates:

```
<h3>Famous Groucho Marx Characters</h3>
<dl>
<dt>Professor Quincy Adams Wagstaff
<dd>Huxley College professor in <em>Horsefeathers</em>
<dt>Rufus T. Firefly
<dd>President of Fredonia in <em>Duck Soup</em>
<dt>Otis B. Driftwood
<dd>sleazy manager in <em>A Night At the Opera</em>
</dl>
```

Again, note that <DD> and <DT> do require end tags. The result is shown in Figure 4.22.

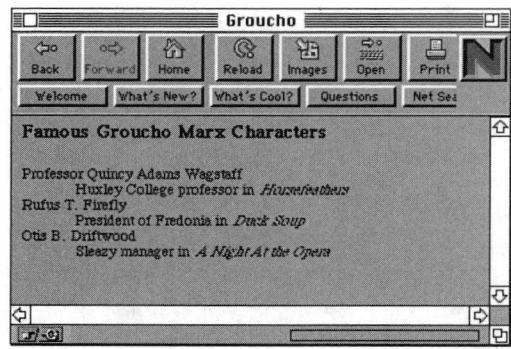

Figure 4.22 Glossary or definition list.

Glossary lists are also useful for "nesting" a series of items in a list beneath a topic heading but without adding a bullet or number before each item (see Figure 4.23):

```
<dl>
<dt><h3>Presidents of the University of Chicago</h3>
<dd>William Rainey Harper 1892-1906
<dd>Harry Pratt Judson 1907-23
<dd>Ernest DeWitt Burton 1923-25
<dd>Max Mason 1925-28
<dd>Robert Maynard Hutchins 1929-51
<dd>Lawrence Kimpton 1951-60
<dd>George W. Beadle 1961-68
<dd>Edward H. Levi 1968-75
<dd>John T. Wilson 1975-78
<dd>Hanna H. Gray 1978-92
<dd>Hugo Sonnenschein 1992-present
</dl>
```

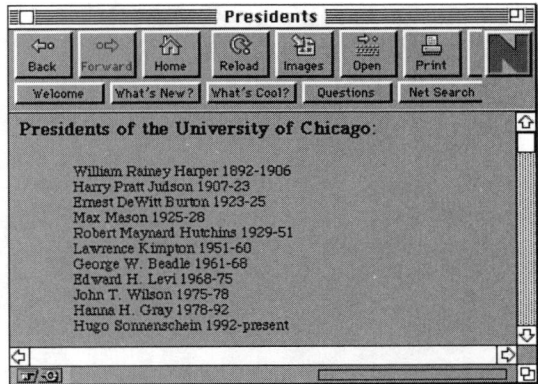

Figure 4.23 Glossary lists: a way to avoid bullets or numbers.

Nested Lists

If you want to create a table of contents or an outline for a long document, try putting a list inside another list. HTML indents or "nests" each list beneath the preceding one. The challenge for you is to keep track of each list and make sure it has the correct start and end tags. One way to keep track is to indent the various levels in your word processor by tabbing them. The tabs aren't readable by your Web browser. You can also add comments as notes to yourself to keep track of the lists.

```
<ul>
<li>Famous Scenes From Marx Brothers Movies
<li>Groucho and Friends
   <ul>
   <li>Groucho and Gummo
   <li>Groucho and Margaret Dumont
   <ul>
      <li>Coconuts: the hotel lobby scene
      <li>Duck Soup: Groucho is named president
      <ul>
         <li>&quot;You can leave in a minute and a huff.&quot;
         </ul>
      <li>A Night At the Opera: Restaurant Scene
      </ul>
   <li>Groucho and Chico
      <ul>
      <li>Monkey Business: In the captain's stateroom
```

```
    <li>A Night at the Opera: Going over the contract
    </ul>
  <li>Zeppo: Was he ever funny?
</ul>
```

The result can be seen in Figure 4.24.

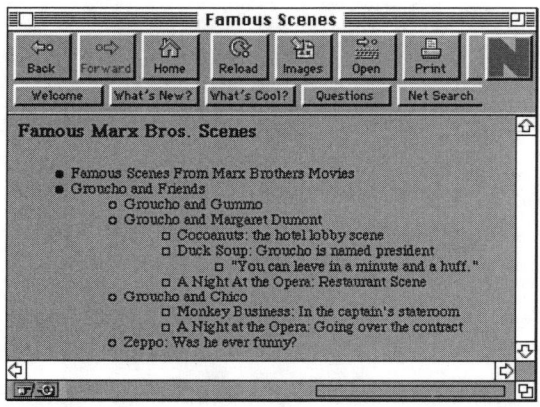

Figure 4.24 A nested unordered list.

Changing all instances of <UL> in the list to the Netscape extension
<UL TYPE=DISC> marks all list items with solid bullets (see Figure 4.25).

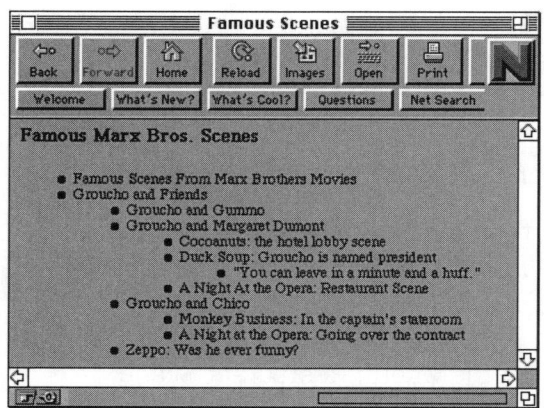

Figure 4.25 The <UL TYPE=DISC> tag in action.

Nested lists can be ordered lists. They can also combine ordered and unordered lists, which begins to get complex.

As in the previous example, here is the general principle: Whenever you want to move in (or to the right), use the start tag <UL> or <OL>. Whenever you want to move back (or to the left), use the end tag </UL> or </OL>.

```
<ol>
<li>My obsession with the Marx Bros.
<li>Early years: childish Groucho imitations
   <ul>
   <li>Grade school: sent home for wearing shoe polish on face
   <li>High school: detention for pinching and chasing
      <ol>
      <li>Attempt at Harpo pantomime fails
      <li>Staging "You Bet Your Life" in theater class
      </ol>
   <li>College: hosting a film festival
   </ol>
<li>Adulthood: Years of therapy to treat my obsession
</ol>
```

The result is shown in Figure 4.26.

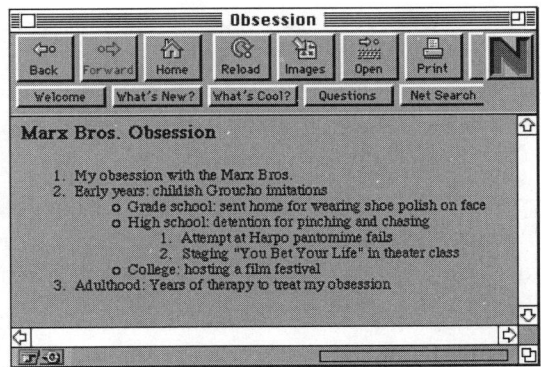

Figure 4.26 A nested unordered/ordered list.

Menu and Directory Lists

These are list tags (<MENU> and <DIR>) that you might see references to in documentation, but that you should ignore because their functions have been

147

replaced by other tags that produce the same effects. Menu and directory lists were included in HTML 1.0 and 2.0, but the current definition for 3.0 does not include them.

Other Netscape Extensions Affecting Text

The following extensions add flexibility to HTML by allowing you to do textual things in Netscape that you can't do otherwise. Remember though, that only readers with Netscape can view these formats!

Changing Font Sizes

Here is the tag:

```
<FONT SIZE=value>. . .</FONT>
```

Like buying a car from Henry Ford—you could have any color you wanted as long as it was black—publishers creating HTML documents are limited to a single point size for text type. This is pretty frustrating for those who use point size variety like a kid in a penny candy shop. Other than using one of the heading tags, there's been no way to control it.

In Netscape, however, you can change the font size with a new extension to HTML, the <FONT SIZE=VALUE> </FONT> tag. The attribute <VALUE> is a number that either increases or decreases the size of any text contained within the start and end tags relative to the normal or "default" font size 3.

You specify if the type is to be 1–4 sizes larger or smaller than the base size (the numbers here aren't "real" point sizes but abstract numbers). Valid values range from 1–7, so the biggest increase you can make is "+4" over the default size of 3.

Warning: Keep in mind that you don't know anything about the way that your client's system is configured, or how it deals with fonts. For example, a Mac without appropriate TrueType or PostScript fonts running will display jagged type if it doesn't have the default font in the modified size you've specified. Macs are the most font-savvy platform. Also remember that type that's smaller than 10 points looks great on the printed page but is illegible onscreen. Netscape's default is 12-point variable-width and 10-point fixed-width.

Chapter 4

It's easy for Web publishers to get carried away with this newfound power and create visual effects they'd rarely produce in print (see Figure 4.27). It's fun to do, but remember, keep it in context and don't get punch happy.

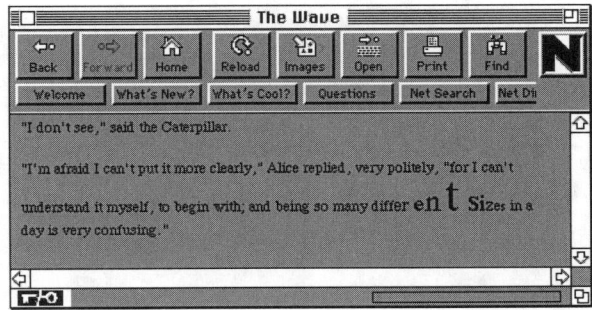

Figure 4.27 An example of overformatting: doing the "wave" with font sizes.

In Netscape, the default font size can be changed using the <BASEFONT SIZE=VALUE> tag. Subsequent font changes will be made relative to it. Here's an example of text marked up with a different base font. The output in Netscape is shown in Figure 4.28.

Where to Find It

Netscape uses its own <FONT> tags extensively on its own pages. Visit http://home.netscape.com/ and look at the source code to get more examples.

```
<html>
<head>
<title>Changing Base Font Size</title>
</head>
<body>
<BASEFONT SIZE="6">Often, in the introductory chapter to a long work, it's customary to present the first paragraph in a larger type size than the rest of the document to highlight it for dramatic effect. This is an example. This would also be useful for creating an advertisement on the Web.
<p>
<FONT SIZE="-2">This is the normal font size minus 2. It can be used for the rest of the document. Or vice versa: the body of the document can be the base size and the introductory paragraph can be &quot;+2&quot;.
</FONT>
</body>
</html>
```

149

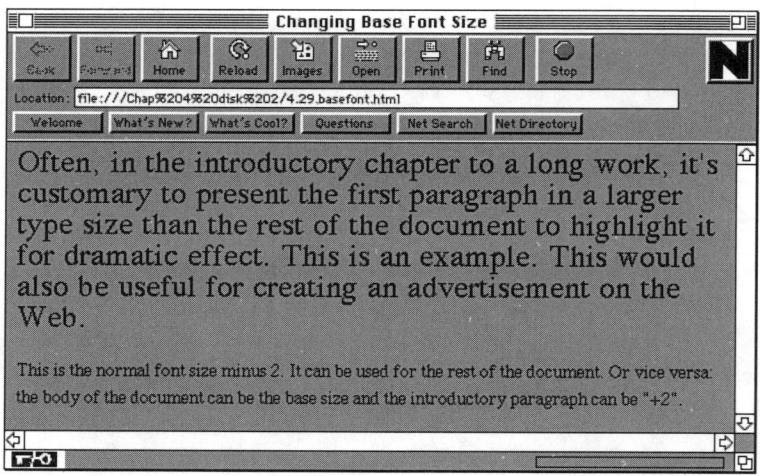

Figure 4.28 Changing the default font size.

 **Warning:** As I pointed out in the last warning, most if not all of these nifty formatting techniques fail to show up when your document is displayed in a browser other than Netscape. You may want to alternate formatting that will show up, such as the formatting styles <EM> or <STRONG>. If your document is full of font size changes, think about providing an alternate document altogether: one for Netscape and one for other browsers that use more widely recognized formatting tags.

Caps and Small Caps

Manipulating Netscape's font size extensions allows you to emulate another commonly used character style in conventional publishing: caps and small caps. Here's an example:

```
<html>
<head><title>Caps and Small Caps</title></head><body>
&lt;FONTSIZE=&quot;+3&quot;&gt; seems to work better with bigger
headings:
<H2>
<FONT SIZE="+3">T</FONT>HE
<FONT SIZE="+3">U</FONT>NIVERSITY OF
```

```
<FONT SIZE="+3">C</FONT>HICAGO<BR>
<FONT SIZE="+3">T</FONT>HE
<FONT SIZE="+3">C</FONT>OLLEGE
</H2>
<pre>
</pre>
&lt;FONT SIZE=&quot;+1&quot;&gt; seems to work better with body
text:<P>
<FONT SIZE="+1">H</FONT>UGO
<FONT SIZE="+1">F.</FONT>
<FONT SIZE="+1">S</FONT>ONNENSCHEIN, President of the University of
Chicago
</body></html>
```

The output is shown in Figure 4.29.

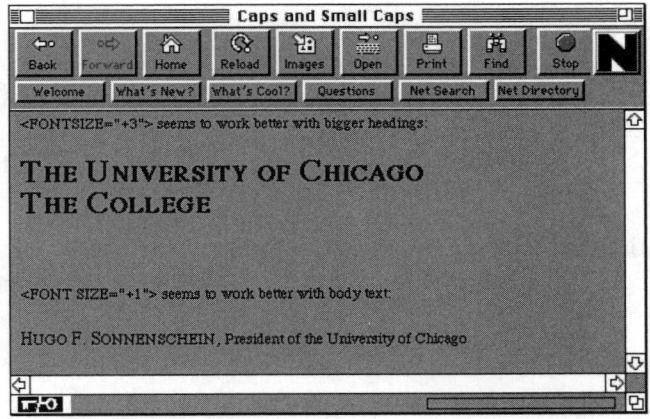

Figure 4.29 Caps and small caps.

<CENTER>

HTML 3.0 proposes using a variation on the paragraph tag, <PALIGN="CENTER">, allow centering of text. But you don't have to wait for HTML 3.0 to become finalized. In Netscape, you can already center any text contained between the <CENTER> </CENTER> tags. Needless to say, from a publishing standpoint, it's wonderful.

<BLINK>

On the other hand, one of the Netscape features that's not so wonderful is this one. I hesitate to even mention it because it is overused—actually, using it once may constitute overuse.

Basically, any text contained within the <BLINK> </BLINK> tags appears with a square area behind it appearing to blink from light to dark. It's one of those things that, the first time you see it, seems "Cool." After that, it's obnoxious. Worst of all, the reader can't turn it off. I have never seen a good use of blink. If you have, please tell me. Don't use it.

Tags for Headings

Heading are used to divide a document into sections. Each heading has its own level of importance within a document and, as such, headings are numbered from H1 to H6. Most browsers (although not all) allow the user to configure how headings appear onscreen. The general rule, though, is that H1 headings are the most important—they introduce major sections of your work—and H6 headings are the least important.

I tend to be a little unorthodox about headings, probably as a result of my newspaper background. I'll give you the orthodox "party line" first and then put my own spin on it.

You might think of headings as levels in an outline, as shown in Figure 4.30.

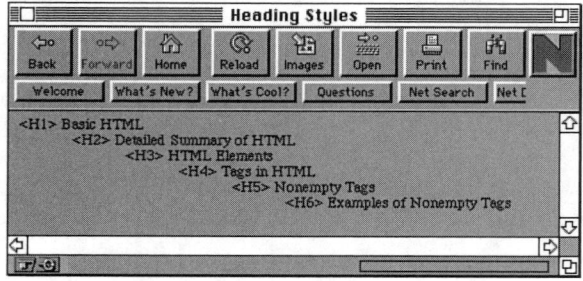

Figure 4.30 Levels of various headings

The "party line" calls for headings to be used hierarchically, from H1 to H6, in order, without skipping from a level H1 to a level H4 heading, for instance.

The reason for this, which makes sense at least in theory, is that someone who is using a on-graphical browser on a UNIX machine, for example, can't see the same progression of headings from "highest" to "lowest," although this might show up well on a Macintosh using Netscape.

In practice, a browser like Lynx doesn't seem to show much difference between levels of headings, whether they progress "H1-H2-H3," or "H1-H3-H6."

Rebel that I am, I don't feel constrained by having to move from H1 to H2 to the exception of all other headings. I don't see the problem skipping headings. What's important is that each heading reflects its relative importance on the page. I would caution you against putting a smaller heading (bigger heading number) above a bigger one (smaller heading number), as follows:

```
<h1>Nonlinear Progression of Headings</h1>
<dl>
<dt><h2>Nonlinear Progression of Headings</h2>
<dd><h4><i>--Controversy or Non-Issue?</i></h4>
</dl>
<h6><i>--Controversy or Non-Issue?</i></h6>
```

The result is shown in Figure 4.31.

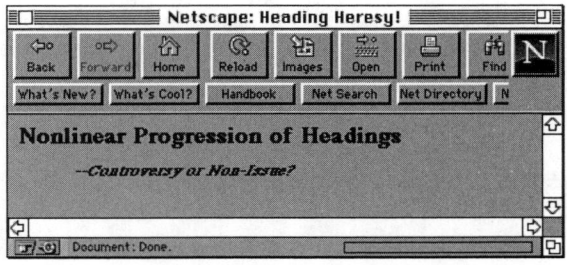

Figure 4.31 An H1 followed by an H6 heading.

My general rules regarding headings are as follows. They should be:

- Short

- Consistent

- If possible, startling or attention-getting

- Contain a specific nugget of information

- A tool to lead the reader into your document or Web site

Greg's Soapbox

I look at headings from a visual standpoint. Why compromise the appearance of your Web site to satisfy someone whose browser will never make it look good anyway? If you really want to get noticed and get a lot of readers, make the best statement you can on your browser of choice and, as long as you don't clutter the page with too many headings, feel free to skip a level to suit your purposes.

I don't think one has to start out one's page with an H1 heading. For a more subtle approach, try an H2. Using all caps might give it as much importance as H1 but convey a different feeling.

In newspapers, headings follow these general rules:

- Major headings go above, less important ones below.

- Don't put big headings under smaller ones.

- Don't clutter up the page with too many styles and sizes of headings.

- Feel free to mix roman (straight up) and italic headings to lend more graphical interest to a page.

Combining Netscape's Extensions with Headings

Once you have made the basic decision to make your document look as good as it can using the Web browser that allows you the most control, and you are aware that you may have to provide an alternate layout to accommodate other browsers, you should feel free to experiment with HTML tags.

By combining heading tags with some of Netscape's extensions to HTML or with style tags, for instance, you can create new options for your document's headings.

By adding the tag <FONT SIZE="+1"> to an <H1> heading, for example, you can take display type (that is, large headings that aren't part of the body text) to new heights. You can also use the caps and small caps style explained before with the italic <I> character style, as shown here:

```
<html><head>
<title>Heading Variations</title>
</head><body>

<h1>Nonlinear Progression of Headings</h1>
<h1><FONT SIZE="7">Nonlinear Progression of Headings</FONT></h1>
<P>
<h2><I>Controversy or Non-Issue?</I></h2>
<h2><I>C<FONT SIZE="-1">ONTROVERSY OR </FONT>N<FONT SIZE=
"-1">ON-ISSUE?</FONT></I></h2>

</body></html>
```

The output in Netscape is shown in Figure 4.32.

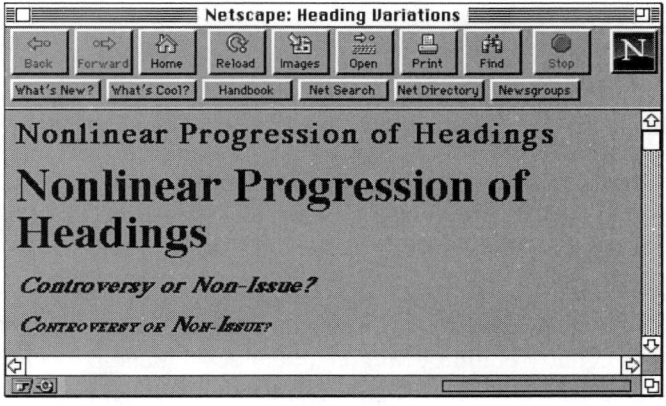

Figure 4.32 Heading variations.

Note: The content of headings is another matter of interest, and is discussed in Chapter 9, "Painless Writing for the Web."

Tags for Graphics

The <HR> Horizontal Rule Tag

This tag basically draws a rule across the width of your window and leaves a blank space above and below it.

However, Netscape has added some nice extensions to the <HR> tag that allow you to vary rules widely in your documents:

- <HR SIZE>
- <HR WIDTH>
- <HR ALIGN>
- <HR NOSHADE>

Netscape's online documentation on these extensions is sketchy. Figure 4.33 illustrates them in greater detail.

The extension is <HR SIZE=N>, where N is the size of the rule in pixels. Increasing N increases the thickness of the horizontal rule.

The default rule thickness is 2, so <HR SIZE=1> actually decreases the rule width to something approximating a one-point or hairline rule. Netscape doesn't specify a limit to the rule size, and I couldn't find one. I experimented up to <HR SIZE=50> and received a rule that was over half an inch thick—although I don't know why one would ever use such a rule in publishing.

To draw a rule that is less than the width of the page, use the extension <HR WIDTH=N%>, where N is a percentage relative to the width of the page. You can also specify an exact width in pixels—for example, <HR WIDTH=20> produces a 20-pixel wide rule.

Note: For most browsers, the width of the page is not fixed, but is determined by the size of your browser window at the moment, the width of the widest graphic on the page.

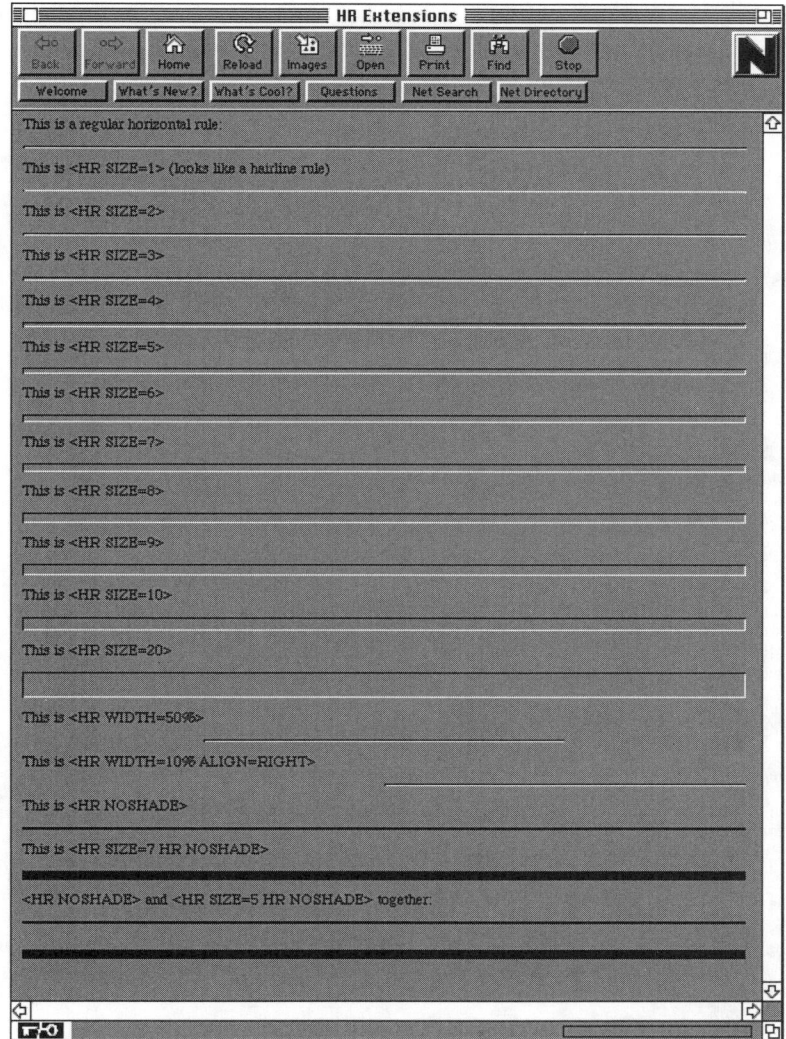

Figure 4.33 Netscape extensions to <HR>.

The <HR ALIGN=LEFT|RIGHT|CENTER> extension allows a horizontal rule to be flush-left, flush-right, or centered on the page. Obviously, this applies only to a rule that is less than a page in width.

Usually, <HR> rules are shaded. To create a solid black rule, use the new extension <HR NOSHADE>.

All of these new extensions can be combined. A size 10 rule can be made flush-right and solid black, for instance. The thing is, you have to use these and other tools sensibly. In general, that means:

- Use rules and type styles sparingly.

- Don't make them too big.

Using these new extensions can create some nice design alternatives for publishers (as long as your readers use Netscape). Some suggestions are shown in Figure 4.34.

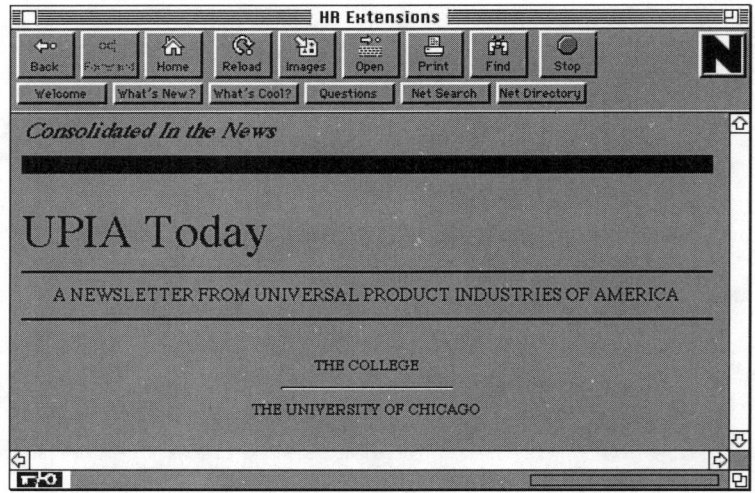

Figure 4.34 Some applications of <HR> extensions.

Images: The <IMG> Tag

One <IMG> is worth a thousand words in HTML. Images, after all, are one of the things that make the Web special. <IMG> is the tag that specifies an image to be displayed by your browser.

There are two kinds of images you can include in your documents: *in-line* images and *external* images. HTML 2.0 has four tags related to images; Netscape has added a number of extensions to the <IMG> tag that allow more control over positioning of both text and images.

<IMG> is an empty tag; there is no </IMG>. This tag has four attributes:

1. SRC, as in <IMG SRC="...">.

2. ALIGN, as in <IMG ALIGN=" ">

3. ALT, as in <IMG ALT=" ">

4. ISMAP, as in <IMG ISMAP=" ">

These are discussed next.

<IMG SRC>

The basic tag for putting an image in your document is <IMG
SRC="*name.of.image.gif*."> This tag tells your browser, "I want to put an image
(IMG) here. The source file (SRC) for this image can be found at the following URL
(="*name.of.image.gif*")."

    <IMG SRC="greendot.gif">

The suffix of the image file won't necessarily be .GIF. JPEG images are becoming
common as well, and are labeled .JPEG. You can also use an image called an X-
bitmap, which has the suffix .XBM or XPM.

The URL that you specify can be either a *relative* or *absolute* URL. A relative URL
gives the address relative to the current document. The absolute URL gives the full
HTTP address for the image file.

You have to use <SRC> in any <IMG> tag, including the three variations that
follow.

<IMG ALIGN>

HTML allows three attributes to be assigned to <IMG ALIGN> that allow the text
that occurs before or after a graphic to be aligned at the top, bottom, or middle of the
image.

To align the baseline of the current line of text with the top of the photo, type:

    <IMG ALIGN="TOP" SRC="../image.gif">

To align the baseline of the current line of text with the middle of the image, type:

<IMG ALIGN="MIDDLE" SRC="../image.gif">

To align the baseline of the current line of text with the bottom of the photo, type:

<IMG ALIGN="BOTTOM" SRC="../image.gif">

If nothing is specified, text and graphic are aligned at the bottom. That's the default. Examples are shown in Figure 4.35.

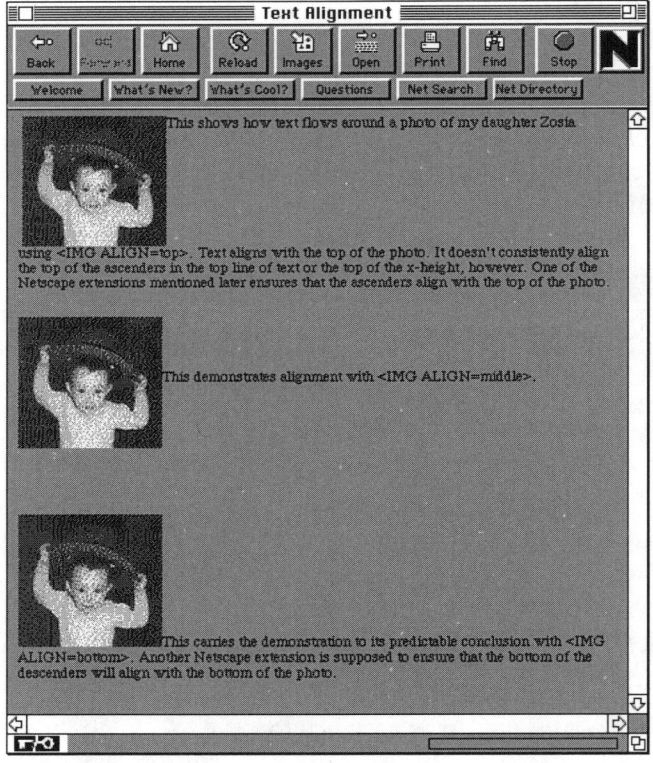

Figure 4.35 Examples of the <IMG ALIGN> tag.

<IMG ALT>

Not all Web browsers can display images and even if they can, users with slow Internet connection often turn off image-loading for faster response. To get the maximum impact for your document or, rather, to prevent your image reference from looking nonsensical on a browser that is not equipped to display it, it is important to provide a text-only alternative.

The attribute <ALT> ("alternative text") is used to specify a text string that a non-graphical browser can display as an alternative to your image. You don't have to do this. It's optional.

If you do use a text-only <ALT>, make sure it's clear what image is being described. Rather than "overview," say, "aerial view of east side of campus," for instance. Also, make sure your <ALT> text doesn't contain HTML tags <STRONG>like these </STRONG>.

Where to Find It

For more information about creating imagemaps, see http://hoohoo.ncsa.uouc.edu/docs/setup/admin/Imagemap.html. You can also try Felipe's Clickable Map Tutorial at http://edb518eaa.edb.utexas.edu/html/gifmap.html. To create a map file, download a copy of WebMap and another essential piece of software, MacMapMaker, at ftp://ftp.uwtc.washington.edu/pub/Mac/Network/WWW. Another source is the Macintosh Archive of the University of Michigan: gopher://gopher.archive.merit.edu:7055/11/mac.

<IMG ISMAP>

The <ISMAP> tag tells Netscape that the image is a clickable map (an "imagemap"). A clickable map is an image that has been set up to act as a map; that is, every pixel is assigned coordinates. Clicking specified areas in the image sends the cursor coordinates to a server, which sends you to a file in another location.

A map is a picture that has been broken into zones. Each zone has its own URL—a new page, a closeup of the picture, and so on. When the user clicks inside the zone, a link is made to the corresponding URL. This process requires extra software running on your server to interpret the user's pointer click and send the client to the right place. This is explained further in Chapter 5.

Clickable maps can be an impressive visual means of accessing parts of a Web site. So impressive, in fact, that the temptation is to scan elaborate color photos and space-age, 3-D graphics that result in the map taking a full five minutes to load onto a screen. When the graphics don't take up a lot of disk space and the map isn't too crowded, though, clickable maps are a useful way of hyperlinking in one place many separate documents and other elements scattered throughout your site.

Netscape Extensions to <IMG>

Netscape's numerous extensions to the <IMG ALIGN> tag allow images to "float" on a Web page while text wraps around it. If you use the <IMG ALIGN=LEFT> attribute, the image aligns with the left margin and the text flows around it. If you use the <IMG ALIGN=RIGHT> attribute, the photo is flush-right and the text flows around it to the left.

Other extensions to the <IMG> tag are supposed to refine its alignment capabilities as explained here (and shown in Figure 4.36). Except for <ALIGN=TEXTTOP>, though, I didn't perceive much difference. These extensions were introduced to help with Netscape's larger-than-usual font sizes.

> The **ALIGN=TEXTTOP>** attribute aligns the top of the image with the top of the tallest text in the line (this is usually but not always the case in <ALIGN=TOP>).

> **<ALIGN=ABSMIDDLE>** aligns the middle of the current line with the middle of the image.

> **<ALIGN=BASELINE>** is the same as <ALIGN=BOTTOM> only with a different name. It aligns the bottom of the image with the baseline of the current line of text.

> **<ALIGN=ABSBOTTOM>** aligns the bottom of the image with the bottom of the current line.

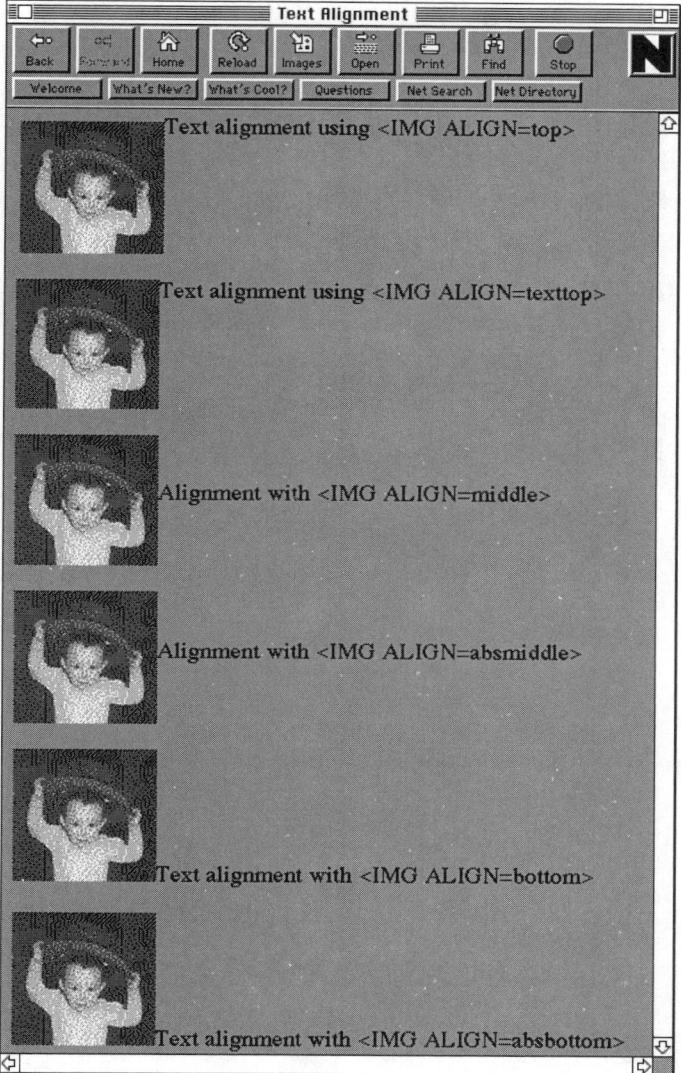

Figure 4.36 Netscape extensions to <IMG>.

<IMG VSPACE=value> <IMG HSPACE=value>

As can be seen in the previous examples, text that wraps around floating images presses up against the image and occasionally even touches it. These two attributes allow some "breathing" room for your image by inserting blank space around it where text will not intrude (see Figure 4.37).

<IMG VSPACE=VALUE> controls the vertical space above and below the image. The number you put in "value" equals the number of pixels.

<IMG HSPACE=VALUE> controls the horizontal space to the left and right of the image. I suggest putting 6 to 9 pixels around an image.

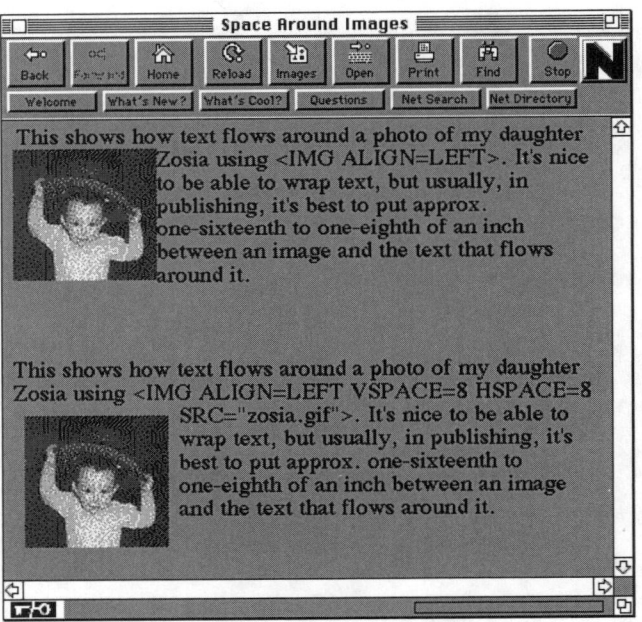

Figure 4.37 Controlling space around floating images.

<IMG WIDTH=value> <IMG HEIGHT=value>

Two other extensions, <IMG WIDTH=VALUE> and <IMG HEIGHT=VALUE>, speed up display of your document. Usually, when a browser such as Netscape encounters an image, it has to calculate that image's size.

If you specify the width and height in pixels in your HTML document, the Web reader doesn't have to wait so long for the image to be loaded over the network and its size calculated. The pixel size can be determined by most programs used to create them, such as Photoshop.

<IMG BORDER=value>

As seen in the HTML tutorial, if an image is used as a clickable link, it is displayed with a border around it. But this border can be hard to see, particularly on a black-and-white monitor. The tag <IMG BORDER=VALUE> lets you control the thickness of the border around a displayed image.

Warning: You are allowed to use the setting <BORDER=0> on images that are also part of anchors, but obviously this will confuse Web readers because they won't see a border indicating that an image is an anchor. If you use <BORDER=VALUE> at all, use it to make the border more visible, not less.

External Images, Sounds, and Animations

External images that take up a lot of room should be kept as separate files so as not to slow down the loading of your main document. Have the reader click text or a smaller, thumbnail version of the larger image.

To include a reference to an external image, use:

<A HREF=image_URL>link anchor text</A>

Here are some of the more common file name extensions recognized by Netscape and other browsers. For some of these, you have to configure your browser to run a helper application to display them, and/or install a system extension like QuickTime to run them. These are some of the files you can serve:

- .TXT (Plain text document)
- .HTML (HTML document)
- .GIF (GIF image)

The following require system extensions as well as helper applications, but are very cool all the same:

- .TIFF (TIFF image)
- .XBM (XBM bitmap image)

- .AIFF (AIFF sound)
- .JPG or .JPEG (JPEG image)
- .MPG or .MPEG (MPEG movie)
- .MOV (QuickTime movie)

This last one is theoretically possible, but there really isn't a good way to display it at present:

- .PS (PostScript file)

If you use a helper application to display one of the external images, set the Preference dialog box in Netscape to recognize it. Basically you are telling Netscape that if it encounters a file with, for instance, a .MOV suffix, it should open the helper application Movie Player to display it.

Links

Links are the way you tie together a group of documents. You can make links from one place to another within a document, from the current document to a local file (a file located on your own computer), or from your document to a remote file (a file located on other computers across your office or across the Internet).

HTML uses the link tag <A> </A> to create links. The <A> tag is often called an anchor tag.

The start tag <A> almost never appears by itself. Other attributes are included within it. The most common attribute is <HREF>, which presumably stands for Hypertext REFerence. The <HREF> tag in an anchor denotes the beginning of a link to another document, another location on the Internet, or to a particular location in the same document. The form is specified by:

```
<A HREF="URL">
```

where URL is the Universal Resource Locator of the file to which the link points.

Any text contained between the <A> and </A> tags is highlighted, either by underlining, in color, or both as the link that, when clicked, will take the reader to the location REFerenced to in the start tag <A HREF>. Get the idea?

Figure 4.38 shows the various parts of simple HTML link tags. The first is a link giving a relative path to a local file. The second is a link giving a path to a file on a remote computer. In either case, the elements of a link tag are the same.

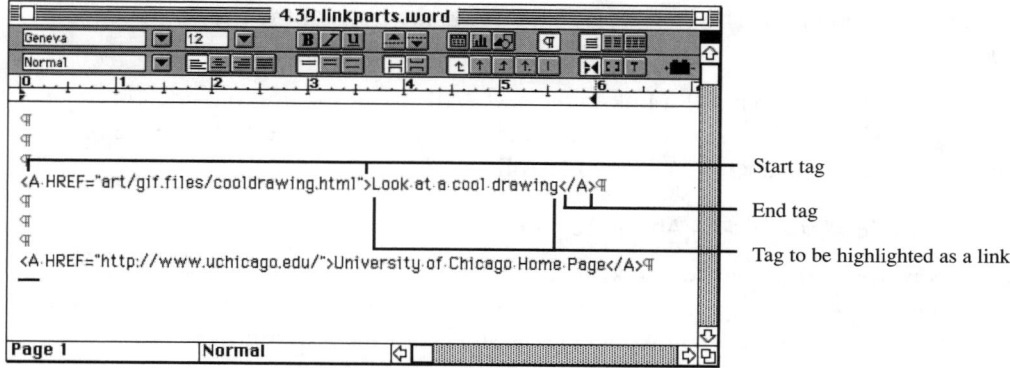

Figure 4.38 Parts of a link tag.

Linking to Specific Sections in the Current Document

Anchors that mark hypertext links within a single document are formed with two tags, <NAME> and <HREF>. <NAME> is used to name or mark the destination or "target" of a link. <HREF> marks the start of the link.

Here is an example of a <NAME> anchor designating the destination of a link within a document. Remember, the beginning link <HREF> has to be in the same document:

<A NAME="*topofpage*">Chapter One</A>

In this anchor, "*topofpage*" is an arbitrary name you assign to the link. When you make the origin link tag using <HREF>, this name is preceded by the pound sign (#):

<A HREF="#*topofpage*">Go to top of page</A>

167

Linking to Specific Sections in Local Documents

The <NAME> tag can also be used to mark a hypertextual link to a specific word or phrase in another document located on your computer or server, or to a document on another computer. This is done by modifying the URL of the file you want to point to.

Let's say you want to make a link to the text "All About Zosia" contained in a file called "Zosia.html." To do this, you use the <NAME> attribute and give the link the name "Zosia." The anchor is formed as follows:

```
<A NAME="Zosia">All About Zosia</A>
```

Let's say you want to make a link to this text from a local document—another document on your computer. You do this by specifying a relative path leading to the document "Zosia.html." You would create an anchor like the following:

```
<A HREF="family/Zosia.html#Zosia">More information</A>about Zosia.
```

In this case, the text More information is the highlighted link that leads to the words "All About Zosia."

Linking to a File on Another Computer

You make a link to another site on the Web by entering its Universal Resource Locator (URL) in your anchor tag. URLs were initially defined in the "Note about URLs" near the beginning of the book. But when you actually start to link your documents to others, some more detailed background information will help. And a little review never hurt anyone. So here's a little more about URLs.

More about URLs

URLs point to any number of different things on a network. They might direct you to a bit of data in a database, results of a search, a posting on Usenet, or a file on FTP or gopher. An URL includes:

- An identifier for the type of Internet service (gopher, FTP, telnet, and so on),
- the Internet address, and
- a file path to the item you want to link to.

There are several kinds of URLs. A file URL might have the form:

file://ftp.yourcomputer.com/pub/files/destination.txt

To point to a location on gopher, you might use the URL:

gopher://gopher.yourcomputer.com/

URLs can also point to a newsgroup, in which case they don't need any backslashes, like this:

news:comp.infosystems.www.providers

Of course, the most common URLs on the Web use HyperText Transport Protocol (HTTP). URLs beginning with HTTP run all through this book. You may, however, encounter a number in the middle of one of these HTTP URLs and wonder what it is. For example:

http://www.yourcomputer.com:1234/pub/files/document.html

The number 1234 refers to a network port on the host's Web server. The default HTTP network port is 80, but if the server resides on a different network port (say, port 1234 on www.yourcomputer.com, as in the previous example), the number shows up in the URL.

If the URL ends with a backslash (/), the server serves up a file set up to act as the "default" file in that directory. If the server is running the WebSTAR (formerly MacHTTP Web server software), for example, the URL dirt.clod.edu/mac.http/ pages serves the default file in the subfolder pages in the folder mac.http on the machine whose Internet nickname is dirt.clod.edu. If no folders are specified and the address ends with a backslash, as in dirt.clod.edu/, the server serves the default file. The name of the default file varies according to the server software.

The path to the file you want to link to can be an *absolute path name* or a *relative path name*.

Relative Path Names

A relative path name is a description of a file's location relative to your current location.

Relative paths are a way of making hypertextual links between documents on your local computer. The simplest kind of relative path is to give the name of a file in quotation marks in an URL. Your browser will then look for that file in the folder that contains the currently displayed document, even if it is looking over the Net from a remote location.

That works fine if the file you want to look for is in the same folder as the current document. Usually, though, that's not the case, and you have to provide a path of folders leading to that file. Examples of relative path names are shown in Figure 4.39.

The examples in Figure 4.39 assume that you are presently working in the document "document.html" and that you want to make links from that document to other files on a Web site.

Folder names are followed by backslashes (/). A folder in the level above the current folder (in this case, "MyWeb") is designated with two dots (..).

> **Note:** Remember not to put blank spaces, slashes, smart quotes, or international characters in the names of any folders or documents on your Web site. When the folders or documents are listed in a path name you are using in an anchor, HTML may not make the link if there is a blank space in that folder or document name.

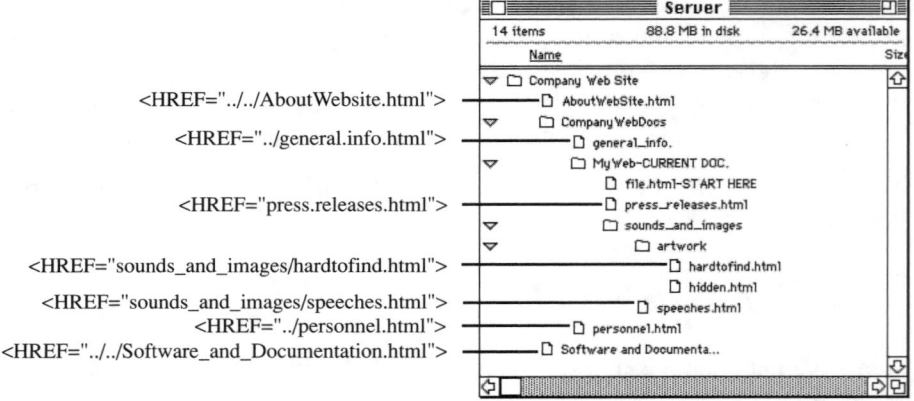

Figure 4.39 Relative path names.

Absolute Path Names

In contrast to relative path names, which point to a destination document or object by detailing its relation to the current document, *absolute path names* lead to a file on your local computer by starting at the top level of your hierarchy of files and folders and working through all the folders in between until you get to the document.

Absolute path names always begin with a slash. After the slash comes all the folders in the path from the top level of the file to which you are connecting.

Keep in mind that "top level" may or may not be name of your computer or the disk where all the files in question are held. It may be the folder that holds your home page, or the file that will be loaded by default if the user specifies a URL that does not include the home page, such as "default.html" or "index.html," for examples.

In almost all cases, when you are linking your documents, it's better to use absolute rather than relative path names. If you should happen to move your HTML documents from one computer or one folder to another, all of your links from the document to the absolute path names will have to be changed. Relative path names, in contrast, work on any system with little or no need to modify them.

Why make more work for yourself?

Check Your Links

Here is a quick reference list of things to check regarding links:

1. Avoid overlapping tags, such as:

   ```
   <A HREF="oops"><i>like this</A></I>
   ```

2. Avoid vague links. Try to indicate as clearly as you can (without making the link too long) what the reader will encounter when selecting the link.

   For instance, a link like <u>Things I like</u> is too vague. <u>Greg's Favorite Movies</u> is better.

3. Organize your links in menus rather than <u>loading up links</u> about loosely <u>related subjects</u> in close <u>proximity</u> in your <u>document</u>.

4. Check your links; check in multiple browsers to see that everything works.

5. Proofread your HTML. This is the most important piece of advice I can give you. Too many documents go out on the Web that just don't work and that look terrible. See Chapter 10 for more information on proofreading Web documents.

Frequently Asked Questions about HTML

What follows is a list of thirteen frequently asked questions (FAQs, pronounced "facks") regarding HTML. Interestingly, most of the questions I hear have to do with how to *not* use HTML, by people who are trying to avoid it somehow. They are most often Macintosh users who fell in love with the Mac environment because it allowed them to write, draw, and publish using friendly point-and-click commands and pull-down menus, so they avoid computer code altogether. Are you one of them? Then read on...

Greg's Soapbox

By the way, who invented the subject of Frequently Asked Questions, and who decided that they should be included on virtually every Web site? I'm not complaining. I use them, too. But don't be a copycat. Create a better and more original heading for your own Web site—something like "Essential Information," for instance.

What Is HTML, Anyway?

HTML stands for **HyperText Markup Language.** It is a language that allows you to mark up your document so that it appears on any number of different computer screens with elements that you have chosen (such as headings and paragraphs) preserved intact.

Each of those computers out there in Cyberspace has its own operating system. When you publish on the Web, your document might appear on a UNIX workstation, an IBM PC, or any number of brands, sizes, or shapes of computers. To make sure your document will look right no matter where it goes, you have to provide generic commands that each one of those computers will recognize.

HTML is just such a set of commands. It conforms to an internationally agreed-upon standard for representing computer documents and exchanging information: International Standard ISO 8879, Standard Generalized Markup Language (SGML).

Why Do I Have to Know about SGML?

You don't *have* to know about it, any more than you have to understand how electricity is made to flick on a light switch. But having some background will make you more confident and competent. For example, if you want to be a Web publisher and not just a Web browser, you should at least know that HTML is a kind of SGML.

SGML was created for IBM in the late 1960s as GML (General Markup Language). It's a computer language that describes *document types* rather than specific documents, thus allowing that document to be defined by a computer and establishing a logical relationship between its parts. It allows a document to be marked up so that it can be translated from computer to computer, but doesn't provide for how it will appear on an individual screen.

Where to Find It

An explanation of the relationship between HTML and SGML can be found at http://www.w3.org/hypertext/WWW/MarkUp/Intro.html. The current HTML DTD is at http:/www.w3.org/hypertext/WWW/MarkUp/DTDHeading.html.

HTML is a *document type* with its own *Document Type Definition* (DTD). It is also a *language* used to mark up documents of the type HTML. DTD is one of those acronyms thrown around casually and often without explanation by techie people writing computer documentation. You don't have to know all about it but you might see DTD written somewhere (as I have) and wonder what it means.

Every SGML document has three parts—a declaration, a prologue, and references:

- The *declaration* simply means that when HTML is declared to be an SGML document, it will conform to the rules for SGML documents, such as "document names can be no longer than 72 characters" or "end tags must begin with (</)."

173

- The *prologue* means that at the beginning of your HTML document there is a DTD specifying what its attributes are. At the beginning of an HTML document, the first tag is (<HTML>).

- The *references* are the tags and other instructions tucked into the document.

Why Do I Have to Use HTML?

The short answer: Marking up a document with HTML is about the only way to get material displayed on a Web browser, and thus, on the Web itself (true, you can display ASCII text on a browser, but the point of this book is to help you present something more attractive).

As of this writing, software is beginning to come out that also allows you to put HTML tags in your documents "in the background," via pull-down menus and other user-friendly commands.

Where to Find It

You can download the latest version of Arachnid from http://sec-look.uiowa.edu/about/projects/arachnid-page.html. Web Weaver is at http://www.potsdam.edu/Web.Weaver/About.html. A list of HTML authoring and editing programs for the Mac is kept by Yahoo at http://www.yahoo.com/Computers/World_Wide_Web/HTML_Editors/Macintosh/.

Why Hasn't Anyone Come Up with Something Better?

I've heard two widely differing opinions as to why it has taken a while. One line of thinking is that it is extremely difficult to embed HTML code-making functions within a proprietary system such as the Macintosh. The other says that it's not difficult at all, it's just that most people in the UNIX and Windows worlds know what they're doing so well that they haven't *needed* a Mac-type WYSIWYG editor.

Whatever the reason, some good programs are beginning to come out. By the time you read this, more new programs to help you write HTML documents will undoubtedly have appeared. And HTML 3.0 does allow more complex formatting of documents. So it's already getting better.

174

Microsoft recently came out with Internet Assistant, but that program includes relatively few HTML commands. And SoftQuad recently released HoTMetaL Pro for the Mac, but it's not without problems (see Chapter 7).

One promising piece of shareware, Arachnid, which is being developed at the University of Iowa, shows how difficult the task is. The program has the right idea, but the beta version available at the time of this writing is extremely large and cumbersome, and full of bugs. My current favorite is Web Weaver. You can use its pull-down menus to produce relatively simple documents as long as they don't go over 32K in size.

Does That Mean I Don't Have to Know Anything about HTML?

If you want to do any kind of serious publishing on the World Wide Web, you are going to have to know something about HTML. And the more you know, the better off you'll be.

Sure, there are utilities to help you write and edit the commands, but you still have to know HTML to edit your own documents and to understand what you are looking at when you call up the source code of a Web page you'd like to emulate. As your mom used to say when she was pushing the green beans your way, "It's good for you."

Well, What's the Minimum I Have to Know?

What are you, lazy? Of course, you're not. You have better things to do with your time than learning a new markup language. The minimum you have to know is this:

- Don't waste the reader's time with useless trivia; be brief and concise.

- Turn off curly quotes.

- Use the <P> tag to break paragraphs.

- Save your documents in text-only (ASCII) format.

- Give a short but specific title.

- Include the suffix ".html" at the end of the name (although it's good to know that this varies from server to server, and some Windows-based servers require ".HTM").

- Break up text with heads, subheads, and lists.
- Include your email address.
- Indicate when your document was last updated.
- Proofread your page.
- Check to see that all the links work.

Why Is It So Ugly?

It's a set of computer markup commands. It's not supposed to be pretty; it's only supposed to tell a Web browser program such as Netscape what functions should be performed by the various parts of a document. Compared to some "real" programming languages, it's simple and easy to understand. So it could be worse.

Why Does Everything in HTML Have to Be Typed Perfectly?

Get with the program—the *computer* program, that is. If you make a typo in computer code, the program won't work. Computers understand things like "yes" and "no," "zero" or "one." They don't read language; they recognize characters that they can process or that instruct them to perform some task.

Actually, most browsers are forgiving of HTML mistakes. For instance, you don't have to type the <HTML> or <HEAD> tag to tell a browser that yours is an HTML document (although it's still a good idea to do so). Just take your time, and proofread your work, and chances are your document will work correctly.

Is It Really Okay to Learn by Copying Someone Else's Code? Isn't It Secret?

It's okay. No one is going to arrest you for this. When authors write commercial software products, they copyright the code and keep it secret so you don't pirate your own program. They want you to buy theirs.

Remember, HTML isn't a program as such. It's a markup language. Long ago, when I was a cub reporter, I used to mark up pages so a typesetter could output type and a keyliner could paste it up. HTML does the same thing. The instructions aren't important; the important thing is what you put onto the Web, and how you present and organize it.

Copying content is another issue. If you want to present material that you've found elsewhere, the usual practice is to set up a link to that material. It's probably not legal, and certainly not "nice," to present back issues of *Wired* on your own server without some sort of attribution.

What's the "Hypertext" Part of HTML?

Where to Find It

There's plenty of information about hypertext on the Internet. A definition can be found at http:// info.cern.ch/hypertext/WWW/ Whatis.html. A short history is at http://info.cern.ch/hypertext/ History.html. A newsgroup on Hypertext, "alt.hypertext," can be found at news:alt.hypertext.

An HTML version of *As We May Think* by Vannevar Bush (July 1945) can be viewed at http:// www.cse.uottawa.ca/ ~dduchier/misc/vbush/ as_we_may_think.html.

Hypertext refers to nonlinear text through which one navigates by means of computer links and anchors. By clicking an object or bit of text, you can skip forward or backward from one point in a document (or from document to document) to another based on your pattern of thought—a desire to know something, to review something, or an inspiration or intuition that just came to you. IMHO (In My Humble Opinion), hypertext is going to change the way we take in information and overturn conventional notions of what "text" is. But we'll have to wait and see.

The concept of hypertext was proposed in the 1940s by Vannevar Bush, an advisor to President Franklin D. Roosevelt. The actual term "hypertext" was first used in 1965 by Ted Nelson. In the late1980s, Bill Atkinson's HyperCard program began to allow hypertext functionality in a Macintosh environment. It's an easy-to-use yet powerful application that was obviously years ahead of its time.

In relation to HTML, Hypertext was seen from the beginning as a way of sharing and displaying graphics, text, databases, and even sound and video, and of moving easily from one element to another.

Who Came Up with HTML?

"...Is coming up with HTML" would be more accurate, actually, because HTML, like the Web, is constantly evolving and improving.

A history of the Web is included in Appendix B, but briefly, the original proposal was written in 1989 by Tim Berners-Lee and Robert Cailleau of CERN (a physics lab) in Switzerland.

The original HTML document type definition was written by Dan Connolly and developed at CERN in 1990. It was released as an Internet draft in 1993.

Berners-Lee and Connolly in particular continue to be active in developing the Web, speaking at conferences, and creating online instructions for how to create home pages and information webs, as are instrumental people like Daniel Connolly.

The new version of HTML, HTML 3.0, is being developed by the W3 Consortium. Groups like the Internet Engineering Task Force, a network of designers and researchers concerned with the development of the Internet, is involved.

What Are HTML's Limitations?

In terms of formatting, HTML is primitive. Those of us who have been doing desktop publishing for a while find it frustrating not to be able to move elements around onscreen—divide a text into columns, justify text, or even indent paragraphs easily, for instance.

I, for one, admit to being a control freak and there's a part of me that refuses to accept not having ultimate control over how a document will look. I hate being at the mercy of each viewer's browser setup.

Don't get me wrong. I'm grateful that HTML lets me put graphics in my documents. But that doesn't stop me from being frustrated by being limited to the resolution of a computer screen for all those elaborate photos and graphics I'd love.

Where to Find It

The latest developments in HTML can be found at the CERN server at http://info.cern.ch/ hypertext/WWW/MarkUp/ MarkUp.html. Another good source is Dan Connolly's HTML Design Notebook, http:// www.w3.org/hypertext/WWW/ People/Connolly/drafts/html-design.html.

Is HTML Changing?

HTML has already gone through a couple of versions—a fact you may also see references to on the Web. The original version, HTML 1.0, contained a number of elements that have since been discontinued ("deprecated," in computerspeak).

The most notable addition to HTML 2.0 was the capability to create forms. HTML 3.0 (also known as HTML+) promises to allow some basic textual formatting commands whose absence is particularly frustrating for publishers.

HTML 3.0 promises to include creation of tables, right-justified text, centered text, and paragraph breaks that do not necessarily add a blank space, for instance (see Chapter 6 for a complete explanation of HTML 3.0). In the meantime, extensions for many of those features have already been developed by Netscape.

Advanced HTML

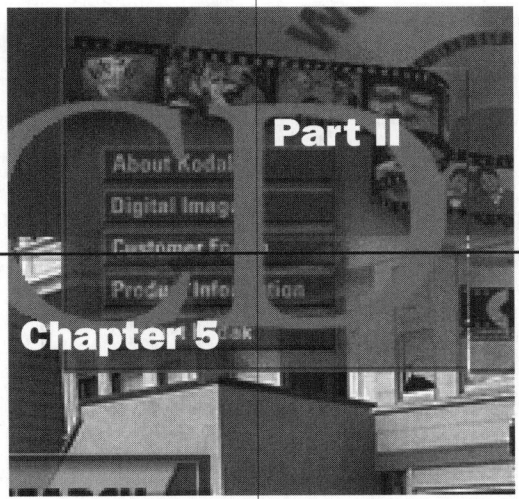

Part II

Chapter 5

Chapters 3 and 4 discussed the basic HTML commands you need to put your message online. As a young lad, I wrote in secret and hid my angst-filled pages so well that even I forgot about them. When I began to write feature stories for my hometown newspaper, however, I discovered the thrill of having an audience.

I became hungry for even the most casual comments on my work—even if it was not the gushing admiration I hoped for. Just having some sort of dialogue with my readers, and knowing they were paying attention, was good enough.

Greg's Soapbox

This reminds me: please remember, when you are surfing and publishing, take a moment to visit the Web site for this book (http://www.mcp.com/ hayden/webmacpublishing) and tell me what you think of it. I haven't gotten over that need for feedback.

On the Web, you can go beyond yelling across the canyon in hopes of hearing an echo. The techniques described in this chapter enable you to interact with Web readers, either directly or indirectly, and to connect with other applications, such as FileMaker and HyperCard, that serve as sources of information.

Scripts that Add Functionality to a Web Site

The direct way is to process data generated by a special computer script by performing an action like clicking a button or filling in a form. Another way is to turn the contents of what you've published into an index that people can search to find information more easily.

The more subtle way is to allow a reader to activate a computer script that performs "on the fly" a function on the server where your data resides. Perhaps visiting your site activates a script that acts as a counter that tracks how many people have visited the site. It might tell readers the current time and date. Or you might provide an "imagemap" visitors can click that activates a script to take them to a file or location you've specified beforehand.

Whether subtle or direct, forms, interface elements, and scripts make your site interactive rather than static. You can extend that interactivity to programs, such as HyperCard and FileMaker, that generate HTML. Using built-in scripting capabilities, you can link your site to an already existing database of information.

Figure 5.1 illustrates the role scripts and database programs might play in a typical client/server interaction on the Internet. The client (that's your reader, on the right) accesses an HTML document that resides on the server (on the left).

The readers can do a number of activities while in the document, such as filling out a form, making a link to an image or another document, or searching for information. Depending on what the readers do, they might access another document or activate a CGI script that retrieves data from a database or other application. (This can get complicated by the fact that CGIs can reside on separate computers, but Figure 5.1 is a simple illustration.)

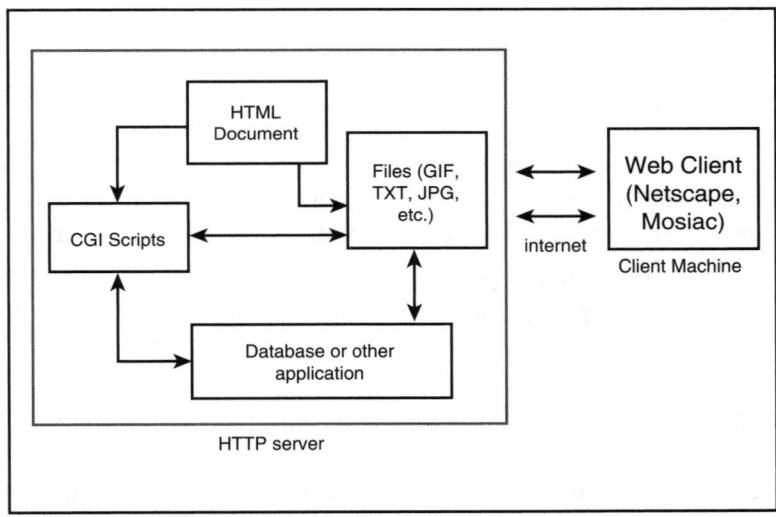

Figure 5.1 The role of scripts in Web publishing

When I was a reporter, I tried to write interesting stories that provoked readers to write letters to the editor or call me on the phone. Now the goal is to make your Web publication useful and well organized so your readers will visit again, request more information, or tell you about themselves.

Scripting (actually writing the computer scripts described above) is certainly better than throwing your message into the ocean in a bottle, but it has drawbacks and is not for everyone. When used well, however, it can turn your Web site into a power-ful interactive communications and marketing tool.

I'm not going to provide a lot of scripts here because my job is to teach you publishing rather than programming. However, I will tell you what the various types of scripts are and point you to places where you can find examples you can copy. Like so many aspects of the Web, scripts are not always secret. Some clever and open-minded programmers have made their offerings available for anyone who wants to use them.

A Simple Search Tool: <ISINDEX>

One of the most useful scripting functions you can set up on a Web site is a searchable index. One way to run a simple kind of search is to use the <ISINDEX> tag along with a script in the server.

The <ISINDEX> tag in an HTML document tells a Web browser that the document can be searched, and activates a browser's searching capability (in NCSA Mosaic, for instance, this is the box next to the "Search" button at the top of the screen). The user types in a keyword or words, and sends them to the server, which accesses a search engine—a program that searches files or databases for information.

An ISINDEX-type of search is useful when the keywords are simple. But most searches are now done using a more powerful and complex HTML function: forms.

Forms

Forms were introduced in HTML 2.0 and will be extended to include more functions in 3.0. Forms are data entry fields in an HTML document that allow a reader to type text, check off boxes and buttons, and "submit" or send the data to the publisher's server to be processed.

As stated earlier, forms are easy to set up in HTML. You use tags to specify checkboxes, radio buttons, multiline text entry fields, and the like. Your browser allows the user to enter data, and then bundles the data and sends it to the address that you specify in the <FORM> </FORM> tag. It may include data to be sent to a specific URL, like this:

```
http://stinking.peat.bog.com/cgi-bin$data
```

or it may simply transmit the data to the URL "stinking.peat.bog.com/cgi-bin" as a separate bundle for processing.

What happens after that gets more complicated. Your Web server is a faithful servant and it will do many things for you, but it will not process your data. For that function you need a CGI.

You may ask for the data with simple HTML, but you can't do anything with it without a supplementary program that will actually help the server to look for it. Fortunately, a growing number of CGIs are available for searching documents, serving text files, accessing databases, and so on. These CGIs reside on your server, not on a client's computer, and are configured to accept data in a certain format, so if you create a custom form, you need custom software to support the form. Because the precise implementation of scripts varies so widely, it's difficult to include specific examples.

Nobody ever said forming relationships was easy, but I will tell you how to set up a basic form. Then I'll include some descriptions of useful CGI scripts, and an example of some simple AppleScript that takes data from a form and outputs it to a text file. Beyond that, it's up to you to write the script, hire someone else to write it, or purchase one of the ready-made CGIs that are beginning to be sold commercially or that come bundled with hardware such as Apple's Web server.

Forms-Based Searches

Remember the morgue of cross-referenced stories in the back of the newspaper office? One obvious application of a searchable index is to provide access to back issues of a publication. A particularly good example is provided by CMP Publications, Inc. (see Figure 5.2).

What's good about this searchable index is that it encompasses a variety of magazines published by CMP Publications so you can find many different articles about a particular subject.

Where to Find It

You can find the CMP Publications Web site at http://techweb.cmp.com/techweb/. Apple Computer's Tech Info Library is at http://www.info.apple.com/til.html

Another useful search form is provided by Apple Computer at one of Apple's Web sites. If you're having a problem with your Macintosh (perish the thought), you can search Apple's extensive technical documentation (see Figure 5.3).

Here is a very brief and untechnical description of how a search works.

The user begins by clicking an anchor such as:

<A HREF="/cgi-bin/sea-file.to.search">Search back issues of our magazine</A>

This opens an HTTP connection to the file and takes the user to a screen containing a data input form. The user types search terms into it and clicks a button such as "Submit Data." This sends a message to the host server and, specifically, to a folder called a "cgi-bin." A **cgi-bin** is a common name for a directory or folder where **binaries** (a term for computer programs, in this case CGI scripts) are stored.

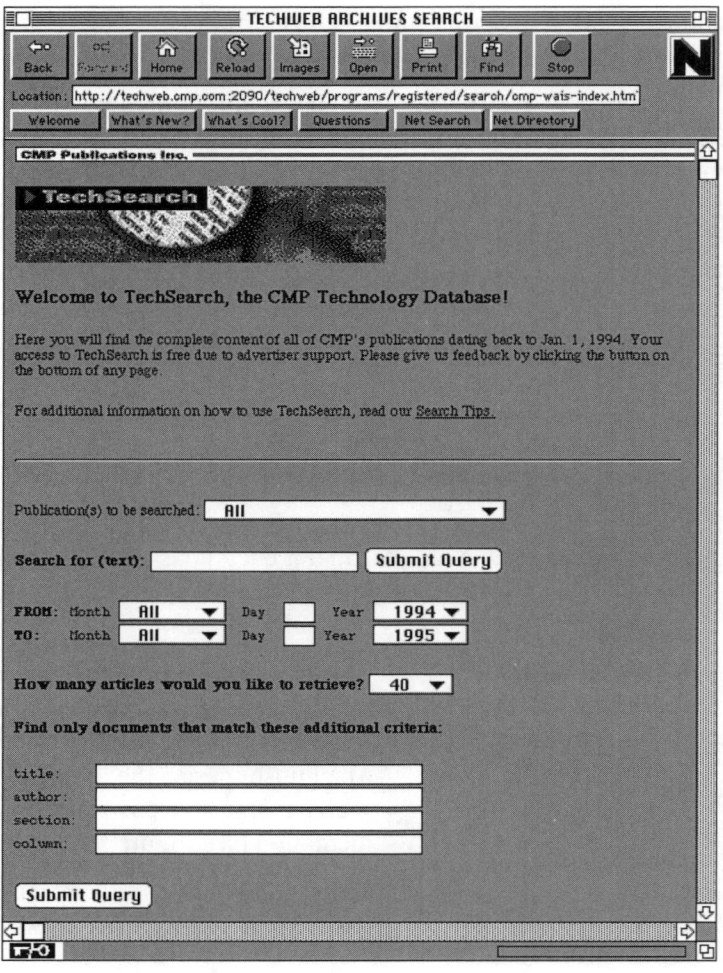

Figure 5.2 CMP Publications search form.

There, a CGI search script is activated that receives the browser's request and gets the search engine to do its stuff. The CGI script, then, is simply a go-between that gets the server to activate a program that actually does the searching, which is called a *search engine*. (One commonly used search engine in the UNIX world is called "grep.")

Figure 5.3 Apple Tech Info Library search form (copyright Apple Computer).

Where to Find It

I'm not including actual search scripts here, but you can find examples yourself at http://www-rlg.stanford.edu/home/jpl/websearch.html, or in Ian Graham's package of HTML documentation, http://www.utirc.utoronto.ca/HTMLdocs/NewHTML/. Graham provides an especially clear and understandable explanation of how to set up a server to perform searches. Also see the description of Tr-WWW later in this chapter.

Other Forms

I'll illustrate some of the following basic form tags and present one very simple method for presenting data collected in a form using the example written by John Casler when he was soliciting membership in a Web-based arts project he called Phusis. Here is the HTML for John's form:

```
<html>
<head><title>Application Phusis
</title></head>
<body>
<h1>Application for
Membership@Phusis</h1>
<hr>
<p>Thank you for your interest in
becoming an active participant
@Phusis. The application process is
mostly intended to generate informa-
tion to be used in a biography page,
supplied by us for your own use in extending research. </p>
<p>Membership is not an open affair, however. Each applicant is carefully
considered. All applicants will receive an electronic confirmation, and an
explanation of our decision in a timely manner. </p>
Upon acceptance, you will be issued a login and password for read/write
ftp access to our server, along with more information on current projects
and collaborations you might want to participate in. Thank you again for
your interest.<br>
<hr>
<FORM METHOD=GET ACTION="membership.exe">
GENERAL INFORMATION<p>
<dl>
<dt>Last Name
<dd><input name="lastname" size=40,12>

<dt>First Name
<dd><input name="firstname" size=40, 12>

<dt>Email Address
<dd><input name="email" size=40,12>
```

```
<dt>Professional Address
<dd><textarea name="proaddress" rows=5 cols=50></textarea>

<dt>Professional Phone Number
<dd><input name="prophone" size=30,12>
<hr>
<dt>Home address <i>(optional)</i>
<dd><textarea name="homeaddress" rows=5 cols=50></textarea>

<dt>Home Phone Number<i>(optional)</i>
<dd><input name="homephone" size=30,12><p>



</dl>
<hr>
Professional Information
<dl>
<dt>Are you affiliated with a university?
<dd><input type="checkbox" name="affiliation" value="1">No
<dd><input type="checkbox" name="affiliation" value="1">Yes
<dd> If yes, please specify...<input name="university" size=34,12>
<dt>Please list your degrees and certificates (include year received). If you
are currently enrolled in a degree program, please note your current status
in the program.
<dd> <textarea name="degreesandstatus" rows=6 cols=50></textarea>
<dt> Professional Organizations and Memberships
<dd><textarea name="orgs" rows=6 cols=50></textarea>
<dt>What is your profession?
<dd><input name="profession" size=34,12>
<dt>Please list a few of your exhibitions, performances, publications, etc.
Please include any relevant information.
<dd><textarea name="shows&publ" rows=10 cols=50>selected works,
Chicago Art Expo, 1989</textarea>
<dt>Related Information.
<dd><textarea name="relatedinfo" rows=8 cols=50>Please use this area
to highlight information you might feel would be of interest.</textarea>
</dl>
<hr>
Personal Information
<dl>
<dt>Date of Birth
<dd><input name="birthdate" size=10,12>
<dt>Please let us know what information you have provided that you would
not like shared with the general public.
```

```
<dd><textarea name="dontshareinfo" rows=4 cols=50></textarea>
<dt>Personal Statement <i>(optional, though recommended). </i> Feel
free to include any proposals for future projects@Phusis you would like to
mediate or participate in.
<dd><textarea name="statement" rows=12 cols=50></textarea>
</dl>
<hr>
Thank you for applying. Click on "Submit Application" to begin the applica-
tion process. We will contact you soon.<p>
<input type=submit value="Submit Application"> <input type=reset
value="Reset"><p>
</form>
</body>
</html>
```

The <FORM> Tag

<FORM> is a closed tag and must be paired with a </FORM> tag at the end of your HTML. The following start tag is taken from the Phusis example:

```
<FORM METHOD=GET ACTION="membership.exe">
```

What's in this tag? Basically, you have two sets of name and value pairs. When a user sends data to a CGI on a server, it is received as a series of these name/value pairs. The name is the value of the attribute; the value is the actual data entered by the user.

(The previous example has name and value pairs but they aren't the kind that get submitted to the CGI; those are in <INPUT>.)

The attribute <ACTION> has as its value the location to which the browser delivers the user's data. In this case the URL is pretty short, because membership.exe is located in the same folder as the form document (which, by the way, is named membership.html). <ACTION> can also point to a location on a remote computer, like this:

```
<FORM METHOD=GET ACTION="http://www.mycomputer.com/MacHttp/
files/membership.exe">
```

The other attribute name used here is <METHOD>, which has the value <GET>, as in

```
<FORM METHOD=GET>
```

190

The <GET> tag causes the form contents to be appended to the URL as if they were a normal query sent to the server. <GET> is the default, but <POST> is the more common method. The server will send the data to the CGI and wait for the CGI's response. <POST> looks like this:

```
<FORM METHOD=POST ACTION="membership.exe">
```

This specifies that the data is a separate package. Your server can't do anything with it, so you must have specified your CGI in the <ACTION> attribute.

The <INPUT> Tag

<INPUT> is the most common tag for data entry in a form. <INPUT> is used with either the <NAME> or <TYPE> attributes. The <NAME> attribute is just a descriptive name for the data being requested. Note that the value for <NAME> that you provide here (lastname, firstname, and email) isn't what people are going to type, and it isn't the blank box people see onscreen. It's the name the CGI uses to process the data. In the example, three tags are used early on:

```
<dl>
<dt>Last Name
<dd><input name="lastname" size="40">

<dt>First Name
<dd><input name="firstname" size="40">

<dt>Email Address
<dd><input name="email" size="40">
```

When the browser sends data to the CGI, it pairs each entry's name with the data in the form <NAME="*data*">.

The <SIZE> attribute, seen in the previous example, allows you to specify the width and height of the box into which people will type their information. In this case the size is 40 characters wide.

> **Note:** The <INPUT> tag only makes sense inside the body of a <FORM> </FORM> pair.

<INPUT TYPE>

The <TYPE> attribute designates the kind of data entry method you are using. (If you leave the <TYPE> attribute out, text will be the default data entry method.) Some common values for <TEXT> are

<INPUT TYPE=TEXT>

This tag creates a single-line text entry field (as opposed to <TEXTAREA>, which provides multiline input).

<INPUT TYPE=PASSWORD>

This is a text entry field in which entered characters usually appear as asterisks or bullets in the browser's window.

<INPUT TYPE=CHECKBOX>

A checkbox is a button that is either on or off. The <VALUE> attribute is used to specify the initial state of a form element; see "<INPUT VALUE>" that follows.

<INPUT TYPE=RADIO>

A group of radio buttons can have only one button checked at a time, and one must be checked; when you check an empty button, the checked button turns off.

Here are some <INPUT> tags from the example form:

```
<dl>
<dt>Are you affiliated with a university?
<dd><input type="checkbox" name="affiliation" value="1">No
<dd><input type="checkbox" name="affiliation" value="1">Yes
<dd>If yes, please specify...<input name="university" size=34>
```

<INPUT TYPE=SUBMIT>

This button instructs the browser to pack up the data and send it to the server.

Note: Elements used with the <NAME> attribute are sent with data, but unnamed ones aren't. If you want your data recorded, make sure to use <NAME>.

<INPUT TYPE=RESET>

This button resets the elements of the form to their default values (which are set using the <VALUE> attribute).

<INPUT VALUE>

This specifies the default value for an input. For example,

<INPUT TYPE=TEXT VALUE="This is an example sentence">

creates a single-line text field with the words "This is an example sentence" entered into the blank. (No quotation marks appear.) Of course, the user may substitute some alternative text.

<INPUT TYPE=SUBMIT VALUE="Hit me!">

Puts "Hit me!" rather than the word "Submit" into the Submit button. Likewise,

<INPUT TYPE=RESET VALUE="start over">

puts "start over" into the reset button.

Just to be confusing, the value attributes of <CHECKBOX> and <RADIO> don't appear onscreen. Rather, they give a new name to the value <ON>, so the checkbox

<INPUT TYPE=CHECKBOX NAME="firstbox" VALUE="activated">

sends something like <firstbox=activated> to the CGI when the user submits the form. The default is on, that is, <firstbox=on>.

<INPUT CHECKED>

This specifies the default state of checkboxes and radio buttons. For example,

<INPUT TYPE=CHECKBOX CHECKED>

causes the browser to display an × in the checkbox when the form is first displayed.

<INPUT SIZE>

The default size of an input blank is twenty characters wide. For multiline text entry boxes, a separate tag, <TEXTAREA> is used. The attribute <SIZE> allows you to specify any size you like; for example,

```
<INPUT TYPE=TEXT SIZE=50>
```

creates a text box that is 50 characters long.

THE <SELECT> Tag

The <SELECT> tag is used to create popup menus and scrolling lists. Like <INPUT>, it only makes sense in the context of a <FORM>. It is a closed tag and must be used with </SELECT>. The basic form is

```
<SELECT NAME="firstmenu">
<OPTION> Line of text without html tags
<OPTION> Second line of text without html tags
<OPTION> Another line of text without html tags
<OPTION> Final line of text without html tags
</SELECT>
```

The <NAME> attribute of the <SELECT> tag functions exactly as in <INPUT>. Note that the text following each <OPTION> tag cannot contain any HTML markup tags; this is because the line of text is what is sent to the CGI for processing. If the users chose the third menu item on the list from the previous example, for instance, the browser would send the CGI the name "firstmenu" and the value "Another line...", or in other words: "firstmenu=Another line of text without html tags."

The <SELECT SIZE> Tag

If no size is specified, the browser displays the option set as a popup menu. If a number greater than one is specified for size, the browser creates a scrolling text field with SIZE lines. For instance,

```
<SELECT SIZE=5>
```

creates a five-line scrolling field. If <SIZE> is greater than the number of options, the browser will fill in the bottom with blank lines.

```
<SELECT MULTIPLE>
```

This attribute allows the user to pick more than one choice from a scrolling text field. (You usually can't pick more than one item from a popup menu—although that's the nature of popup menus, it isn't strictly supported by all browsers.) For example,

```
<SELECT NAME="fruit" SIZE=5 MULTIPLE>
<OPTION> Apple
<OPTION> Banana
<OPTION> Orange
<OPTION> Kiwi
</SELECT>
```

presents a scrolling list that allows the user to pick as many options as needed. If, for example, the user selects the first and second items, the browser sends these tags to the CGI:

```
fruit=Apple
fruit=Banana
```

The <TEXTAREA> Tag

The <TEXTAREA> tag simply creates a big, multiline blank for the user to fill in. Like <INPUT> and <SELECT>, it works only within the <FORM> tag, and it must have a name. It is closed. It uses the attributes <ROWS> (number of lines) and <COLS> (width in characters) to define its size. For example,

```
<TEXTAREA NAME="Textblock" ROWS=5 COLS=20>
</TEXTAREA>
```

specifies a five-line by twenty-character block. A <TEXTAREA> blank always has a scroll bar so that users can enter as much text as they like. Any default text goes between the tags, like this:

```
<TEXTAREA NAME="Textblock" ROWS=10 COLS=65>...By Mr Silvero
With caressing hands, at Limoges
Who walked all night in the next room;
By Hakagawa, bowing among the Titians;
By Madame de Tournquist, in the dark room
Shifting the candles;
Fraulein von Kulp
Who turned in the hall, one hand on the door.
Vacant shuttles
Weave the wind.
</TEXTAREA>
```

Notice that line breaks are preserved, unlike the usual HTML text that would require <BR>. As with <SELECT>, no markup tags may be used in the text, as it is sent to the CGI for processing. Most <TEXTAREA> fields do not allow word wrap, although this varies from browser to browser.

The result of the HTML used in the Phusis form is shown in Figure 5.4.

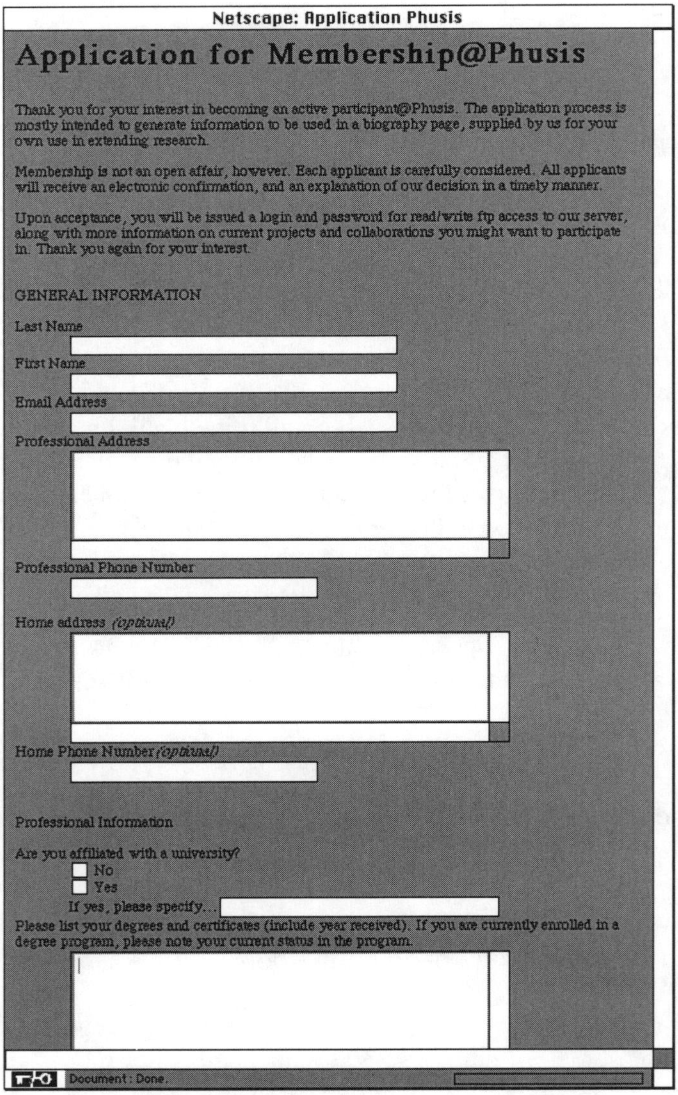

Figure 5.4 Phusis registration form.

Putting It Together with CGI Scripts

Now that you have created the form, you have to be ready to collect and report the data you receive. That's where CGIs come in. As stated earlier, CGIs are powerful tools for your Web site, but they have a few potential drawbacks. Let's start with the most abstract analysis of CGIs first.

HTML versus CGI: A Comparison

HTML is not a programming language.

HTML documents provide data, addresses where more data can be found, and local annotation of that data. A programming language is characterized by its capability to make decisions (with statements like IF...THEN...) and to repeat instructions (with statements like FOR...DO...). A computer program uses these tools to perform functions such as search text, sort databases, do arithmetic, and so on.

A browser *is* a program, however, because it uses decision-making and iteration tools to display an HTML document. A server program, such as WebSTAR, is also a program because it processes the requests that it receives from browsers.

Because HTML does not have these programming tools available, an HTML document does not have the capability to interpret data that a user may send to the server by, say, filling in a form or clicking in a map. What an HTML document *can* do, however, is to serve a form with instructions to pass off the user's data to another application on the server that *can* process the data. These programs are CGIs (Common Gateway Interfaces).

Things to Consider before CGI-ing

In college, we English majors used to think it was amusing to ask each other, "Do you like Kipling?" The answer, of course, was: "I don't know. I've never Kipled." Well, if you've never done any CGI-ing, what follows are some drawbacks you should consider to help decide whether you will like it.

CGIs can consume a lot of computational horsepower. Very little CPU time is required for a Web server to serve HTML documents. It simply finds the file that the browser has asked for and sends the file over the Internet. It doesn't have to do anything to the file.

A search, a sort, or a computation requires your server to do some work on a file or files. That work uses more of the computer's basic resources: RAM (memory) and CPU time. As these are limited, use of CGIs will make your server respond more slowly and, in worst-case scenarios, to *hang* (not respond to any input) or to crash. Well-constructed CGIs rarely exhibit such problems. But it's best to test them out under stressful, rather than ideal, conditions.

Furthermore, if your server software handles its requests to the CGI program *synchronously,* it must wait for the CGI program to reply before it can do anything else. Happily, servers and shareware CGI software are beginning to support *asynchronous* calls, so that the server can proceed while the CGI program is thinking about your request.

CGIs can pose a security risk. A CGI does not necessarily confine its activities to a certain folder in your hard drive. It is remotely possible that someone may tamper with your files by sending cryptic requests to your CGI program. Also, a small mistake in a CGI script can cause it to serve, say, your financial data rather than the information you wanted. To be honest, these possibilities are extremely unlikely, but you should consider your individual circumstances carefully before deciding to take the risk.

CGIs are machine-specific. An HTML document is extremely "portable." You can take an HTML document served on, say, a UNIX workstation, and serve it on your Apple Internet Server with a minimum of fuss. (You might have to tweak the names of the local files if you move from platform to platform.) Adding CGIs to the picture makes changing platforms far more complicated; the analogous CGI may not even exist on more than one platform.

Despite all this, I don't want to discourage you from using CGIs. My opinion is that a great deal of the Web's popularity and utility comes from Netscape, MacWeb, and Mosaic's support for forms. Besides, your competition is probably using them, so you should, too. And CGIs do a lot of things besides process form data.

AppleScript and CGI

In many cases, a Macintosh HTTP server will communicate with a CGI program written in AppleScript. AppleScript is a way for two Mac programs to communicate with one another. (It does a lot of things in addition, but this is the most relevant function for our purposes.) In this case, the server is communicating with the CGI program. AppleScript is built into System 7.5 and is available as a commercial extension to System 7.x.

> **Note:** Although AppleScript is often used to create CGIs in the Mac environment, there are other programs that are in many ways more powerful, such as MacPerl, C, C++, or HyperCard. Frontier (also known as Aretha) is native to the Power Macintosh and multithreaded.

For our purposes, AppleScript can be thought of as one way to implement CGI programs on a Macintosh Web server. Here is an example of a very simple, fundamental AppleScript used to gather the contents of the Phusis form shown in Figure 5.4 and write the results to a text file:

```
on «event WWW sr ch» http_search_args
    set crlf to (ASCII character 13) & (ASCII character 10)
    set http_20_header to "HTTP/2.0.1 200 OK" & crlf & "Server:
MacHTTP" & crlf & ¬
    "MIME-Version: 1.0" & crlf & "Content-type: text/html" & crlf & crlf
    -- Change the following to be the appropriate file. Note that it must
    -- exist before running the script (create an empty text file first.)
    set f to open file alias "http://128.135.26.63/applicants.txt" for
update
    position file f at (get file length f)
    write file f text http_search_args
    close file f
    return http_20_header & "<title>Confirmation</title>
<h1>Application Confirmation</h1> Thank you for applying to Phusis. You
will be emailed further information.<p><i>Phusis staff</i><p>"
end «event WWW sr ch»
```

To make this work, you have to put all the files in the appropriate places on a Web server that has AppleScript and related system extensions installed. You must also have a text file created into which the data will be output. And you have to describe a path name leading to that text output document (in this case I specified a path that includes our office server's IP address: http://128.135.26.63/applicants.txt).

There are three documents working together here:

1. The actual HTML form (membership.html).

2. A text document containing the AppleScript (membership.exe), which takes the data and specifies that it will be output to.

3. The empty text file you have set up (applicants.txt).

What happens is that when someone fills out the form and clicks the Submit button, the data is sent to a server, where the script contained in "membership.exe" (the Common Gateway Interface) acts on it and writes the results to the file "applicants.txt."

Can You Do It Yourself?

This raises a bigger question: are you going to write your own CGI scripts? You can, of course, in the same way that you can run from New York to Los Angeles. But, why would you want to? Even a simple script that works under ideal circumstances may not be suitable in real-world situations. There are simply too many variables flying around.

If you value your personal hygiene, it's best to use one of the many ready-made CGIs available on the Web, or to find a consultant to write one for you.

Where to Find It

John Wiederspan's Mac WWW development site is located at http:// www.uwtc.washington.edu/ Computing/WWW/Mac/ Directory.html. The CGI-specific information for WebSTAR and MacHTTP is located at: http:// www.uwtc.washington.edu/ computing/www/lessons/.The FTP site related to this material is ftp://ftp.uwtc.washington.edu// pub/Mac/Network/WWW.

Where to Find Ready-Made CGIs

John Wiederspan's Mac WWW development site is an excellent source for shareware and freeware CGI software for the Mac. In fact, this a great site for all kinds of information relating to the Macintosh and the Web. Here are some of the important CGI applications available at this site.

Mac-ImageMap

Mac-ImageMap is an essential CGI application for creating clickable imagemaps, which are discussed in the following section "Clickable Imagemaps." It works with MacHTTP/WebSTAR to process imagemap data.

Email.cgi

Email.cgi is a utility that caters to browsers who cannot send mail. It sends the browser a form that the Web reader can complete. Then it mails the completed form to the user-designated recipient. It requires MacHTTP or WebSTAR, AppleScript, and a few AppleScript extras called OSAXen. The extras are not included with Email.cgi, but hyperlinks pointing to them are specified in the documentation materials.

Fmpro.acgi

Fmpro.acgi allows a MacHTTP/WebSTAR server to access FileMaker Pro databases. You can add, delete, and edit records in your FileMaker document. (Fmpro.acgi accomplishes this by remote-controlling FileMaker, so make sure you have plenty of memory available.) It requires MacHTTP, FileMaker Pro, AppleScript, and AppleScript extensions that are not included, but are freely available on the Web.

FMProCGI

FMProCGI is a very similar utility for using MacHTTP to control FileMaker Pro. Its documentation is more extensive than that of Fmpro.acgi. It requires MacHTTP, FileMaker Pro, AppleScript, and AppleScript extensions, which are not included with FMProCGI, but are hyperlink-specified in the documentation materials.

GIFServ

GIFServ provides rudimentary animation for Netscape 1.1. Essentially, it is an application that serves a series of GIF files using Netscape Navigator 1.1 server-push/client-pull technology to do simple multiframe animations. It's cool, but you won't mistake the results for a QuickTime movie—each frame must be transmitted over the Internet, and frames don't come in at twelve frames per second. GIFServ simply serves all the GIFs it finds in a specified folder in alphabetical order as a multipart GIF.

Where to Find It

Two shareware products, NetCloak and NetForms, are CGI add-ons for MacHTTP/WebSTAR servers. They allow you to add functionality to your Web site (including processing of form data, time and date stamps, client information, or passwords) without having to know how to write the actual CGI scripts. Find out more at http://www.maxum.com/maxum/.

Netcloak

NetCloak is conceptually different from most of the other CGIs discussed here. Rather than processing data from the user or allowing the user access to data in non-HTML formats, NetCloak effectively extends the HTML language to include new commands. Essentially, NetCloak edits your HTML document according to the conditions under which it is viewed, and sends the edited, standard HTML document to the browser.

These commands involve hiding parts of your HTML page from the user and revealing them under special conditions that you define, using nonstandard, NetCloak-specific HTML extensions such as the <HIDE> and <SHOW> tags.

Where to Find It

TR-WWW is shareware; find out more at http://informatics.med.monash.edu.au/tr-www.html.

TR-WWW

TR-WWW is a search engine that processes text, HTML, and Microsoft Word files. It doesn't require that you preformat your files for searching and it can search huge documents quickly. (It processes the text, although not the formatting, of Word files.) This is an ideal tool for publishing large text documents on the Web in a searchable format. TR-WWW is extensively documented, and the documentation states that it requires only the latest version of MacHTTP to run.

Clickable Imagemaps

A clickable imagemap is a graphic image that has been "mapped" so that each pixel has been assigned x, y, or similar coordinates, as in a graph. Each pixel can, in theory, serve as a link. You click a predefined region of the graphic—a square or circle you have mapped out on it and designated with a destination (a file name or URL). A link is made to that destination file or a URL, taking you to the new location.

Greg's Soapbox

Imagemaps, while undeniably "cool," often take a long time to load onscreen because of the information contained within them. As much as possible, keep the file size manageable. Also, the links they contain need to be duplicated on the same page, either by textual or button anchors, for nongraphical browsers.

There is no standard way to create an imagemap. There are a number of software programs you can use. You don't have to use WebMap or Mac-ImageMap, for instance; MapServe or MacMapMaker are also appropriate.

The techniques also vary depending on whether you have an NCSA or CERN server. Here's a brief rundown on one way to create an imagemap, to give you an idea of what is involved:

1. Create a graphic image and save it in GIF format.

2. Define the clickable regions of the image by using a program such as WebMap to define clickable regions of the image.

   To do this, you open up your already-saved GIF image within WebMap and use WebMap's drawing tools to create clickable regions in the shape of a circle, square, or polygon by drawing them "on top" of your image.

   WebMap assigns a set of x,y coordinates to each region you create. (The 0,0 point is at the top left-hand corner of your image.) Each region you draw is assigned x,y numbers describing its boundaries. Depending on how many of these regions you draw, you will wind up with a list of these regions and coordinates. That list is called an *imagemap configuration file*. Any user who clicks within the boundaries of a particular region will be taken to a file you assign to it. (See the next step.)

3. Now that you have a set of clickable regions, each with its own coordinates, you set up the destination files on your server. You have to determine whether you are using a CERN or NCSA server. Ask your Internet provider if you're not sure.

   Each region is assigned a destination URL where a user will be taken. It's okay to have several regions pointing to the same URL, but each region can have only one destination.

4. Enable a CGI program to carry out the actions specified in your Configuration File. I am familiar with one called Mac-ImageMap. This comes with a CGI application called imagemap.cgi. This application needs to be running in the background when you start testing the map.

   Mac-ImageMap also comes with a configuration file. You have to change a line in the code to point to your map and your map file. (This is explained further in the section entitled "A Personal Example," which follows.)

5. Test, correct errors, and retest until it all works correctly. Make sure the folders are in the correct folders in the server so that the pathname specified in the map file actually takes the user to those files.

Where to Find It

WebMap contains online instructions on creating clickable regions. It's now a commercial program, but a shareware beta version can be found at ftp://ftp.uwtc.washington.edu//pub/Mac/Network/WWW/WebMap2.0b7.sit.bin. You can also find a version of MacMapMaker at ftp://ftp.uwtc.washington.edu//pub/Mac/Network/WWW/.

A Personal Example

In my own illogical way, I created an imagemap on a server before I knew very much about HTML. I found it to be a difficult and tedious experience, which may explain some of my skepticism about imagemaps; but when the map began to work, it was a tremendous thrill that made all the effort worthwhile. Here's what I did.

I wanted to create a visual map of a group of my stories and poems arranged in the shape of a Tibetan mandala. After I picked out the works I wanted to include, I made a rough drawing on paper, and then created the graphic in MacDraw. I saved the original in PICT format and later converted it to GIF using a program called GIFConverter.

It's a crude image, to be sure (I'm no artist), but it's also pretty simple. It is only about 13K in size and doesn't take long to load onscreen; see Figure 5.5.

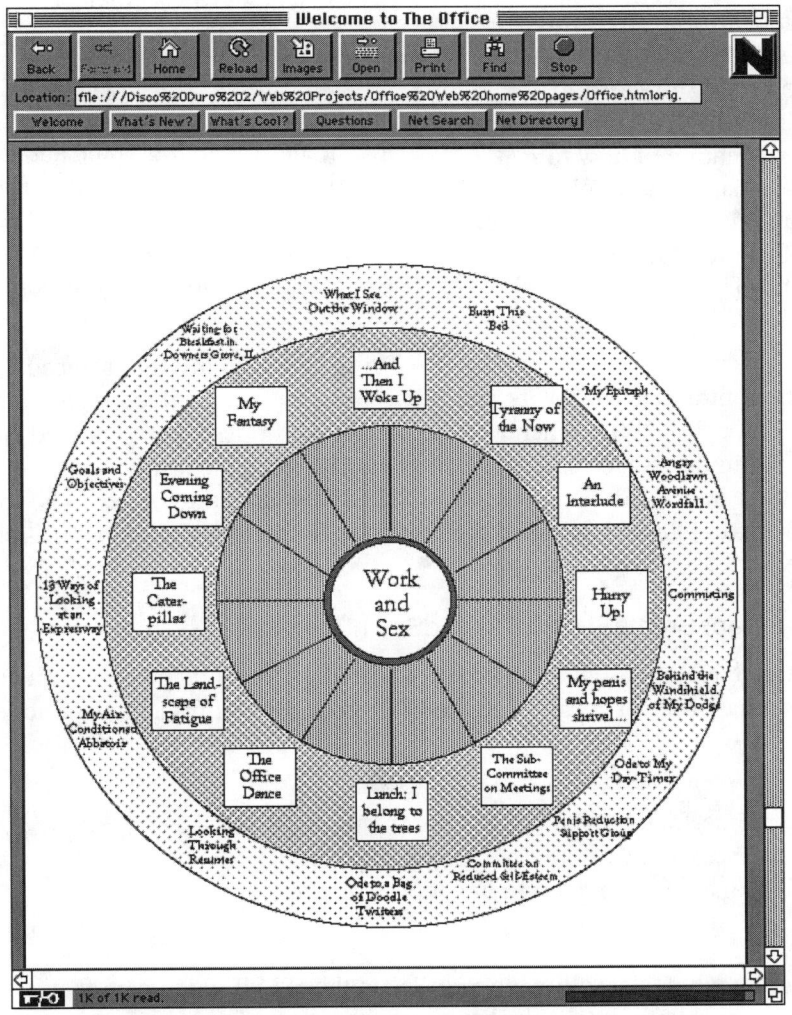

Figure 5.5 Original imagemap GIF image.

Where to Find It

WebMap, by Rowland Smith, is at http://www.city.net/cnx/software/webmap.html. Mac-ImageMap is at http://weyl.zib-berlin.de/imagemap/Mac-ImageMap.html. An excellent explanation of how to make an imagemap is on Jon Wiederspan's site, http://www.uwtc.washington.edu/Computing/WWW/Map.html.

Next, I downloaded the shareware program WebMap and opened my GIF file in the program. Using WebMap's drawing tools, I "traced" squares, circles, or polygons around the titles in the drawing. These shapes, while visible in WebMap, don't show up when the file appears in a Web browser.

What WebMap does is map out the regions you "trace" on your graphic and assign numerical coordinates to them. For each region you draw, you type the URL of the file you want to take the user to after the user clicks within the mapped-out coordinates.

For instance, in my file, I traced a circle around the central region, "Work and Sex." WebMap assigned the region the coordinates "230,306 320,396." Whenever the Macintosh finder's arrow moved atop pixels that fell within those coordinates (in other words, when the arrow was inside the circle in the center) and the mouse was clicked, I wanted the viewer to go to the poem "Work and Sex." I assigned the poem the following relative path, as shown in Figure 5.6.

    /imagemap/Greg'sStuff/WorkandSex.html

I also had to have an essential bit of software called imagemap.cgi, which comes with Mac-ImageMap. This allowed the CGI processing of my map instructions.

Note: Mac-ImageMap applies only if you're using MacHTTP/WebSTAR from a Mac server; if you're using a UNIX or other server, it's not required and the methods for serving imagemaps are different.

I then had to include the following *maplink* in the HTML document that included my imagemap. This maplink tells the browser where to find the map processing CGI application. Specifically, these lines instruct imagemap.cgi to process the instructions in the imagemap configuration file "officemap" when someone clicks within the imagemap "office.gif2." The computer referred to is a Macintosh running MacHTTP:

```
<A HREF="http://upubs-63.uchicago.edu/imagemap.cgi$officemap">
<IMG SRC="http://upubs-63.uchicago.edu/office/office.gif2" ISMAP>
</A>
```

The last thing I did was change some lines in the configuration file that enable the imagemap.cgi application to recognize my configuration file and act on it:

```
officemap : :office:office.gif2.map
```

(The leading colon ":" indicates that my map, "officemap," is a subfolder of the Mac-ImageMap folder, wherein the map-file "office.gif2.map" resides.)

Figure 5.6 WebMap configuration file.

The map didn't work the first time, or the second. The problem was the relative path names had to point through exactly the right sequence of folders and point to exactly the right files in not one, but in three places: the configuration file, the lines of CGI in the HTML page in the configuration file, and the imagemap.cgi file.

Imagemaps can work if the files are of a manageable size and the clickable "hot spots" are well defined. A good, yet simple, imagemap is found on Stanford University's Web site (see Figure 5.7).

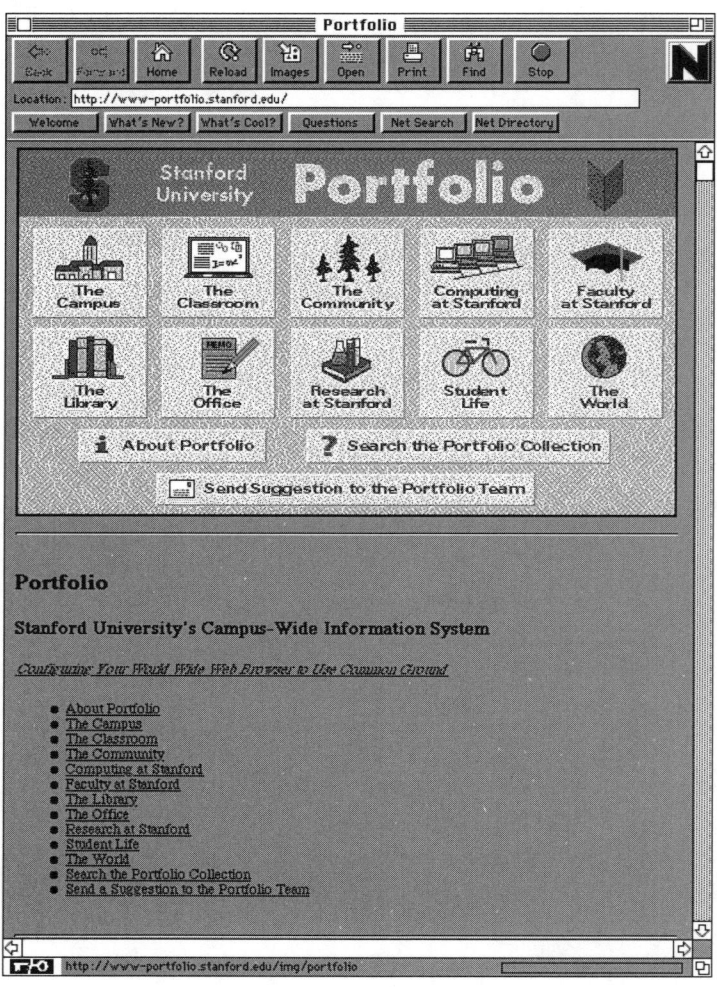

Figure 5.7 Imagemap used by Stanford University.

It works well not only because the clickable regions are well defined, but because, with the flat colors, it compresses well (only 10K in size) in GIF format. This shows that an imagemap doesn't have to be small to work well. It's the file size that counts, not the total size.

Using Other Programs to Generate HTML

Converting your press releases and other textual documents from their original format to HTML isn't overly difficult, especially if you use one of the converter or editing programs described in Chapter 7.

But what if you have an extensive inventory or catalog of data held in a database file, and you want to make that inventory readable on the Web so that potential customers can see what you have for sale?

Creating dozens or hundreds of individual HTML documents, one for each record in your database, is impractical at best. It's also not necessary because you might be able to use the actual database program to generate HTML versions of your records.

Any program that has scripting capabilities, such as HyperCard or FileMaker, can be used to generate HTML. This book can't teach you how to program in HyperCard, for example, but if you are proficient in these applications, you only have to modify your routines to generate HTML tags. The following examples were developed by the aforementioned HyperCard guru, John Casler.

A HyperCard Script that Generates HTML

John is a real-life artist in addition to being a computer consultant, and he created this HyperCard stack to catalog his work (see Figure 5.8).

Note: The HyperCard stack shown in Figure 5.8 and its script are freeware and available on the Web site for this book, so you can adapt them to your own cataloguing needs.

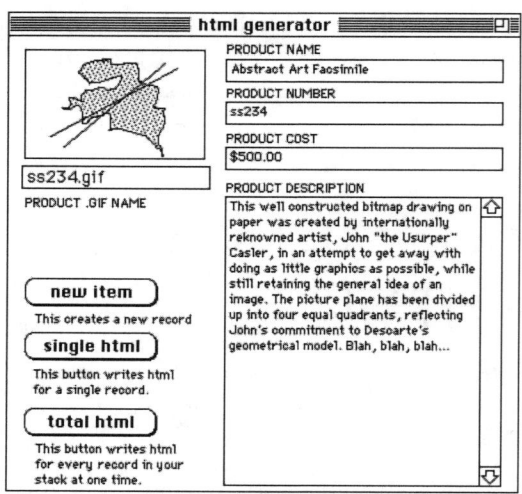

Figure 5.8 HyperCard stack that generates HTML.

There are two separate HTML-generating functions in this stack. They are represented by the two buttons, "single html" and "total html." The first generates an HTML document containing the information for a single record. The second generates an ASCII file with HTML tags and places it in the same folder as HyperCard, unless you specify another destination.

If you try this, remember to keep all names single entities, and to put all GIF files and other documents in the right location on your server. John's comment lines (any lines that begin with "- -") explain how the rest of the script works. The script, in fact, starts out with several general comments:

- -the "& return" string concatenated to end of our put statements is strictly for ease of reading the final ASCII, HTML documents. The Web needs no such pretty print for this script to still function correctly, but one should consider little interface issues such as this to really take advantage of the stack, make one's own life easier, and make allowances for future edits.- -
- -this stack is meant to produce locally viewable HTML documents. For actual, HTTP-served documents, one needs to extend the string literals to include the "http://someDirectory/..." materials, particularly in the case of .gifs and other anchors, that is, hrefs.- -
- -also, don't forget to place the actual gif files, with the correct names, into the appropriate locations on your server.- -

Now the script begins:

```
on mouseUp
  put "<title>" & field "product_name" & "</title>" & return after htmlVar
  - -this creates a variable "htmlVar" in which you hold all info- -

  put "<h1>" & fld "product_name" & "</h1>" & return after htmlVar
  - -this starts to write the html code for you- -

  put "<img src=" & quote & fld "gif_name" & quote & "><p>" & return
after htmlVar
  - -this puts the img tag into your variable htmlVar, and points to the
correct gif file- -

  put "<dl><dl>Product Number:" && fld "product_number" & "<br>" &
return after htmlVar
  - -the <dl> formats an indent into your html, the <br> sends a line break- -

  put "Cost:" && fld "product_price" & "<br>" & return after htmlVar
  - -add another item to the variable, send another line break- -

  put "Product Description:" && fld "product_description" after htmlVar
  - -you are now ready to write the file. These will be individual HTML docu-
ments, but with a simple change to the repeat loop, one could write an
entire series of records to one file, complete with indexing if one desires!- -

  put fld "product_number" & ".html" into docName
  - -here you create the HTML document name variable, and add the all
important suffix .html. You could use fld "product_name", but then you
have to restrict the fld to single-word entries, a restriction that also applies
to the "product_number" field as well!- -

  put "</dl></dl>" & return after htmlVar
  - -this closes up the indentation in our HTML formatting- -

  open file docName
  write htmlVar to file docName
  close file docName
  - -and that's all there is to it! Remember, the ASCII file will be put auto-
matically to the same folder as HyperCard, unless you give it a specific
path as an alternative. For example: open file "polis:Desktop folder:" &
docName places the new ascii file on my desktop!- -
end mouseUp
```

Sticklers for detail will notice that John violates some of the basic HTML rules spelled out elsewhere (but that are commonly violated all over the Web) such as not using the <HTML>, <HEAD>, or <BODY> tags. It's not proper HTML, but it works.

The results are shown in Figure 5.9.

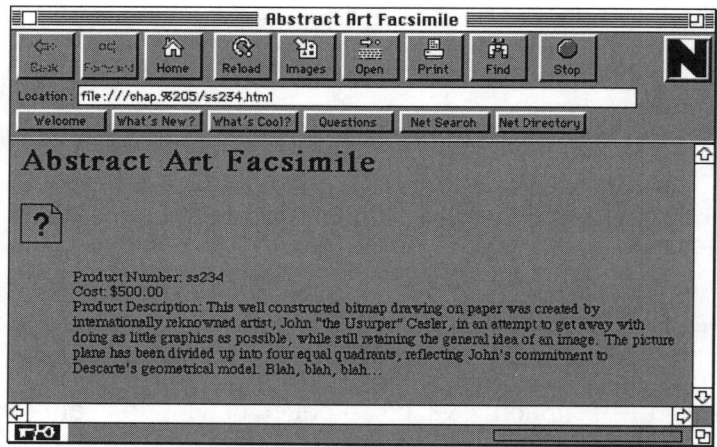

Figure 5.9 Single record output in HTML.

Now for the script that generates an ASCII file coded for all records in your stack. First some general comments as those above apply here, so I won't repeat them.

Here's the script:

```
on mouseUp
  lock screen
  - -this keeps the user from having to look at a lot of cards flashing by- -

  repeat with i = 1 to the number of cds
  put empty into htmlVar
  - -this flushes the variable htmlVar with each new card, and initializes it to
empty- -

  go to card i
  - -this loop will essentially mimic the single card but apply to every record
in your stack

  put "<title>" & field "product_name" & "</title>" & return after htmlVar
  - -this creates a variable "htmlVar" in which you hold all info.- -
```

```
    put "<h1>" & fld "product_name" & "</h1>" & return after htmlVar
    --this starts to write the html code for you--

    put "<img src=" & quote & fld "gif_name" & quote & "><p>" & return
after htmlVar
    --this puts the img tag into our variable HTMLVar, and points to the
correct gif file

    put "<dl><dl>Product Number:" && fld "product_number" & "<br>" &
return after htmlVar
    --the <dl> formats an indent into our HTML, the <br> sends a line break

    put "Cost:" && fld "product_price" & "<br>" & return after htmlVar
    --add another item to the variable, send another line break--

    put "Product Description:" && fld "product_description" after htmlVar
    --you are now ready to write the file. These will be individual HTML docu-
ments, but with a simple change to the repeat loop, one could write an
entire series of records to one file, complete with indexing if one desires.--

    put fld "product_number" & ".html" into docName
    --here you create the HTML document name variable, and add the all
important suffix .html
    --you could use fld "product_name", but then you have to restrict the fld
to single-word entries, a restriction that also applies to the
"product_number" field as well!--

    put "</dl></dl>" & return after htmlVar
    --this closes up the indentation in our HTML formatting

    open file docName
    write htmlVar to file docName
    close file docName
--and that's all there is to it! Remember, the ASCII file will be put automati-
cally to the same folder as HyperCard, unless you give it a specific path as
an alternative. For example: open file "polis:Desktop folder:" & docName
places the new ASCII file on my desktop.--

    end repeat
--that's it! You now have as many HTML documents as you have records in
your stack.--

    unlock screen
--always nice to tidy up!--
end mouseUp
```

Using FileMaker to Generate HTML

Along with the CGIs listed earlier that allow your browser or MacHTTP to access FileMaker Pro databases, there are scripts you can write within FileMaker that generate HTML from a database.

John Casler did this with the University of Chicago College Research Opportunities Program Directory, which was described in Chapter 2. To generate HTML, he went into FileMaker Pro's "Define Fields" window and turned the fields that were to be output to HTML into calculation fields. He added the script to generate HTML into those fields as pseudocalculations (see Figure 5.10).

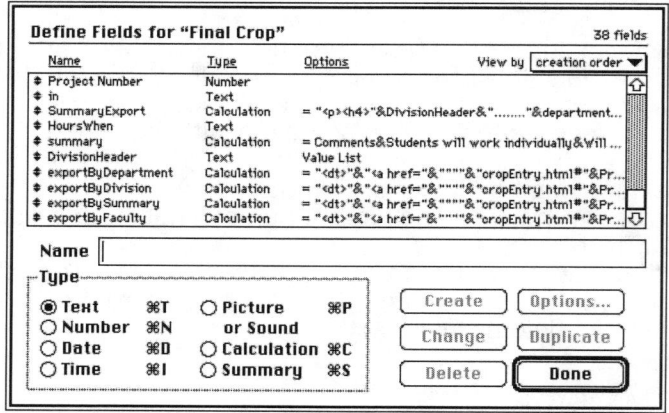

Figure 5.10 Calculation fields used to generate HTML.

He then used FileMaker's script utility to create a script called "Export," which gathered the contents of the calculation fields and exported them to an HTML document when the Export button was clicked (Figure 5.11).

The output in Netscape can be seen in Figure 5.12. (I realize that the contents of Figures 5.11 and 5.12 don't match exactly, but the arrangement of the data is the same.)

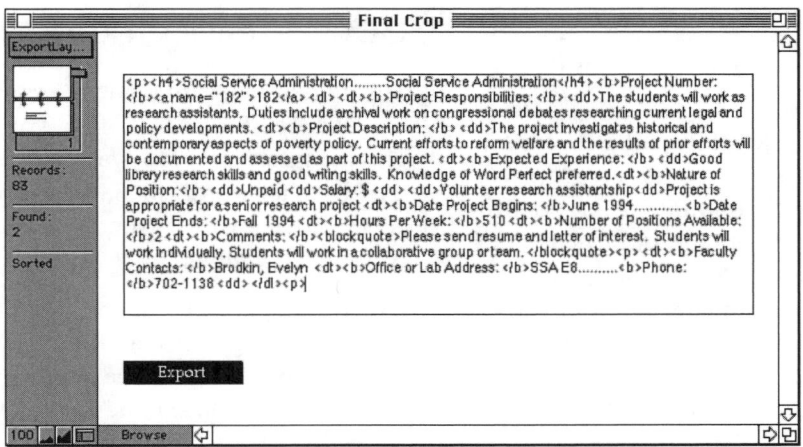

Figure 5.11 Export Script document.

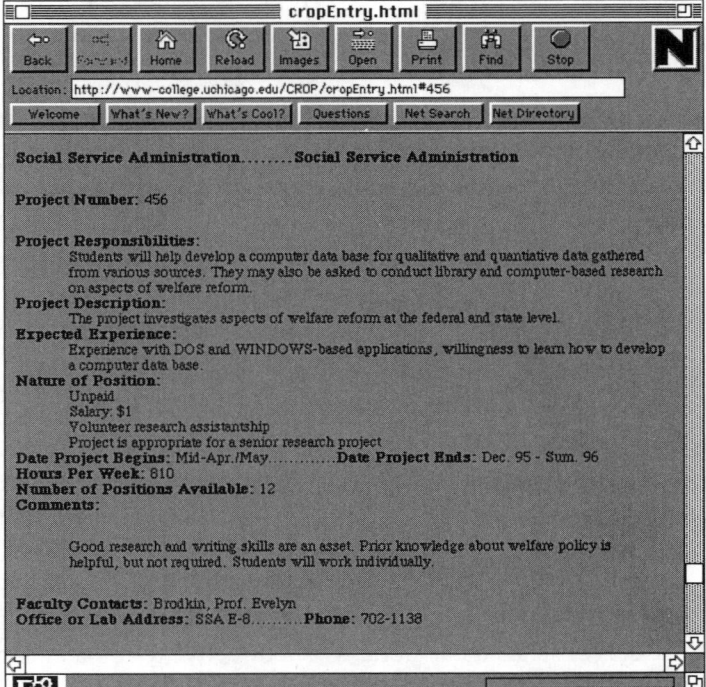

Figure 5.12 FileMaker data displayed in Netscape.

Where to Find It

The basic information source for server side includes is http://hoohoo.ncsa.uiuc.edu/docs/tutorials/includes.html. (It focuses on NCSA HTTPD and Netsite.) Another set of instructions (primarily useful for readers configuring UNIX Web servers) is at http://www.webtools.org/counter/ssi/step-by-step.html.

Server Side Includes

This rather inelegant name refers to scripts on your Web server that allow you to provide information to Web readers "on the fly." In other words, the information is generated anew every time a visitor connects to your site.

Examples of server side includes are scripts that might display the current date and time to the visitor, the date when the file was last modified, the email address of the Webmaster, or a signature generated fresh with every visit so that it doesn't have to be rewritten on every document.

Another example is an access counter that records the number of visitors to a particular Web site. A script that does this (on UNIX computers, at least) is found at http://www.webtools.org/counter.

The same cautionary statements made earlier about CGIs apply to server side includes. Be aware of the programming power they require. They might conceivably cause trouble on a site whose Internet connection is inadequate or barely adequate to handle the traffic it receives.

Server Push-Client Pull

This is a Netscape extension that allows you to refresh the client data at regular intervals, or even to put a crude sort of animation into your Web documents.

This is another way in which a Web reader can get information from a server. Along with the traditional method—the user clicks a link and gets information—this gives the server the capability to "push" data to the browser.

In server push, the server sends down a bundle of data, and sends more data at predetermined intervals.

In client pull, the server sends data, along with a directive to reload the data in a specified amount of time (for instance, "load this data in five seconds"). After the five seconds elapses, the client does what it has been told.

In server push, the connection between server and browser is always open; in client pull the information is sent once, and the client performs the action after time has elapsed.

The following HTML code refreshes a screen once every second. It uses an HTML 3.0 tag (<META>) that (as of this writing at least) is recognized only by Netscape 1.1. The <META> tag gives general information relating to the HTML document as a whole. When used with the <HTTP-EQUIV> attribute, as it is in the following HTML example, <META> simulates an HTTP response header.

```
<html><head>
<META HTTP-EQUIV="Refresh" CONTENT=1></head>
<title>A Refreshing Document</title>
<body><h1>This is a refreshed document!</h1>
<p>Here's some text that can be updated regularly.</p>
</body><html>
```

Where to Find It

The basic information on server push and client pull is at Netscape's Web site: http://home.netscape.com/assist/net_sites/pushpull.html.

You can use server push or client pull to refresh in-line images on a regular basis, thus giving the effect of crude animation. You can also update stock tickers or take periodic images of the fish swimming in your aquarium. Be aware, though, that this only works on Netscape 1.1, and that server push consumes some of your server's computing capacity.

Now that you've seen some ways in which HTML's capabilities can be extended to make a Web site more interactive and powerful, you're ready to get a glimpse of the next stage, HTML 3.0, where the markup language's capabilities are developed a step further.

HTML 3.0: New Tools for Web Authoring

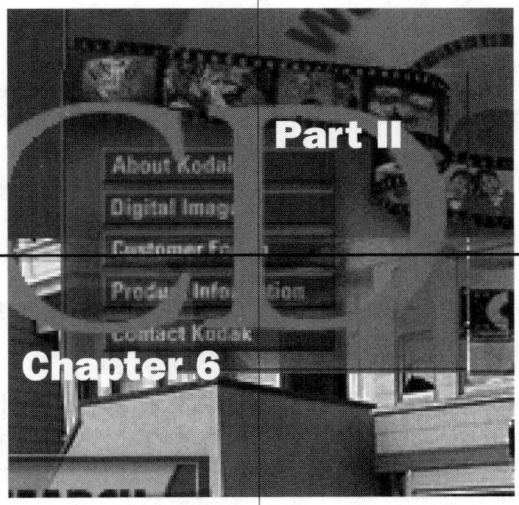

Part II

Chapter 6

If you like to be entertained by fast-moving adventure stories, you'll love hearing about the evolution of the HTML markup language. Just a few years ago, it was an experimental subset of SGML used by a handful of computer visionaries.

Where to Find It

Discussions about HTML 3.0 as well as other HTML-related subjects are taking place on the mailing list www-html. To subscribe, send an email message to: listserv@info.cern.ch. The body of your message should be: subscribe www-html (your full name). Archives of recent discussions can be reviewed on the Web at http://gummo.stanford.edu/html/hypermail/.

Where to Find It

The HTML 3.0 specification can be found at http://www.hpl.hp.co.uk/people/dsr/html3/CoverPage.html. An index to all HTML 3.0 tags is at http://www.halsoft.com/sgml/html-3.0/DTD-HOME.html.

Now (drum roll, please) it's an increasingly powerful tool that allows increasingly complex document formatting and allows clients to work with multimedia and helper applications in creating their Web presentations. Developers (applause, applause) are to be found everywhere around the globe. HTML's simplicity and ease-of-use are two big reasons why the Web has grown at such a spectacular rate.

Perhaps the most amazing thing about HTML's development is that you can participate in it at home. It is occurring not in a single programmer's workstation, but online. You, too, can watch the latest innovations and "listen in" on current debates about rules and standards.

That's what HTML is, after all: a set of standards that we agree to observe. HTML doesn't come in a box like a computer's operating software; you can't buy it in a store. It is built into the Web browsers. The browsers are programmed to recognize HTML tags and other commands and will display them the way the HTML developers intended.

David Raggett is the primary author of HTML 3.0, which can be defined as an extensive set of proposed extensions to HTML 2.0. He is assisted by the HTML workgroup of the Internet Engineering Task Force (IETF).

Note: Some of the Netscape extensions to HTML described in the previous chapter are not in the current draft of HTML 3.0. Most of the extensions have HTML 3.0 equivalents, but some do not. Which ones should you use?

In general, I favor the HTML 3.0 commands because Netscape has pledged to support them. In particular, beware of using Netscape's <CENTER>, <FONT>, and <BASEFONT> extensions. The first is being superseded by HTML 3.0's <ALIGN=CENTER> tag. The others apparently will not be included in HTML 3.0 and will not appear on browsers other than Netscape. Although these tags are useful, they may not be supported by future browsers.

Where to Find It

Dave Raggett's home page, http:/ /www.hpl.hp.co.uk/people/ dsr/, contains links to the current description of HTML 3.0, as well as general information about the W3 Organization and IETF.

Although the document type Definition (DTD) of HTML 3.0 is not yet final, its proposed rules have been published on the Web for a while and, at this writing, the table elements have been adopted by browsers such as Netscape Navigator 1.1 and the version 2.0 beta releases of NCSA Mosaic.

This chapter briefly outlines some of the new features of HTML 3.0 that are of particular interest to information providers. When these features are supported by browsers, they will allow you to do wonderful things with your online publications.

Note: Because HTML 3.0 is still under development, many of these tag names mentioned here will change, or may have changed already. This section is intended to give a general idea of what HTML 3.0 will allow you to do. I'm using the March 28, 1995, description of HTML 3.0, which was the latest one available at the time this book was being written.

Specifying the Document as HTML 3.0

It is suggested that you start an HTML 3.0 document with the following comment line so that a browser will be able to identify its document type definition and will know which HTML extensions are used:

```
<!doctype HTML public "-//W3O//DTD W3 HTML 3.0//EN">
```

When you save your HTML document, consider giving it the suffix ".html3" for the same reason.

Tables

The most immediate impact of HTML 3.0 can be seen when creating tables.

The following HTML was used to generate the simple table shown in Figure 6.1. Note that:

- The <BORDER> tag tells the browser to draw lines around each cell in the table.

- The <CAPTION> </CAPTION> tag is used to place a caption above or below the table.

- The <TR> tag denotes a table row. It need not have an end tag </TR>.

- The <TH> tag appears before table header cell text. This text is emphasized to distinguish it from data text.

- The <TD> tag is used with table data text.

```
<table border>
   <caption>Recent Presidents</caption>
   <tr><th>President<th>Term Started<th>Ended
   <tr><td>Kennedy<td>1961<td>1963
   <tr><td>Johnson<td>1963<td>1969
   <tr><td>Nixon<td>1969<td>1974
</table>
```

A more complex table is shown in Figure 6.2. This is a real-life example taken from the University of Chicago College course catalog. It shows how one of the alignment tags (<ALIGN=CENTER>) under development in HTML 3.0 is used with table text, and how line breaks can be used in a cell. I inserted a blank line between the code for each row to make it easier to read.

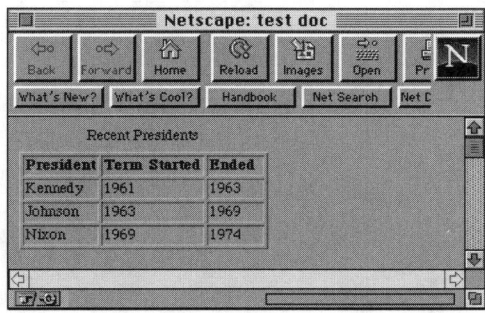

Figure 6.1 A simple table.

Greg's Soapbox

You'll notice that I have used the Netscape extension <FONT SIZE> to increase the size of the chart number 1B even though it isn't part of the HTML 3.0 description. Some discourage the use of <FONT SIZE> and other Netscape extensions, but I find it useful so I'm employing it in this example. In the future, we will probably be able to use style sheets to change font size in HTML 3.0. Personally, I hope the <FONT> extensions will be officially adopted.

The HTML tags for Figure 6.2 follow:

```
<table border>
     <tr><td><td><td><td><td align=center>Spring Quarter<p>195.
     Biological<br>Diversity. Staff.

     <tr><th align=center><p><font size=6><b>1B</b></font>
          <td align=center><i>PQ: Chem<br>111-112-113<br>&amp;
          two<br>quarters<br>calculus.
          <td align=center>Autumn Quarter<p>196. Cell and
          Molecular<br>Biology. L. Mets<br>Required discussion.<td
          align=center>Winter Quarter<p>197. Genetics. B.<br>Strauss, A.
          Mahowald<td align=center>Spring Quarter<p>198.
          Evolutionary<br>Biology. B.<br>Charlesworth, J.<br>Coyne.
</table>
```

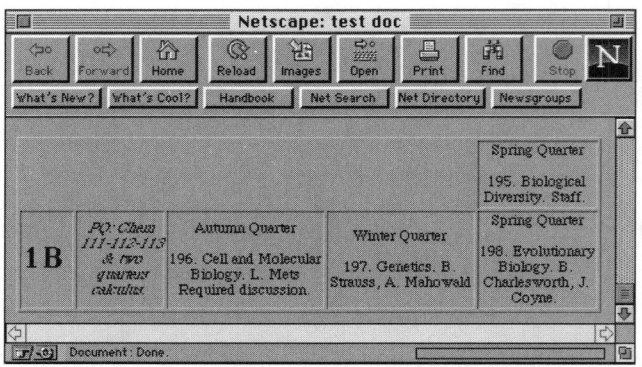

Figure 6.2 A not-so-simple table.

A table can include more than just data. It can contain text, images, multiple paragraphs, lists, and headers. This brings up the possibility of "columns" of text.

Figure 6.3 depicts a table without the <TABLE BORDER> tag. The first two paragraphs of text were preceded by the <TD> tag and the "sidebar" was preceded by <TH> to give it emphasis. All the text was contained in the <TABLE> </TABLE> tag.

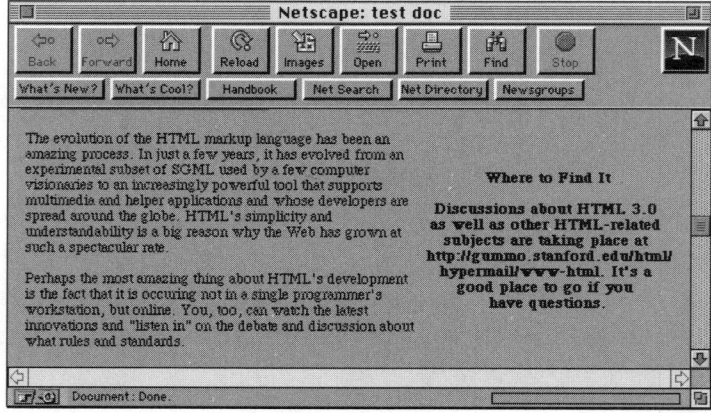

Figure 6.3 Text used in a table.

Character Formatting

The following minitable includes the character formatting tags adopted in HTML 3.0.

Tag	Purpose
<U> </U>	Underlining
<I> </I>	Italics
<B> </B>	Bold
<TT> </TT>	Monospace font
	Subscript
	Superscript
<STRIKE> </STRIKE>	Strikethrough

Note: The danger of using the <U> </U> tag to underline text is that people assume underlining is saved for hypertext links and they will be confused when they click it and nothing happens. Many Web users are either color-blind or (like myself) have monochrome monitors, so underlining is the only way they can identify a clickable link.

Character Entities

HTML 3.0 proposes recognition of character entities for new symbols, including:

  for an em space

  for an en space

— for an em dash

– for an en dash

Other Textual Elements

HTML 3.0 covers a number of other ways of formatting text as covered in the following sections.

Centering Text

HTML 3.0 uses the <CENTER> tag with <P> and/or heading tags to center text, as in <P ALIGN=CENTER> to center a paragraph, or <H1 ALIGN=CENTER> to center a heading. As stated previously, this is different from Netscape's <CENTER> </CENTER> tag.

Aligning Text

The <ALIGN> tag is used to align either paragraphs or headings:

> **<P ALIGN=LEFT|RIGHT|CENTER> </P>** for paragraphs

> **<Hn ALIGN=LEFT|RIGHT|CENTER> </Hn>** for headings, where n is a number from 1 to 6

The <NOWRAP> tag prevents the browser from automatically wrapping lines of text. You then use the <BR> tag to specify line breaks.

The <CLEAR> tag moves text down until the left, right, or both margins are clear (<CLEAR=LEFT>, <CLEAR=RIGHT>, and <CLEAR=ALL>, respectively). You can also specify <CLEAR="50 pixels">, which moves text down until there are 50 pixels of clear space. <CLEAR> can be used with most block-like elements such as <P>, <Hn>, and <DIV>.

Captions

The <CAPTION> </CAPTION> tag creates a caption for a table or figure.

Divisions

The <DIV> tag can be used with an attribute, <CLASS> to designate different textual elements in a long or multipart document such as a chapter, section, or appendix. For example:

```
<DIV CLASS=Appendix>
<P>Here is a complete list of all tags currently in use (that is, supported
    by browsers) in HTML 2.0, HTML 3.0, and Netscape's Extensions to
    HTML.</P>
. . .
</DIV>
```

In-Line Quotes

The <Q> </Q> tag is used for a short quotation (in contrast to <BLOCKQUOTE>). It is typically shown enclosed in quotation marks as appropriate to the language. For English, these are matching double or single quotation marks, alternating for nested quotes.

<TAB> Tag

The <TAB> tag allows you to set a tab stop in a paragraph. For those who are used to simply hitting a Tab key on a keyboard, the process might seem cumbersome. The purpose, though, is to allow creation of tabs no matter what font you used, and to have conversion software preserve the tabs. <TAB> is an empty tag; there is no </TAB>.

The <TAB> process is actually similar to setting a tab on a low-tech typewriter (if you can remember that far back). First, you specify a tab stop; then, you actually create the tab in your document.

In HTML 3.0 first you "create" a tab stop with <TAB ID=*name*>. Then, you "insert" the tab where you want it with <TAB TO=*name*>.

<TAB> also has an <ALIGN> attribute with a number of options that allows you more control over specifying exactly where the tab stop should be.

> **<ALIGN=LEFT>** makes the following text come immediately after the designated tab stop. (This is the default.)

> **<ALIGN=CENTER>** centers text on the designated tab stop, unless the <TO> attribute is missing; in that case it centers the text on the page.

> **<ALIGN=RIGHT>** aligns text flush right with the designated tab stop. (If the <TO> attribute is missing, it makes text flush-right on the page.)

> **<ALIGN=DECIMAL>** aligns text with a decimal point. (If the <TO> attribute is missing, the tab acts like a blank space.)

An example showing the proposed use of tabs is next. At the time this was written, most browsers did not yet support tabs, so I am simulating the effect in a word processing document (there are other ways to center text, but for this example I used the <ALIGN=CENTER> attribute, as follows):

```
<p><b><tab align=center>UNIVERSITY CALENDAR 1995–96</b></p>
<p><i><tab id=t1>SUMMER QUARTER</i></p>
<tab to=t1>Registration for summer quarter<tab align=right>June 19<br>
<tab to=t1>Classes meet<tab align=right>June 19<br>
```

The output should look like Figure 6.4.

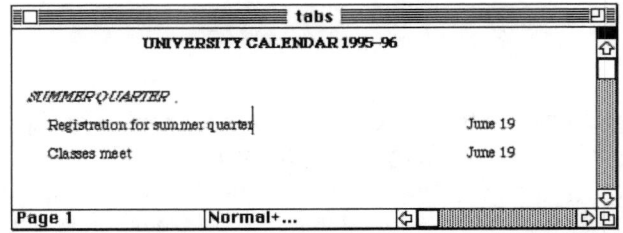

Figure 6.4 Tabs in HTML 3.0.

Style Sheets

HTML 3.0 can be used with style sheets containing detailed information about typefaces, font sizes, line spacing, and other formatting instructions.

Using the <LINK> tag in the <HEAD> tag, you can link your document to a style sheet specifying that the font used will be Times, the size 12 point, that an H1 heading will be three points larger, and so on.

You can also use the <STYLE> </STYLE> tag to allow for overrides of the standard style. If you do specify a font other than the common Times or Helvetica, for instance, realize that not all users have the font in question.

Footnotes

The <FN> </FN> tag can be used to create simple footnotes. When possible, they are presented as popup notes; otherwise you put them at the bottom of the page. The reader is taken to the footnote by clicking an anchor pointing to that footnote.

The way the <FN> </FN> tag works is similar to the <TAB> tag. You specify a footnote using the <ID> attribute, as in:

```
<FN ID=FN1><i>Specified in HTML 3.0 DTD</FN>
```

That's the destination. Earlier in the text, you create an anchor like this:

We are all awaiting browsers that support elements like <A
HREF="#FN1">footnotes, tabs, styles, and math equations</A>

The <MATH> Tag

This tag can describe a wide range of math expressions. Because the Web was
created by physicists and is used for many scientific applications, this is far from a
trivial use. Subscript and superscript elements in an equation are supported, among
many other elements. A <BOX> tag would be provided for brackets, delimiters and
integral signs, and placing one element over another.

Again, I can't display the <MATH> element in a Web browser on the Mac, so I will
borrow an example from Dave Raggett's HTML 3.0 DTD. This gives as an example
the following HTML:

<MATH>∫_a_^b^{f(x)<over>1+x} dx</MATH>

The brackets { and } are used to place one element over another. The output can be
displayed in a fixed-width font like this:

```
b
/   f(x)
| -------- dx
/   1 + x
a
```

The <NOTE> Tag

The <NOTE> </NOTE> tag is proposed as a way to highlight (typically, by indent-
ing) warnings, tips, errors, and other text that needs to be emphasized from the text
around it.

When the <CLASS> attribute is used with <NOTE>, it can specify different types of
"notes," such as:

<NOTE CLASS=WARNING> If you have been running on a battery, be
sure to choose Shut Down from the Special menu before you stop work for
the night, or else you will drain and possibly damage the battery.
</NOTE>

<NOTE CLASS=CAUTION> You can try out these HTML 3.0 tags in a text document, but they may not be displayed by all browsers, and the names might still change.</NOTE>

Other Text Markup Tags

- The <DFN> tag indicates the defining instance of a term. *Example*: A <DFN>modem</DFN> is used to demodulate digital signals.

- The <AU> tag indicates the name of an author. *Example*: The elements have been proposed by <AU>David Raggett</AU>, who is developing HTML 3.0.

- The <PERSON> tag allows these names to be extracted automatically by indexing programs. *Example*: More information about <PERSON>The Dalai Lama</PERSON> can be found at this site.

- The <ACRONYM> tag is used to mark up acronyms. *Example*: The Internet Engineering Task Force <ACRONYM>(IETF)</ACRONYM> is the protocol engineering arm of the Internet Architecture Board <ACRONYM>(IAB). </ACRONYM>

- The <ABBREV> </ABBREV> tag is used to mark up abbreviations.

- The <INS> </INS> tag is used for inserted text, for instance in legal documents.

- The <DEL> </DEL> tag is used for deleted text, for instance in legal documents.

Lists

HTML 3.0 allows more control over the appearance of lists in a document.

A <COMPACT> List

The <COMPACT> tag, when used with a list tag, for example <DL COMPACT> </DL>, <UL COMPACT> </UL>, <OL COMPACT> </OL>, presents the list so that it takes up less space (see Figure 6.5).

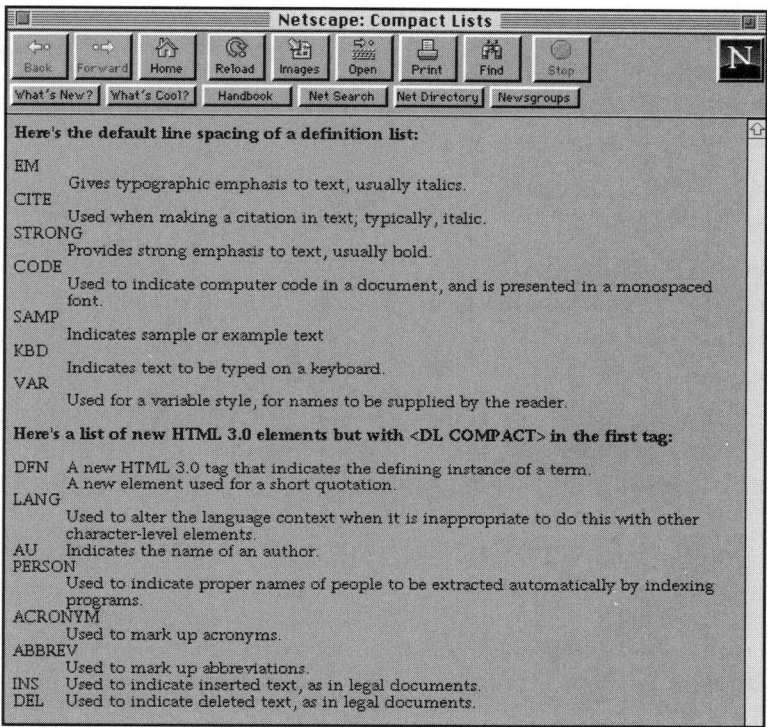

Figure 6.5 Comparison of default and "compact" lists.

Attributes to <OL> Ordered Lists

The following attributes have been proposed to ordered lists:

The <OL CONTINUE> </OL> prevents restarting of a numbering sequence.

The <OL SEQNUM=*number*> </OL> allows you to determine the number at which a list starts.

The <OL COMPACT> </OL> was mentioned previously. It makes a list more compact.

Extensions to <UL> Unordered Lists

Three variations on the <WRAP> tag (<WRAP=VERT>, <WRAP=HORIZ>, <WRAP=NONE>) control the direction in which multicolumn lists flow. (The number of columns depends on your browser.)

The **<PLAIN>** tag, as in <UL PLAIN> </UL>, eliminates bullets from an unordered list.

The **<DINGBAT>** tag, as in <UL DINGBAT> </UL>, allows you to use an icon or other image to mark each list item rather than a bullet. The icon is specified with a character entity: <clock> would indicate that an item is displayed with a clock icon, <diskette> with a diskette icon, and so on.

The **<SRC>** tag, as in <UL SRC="image.gif"> </UL>, allows a bullet to be defined by a graphic.

Images and Graphic Elements

The big change in the way HTML will handle graphic elements is the addition of the <FIG> tag for complex images with clickable hotzones, captions, or credit lines, and the designation of the existing <IMG> tag for simpler in-line images.

The <FIG> Tag

A new tag called <FIG> </FIG> (for figure) allows overlays, captions, and ISMAPs, as well as the intriguing future possibility of virtual reality-type images. The <ALIGN> attribute, one of Netscape's extensions to the <IMG> tag, also works with this tag.

The <FIG> tag allows authors to mark captions and credit lines with headers and other elements. It works faster than <IMG> with complicated graphics such as clickable imagemaps because it supports caching—the storage of information in memory. <FIG> also allows the cursor to change shape as it passes over a clickable region.

The basic use of <FIG> is different from <IMG>. For example:

```
<FIG SRC="campus.jpeg">
<p>The central quadrangles</p>
</FIG>
```

A number of attributes is proposed for <FIG>, including:

232

<NOFLOW>, which keeps text from flowing around a figure.

<ALIGN>, which not only aligns the image with the left or right margins or in the center of a page, using the values <ALIGN=LEFT>, <ALIGN=RIGHT>, and <ALIGN=CENTER>, but also supports <ALIGN=JUSTIFY>, which causes the figure to fill the space between the left and right margins, and <ALIGN=BLEEDLEFT> and <ALIGN=BLEEDRIGHT>, which make the figure flush left or flush right with a window border.

The **<WIDTH>**, **<HEIGHT>**, and **<UNITS>** tags are also supported (see the attributes to the <IMG> tag in the next section).

The **<IMAGEMAP>** tag specifies a clickable map for processing mouse clicks and drags.

The <IMG> Tag

The <IMG> tag is used primarily to display in-line images in HTML 3.0. Some of Netscape's extensions are included, including the attributes:

<WIDTH> and **<HEIGHT>**, which specify the suggested width and height for the image, in pixels; a new **<UNITS>** attribute refines this by allowing you to specify the measurement in pixels (<UNITS=pixels>) or an en space (<UNITS=en>).

<ALIGN=LEFT|RIGHT>, which makes an image align with the current left or right margins.

<ISMAP> is still supported for clickable imagemaps, but **<FIG>** is preferred because <FIG> works faster due to caching and allows the cursor to change shape as it passes over a clickable hotzone.

The <HR> Tag

The <HR> tag is being extended to include the tag <SRC>, which can be used to designate a custom graphic instead of the old horizontal rule. For example,

```
<HR SRC="graphic.gif">
```

might spice up a home page, although making it more time-consuming to load.

However, Netscape's extensions to <HR> are not included in the current draft: that includes the <SIZE> tag to make a wider rule, or the <WIDTH> tag.

The <BANNER> Tag

A new head tag, <BANNER>, provides an alternative to using the <LINK> tag to make a reference to an externally defined banner. For instance, a tag like

    <LINK REL=BANNER HREF="image.gif">

provides a zone at the top of each document for a navigational aid, disclaimer, or other information. Banners don't scroll with the rest of the document. It then doesn't have to be reinserted in each document but can reside outside, which saves on memory and speeds up document loading.

Backgrounds

HTML 3.0 does provide support for backgrounds as a tag of the <BODY> tag. However, Netscape's extension <BGCOLOR> is not included. It should be used with caution because it shows up only on Netscape (this extension is explained further in Chapter 12).

Head Elements

The <META> Tag

The <META> tag is used to embed generic information about your document that can be extracted for use in searching, indexing, and cataloging. The <NAME> tag in <META NAME="SearchType">, for instance, can be used to identify the document's author, publication date, or other general information.

The <ID> Tag

In HTML 2.0, the <NAME> tag is used with an anchor to create a link to a specific location in a document. In HTML 3.0, <NAME> is replaced with <ID>. The destination doesn't have to be specified with the anchor tag, necessarily, as <A NAME="name">.

234

An entire paragraph or other element can be the destination, as in:

<P ID="attributes">The ID attribute replaces NAME in HTML 2.0; alas, farewell to poor old deprecated NAME.</P>

The originating anchor would be specified as usual:

<A HREF="#attributes">ID attribute</A>

The <LINK> Tag

The <LINK> tag associates a document with a style sheet to provide greater control over formatting. By specifying a style sheet language, such as DSSSL in the <LINK> tag, you can override the DSSSL settings later and provide variations in textual formatting throughout a document. Besides DSSSL, you might be able to use <LINK> to point to your "house" style sheet. This process is explained further in the next section.

Links

The <LINK> tag will be a generalized way of defining the HTML document's relationship with other files on the Internet. Such files can include:

- Supplementary information, such as a copyright notice, toolbars, or directions to the next step in a guided tour of pages.

- A style sheet.

- Banners that float at the top of the window as the user scrolls down the page.

One much-anticipated new tag proposed for HTML 3.0 is <LINK STYLE>. This tag provides the browser with the address of a style sheet, so that you can specify such things as character size, character weight, **tracking** (space between letters), **leading** (space between lines), or type color.

It's possible that a document can have more than one style sheet to draw on. Perhaps Web publishers will create a single style sheet for all the pages on the site to ensure site-wide consistency, designers will create special style sheets for individual pages, and users will create their own style sheets to accommodate their own special needs.

The unresolved question is: how does the browser decide which style sheet to use? There isn't really a consensus on this problem: designers like to control the look of a page, and the computer people like the idea that users can customize the page.

The <LINK> tag also plays a key role in defining navigational buttons. Such buttons will act in a fashion similar to the linked GIF files and clickable maps used in HTML 2.0, but will not be anchored to the page; rather they will be assigned to things like toolbars, browser menu items by reserved relation keywords, or keyboard shortcuts.

For example, an HTML 3.0-compatible browser might have a floating navigational palette with a button called Help; an HTML 3.0 tag that looked something like <LINK REL=Help HREF="assistance.html"> would send the browser the file "assistance.html" when the user clicks the Help button.

Forms

HTML 3.0 extends the <FORM> tag with new kinds of input and allows for some processing to be done on the browser's, rather than the server's, CPU.

In addition to the form input types discussed in Chapter 5 (text, radio buttons, checkboxes, submit buttons, and menus), HTML 3.0 will support range controls (probably with slider-like controls), allow the reader to input graphic data by drawing on an image, and allow users to submit files. Attributes for these input types had not yet been designated at the time this was written.

Most modern applications check the data a user enters and give some sort of feedback. If you enter a letter where a number should be, the application might beep and tell you to enter a number instead. HTML 2.0 does not provide for checking the data as it is entered by the user; such error-checking must take place as a CGI or other server-side software.

HTML 3.0 does not provide for direct screening of data in an HTML document, but it does allow you to specify the address of a script to be executed by the browser that can check the form.

Remember that some data-crunching has taken place in CGIs on the server's end. A script sent to the user's machine can offload a great deal of work to the user, reduce network traffic, and allow you to process forms in simple ways, and with a much simpler set of tools than CGIs use.

Scripts *will* be limited in power for some pretty sensible reasons. It's not difficult to imagine the havoc that a virus or a poorly written script could cause: it might accidentally erase critical system files or get caught in a loop and send hundreds or thousands of files, probably your personal correspondence, over the Web. Scripts will be able to look at the data that the user has entered into a form and to look at some basic information about the user—probably the things that have been entered into a Preferences dialog box.

Of course, browsers will have to support not only HTML 3.0 but also the scripting language for such scripts to support your HTML document. HTML 3.0 does not specify what the scripting language must be, and it may be that several competing languages will be developed and used.

The early contender is probably Sun Microsystems' Java. In May, 1995, Netscape Communications Corporation and Sun Microsystems, Inc. announced that Netscape intends to license Java to implement in Navigator.

Pointers to both of these products, as well as a number of other HTML authoring and editing programs, are included in the next chapter.

HTML Authoring Assistants

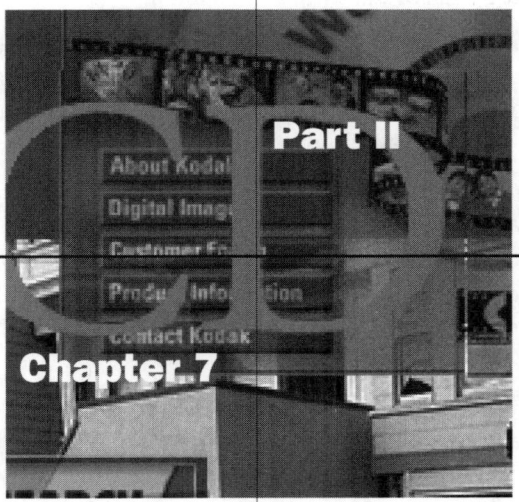

Part II

Chapter 7

If I've done my job as an author and you've done your job as a reader, by now you have a working knowledge of how to write basic HTML documents that can be published on the Web.

But no matter what stage you are in HTML—or in life in general—you can always use a little help from your friends. Consider using one or more of the HTML authoring assistants to supplement your own expertise. You might regard them as the equivalent of copyeditors and proofreaders in your Web "publishing house" (although, as you'll see, there's no substitute for using your own two eyes, and many people believe it's easier and more reliable to enter and edit the "raw" HTML).

Authoring Assistants: A Quick Introduction

There are three categories of authoring assistants:

- *HTML converters* take files created in another program (such as a word processor) and add the HTML tags for you. You don't have to remember every single tag yourself, and you don't have to enter all the tags one by one; the converter does much, although not all, of the work.

- *HTML editing and authoring programs* allow you to create and edit Web documents without having to enter all the tags, anchors, and other commands individually. HTML editors (such as HTML Editor) allow you to insert and change tags easily. HTML authors (such as Arachnid) allow you to create a document from scratch—or open an existing HTML document and edit it.

- *HTML validation or checking services* review your HTML files and point out errors or inconsistencies.

Freeware versus Commercial Products

Many of the programs are freeware (free) or shareware (you pay a small fee after you have tried it out and decide to keep it) and can be tried out by downloading them from the Internet. Of these, several have gone through a number of versions to add features, correct bugs, and keep up with new versions of other software (such as word processing programs whose output they use), and are thus pretty reliable.

A growing assortment of commercial editors and authoring programs are also available. Some come bundled with commercial Web browsers such as Enhanced Mosaic.

Should you download a free program from the Web or shell out a hundred dollars or more for a commercial program? Most committed Web surfers aren't going to wait

Where to Find It

At the end of the chapter I've listed some very impressive-sounding HTML authoring and editing programs that were just being released as this book went to press. (There will undoubtedly be more out there by the time you read this.)

to buy a program or go through the effort of finding an "authorized reseller." As soon as they are interested in a product, they'll search for a freeware version on the Web and get it, if they can. After a while, though, the limitations of freeware programs cause them to consider buying something more powerful.

It seems sensible to try out the freeware first and then to spring for a commercial editor if you like using editors and want to implement more complicated pages with forms, for instance.

Most of this chapter is devoted to comparing the shareware products because they are what you are likely to start with, and because what they attempt to do is basically the same as what the commercial ones offer.

Why Use an HTML Authoring Assistant?

Yes, you should pat yourself on the back for putting forth the effort to learn HTML. But you don't have to do all the work yourself, necessarily. There are a number of ways in which authoring programs can help Web publishers:

- If you have a substantial number of published documents that need to go online, using a converter considerably speeds the process by translating some (although probably not all) of the basic formatting commands in your original document into the all-important HTML "cookies."

- If you've created or converted a document and it doesn't work the first time (don't take it personally; this happens *most* of the time), an editor can help you quickly preview the changes you need to make.

- If you find writing HTML to be tedious and time-consuming, using an authoring assistant's shortcuts can make you feel less like a programmer and more like a Macintosh user again.

- A converter allows you to work in the word processor you prefer (Microsoft Word, for instance) to do the actual writing, if you feel more comfortable doing so.

This chapter describes a number of the more popular shareware HTML editors and converters for the Macintosh. It's not meant to be a comprehensive list, because there are a lot of programs already and new versions of software are coming out nearly every day. (See the end of this chapter for a list of places to find the latest products.)

The goal of this section is to acquaint you with what authoring assistants can and cannot do for publishers, to suggest some software that has particular advantages, and to list places where you can download some of the programs.

Note: If you download a shareware program, be sure you read the distribution agreement. If you decide to keep the software, be a good citizen and pay the specified shareware fee.

The Ideal HTML Editor

As of this writing, at least, there does not yet seem to be a perfect, commercially available HTML editing or authoring program. My wish list for the ideal program includes these features:

- Operates in Mac, Windows, and UNIX environments (and not just on a Power Macintosh, but on most kinds of Macintosh computers);

- Runs directly from within a word processing program such as Word or Word-Perfect using pull-down menus and buttons. For instance, you'd pull down the Edit menu, choose **HTML**, and the tags would be generated for you;

- Instantly previews and edits your work in a Web browser window; and

- Inserts anchors and images easily, without having to type in long relative addresses or URLs.

Some of the shareware HTML editors perform some of these functions already. None, however, runs "invisibly" from within a word processor or page layout program to spare you the agony of having to look at raw HTML. Software developers, though, are scrambling to create such a program.

Press releases describing SoftQuad's HoTMetaL Pro 2.0 and InContext's Spider sounded promising, but these products hadn't been released when this book went to press. Also exciting was the announcement that Adobe was planning to add HTML generating capabilities to its PageMaker page layout software. And giant Microsoft continued to lurk in the background with promises that soon, very soon, just around the corner (in other words, don't hold your breath), we will be able to generate HTML directly from within a Word document with its long-awaited Internet Assistant.

Note: A number of URLs is given in this chapter (and throughout this book) for information about software or other resources. At the end of each address I've typed a period to avoid being cited by the grammar police. Be aware, though, that the period is not part of the address. For instance, a correct address would be in "http://www.sgi.com" and not "http://www.sgi.com."

At the end of this chapter I've included several URLs that contain links to these tools for use in Macintosh, Windows, UNIX, and other systems. When the "perfect" HTML authoring assistant is developed, these will be the places where you can find it—as well as the other utilities that have inevitably been released since this book was published.

Shareware Authoring and Editing Tools: A Comparison

Table 7.1 compares some of the HTML editors for the Macintosh.

Table 7.1 Macintosh HTML Editors

	Pull-Down Menus	Net-scape Exts.	Search and Replace	View work in Browser	Support Forms	Other HTML 2.0	Create Anchors Easily	Open 32K + Files	Program Size
HTML Editors									
Arachnid	✔	✔		✔	✔	✔	✔		1,026K
BB edit extensions						✔	✔		

continued

Table 7.1 Continued

	Pull-Down Menus	Net-scape Exts.	Search and Replace	View work in Browser	Support Forms	Other HTML 2.0	Create Anchors Easily	Open 32K + Files	Program Size
Bob's HTML Editor	✔			✔	✔		✔		
HTML.edit	✔						✔		1,133K
HTML Editor	✔			✔				✔	975K
HTML Grinder			✔	✔			✔		983K
Simple HTML Editor	✔	✔	✔	✔	✔	✔	✔		273K
HTML Pro	✔			✔			✔		125K
HTML Web Weaver	✔	✔	✔	✔	✔	✔	✔		983K

Some explanation is in order in Table 7.1. I list file size because some of these programs (even if they are sent across the Net as a self-expanding archive) can get pretty huge if you are downloading them from the Internet.

The thing about URLs is that in some text editors you have to type a long file name or URL address, whereas in others there is a shortcut that makes this easier. (For instance, if you are working on a Web server running MacHTTP, Bob's HTML Editor automatically incorporates relative paths to IMGs and URLs into its palettes.) A check mark indicates that there is such a shortcut.

Converting a Word Processing File to HTML

Let's say you have your text and images ready to be placed before 13.5 million or more World Wide Web users (scary, isn't it?). You have copyedited and proofread your text and it's ready to go. You have decided not to hire someone to set up your home page for you but are committed to doing it in-house (or more likely, you don't have the money to hire a consultant and have to do it yourself whether you like it or not). Where do you start?

What I would like to do is list the two programs I use most often (rtftohtml and HTML Web Weaver), and then list the others. There are a number of programs you can use, which I describe a little later. But, rather than go through them all to begin with, let me jump right in and show you what I do most often with the program I prefer, which is called "rtftohtml."

An HTML Converter: rtftohtml (✔ Greg's Choice)

This is a reliable, easy-to-use utility by Chris Hector that converts word processing files to HTML. It's a Mac version of a UNIX utility, freely distributed on the Internet, and everyone I know of who has ever used it recommends it highly.

You may remember from Chapter 4 that any instances of four characters of the ASCII character set—the left angle bracket (<), the right angle bracket (>), the ampersand (&), and the double quotation mark ("), as well as accented characters, cannot be used "as is" in HTML and must be replaced with an HTML character entity.

Instead of having to remember to type that HTML character entity, however, the editors and converters you are going to use make those adjustments automatically, as well as the following changes:

- All those nice double "curly" quotes you inserted are changed back to "straight" ones.

- En- and em-dashes are changed to two hyphens.

- Centered text becomes flush left.

- A "nested" paragraph becomes flush left.

- Caps and small caps become all caps.

I've typed the sample text in Microsoft Word 5.1, shown in Figure 7.1. Let's take this text and run it through rtftohtml and several other programs to demonstrate the process of converting an existing file to HTML and then editing it.

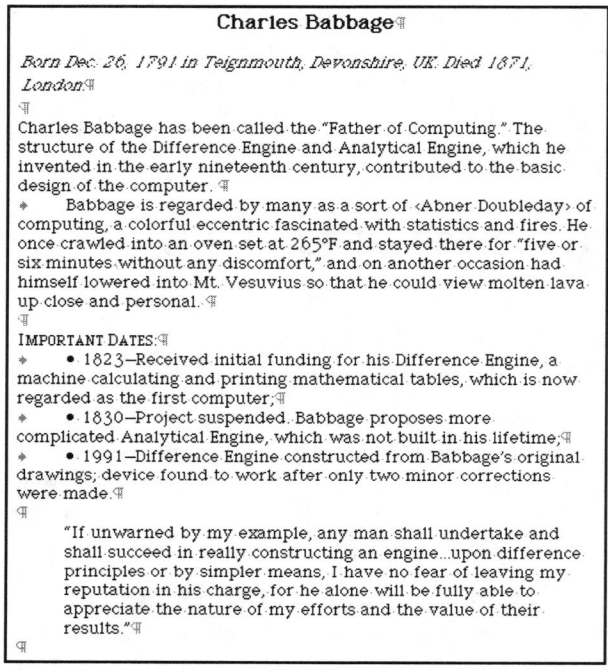

Figure 7.1 A test Word document.

As you can see, this passage is loaded with gratuitous formatting challenges I've inserted for this test: greater-than and less-than symbols; an ampersand; a list; quotations; em-dashes; an ellipsis; and so on.

Where to Find It

To find out more about the amazing life of Charles Babbage, as well as a web of images and notes for the television series "The Machine That Changed the World," go to http://ei.cs.vt.edu/~history/TMTCTW.html.

Now you have to do some reformatting of your original document before running it through the converter. This might seem like a lot of work, especially for our brief test passage, but if you are preparing to mark up a 100-page booklet (or my university's 500-hundred-page course catalog) with many styles, lists, and so on, for HTML, believe me, a little preparation up front will save a lot of time and effort in the long run.

First, make sure that the document is formatted with styles.

Note: If you've been avoiding your word processor's styles feature, it's time to cast off your inhibitions. Styles are sets of instructions that a word processing program uses to format text. For instance, if you assign the style names H1 or H2 to your text document, after the document is converted to HTML, the designated text is interpreted as H1 and H2 headings.

The styles you use should have specific names. You can leave body text as the style name "Normal." However, the title should be formatted as header 1 (not H1), and subsequent headings and subheadings should be formatted as header 2, header 3, and so on, through header 6.

After you select text and assign it a style name, the appearance of that text might change onscreen because of the formatting instructions included in the style. Don't worry about how the headings look onscreen while you are still working in your text editor or word processor. The important thing is that the correct style names are embedded in your document. When you run your document through the converter, the styles are changed automatically to H1, H2, and so on, and can thus be recognized and displayed as headings by a Web browser.

Because I have a bulleted list in my passage, I have to select each paragraph in the list and assign it the standard HTML tag <UL>. (I can also give it a name of my own and change the rtftohtml translation table to include the new name.) I also take the last paragraph and assign it the tag <BLOCKQUOTE>.

At this point the prep work is done. After this, the converter is in the driver's seat. (Note that one thing I didn't have to do was change "smart" quotes back to straight ones. The program does that automatically.)

Where to Find It

A fascinating list of material related to the history of computing is at http://ei.cs.vt.edu/~history/index.html.

Save your document in Rich Text Format (RTF). RTF is a standard interchange format that can be output by many word processing programs. In Word, this is done by choosing Save As from the File menu and selecting "Interchange Format (RTF)" from the menu at the bottom of the window (the Save As File Type menu).

Give the file a new name, for example, "Babbage-rtf." The resulting file will look like gibberish, but don't let that worry you. Close the file. Go to the desktop and drag-and-drop the icon for your RTF file on top of the rtftohtml alias that you created on your desktop.

> **Note:** Drag-and-drop is a feature that enables an application to activate or open a file by dropping it on the application's icon. A fast way to open an HTML file to preview it, for instance, is to drag-and-drop the file to your Web browser icon. It works only if the application recognizes the file type of the document. If you double-click your HTML document, it is opened by the authoring program rather than by Netscape/Mosaic.

A new file is created with the appendage ".html" in its name (such as "Babbage-rtf.html"). The file has now been coded for HTML; you can look through it and see the tags.

Where to Find It

You can get the latest version of rtftohtml at ftp://ftp.cray.com/src/WWWstuff/RTF/rtftohtml_overview html. Note that this URL is case-sensitive; you have to type in the capital letters.

If this was a WYSIWYG editor, you'd be able to see your file with its formatting intact; but this is only a converter. To see what you have wrought, select the file and drag-and-drop it onto your Web browser. In my case, I drag "Babbage-rtf.html" onto the Netscape alias icon on my desktop. Netscape opens and I see the file as it has been formatted for the Web. (Of course, it has not appeared on the Web yet. This is a local file that can be seen only on your computer.) It looks like Figure 7.2.

Another Converter: rtftoweb

A converter called "rtftoweb," by Christian Bolik of the University of Hanover, Germany is an extension of rtftohtml. It's a UNIX utility, but worth mentioning at least in passing because it is related to rtftohtml and seems useful. (I haven't used it, myself.) It purports to convert an RTF document into a fully hypertextual set of HTML documents and provides automatic generation of active table of contents and index, navigation panels, and active cross-references to headings.

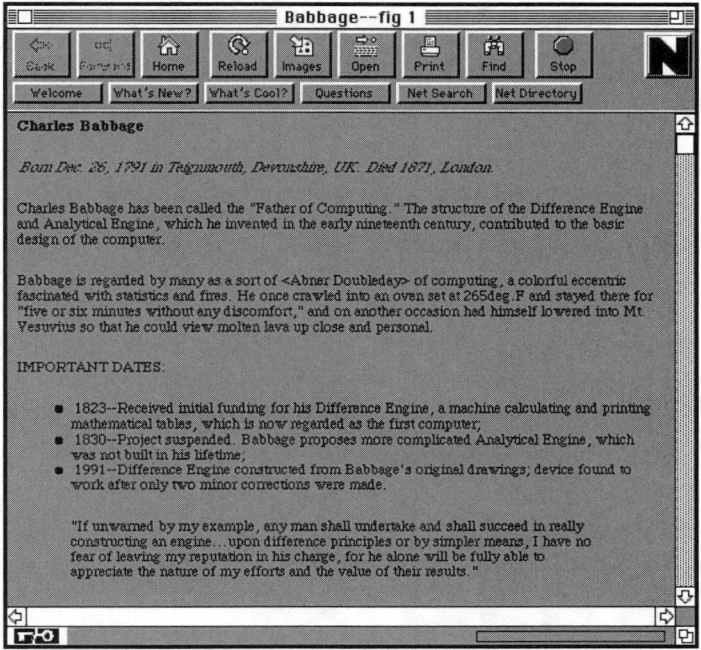

Figure 7.2 An HTML file converted with rtftohtml.

Most of the formatting of the "Babbage" document was retained by rtftohtml, but the program doesn't do everything. The main title wasn't centered, and the degree symbol was replaced by the abbreviation "deg."

To make further corrections, you have to open the "Babbage-rtf.html" document and make changes and/or type the new tags. Any revisions would not be saved in the original "Babbage" text file, however. To be accurate, you should update both the original and the HTML version. That's one of the problems with using converters—you create a second version of your file and thus have to make revisions in two places.

Because the purpose of this exercise is to try out authoring assistants, however, you use an HTML editing program to make the changes to "Babbage-html."

Where to Find It

You can get the latest version of rtftohtml at ftp://ftp.rrzn.uni-hannover.de/pub/unix-local/misc/rtftoweb/html/rtftoweb-1.html.

Correcting a File with an HTML Editor

What follows are brief rundowns of a few editing programs you might use. The one that's best for you depends on the programs with which you're most comfortable:

- If you regularly use a text editing program like Alpha or BBEdit, you will probably want to download from the Web a set of HTML extensions for it.

- If you just want to add some tags or change a link, you might pick HTML Editor.

- If you're particularly *codaphobic* (a word I just coined, meaning "averse to writing code"), try a program with a friendly interface like HTML Web Weaver.

- HyperCard enthusiasts might pick S H E or Bob's HTML Editor.

Again, I'll start out with the one I like best and summarize the rest in alphabetical order.

HTML Web Weaver (✔ Greg's Choice)

HTML Web Weaver, by Robert C. Best III of SUNY Potsdam, has the friendliest interface of any shareware HTML editor I've seen. (In other words, it closely follows the Mac interface.)

Where to Find It

Alpha is at http://www.cs.umd.edu/~keleher/alpha.html. BBEdit Tools is at http://www.york.ac.uk/~ld11/BBEditTools.html.

It's extremely easy to create tags in HTML Web Weaver. You select tags either from windows that "float" onscreen (and whose contents you can configure), or from a **Tags** menu at the top of your screen. The list of tags is quite extensive and includes Netscape extensions such as <FONT SIZE> and <CENTER>.

Links are made in typical Mac fashion as well, by choosing **Link** from the same

Tags menu (it's an extensive menu). Links can be made to gopher servers or FTP URLs as well as HTTP URLs.

To preview a file, you configure HTML Web Weaver to open a browser and choose **Preview** from the **File** menu or click a Preview button. Other features include:

- You can scan for special characters when a file is imported to automatically replace them with HTML entities.

- You can summon balloon help.

- You can perform text search and replaces.

To edit the "Babbage" file, I opened the "Babbage-html" file from HTML Web Weaver. I allowed HTML Web Weaver to rewrite the tags in its own generic fashion. I then selected the heading "Charles Babbage" and chose **Header - Size 1** from the **Tags** menu. I selected the first paragraph and chose **Italic** from one of the floating menus.

I made a link by selecting the words "Charles Babbage" at the beginning of the second paragraph and typed in the address of the Charles Babbage Institute. After clicking OK, HTML Web Weaver inserted anchors around the text I had selected. See Figure 7.3.

Where to Find It

For general information about the program, and a list of sites from which HTML Web Weaver can be downloaded, go to http://www.student.potsdam.edu/web.weaver/about.html (new version 2.5.2 is now available for downloading). A review of the program in *MacWEEK* magazine is at http://www.ziff.com:8006/~macweek/mw_041795/gw3.html.

I was particularly impressed with the ease of creating the effect of caps and small caps by selecting various characters in the heading "Important Dates" and choosing either Font Size 4 or Font Size 3.

HTML Web Weaver does have some drawbacks. It can't open files bigger than 32K (this limit will be lifted in a future release), and search-and-replace works erratically. Our office's HTML expert, Susan Soric, endorses the program enthusiastically and uses it on a daily basis.

HTML Web Weaver requires Mac System 7.0 or later and at least 700K of available RAM. The shareware fee is $25, $14 for educational use.

This button allows you to preview the document in a Web browser

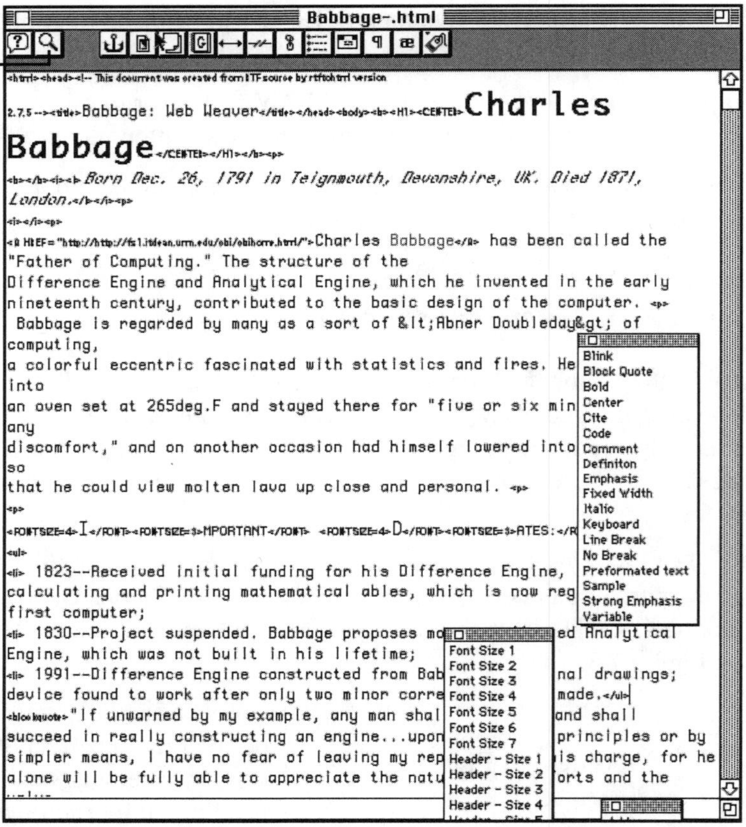

Figure 7.3 HTML Web Weaver window.

The edited version of the Babbage text can be seen in Figure 7.4.

A Case Study: Using an HTML Converter and Editor

Every year, the Office of the University Publications (where I am assistant director) is responsible for producing the course catalog for the College of the University of Chicago.

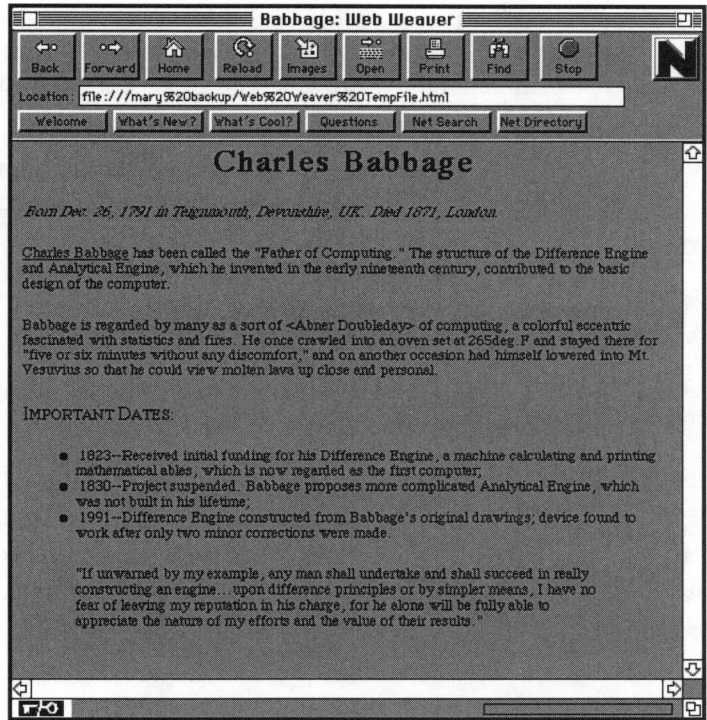

Figure 7.4 Sample HTML file after editing with HTML Web Weaver.

As anyone who has worked in a university publications office can tell you, compiling and printing a course catalog booklet is quite an undertaking. In our case, the course catalog is a 496-page document consisting of over 60 Microsoft Word files, one file for each chapter or academic program of study.

This year, we posted the catalog on the Web for the first time. To do this, we converted the original Word files to HTML documents using rtftohtml. Before running the files through the converter, though, all nonstandard typefaces were changed to Times Roman and all nonstandard styles were changed to "heading 1," "heading 2," and so on, as explained earlier. We also edited out any nonstandard characters (such as those formatted with "hidden text") using Word's search-and-replace feature.

We also felt it was wise to split each chapter into smaller files, because many were over the 32K capacity of most HTML editors, and because they would then require less time to load on a Web reader's computer.

This left us with over a hundred separate HTML files which were edited individually using HTML Web Weaver. Susan Soric added links to facilitate navigation through all the documents, and posted them on our office's Web server (http://www-upubs.uchicago.edu).

We hope to automate the process even further in the future by converting the catalog to a database program such as FileMaker Pro, from which we could generate HTML automatically using the scripting techniques described in Chapter 5.

Other HTML Authoring Assistants

What follows are brief descriptions of some of the more popular shareware HTML editing/authoring programs available on the Web.

Arachnid

Arachnid, by Robert McBurney of the University of Iowa, is an ambitious program developed in SuperCard that describes itself as an HTML "file builder" rather than an editor.

It has an excellent approach in theory, but falls short in practice, at least in the Beta 1.3.2 version that was available when I tested it. The theory is that the process of "building" pages happens graphically, without ever having to type HTML codes. Images and text are aligned graphically, by dragging them as objects.

Arachnid allows the testing of links and playback of audio and video files from within the program rather than having to preview them in a browser. It comes with an Arachnid Player application that allows files to be distributed and read by others who don't have the application. The danger of this approach is that the way Arachnid's Player displays an HTML may differ significantly from another "standard" browser—it forces the author to test the document in several formats (which in itself is not bad practice).

Where to Find It

I wasn't able to test the 1.5.4 release of Arachnid as this book went to press, but you can check it out at http://sec-look.uiowa.edu/.

I encountered several bugs in this release (they may have been fixed by the time you read this, however). Images jumped around onscreen, and when exporting files to HTML, Arachnid didn't give you a chance to designate where the file was supposed to go. Experienced Web page designers may not like having the HTML removed completely. Keep an eye on future versions, with some work it could be impressive.

Bob's HTML Editor (BHE)

Bob's HTML Editor (BHE), by Bob Matsuoka, is a multiwindow text editor that provides a set of tools for quickly adding HTML commands to blocks of text. Many of the most frequently accessed commands can be accessed via command keys and/or icons on a bar that runs across the top of the application window, or from a palette.

BHE also provides palettes that let you store locations of IMG and URL files and incorporate them into your HTML file. For those working from MacHTTP servers and some UNIX servers with AFP (AppleTalk File Protocol), relative paths to IMGs and URLs are automatically incorporated into the palettes, as are local anchor points. The program also lets you import URLs from hotlists and HTML files, as well as strip out HTML commands from text.

BHE lets you view files with the Web browser of your choice while simultaneously editing them. Files can be no more than 32K in size. Most HTML 2.0 commands and options are supported. Forms will be supported in a future version.

Where to Find It

Documentation for Bob's HTML Editor is at http://www.ilt.columbia.edu/public/macintosh/Bobs_HTML_Editor/readme.html.

HTML.Edit

HTML.edit, by Murray M. Altheim, helps insert HTML commands into documents and also performs some project-management functions. It is a HyperCard-based application, but HyperCard is not required to run it. See Figure 7.5.

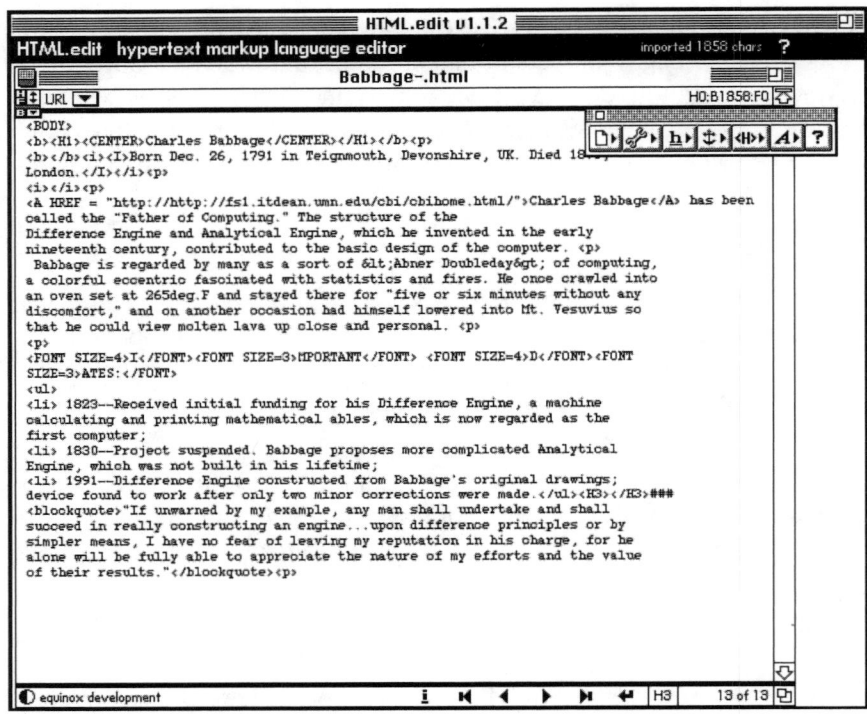

Figure 7.5 HTML.edit window.

Like most tag editors it provides automatic conversion of special characters like ü, &, and so on. One of its best features is its linking capability by use of an anchor utility and index pages. Index pages allow you to collect a group of related documents to which you might be likely to create many links. Those files appear on a list so you can select them and create the links easily. It does not work with documents larger than 30,000 characters. The 1.7b3/4 version, however, does include support for forms and tables.

Where to Find It

The home page for HTML.edit is http://ogopogo.nttc.edu/ tools/HTMLedit/ HTMLedit.html. You can download the 1.6beta3 version of the program from ftp:// ogopogo.nttc.edu/pub/tools/.

Drawbacks: Doesn't support forms or tables. I found it to be very s...l...o...w in operation.

HTML Editor

HTML Editor for the Macintosh, by Dr. Rick Giles of Acadia University, is a useful program for editing or inserting HTML commands into a document. It is virtually the only shareware HTML editor that works with files larger than 32K. See Figure 7.6.

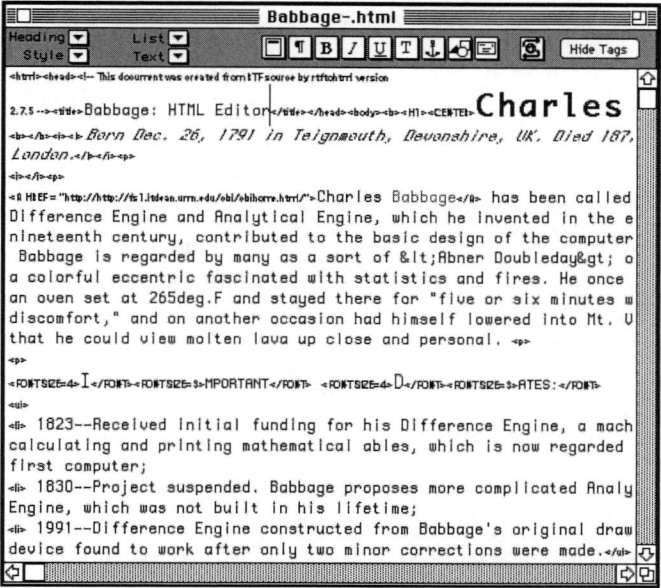

Figure 7.6 HTML Editor window.

The program allows you to insert common HTML tags by button clicks, menu selections, or keystrokes. It has search-and-replace commands for text editing, and lets you change the formatting of any style and apply the new style throughout the document. It allows you to hide tags for a quick preview of your document or, by clicking a button, to open Mosaic 2.0, Netscape 1.1, or MacWeb to see how the document actually looks on a browser.

Drawbacks: Your document must be in text-only or HTML format to open it in HTML Edit.

Where to Find It

You can read the documentation for HTML Editor at http://dragon.acadiau.ca/~giles/HTML_Editor/Documentation.html. You can get the program at ftp://cs.dal.ca/giles/.

Where to Find It

You can download HTML extensions to Alpha from ftp://cs.umd.edu//pub/faculty/keleher/Alpha/.

HTML Extensions to Alpha

Alpha is a very powerful, multipurpose editor that gives longtime Macintosh users like myself a glimpse into another world, the world of LaTeX. HTML Mode (suffix ".html") is for editing HyperText Markup Language documents. It is not a previewer, nor is it a verifier. It allows any program- or user-defined function to be bound to any keystroke, or placed into user-defined menus.

Alpha uses Dr. John Ousterhout's Tool Command Language (TCL) as an extension language. It has very impressive help features and menus right above the vertical scroll bar.

Drawbacks: Frankly, I couldn't figure out what it all meant. Users who've had experience with programmers, editors, LaTeX, or the UNIX editor emacs and like to have complete control over the behavior and functions of their editing environment (or like menu items entitled "Yank" and "Twiddle") will have a field day with this. The rest of us should use something simpler.

HTML Extensions to BBEdit

This popular set of extensions, written by Carles Bellver of the Universitat Jaume I in Spain, is designed for use with the BBEdit text editor. The extensions let you convert plain text files into HTML documents and insert HTML tags inside of them. Your work can be previewed with a Web browser. Drag the extensions files onto the 'BBEdit extensions' folder that comes with BBEdit (BBEdit is a commercial program, but BBEdit Lite is shareware. The extensions work with both.) From then on the HTML extensions will show on BBEdit **Extensions** menu.

Where to Find It

A description of BBEdit extensions is at http://www.uji.es/bbedit-html-extensions.html. You can download the program from ftp://ftp.uji.es/pub/mac/util/.

You can find BBEdit Lite at ftp://ftp.std.com/pub/bbedit. BBEdit Lite is at ftp://ogopogo.nttc.edu/pub/tools/. By the way, both BBEdit and the HTML extensions are being bundled with Apple's Internet Server.

Another set of extensions, BBEdit HTML Tools, by Lindsay Davies, is available at http://www.york.ac.uk/~ld11/BBEditTools.html.

Where to Find It

HTML Grinder is located at http://www.matterform.com/welcome.html.

HTML Grinder

The Grinder is a powerful utility that assists with intelligent link building. It automates such tasks as find-and-replace, maintaining glossaries of replaceable text, replacing chunks of tagged text, and accessing special plug-in tools called "wheels" to modify HTML pages.

The Find and Replace Tool, for instance, lets you search-and-replace text on all of your HTML pages at once by typing the new text in the Find and Replace window and dragging all the pages onto the Grinder icon.

HTML Pro

HTML Pro, by Niklas Frykholm, is a clever HTML editor that allows you to see a WYSIWYG display of your document in a "Source" window while viewing the actual HTML code in another window (see Figure 7.7). Again, the danger with having an editor interpret and display HTML for you is that the "standard" browsers may display them differently.

A trial run in my office uncovered a number of bugs, which will probably be corrected in future releases. One big advantage is that the program is relatively small (only 125K) and fast. However, it does not yet support Netscape extensions or forms.

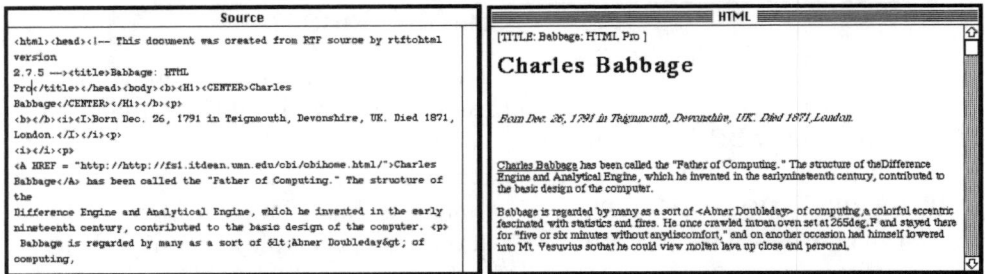

Figure 7.7 HTML Pro's two editing windows.

Simple HTML Editor (S H E)

If you like HyperCard, you'll love Simple HTML Editor (S H E).

S H E is a HyperCard-based editor, but it doesn't require HyperCard to run. It allows you to insert tags by pointing and clicking buttons or pull-down menus and its list of menu commands is more extensive than other programs. See Figure7.8.

Where to Find It

You can find HTML Pro at http://www.ts.umu.se/~r2d2/shareware/htmlpro_help.html.

Where to Find It

Documentation for S H E is at http://www.lib.ncsu.edu/staff/morgan/simple.html. The program is at ftp://ftp.lib.ncsu.edu/pub/software/mac/.

It allows you do centering of text as well as many other Netscape extensions. One of the menus covers the creation of forms. S H E has an online help file and allows the opening of text files via drag-and-drop. Its extensive formatting capabilities and its user-friendly interface are big points in its favor.

Drawbacks: This is not a WYSIWYG editor. Undo doesn't always quite work correctly. I had some problems seeing the entire window on my PowerBook (the version 2.9 release added a "small" version for smaller monitors). Documents must be less than 30,000 characters in length. "I could fix this, but the Editor would no longer be 'simple,'" author Eric Lease Morgan admits. I'm hoping for a Not-So-Simple HTML Editor (NSSHE), myself.

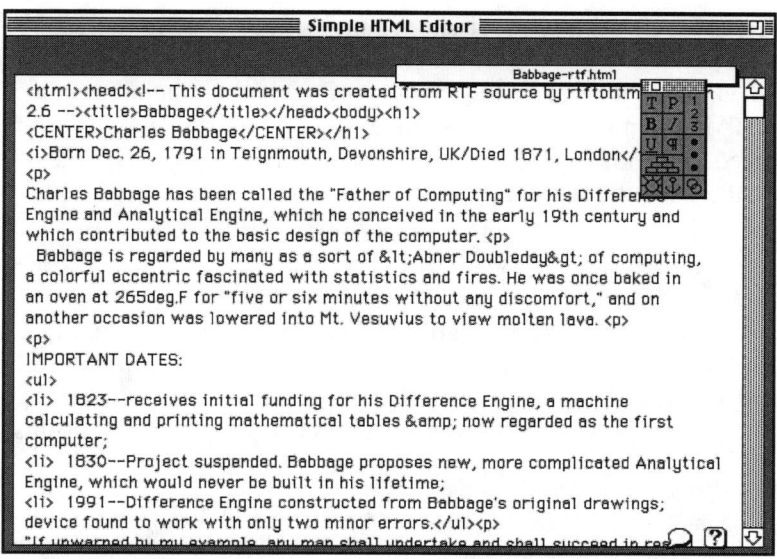

Figure 7.8 Simple HTML Editor window.

Aretha/AutoWeb

Aretha is a shareware release of Frontier, a system-level scripting environment for the Mac that is reputed to be better than AppleScript itself. Aretha is not for the codaphobic, but for those with the appropriate technical experience, it does allow some powerful scripting applications for a MacHTTP/WebSTAR server.

One component of the beta release of Aretha, called AutoWeb, is designed to handle many of the functions of managing a WebSTAR site, including creating home pages, generating anchors and links, and keeping track of graphics files.

Where to Find It

Aretha was, as of this writing, being offered on HotWired's Web site: http://www.hotwired.com/ Staff/userland/aretha/. A very positive review of Aretha can be found in TidBITS number 279: http://www.dartmouth.edu/ pages/TidBITS/issues/ TidBITS-279.html.

Coding Page Layout Documents for HTML

As I stated earlier, Adobe plans big things for PageMaker, including the capability to generate HTML from within the program. (At this writing, Version 6.0 was expected to be released in summer, 1995 and was supposed to include an HTML plug-in.) Until then, there are the following products.

Dave

Dave is an AppleScript conversion utility that converts PageMaker 5.0 text to HTML. Jeff Boulter of Bucknell University wrote this in order to create on online version of *The Bucknellian* magazine (described in Chapter 2). A non-AppleScript version was in the works as this was being written.

Drawbacks: Only converts text. Not very fast. Won't replace multiple characters such as ellipses. Files have to be less than 32,000 characters.

Where to Find It

You can find Dave at http://www.bucknell.edu/bucknellian/dave.

PageMaker WebSucker

This HyperCard stack takes stories from PageMaker 5.0 documents and translates them to HTML. Like "Dave," it was written for a university newspaper: the Clark University *Scarlet*. It creates a table of contents for the stories and categorizes them as well.

Where to Find It

You can find PageMaker WebSucker at http://www.iii.net/users/mcohen/websucker.html.

Quark to HTML: Gateway

Gateway is an application under development recently released in beta version by Acrobyte. The Document Content Palette, which Gateway adds to QuarkXPress, displays the content elements of a document (text boxes, linked stories, pictures,

Where to Find It

Gateway can be found at http://www.w3.org/hypertext/WWW/Tools/Gateway.html.

and anchored boxes). Users can choose which content elements they want to export, and arrange them to form a linear "article," or HTML page. Users can also create hyperlinks in their QuarkXPress documents, which are exported as HTML links.

For text chains, users can set up a mapping from their QuarkXPress style sheets to HTML tags, and also tag individual text selections by hand. Gateway will convert pictures to 72 dpi images, cropped and scaled as in the QuarkXPress layout.

Where to Find It

Documentation is at http://the-tech.mit.edu/~jeremy/qt2www.html. The program is at ftp://the-tech.mit.edu//pub/WWW/.

Quark to HTML Conversion Version 1.0 Beta

This utility, by Jeremy Hylton, converts QuarkXPress-tagged text to HTML.

Byte Productions Filter for Quark

A "modest, but working" filter for QuarkXPress is available at ftp://mars.aliens.com//pub/Macintosh/.

ClarisWorks to HTML Converters

The XTND HTML Translator allows Web publishers to create documents in ClarisWorks and save them in HTML format. Go to http://ai.eecs.umich.edu/highc/software/translator.html.

Another converter by Leonard Rosenthal can be found at ftp://pub/info-mac/text/html/html-plus-xtnd.hqx.

HTML Validation and Checking Services

A number of services on the Web actually purport to check your HTML files and report errors to you. Each site comes with a form into which you can type or paste HTML and submit it to the service for review. As a test, I sent the following bit of HTML to one such checker, VILSPA HTML Validation service:

```
1          <HTML>
2          <HEAD>
3          <TITLE>Bad HTML</TITLE>
4          </HEAD>
5          <BODY>
6          <H2> This is a sample of bad html. <H3>
7          <IMG SRC = "http://www-upubs.uchicago.edu/
           Master_Alumni_Page/nonexistent.gif">
8          Here are two lines
9          <P>
10         separated by a paragraph tag.
11         <SANDBOX>
12         </BODY>
13         </HTML>
```

As you can see, the <H2> and <H3> tags in line 6 don't match. The image that I refer to in line 7 does not exist, as the name suggests. The <P> tag in line 9 is used as a separator, rather than the preferred "container," of text. I made up the tag <SANDBOX> in line 11, and I'm pretty sure that no variation on HTML contains references to sandboxes. This is what VILSPA returned:

```
sgmls: SGML error at -, line 7 at ">":
   H2 end-tag implied by H3 start-tag; not minimizable
sgmls: SGML error at -, line 10 at ">":
   H3 end-tag implied by P start-tag; not minimizable
```

Both these messages refer to the mismatch of tags in line 6. The validation software recognizes that something is wrong with these tags, and seems unable to pin down where the problem is—it refers to lines 7 and 10 and it's actually line 7. It also sent back the following report:

```
 sgmls: SGML error at -, line 12 at ">":
```

VILSPA only recognizes <P> as half of the <P> </P> container pair, and so finds an error here. Of course, as of this writing, this use of <P> is perfectly valid.

Where to Find It

Get your HTML checked for free at VILSPA HTML Validation service, http://www.vilspa.esa.es/div/help/validation-form.html.

Not surprisingly, the software has discovered my imaginary tag:

> Undefined SANDBOX start-tag GI ignored; not used in DTD

Note that the software did not check to make sure that a file called "nonexistent.gif" exists at the location specified in the <IMG> tag. VILSPA checks your HTML for well-formed expressions, rather than for content. It doesn't spell check your copy or make sure that your links work in the way that you imagine they work. If the HTML grammar is correct, VILSPA does not display any error messages.

VILSPA also returns a rendering, or preview of your page. This is helpful, of course, but it's the same preview you'll see by dragging your HTML document onto your browser program.

Just for laughs, I sent the Netscape home page (http://home.mcom.com/home/welcome.html) for validation. (Note that this is the April 1995 home page, which has long since been replaced.) VILSPA returned:

```
sgmls: SGML error at -, line 4 at ">":
    Undefined CENTER start-tag GI ignored; not used in DTD
sgmls: SGML error at -, line 6 at "8":
    WIDTH = "468" attribute ignored: not defined for this element
sgmls: SGML error at -, line 6 at "1":
    HEIGHT = "171" attribute ignored: not defined for this element
sgmls: SGML error at -, line 7 at "0":
    BORDER = "0" attribute ignored: not defined for this element
sgmls: SGML error at -, line 11 at "S":
    Possible attributes treated as data because none were defined
sgmls: SGML error at -, line 11 at " ":
    Undefined FONT start-tag GI ignored; not used in DTD
sgmls: SGML error at -, line 11 at ">":
    No element declaration for FONT end-tag GI; end-tag ignored
sgmls: SGML error at -, line 12 at "S":
    Possible attributes treated as data because none were defined
sgmls: SGML error at -, line 12 at " ":
    Undefined FONT start-tag GI ignored; not used in DTD
sgmls: SGML error at -, line 12 at ">":
    No element declaration for FONT end-tag GI; end-tag ignored
sgmls: SGML error at -, line 14 at ">":
    No element declaration for CENTER end-tag GI; end-tag ignored
sgmls: SGML error at -, line 18 at ">":
    DL end-tag implied by B start-tag; not minimizable
sgmls: SGML error at -, line 19 at ">":
    B end-tag implied by DT start-tag; not minimizable
sgmls: SGML error at -, line 19 at ">":
    Out-of-context DT start-tag ended HTML document element (and parse)
```

Where to Find It

A number of other validation services are available besides VILSPA. I've listed addresses at the end of this chapter, but you can find links to them at http://www.yahoo.com/Computers/World_Wide_Web/HTML/Validation_Checkers. Be sure to read the useful essay "Why Validate Your HTML" at http://www.earth.com/bad-style/why-validate.html.

What does all this mean? Let's start by looking at the source. On Netscape's home page, line 19 reads as follows:

```
We want to <A HREF="/
welcome.html">welcome</A> you to
our new home!
```

This doesn't make any sense—there aren't any <DL>, <DT>, or <B> tags here. However, this looks like our mismatched tags from the "Bad HTML" example, and the problem turns out to be similar. I found the actual mismatched tags in lines 13 to 17:

```
<B>
<DT>
W<FONT SIZE=-1>E'RE</FONT>
N<FONT SIZE=-1>EW</FONT>!
</B>
```

The <DT> tag is incorrectly embedded in the <B> </B> pair. Style tags should be inside other elements; they should not contain other elements. The proper HTML has the style tag inside the list item tag:

```
<DT>
<B>
W<FONT SIZE=-1>E'RE</FONT>
N<FONT SIZE=-1>EW</FONT>!
</B>
```

Thanks to VILSPA, I found a minor error in Netscape's own HTML. Of course, Netscape's browser interprets this page without problems, but seemingly insignificant errors like this might cause a more unsteady browser to produce an unexpected display.

Such validation services will become more useful when HTML 3.0 becomes standard. Tags like <DL> and <DT> are treated like containers, and HTML documents in general will become more complicated.

Where to Find It

WebMagic Author is a dynamic WYSIWYG Web authoring program that comes with Silicon Graphics' powerful WebFORCE environment and Indy workstation. At the time this book went to press, there was no version of the program for the Mac. (SG requires you to buy the entire workstation to run it correctly.) I mention the program because the Indy workstation is so impressive and WebMagic does have many of the features of an "ideal" editor. Check out SG's Web site (http://www.sgi.com/) to find out more.

A Commercial HTML Editor: HoTMetaL Pro

The title of HoTMetaL Pro's online help file is telling: "A Guide For the Perplexed." I was, to an extent.

It's not that SoftQuad's product isn't powerful. It is. Or that its manual isn't well-written and organized. No problem there. It's just that the program isn't intuitive, like many Mac programs. (It was developed originally for Windows). Its learning curve is steep and, for beginners at least, pretty long.

HoTMetaL Pro is a versatile editor best-suited for users who are already adept at working with HTML. It has plenty of features, including a spell-checker, thesaurus, macros, and table editor. It will recognize Netscape's extensions after you change a line in the preferences file.

HoTMetaL Pro, however, is not forgiving. If you are opening an existing HTML file, the program forces you to correct any serious errors in your file before it will open. As shown in Figure 7.9, it replaces the familiar "cookie" tags with big icons that tend to clutter your work screen (you can hide these, however).

The program (which by itself amounts to 2,078K) requires 6 MB of available RAM to run, and a 68040 processor is recommended. I tried out the 1.0 version; as this book went to press the 2.0 version was about to be released.

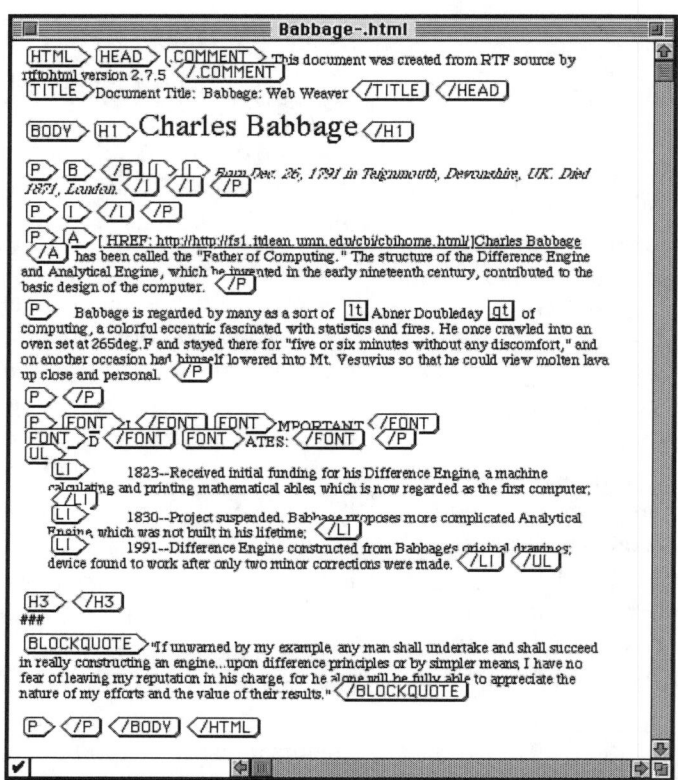

Figure 7.9 HoTMetaL Pro working window.

Resources

HTML Editors and Converters

Try these sites:

- At CERN: http://www.w3.org/hypertext/WWW/Tools/Filters.html.

- At the Library of Congress: http://lcweb.loc.gov/global/html.html.

- At Yahoo: http://www.yahoo.com/Computers/World_Wide_Web/ HTMLConverters.

- A list of QuarkXPress to HTML utilities can be found at http://www.w3.org/ hypertext/WWW/Tools/QXP.html.

HTML Validation Services

Try these sites:

- html_analyzer is at http://wsk.eit.com/wsk/dist/doc/admin/webtest/ verify_links.html.

- htmlchek is at http://uts.cc.utexas.edu/~churchh/htmlchek.html.

- WWWeblint is at http://www.unipress.com/weblint.

- "Why Validate Your HTML" is at http://www.earth.com/bad-style/why-validate.html.

Commercial HTML Editors

Try these sites:

- In Context Spider: http://www.incontext.ca/.

- HoTMetaL Pro 2.0 is at SoftQuad's site: http://www.sq.com/.

Preserving Your Publication with Portable Document Software

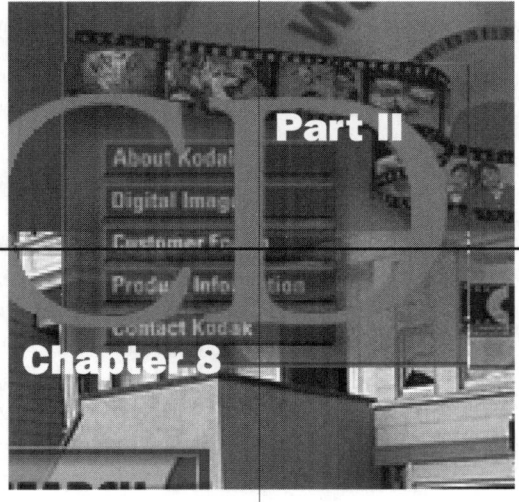

Part II

Chapter 8

Publishers are in the business of communication, and much of what we communicate is conveyed through something more than words and headlines. Our goal is to make an impact through the choice of a particular typeface, the way the text wraps around a photo, the spacing of text and different type sizes, the balance of tone and words, or the juxtaposition of images and white space. If it is important to you to preserve these elements while reaching the widest possible audience, consider converting your publication using "portable" document software.

Why Buck the Trend?

The idea of "preserving" or fixing a document online runs counter to the concept that everything on the Web should constantly be in a state of flux, so it deserves some explanation.

The nature of online publishing is toward modularity and interchangeability of information, and away from a presentation that uses a fixed page size and unchangeable type fonts.

Where to Find It

Guess who's getting into the PDF game? The Internal Revenue Service, which provides Acrobat PDF versions of all tax forms that you can download. Go to http://www.ustreas.gov/treasury/bureaus/irs/taxforms.html for more information.

Documents have to be described in standard ways so that they can be read over the Internet and displayed on as many different types of computers as possible. You can't expect to have much control over a file's appearance if you created the original page on your Mac in Australia and my brother-in-law, for instance, calls it up on his Packard Bell computer in Chicago. It has to be described in a generic markup language that a wide variety of computers and browsers can recognize, like HTML (or its parent language, SGML).

What happens, though, if your company has spent a lot of time and money designing a promotional brochure that uses just the right tone and appearance to convey exactly the message your president and vice president want to broadcast to the world? What if you think a three-inch wide column, a special typeface, and a particular shade of gray are perfect and can't be improved upon? Is there some way to put the existing brochure on the Internet while preserving its original layout?

Here's one more question: Is there some way to make your document really secure, so that it can be read online but not copied onto anyone's computer? Perhaps your agreements with your writers or photographers call for one-time only use of their work, and you want to protect their copyright (not to mention your own). You can't do that on the Internet, where everything is available to be plundered and recycled, right?

I wouldn't be writing this chapter if the answers to the preceding questions were "no." By using one of the software programs I'm about to describe, you can preserve and protect your publications from modification, without having to convert them to HTML.

Note: At the moment, only whole pieces of publications in electronic form (on a computer) can be converted to a portable document format. (Adobe has, however, announced an impressive-sounding product for Windows called Capture that allegedly converts any scanned publication into a PDF file.) Perhaps your company has been reprinting a brochure for years and not all the photos are in the electronic file because the printer has been simply picking them up from standing film. You'll have to scan in any of these "missing" images and add them to the file before putting the publication on the Web whether you use HTML or a PDF program such as Acrobat.

This chapter discusses several applications that allow you to take a computer "snapshot" of a document and convert it to a portable document format (see Figure 8.1). The portable version of your document can then be read by another computer even if that computer does not have the original software. This means that a complex publication with scanned color photos and elaborate design elements can be viewed on the Internet with all of its graphics and formatting commands intact.

Figure 8.1 A "real" college information brochure, left, and the PDF version viewed with Acrobat reader.

Portable Document Software Options

Competition is currently fierce among companies that produce portable document software. This is because the technology is used for transmitting one's work "intact" between different kinds of computers in a workgroup or large organization. They also provide a way to "publish without paper" and save some trees.

Anyone shopping for a program naturally benefits from wider choices and lower prices brought about by the competition. There are currently five software options for producing portable documents:

- Acrobat (Adobe Systems)
- Common Ground (Common Ground Software, Inc.)
- Envoy (The Novell Applications Group)
- Replica (Farallon Computing, Inc.)
- Apple System 7.5's PDD feature (which uses QuickDraw GX)

Where to Find It

A brief list of links to Macintosh portable document readers is at http://www.astro.nwu.edu/lentz/mac/software/pdd.html.

Each of these options has essentially the same capacity: to make a document portable by taking a computer "snapshot" of it and duplicating, as closely as possible, its type fonts and graphics. Some of the programs go a step or two further and allow you to create such navigational features as hypertextual links, thumbnails of each page, a table of contents, and so on.

For transmitting a file, you don't need to get too fancy. In fact, what we Web publishers need from a good portable document program is

- To preserve the look of the document.
- To provide a security (read-only) option.
- To make the file as small as possible for easy downloading.
- To make it easy for the reader to view and use the document using a program's viewer software.

All of the programs mentioned here do the job, but the degrees of success vary. Which one you choose depends upon your needs and the software you use. If you have System 7.5, try using QuickDraw GX to create a portable document. There are potential disadvantages to these PDDs, however, because they're Mac-only. If you have other Novell software, use Envoy. If you like Farallon's products and are familiar with its program Timbuktu, go for Replica.

That said, most informed sources believe that Acrobat is becoming the industry standard, because the company is visible and well-established and because Acrobat documents will soon be coordinated with both Netscape and PageMaker (which Adobe acquired with its purchase of Aldus Corporation).

Greg's Soapbox

I've heard objections to using Acrobat and other portable document programs because of the extra work they require and because they aren't "friendly" to Web users who use computers that don't display color or graphics very easily. When you open one of these documents and watch a page load on a color screen, it's an amazing experience, and to my mind, well worth the effort. Another helpful feature of these programs is that they allow you to transport and print complex documents across different computer platforms. Download the spring 1995 edition of the *Oberlin Alumni Magazine* (see Figure 8.6) and see for yourself.

As this book was being written, Adobe released a beta version of Acrobat Weblink, a plug-in for Acrobat Exchange that allows Web readers to link PDF files to other documents on the Web (see the section at the end of this chapter entitled "A Glimpse of the Future: Weblink/InternetLink"). A future version of Netscape is expected to allow users to read Acrobat documents. Acrobat's presence on the Web makes it the most reliable choice for portable document production—plus, its option for work-groups and other non-Web users makes it even more attractive.

However, for most Web publishers, Common Ground's features are nearly as good as Acrobat's. The program is more affordable, simpler, and smaller than Acrobat. If your natural inclination is to go with the "little guy," this is the choice for you.

Here's a rundown of the various programs and how they work. I went into more detail in my Acrobat description because that's what I use and am most familiar with. Wow, I just love the power of being the author.

Acrobat

Adobe Acrobat comes in several different flavors. Acrobat Reader is the basic vanilla program. It's free and it's the part of Acrobat that you are most likely to encounter, because it lets you read documents saved in Acrobat's PDF format after you download them from the Internet.

To convert PostScript files (such as those commonly generated from PageMaker or QuarkXPress for service bureaus or distribution on the Net) into PDF format, there's Acrobat Distiller. You have to buy it with one of the commercial packages such as Acrobat Pro, however.

Then there's Acrobat Exchange, which is more of an authoring tool for working on PDF files. It lets you generate search indices and add links, tables of contents, electronic notes, and so on.

Acrobat Distiller and PDF Writer let you "print" a document into a PDF file. The PDF version contains the original document's text and images and can be viewed by anyone who has Exchange or Adobe's free reader software.

Just for the fun of it, let's imagine that there are ten people sitting in front of ten computers who want to create, share, and review documents electronically, even though they all have very different hardware or software. Hey, guess what? Adobe offers a ten-user Acrobat for Workgroups package that includes Distiller, as well as Acrobat Catalog, and can give a PDF file full text search capabilities.

Here's an example that shows how Acrobat came to the rescue in my office. We needed to insert a computer visualization of a molecule (see Figure 8.2) into a newsletter. The original image was created on a Silicon Graphics workstation and came to us as a 300-dots-per-inch bitmap PostScript image.

The problem was that my office doesn't have a Silicon Graphics workstation. Our production czar, Tim Webster, made a PDF file of the image using Acrobat Distiller. He was then able to import the image into Illustrator, and then into Photoshop for some cleanup, and finally into the PageMaker version of the newsletter that was turned into a PDF file using Acrobat Distiller (see Figure 8.3).

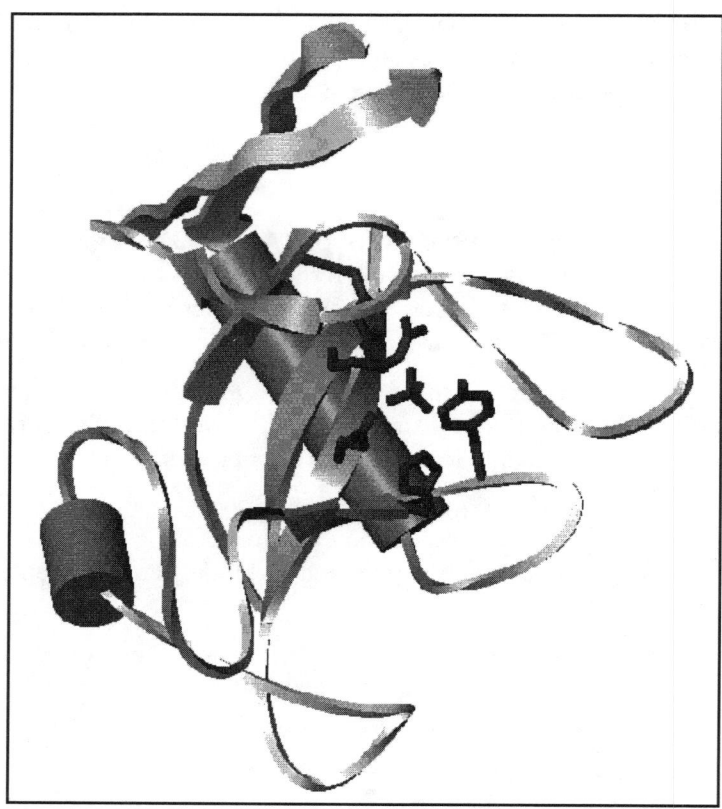

Figure 8.2 A PDF file created with Acrobat.

For transmitting and viewing files on the Web, the publisher creates a PDF version of the original using PDF Writer or Distiller, and then uses Exchange to add "sticky" notes, bookmarks, a table of contents, or hypertext links either within the document or between that document and others.

The viewer has to do three things before reading this file:

1. Download Adobe Type Manager (either version 3.8 or an LE version), which is what the reader uses to simulate your original fonts.

2. Install Acrobat Reader.

3. Configure Netscape, Mosaic, or MacWeb to run Acrobat Reader as a helper application.

ATM (Adobe Type Manager) creates rasterized images of PostScript, QuickDraw GX, or Multiple Master fonts that it keeps in memory for display as bitmaps. This doesn't always work well with symbols or very stylized fonts (see Figure 8.4). In that case, you have the option of embedding the original fonts in your document, but that dramatically increases the file size. Figure 8.5 shows fonts emulated using Replica.

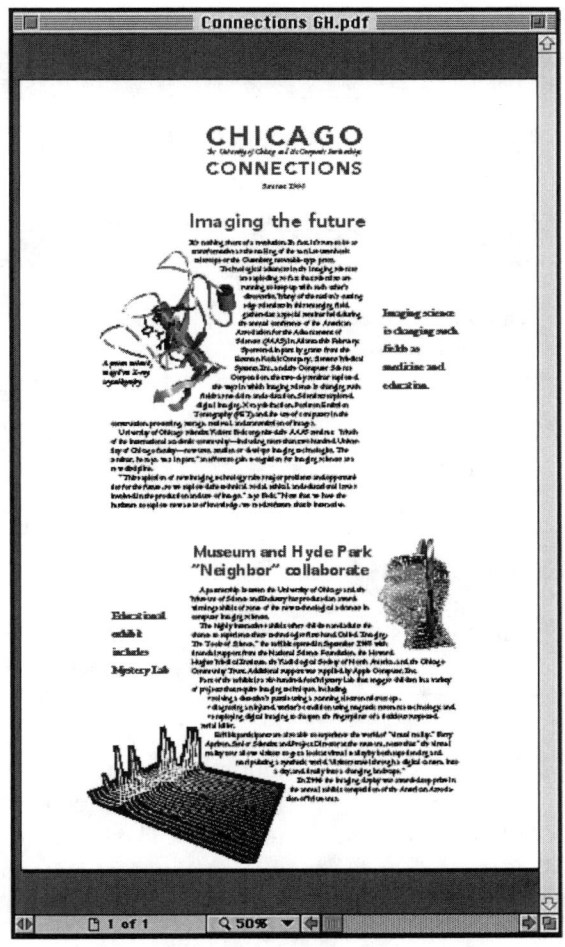

Figure 8.3 PageMaker file distilled using Acrobat.

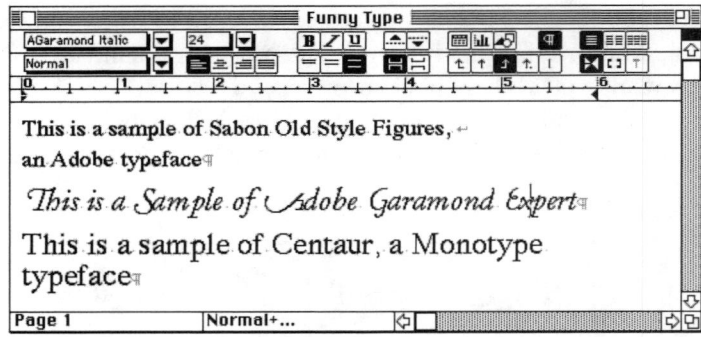

Figure 8.4 Fonts that might be hard to emulate.

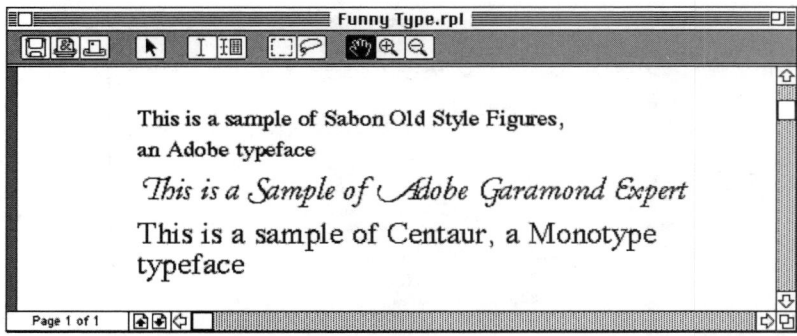

Figure 8.5 Fonts emulated using Replica.

One of Acrobat's best features is that it lets you follow the flow of a story through a newsletter or other publication even when the story has been broken into discontinuous pieces. As seen in Chapter 2, Linda Grashoff, who publishes the Oberlin alumni newsletter in Acrobat, also makes use of Acrobat's capability to attach notes to a story. The notes provide her with a way to get more material in the online version than existed in the printed piece (see Figure 8.6).

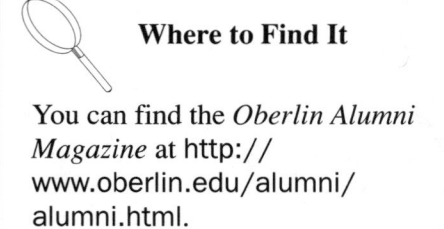

Where to Find It

You can find the *Oberlin Alumni Magazine* at http://www.oberlin.edu/alumni/alumni.html.

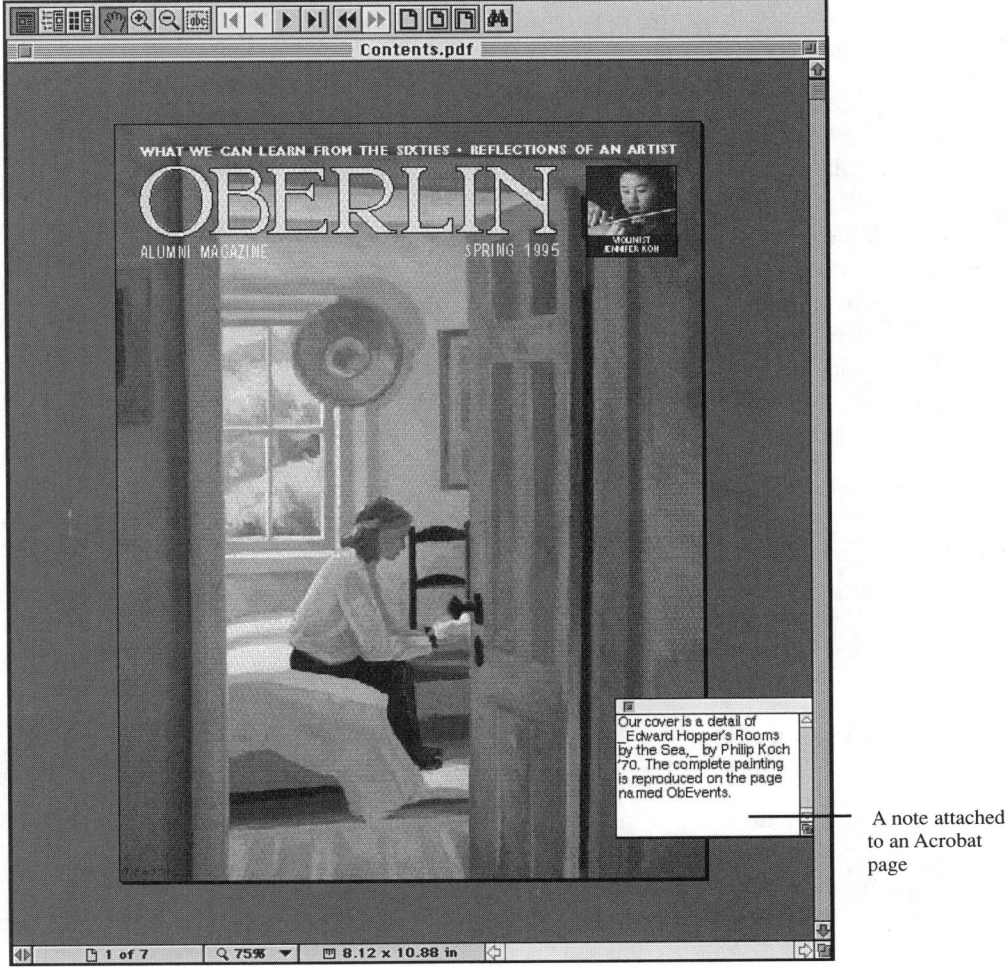

Figure 8.6 Cover of online *Oberlin Alumni Magazine*.

On the downside, Adobe's ATM software also requires a sizable amount of memory: a minimum of 4 MB of RAM, which increases depending on the number of fonts and point sizes you ask it to rasterize.

Where to Find It

Practically all you need to know about Acrobat can be found at Adobe's Web site, http://www.adobe.com/. Acrobat Reader can be downloaded, as well as a beta version of Weblink. There's also a list of links to other organizations that use Acrobat so you can see why others like PDF files.

What's good about Adobe is its marketing commitment to users who share documents on the Web. Because the company is already so well established, Adobe people are easy to reach, reliable, and certain to upgrade their products on a regular basis. The explanation of Adobe's Acrobat product line seems more complicated than it really is. In practice, it's not overly difficult to distill, annotate, and read files.

When the complicated brochure shown in Figure 8.3 was run through Acrobat distiller, the file size was reduced from over 16 MB to 2.3 MB.

Common Ground

Common Ground is produced by Common Ground Software, a small company in California that actually came out with portable document software before Adobe did.

Where to Find It

For more information about the latest release of Common Ground, call Common Ground Software, 1-800-598-3921 or 1-415-802-5800. Stanford University's Web site uses Common Ground versions of many documents and provides general information about the program, as well as the MiniViewer software for downloading, at http://www-portfolio.stanford.edu/100854.

When transmitting and displaying documents on the Web, smaller and simpler is often better. In general, Common Ground performs the same basic functions as Acrobat, while being more manageable than its competition.

Common Ground has one big advantage over Acrobat: it allows the option of embedding a Mac or Windows viewer into a Common Ground document. So, while the Acrobat user is stuck with having to go through the work of downloading a separate reader program, the lucky duck with Common Ground could be home free. Each Common Ground document can contain not only the material to be viewed

Where to Find It

If you want to get another perspective, you can read a very favorable review of Common Ground in *NCT Web* magazine: http://www.awa.com/nct/software/commong.html. A review in the April 1995 issue of *Macworld* magazine was also thumbs up.

but also the application with which to view it. Embedding Common Ground's MiniViewer can add approximately 100–150K to a file, however.

The good news is that Common Ground software plans to incorporate Bitstream's TrueDoc font display technology in Common Ground 2.0, which was due for release as this book was being written. This will allow Common Ground to print or display fonts at any resolution without requiring the font to be embedded in a document. An extension to version 2.0 will deliver pages on demand rather than having to wait for the entire document to download.

Common Ground also allows password protection of its documents. Like Acrobat, it allows users to include bookmarks, hyperlinks, and a table of contents. It also allows searches through the Verity search engine.

Common Ground is a very good program, but it's not used by Web publishers as often as Acrobat. Accessibility is its Achilles' heel. Common Ground does not have its own Web site, and you can't download the program to try it out. I was able to download the MiniViewer from one of my own campus's archives, but only after searching for it long and hard.

Envoy

Novell's Envoy 1.0 performs the same kinds of functions that Acrobat does, but in a less complex fashion. Envoy consists of three main components:

- Publisher software, which creates the portable documents.

- Viewer, which allows viewing, annotating, and printing of Envoy files.

- Runtime, which allows creation of a standalone Envoy document that can be read by someone who doesn't have the program's viewer software.

Where to Find It

You can read more about Envoy at Novell's Web site, http://www.novell.com/, or call 1-800-861-2551 or 1-801-229-1667.

With Envoy, you can create bookmarks, thumbnails, and hypertextual links, as well as highlight text and objects in its documents. It also has extensive annotating capabilities that allow a viewer to add notes and comments to a document and send it back to the originator. Drag-and-drop file creation is another feature of Envoy publisher.

The program requires only 900K of available RAM, so if your hardware is limited and your needs are limited to simple transmission of published documents over the Web, Envoy might be a good alternative to Acrobat.

Replica

Replica is the simplest of the four PDF programs. It handles the basic functions: font duplication, file size compression, freely distributed viewer software, text search, and navigation tools.

One unique feature about Replica is that you can download a trial version of the program from Farallon's Web site and work with it immediately (see Figure 8.7—compare this to the Acrobat version of the same document in Figure 8.3).

Where to Find It

To find out more about Replica, and to download the program for a five-document trial period, go to http://www2.farallon.com/www/www2/rep/repmac.html.

Replica consists of two pieces of software, their functions are probably self-explanatory: Creator and Viewer. The program offers automatic file encryption, as well as optional password protection and view-only options for documents. Replica requires 4 MB of RAM on a Mac running System 7 or later.

Replica files tend to be smaller than those created by the other programs. The page shown in Figures 8.3 and 8.7 was over 3 MB in the original PostScript file; Acrobat distilled it to 540K and Replica reduced it to only 135K.

Figure 8.7 Replica's version of our newsletter.

Apple System 7.5/QuickDraw GX

If your Macintosh is running System 7.5, you don't have to buy one of the aforementioned programs to create a portable document. The QuickDraw GX imaging technology, which ships with System 7.5, allows the creation of Portable Digital Documents (PDDs).

All you have to do is select **Print** from the File menu and then select **PDD Maker GX** from the popup menu. The resulting PDD can then be opened, viewed, and printed from any other Macintosh with QuickDraw GX installed.

So how do all these puzzle pieces fit together? Let's ask Don Crabb, whose name is on the publishing library that this book belongs to. He believes the QuickDraw GX PDDs will be the virtual document architecture for low-end, basic documents, whereas Acrobat will become the default choice for middle- to high-end documents. QuickDraw GX is certainly a viable, no-cost solution for Mac-only workgroups, while Acrobat is the cross-platform solution and is more immediately useful to Web publishers.

Special Considerations when Publishing a "Portable" Web Document

No matter what software program you use, there is a price to pay in both time and effort by Web publisher and reader alike. In return for preserving your document, you have to take into account several significant considerations:

1. You have to buy the software and learn how to use it.

2. Anyone who wants to read your publication may have to install a "reader" program. In the case of Acrobat, you can either set up the viewer software as a link on your site so that it downloads when the users click it, or direct the users to the vendor's Web site, where they can download the reader and find plenty of other documentation.

3. Not all browsers or computers can be expected to run the "reader" software.

4. Once your Web readers have the viewer software, they'll have to configure Netscape, MacWeb, or Mosaic to run Acrobat as a helper application if they want to view a portable document while still connected to a Web browser. This means that when a link to a file has the suffix .PDF in its name, the browser knows that it needs to open the Acrobat Reader "helper" application to view that file. (You can, of course, simply download the .PDF file to your computer and view it with Reader separately after disconnecting from the Web to conserve memory.)

5. You will probably have to provide "generic" HTML or even ASCII versions of the same publication for Web readers who either can't or won't read the portable version. As a result, you might have to prepare two or even three versions instead of just the usual HTML one.

6. There is also the question of how much to embed in the file. If you embed a product's reader software, you make it easier for others to scan your file. That's the good news. The bad news is that you substantially increase the size of that file. In the case of Common Ground, installing the simpler Mini-Viewer adds 150K to the file, while installing its "Pro Viewer" adds as much as 500K.

7. If you want to ensure that the look of the original's type styles is preserved exactly, you can embed the font with the program. This means that the user doesn't have to depend on the portable document program to emulate fonts. If you are using Acrobat and you use typefaces from Monotype rather than Adobe, this might be a good approach. But be ready for your file size to grow substantially, thus making it more time-consuming for your impatient readers to download.

8. You should consider the fact that the design you are endeavoring to preserve may look great as, say, a 4"× 9" printed brochure, but may be difficult to read on a 9" laptop display. Ideally, you may want to redesign your publication to appear exclusively onscreen.

9. Do you "lock" your document to be read only? The security feature will, once again, add to the file size. Preserving your documents online, then, is not a straightforward matter, but one that requires an assessment of your goals.

10. Having created a document, do you want to add hyperlinks within it, or notes, or bookmarks? These can greatly enhance one's navigation, but they can also increase the work required to prepare the file before going online.

Why Go Through All This Trouble?

While I was writing this book, a couple of major newspapers closed in Wisconsin and Texas. One reason for their demise was the dramatically increasing cost of newsprint.

Remember *Omni Magazine*? It used to be found on magazine stands, but today is available only in electronic format.

If enough people show interest in reading your PDF document, you might be able to save on paper costs and simply publish online. If paper costs continue to rise, this may become more of a necessity and less of an option.

One Publisher's Approach

Here's an example that illustrates one way to approach the issues involved in creating portable documents.

I'm assistant director of a publications office that publishes real-life promotional literature for the University of Chicago. We want to put our color viewbook and general information brochure on the Web. We want to preserve the graphics, photos, and general look-and-feel that we've developed over many years, the result of the combined effort of many professional photographers, writers, and designers.

We are also concerned that the photos we put out on the Web might be copied and misused, resulting in strong complaints and ill-will (or, at the worst, lawsuits) by the freelance photographers who regularly work for us.

Our office has decided to put out our primary publications for prospective students, such as our college viewbook, by converting them with Acrobat. We also plan to "lock" the publications so they can be read but not copied. (Although, you have to be aware that people can still take a "picture" of what's onscreen even if the document is read-only.)

In making this decision, we have had to consider the fact that anyone who wants to look at our primary publication for prospective students has to go through a bit of work before they can be read. In the fast moving, point-and-click world of the Web, those few minutes of work may turn off a lot of viewers.

But to put a positive spin on the situation (so our reasoning goes), the potential reader we lose may be, in fact, the casual Web surfer who isn't at all interested in attending the college of the University of Chicago. We may be building in some insurance that our message will only go to "serious" readers.

We've not yet decided whether to also provide the same publications in the HTML format so that they can be viewed by anyone on the Web.

We also have to listen to objections from those who say that a UNIX or Sun computer will never be able to read our document (although there are both Windows and UNIX versions of Acrobat's Reader). Those with anti-exclusionary philosophies argue that restricting access to information runs against the fundamental open nature of the Internet.

Assess Your Goals

You have to ask yourself the following question (one that you can never ask too many times): *What are my primary goals and objectives in publishing on the World Wide Web?* Is my goal to reach the widest possible audience, or to attract only "serious" readers who are willing to put out the effort to see my published document the way I want it to be seen? What are my real communications goals?

For that matter, it doesn't have to be an all or nothing approach. You may choose to take both the high road and the low road by putting out basic information about your organization as conventional HTML format, while also putting your most important public relations piece out using a program like Acrobat.

A Glimpse of the Future: Weblink/InternetLink

Weblink, a new product from Adobe, opens up a new level of interactivity between portable documents and the Web. The program allows you to embed hyperlinks to URLs around the Web within an Acrobat document. Click a hyperlink, and Netscape launches automatically to take you to the appropriate URL.

The beta version didn't support hyperlinks from within the free Acrobat Reader. That means you have to use the Acrobat Exchange program to read a PDF file, see the hyperlinks the author has embedded in it, and click them to go to a site around the Web (see Figure 8.8).

Note: Another product that has been out for a while already performs the same functions as Weblink: it's InternetLink, a plug-in module for Acrobat Exchange from the University of Minnesota. It also lets you embed URLs as links in PDF documents. When the user clicks such a link, InternetLink launches an appropriate helper application and requests to retrieve the item.

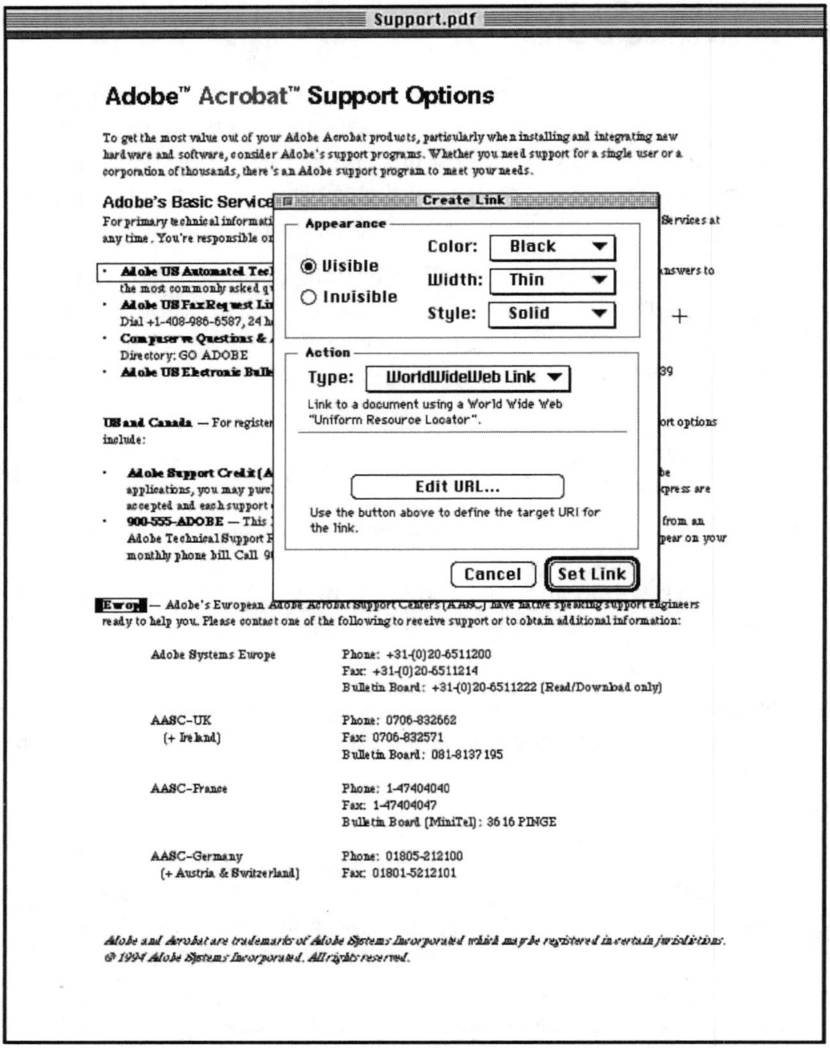

Support.pdf

Adobe™ Acrobat™ Support Options

To get the most value out of your Adobe Acrobat products, particularly when installing and integrating new hardware and software, consider Adobe's support programs. Whether you need support for a single user or a corporation of thousands, there's an Adobe support program to meet your needs.

Adobe's Basic Service

For primary technical information ... Services at any time. You're responsible on ...

- **Adobe US Automated Tec** ... answers to the most commonly asked q ...
- **Adobe US Fax Request Li** Dial +1-408-986-6587, 24 h ...
- **Compuserve Questions & A** Directory: GO ADOBE
- **Adobe US Electronic Bulle** ... 39

US and Canada — For register ... ort options include:

- **Adobe Support Credit (A** ... be applications, you may purc ... cpress are accepted and each support ...
- **900-555-ADOBE** — This ... from an Adobe Technical Support R ... pear on your monthly phone bill. Call 9 ...

Europe — Adobe's European Adobe Acrobat Support Centers (AASC) have native speaking support engineers ready to help you. Please contact one of the following to receive support or to obtain additional information:

Adobe Systems Europe   Phone: +31-(0)20-6511200
Fax: +31-(0)20-6511214
Bulletin Board: +31-(0)20-6511222 (Read/Download only)

AASC-UK   Phone: 0706-832662
(+ Ireland)   Fax: 0706-832571
Bulletin Board: 081-8137195

AASC-France   Phone: 1-47404040
Fax: 1-47404047
Bulletin Board (MiniTel): 3616 PINGE

AASC-Germany   Phone: 01805-212100
(+ Austria & Switzerland)   Fax: 01801-5212101

Adobe and Acrobat are trademarks of Adobe Systems Incorporated which may be registered in certain jurisdictions.
© 1994 Adobe Systems Incorporated. All rights reserved.

Create Link

Appearance

- ● Visible
- ○ Invisible

Color: Black ▼
Width: Thin ▼
Style: Solid ▼

Action

Type: WorldWideWeb Link ▼

Link to a document using a World Wide Web "Uniform Resource Locator".

Edit URL...

Use the button above to define the target URI for the link.

Cancel   Set Link

Figure 8.8 The hyperlink option in Acrobat Exchange.

Where to Find It

Weblink can be downloaded from Adobe's Web site: http://www.adobe.com/Acrobat/Weblink.html. InternetLink performs basically the same functions and can be found at ftp://boombox.micro.umn.edu/pub/gopher/Macintosh-TurboGopher/.

Nevertheless, it seems reasonable that Adobe will include Weblink support for Acrobat Reader in the future. When that happens, it means that Web publishers will be able to put out, along with their conventional HTML documents, alternate versions of those documents as PDF files, complete with hyperlinks.

These PDF "home pages" can retain the complex formatting of a printed publication, but behave like a hypertextual HTML page and interact with Netscape and the Web. It gives you the exciting option of creating a home page with truly professional design and typography that acts like an HTML page. Consult Adobe's Web site for the latest information on this promising software.

Part III

Making Your Web
Page Look and
Read Professionally

Painless Writing for the Web: Style and Content

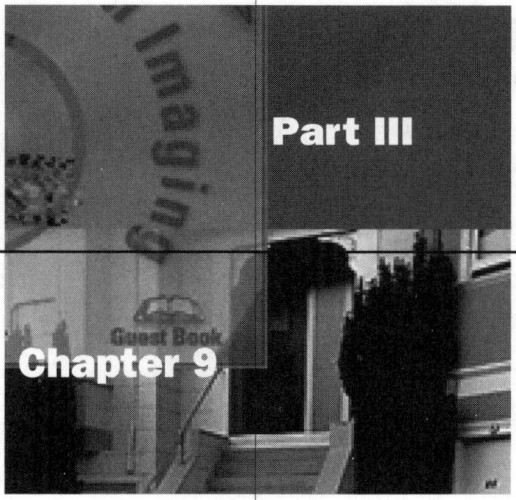

Part III

Chapter 9

Now that you have an overview of the various Web authoring and editing tools, you are probably wondering how you come up with the content that you will code in HTML. What special techniques should you use when writing for your Web site? How is reading onscreen different than reading on paper?

In a nutshell, the most important points about writing for the Web are

- Be as brief and focused as possible.

- Grab the reader's attention immediately—and keep grabbing it.

- Direct the reader's eyes through a well-organized and well-presented document or hypertextually linked web of documents.

Yes, I plead guilty to the charge that I make my living by editing. But the need for clarity is not just the over-anal-retentiveness of an old fuddy-duddy. Cyberspace abounds with evidence of poor or misdirected writing. In the rush to get online, companies and individuals often don't give much thought to basic principles of style, copyediting, proofing, updating, or the needs of the special audience in this new medium.

This chapter shows you how to write for the Web and how this is different from writing for print media. It suggests ways to get and keep the Web surfer's attention by using headlines, captions, design elements, and writing styles that practically leap off the screen.

Topics discussed in this chapter focus on stylistic issues related to writing and editing, and include:

- How to write for the Web;

- How to structure text for the Web;

- How to organize text with subheads, callouts, and other formatting; and

- How to add style to your content.

Chapter 10 addresses the basics of proofreading and copyediting, and how these skills apply to the Web.

Why Mess with Success?

You might well ask: Why go through the trouble of rewriting for the Web? Why not simply publish on the Internet exactly the same material you put out in your fabulously successful printed pieces?

Painless Writing for the Web:
Style and Content

Where to Find It

"Pointers: A Webwide Collection of Cultural Treasures" is part of MasterCard International's Web site: http://www.mastercard.com/. Another commercial site, public.com, invites customers to submit (for a fee) their own personal ads (http://www.public.com/). A very funny site, Joe's AMAZING problem solver, invites everyone from the love-lorn to World Wide Web newbies to tell their problems and get free advice (http:/studsys.mscs.mu.edu:80/~carpent1/probsolv/).

Sounds like a loaded question, but it's not. In the following cases, what you put out on paper should be easily translated to the Web:

- You don't have the money or staff to do a lot of rewriting;

- Like a newspaper reporter, you need to get information out fast, and it's timely only for a short period; or

- Your university, corporation, or large organization has finely crafted its message so as to convey the proper image.

In most cases, however, the text you used for your printed piece will have to be reorganized and reworked for the Web. The problem lies not with your words, dear information providers, but with your readers.

Tip: *Have somebody else do the writing for you.* Look at MasterCard International's site, in which they are inviting anyone to submit stories from around the world, "linking people and generations to timeless truths." Sounds high-minded, but it's also a clever way to provide free content from which the company can advertise its own name and logo on virtually every page.

Hitting a Moving Target

A study recently conducted by the Georgia Institute of Technology indicated that most people who use the Internet are browsing for information randomly, rather than heading to a specific site. This is only one of the ways in which writing for the Web is different from writing for a print audience.

Usually, you identify your audience before beginning to work on a printed piece. Then, you print a specific number of copies that you distribute to people on a mailing list.

In contrast, a Web audience defines itself. Those who are genuinely interested in what you have to say will find you if you provide the right hooks and keywords (see Chapter 11, "Organizing Your Web Site," for tips on naming your site). Browsers who genuinely aren't interested will take a brief glance and move to a surfing stop more to their liking.

It's the group between those two extremes, the ones who *might* be interested, that you can attract to your Web site with snappy writing, effective design, and attractive graphics.

Writing for the Web in Six Easy Steps

Here's a quick summary of the steps to creating effective, audience-oriented content for your Web site. Following the steps is a more detailed examination of how people are using these techniques online, including some specific examples from the Web.

Before You Start Typing

If you are composing your text directly onto a word processing document such as Word or WordPerfect, you'll save yourself time by following these guidelines beforehand:

- Set up your document with styles that will be easily translated into HTML tags. Headings should be assigned the style Heading 1 (or H1), Heading 2, Heading 3, and so on. Body text should have the style Body or Normal.

- Don't use any Adobe or other third-party typefaces, but choose something generic like Times or Helvetica.

- Put one space after colons and after periods at the end of sentences.

- Turn off your word processing program's curly or "smart quotes" feature and use straight quotation marks (").

- Use two hyphens instead of an em-dash (command-option-hyphen).

- Avoid characters that are used in HTML tags (in particular, ampersands, angle brackets, or straight quotes), or other characters such as accents, umlauts, or ligatures that many computers or Web browsers can't display.

See Chapter 10 for more on information on formatting what you've written.

Step One: Be Clear

Don't lose viewers by telling jokes nobody will get. You can be clever, of course, but be sure you:

- Give the name of your Web site;

- Identify yourself or your organization (especially useful if your home page is obviously part of a large institution such as a university, and it's not clear from your URL what university it is);

- Say something about the purpose or goal of your Web site;

- Provide a "hook" or lead to entice the reader to investigate *your site* rather than someone else's (see the section entitled "The Front Page Meets the Home Page," later in this chapter).

Greg's Soapbox

Although Cyberspace breaks down geographic, cultural, and political boundaries in a truly new and profound way, I personally find it helpful if people identify where in the world they are located by something more specific than their email suffix ("de" for Germany, "uk" for United Kingdom, and so on). Consider giving your actual city, state, or country location somewhere on your site.

Step Two: Be Brief

Back in the good old days, people had meals of several courses and then curled up in a big chair with a good book for an entire evening. Now they are more likely to nosh or graze on the run and when they sit down to the computer, they only want to consume what's on their computer screen in little bits, and then move on to something else. It's as though, now that they have the ability to make a hyperlink, Web surfers *need* to click and move somewhere every few minutes they are connected.

Keep your message as brief as possible, and after one subject has been presented, start the next subject on a new page and provide a link to it.

Step Three: Strike the Right Tone

Adopt the right tone for the audience you want to attract. If you want to be business-like, adopt a businesslike tone. If you want to have fun, don't hold back! Whatever approach you take, be consistent from page to page—you might even repeat the same "joke" or style of heading to develop a "theme." If you decide to use the second person "you" in one document, don't suddenly switch to "they" in the next.

Step Four: Write Headings that Stop the Clicker-Finger

The average Web surfer has an itchy clicker-finger. (I confess that my attention span is as short as they come.) The Web publisher's challenge is to attract an audience that's driving by at high speed, as if whizzing along an interstate highway with a number of towns or roadside attractions passing by in a blur.

One way to get the reader to focus on your message is through headlines that catch the eye. Remember those Burma Shave advertising signs that used to be spaced along the road at strategic intervals? They had two or three words on each sign, so the message said something like:

> The Whale
>
> Put Jonah
>
> Down the Hatch

But Coughed Him Up

Because He Scratched

Burma Shave[1]

The same idea of a series of headings (poetry optional) can be used to attract the quickly-moving Net surfer. Figure 9.1 illustrates traveling down the information superhighway.

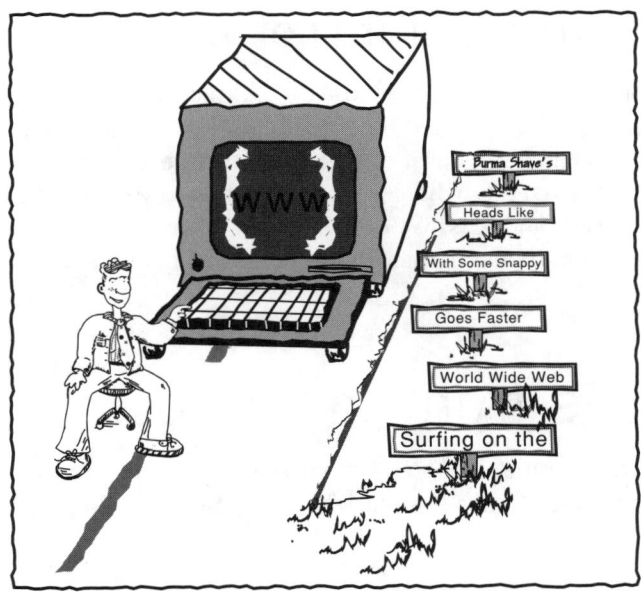

Figure 9.1 Traveling down the information superhighway.

Step Five: Think Like a Journalist

I learned a few useful tricks of the trade during my years as a journalist. For example, how do you stop someone who is walking down the street dead in their tracks when they pass a newsstand? Write headlines that scream, "There's an astonishing and important thing happening right now. Read all about it!"

How do you wake up a sleepy-eyed reader sitting at the breakfast table, paging through your thick Sunday edition, who might not pay attention very long? Write a great lead sentence, and put all the pertinent information in the first paragraph or two.

The average Web surfer is not unlike the parent driving through an unfamiliar town past dinnertime. To meet the need as the howls of discontent from the back of the minivan increase, one has to put up the equivalent of a statue of Paul Bunyan waving a sign with flashing lights that reads "Eat at My Family Restaurant!"

In other words, give something away; have a contest. At the least, provide a tantalizing way to promise great benefits if only the reader will click a step or two further into your Web site.

Step Six: Arrange a Trail of Words

In terms of writing, this means: *Direct the eye*. Attract readers with headlines and leads and, when you have captured their attention, lead them along, deeper and deeper into the substance of your message. Give them brief, concise, snappy copy to read, and show them visually where you want their eyes to go. Give them a path to follow using subheads and lists. We don't need to discover a new world here, but only to follow the trail that experienced journalists and advertising professionals have blazed for years.

Examples from the Web

Now you can look at some sites on the Web to learn how others who are using (or not using) these techniques summarized in my Six-Step Program for Web composition.

The Front Page Meets the Home Page

An online newspaper is the perfect place to see how journalistic approaches apply to the Web. Let's go back to the Mercury Center server of the *San Jose Mercury News,* shown in Figure 9.2 (Reprinted with permission of Mercury Center, http:/ www.sjmercury.com).

Look at the Today's Newspaper screen in Figure 9.2. It doesn't hit you with a lot of words at once. Rather, you see the art of the headline in action: a series of teasers designed to draw your eye into a topic and tell you what it's about in a flash.

Painless Writing for the Web:
Style and Content

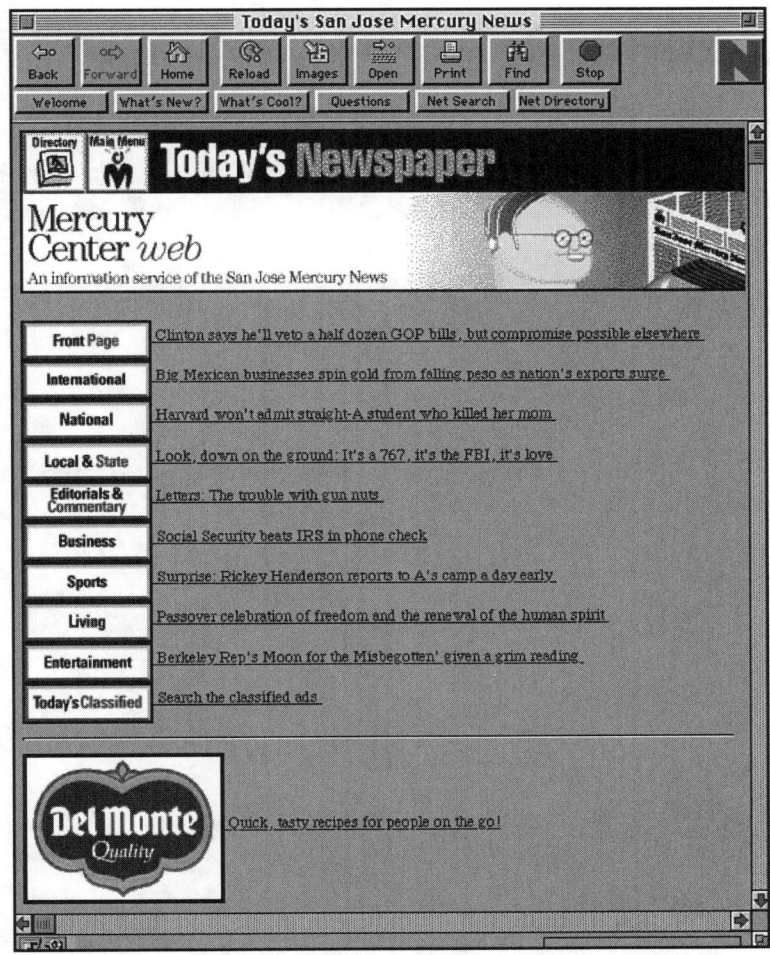

Figure 9.2 Mercury Center "Today's Newspaper" page. Note the interactive ad at the bottom.

Click the heading "Today's San Jose Mercury News" and you still don't get a large block of type, but rather, a new series of headlines, each one a link to the full story, and a one- or two-sentence lead for each story, as shown in Figure 9.3 (also reprinted with permission).

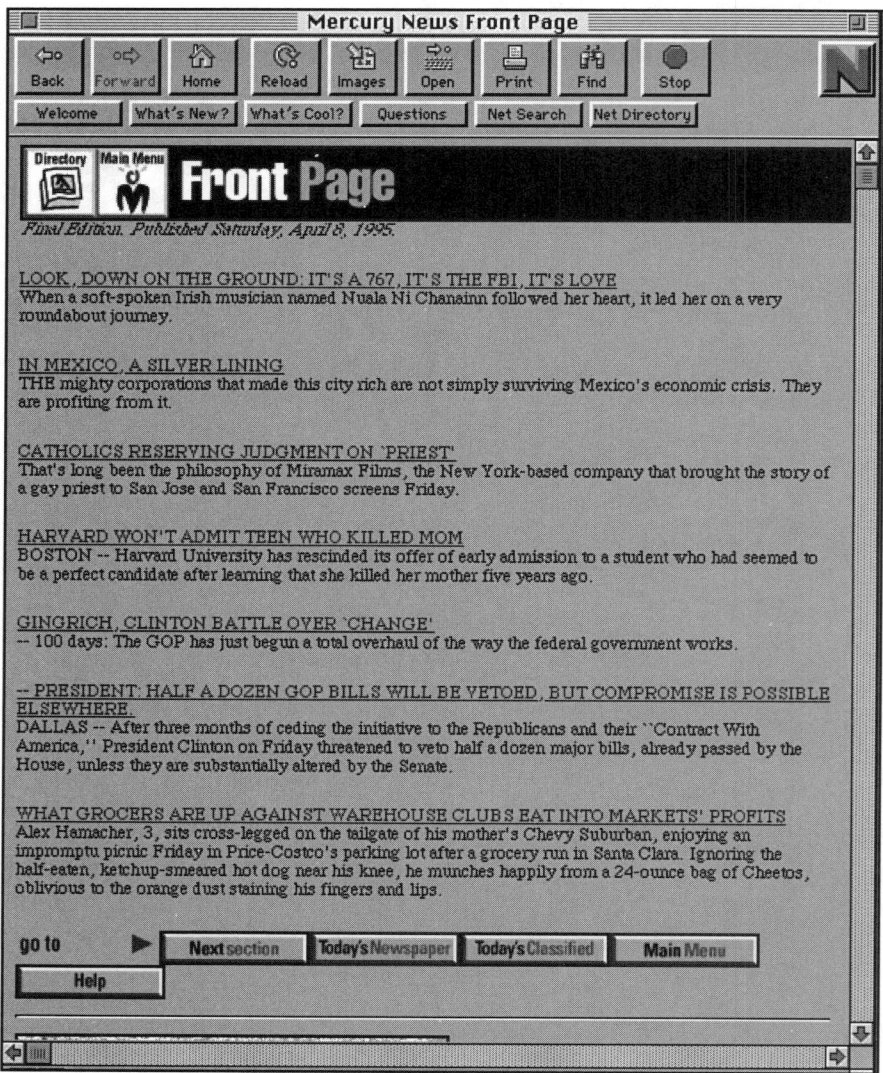

Figure 9.3 Mercury Center "Front Page." Note the well-written leads, particularly in the last story.

What this indicates is that it might be a good idea to lead your reader gradually into your text. Of course, you run the risk of making the readers click so many pages that they will lose interest and go elsewhere, but even if that happens it was better to have had them for a few brief shining moments than to never have captured them at all (besides, they might come back later).

Headlines that Kick, Startle, and Grab

Where to Find It

After offering its online service for free for several months and building up a sizable readership, the *San Jose Mercury News* now charges a monthly fee for full access. You can access headlines and news summaries at http://www.sjmercury.com/.

Where to Find It

You can access a list of some newspaper publishers with online services in operation or under development at http://marketplace.com/e-papers.list.www/e-papers.home.page.html.

Another idea you need to understand is what makes a good headline. My ideal headline:

- Is short ("Wall Street Lays Egg").

- Tells you at a glance what's happening ("President Killed").

- Startles and entices ("Browsing the Web: Better Than Sex?").

- Whenever possible, puns or refers to something other than its story ("The Rhodes Not Taken," a story about fellowships; "Strokes of Genius," a story about a college crew team).

- Conveys a sense of the emotion or feeling associated with the event or topic ("At Last—The 4-Minute Mile").

Although you probably aren't describing a news story, many of the same principles apply to the Web. Announce yourself clearly; *shout* to readers why they should be interested in you.

Put yourself in the reader's place. Try to answer these questions:

- Why would someone want what I have to offer?

- How am I different from all the others who are similar to me?

Keep in mind that the Web readers will be asking:

- What can I gain or learn by looking at this Web site?

- What's in this for me?

You can spice up virtually any straightforward heading by telling your audience something specific about your product or service. You also can divide the heading into two parts by a colon or a smaller, secondary head called a "kicker." Here are some examples:

- For an electronic shopping mall:

    Dull: *Online Shopping Mall*

    Better: *Your One-Stop Shopping Place for Electronic Wonders*

    With a pushy but attention-getting kicker:

    Online Shopping Mall

    Warning: Our Electronic Deals Will Shock You!

- For a law firm:

    Dull: *John Q. Advocate, Attorney at Law*

    Better: *The Best Little Law Firm in Santa Monica*

    Classier: *The Peoples' Legal Advocate: John Q. Advocate, Probate/Legal Expert*

- For a newspaper:

    Dull: *The Chicago Tribune Home Page*

    Better: *Chicago's Premier Information Source: The Chicago Tribune*

    Clever: *News Without Paper: The Tribune Online*

- For a small business:

    Dull: *Steve Quick Jewelers*

    Better: *Chicago's Electronic Jewelry Store*

    Mysterious: *Diamonds in the Web*

Provide More than a Row of Buttons

Now you can look on the Web for some more examples of good and not-so-good headings and how they can be integrated with a home page layout to inform and attract the viewer.

One ineffective technique commonly seen on the Web is the "row of buttons" syndrome. Look at this well-known company's home page, shown in Figure 9.4 (Web page is copyright of FedEx, Inc.).

Figure 9.4 FedEx home page in Spring, 1995.

This page needs some good headlines, especially because there are no flashy photos or logos to call attention to it. Instead, you see a row of buttons. There isn't a problem with lining up the buttons, themselves, but with the lack of information

307

Where to Find It

I may not like its home page, but I use FedEx all the time. They can be found at http://www. fedex.com/.

accompanying them. What reason other than blind curiosity (or a need to complain about an undelivered package, in which case you might as well use the phone) would make you want to click here? The dull headings don't provide any enticement to do so. And when you do click the first one, what do you get? Another row of buttons, only this time with a set of links, shown in Figure 9.5.

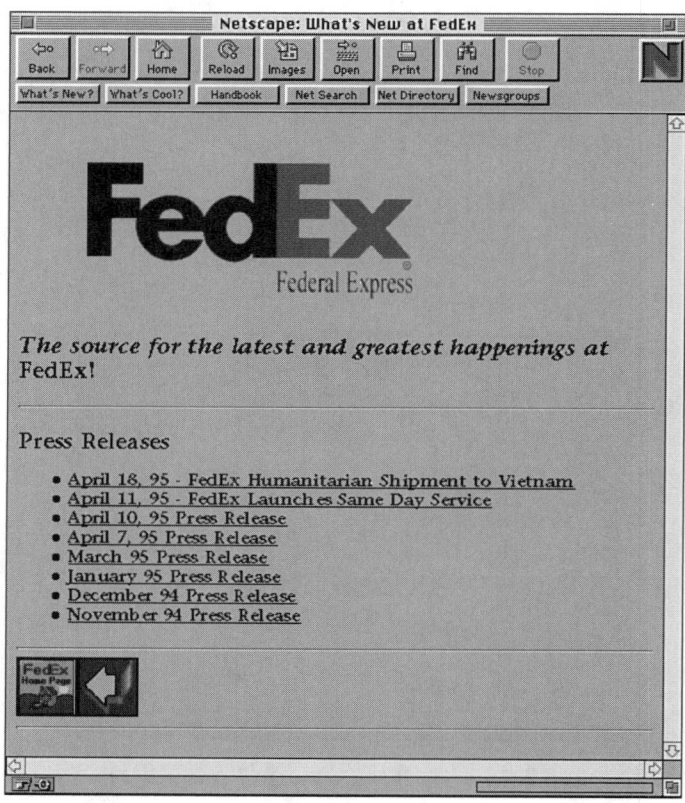

Figure 9.5 "What's New at FedEx" page. (Copyright of FedEx, Inc.)

Painless Writing for the Web:
Style and Content

Unless viewers are looking for a specific person or office in the company, they will move on after confronting this.

Figure 9.6 contains an example of a more user-friendly home page that promises benefits with the first click.

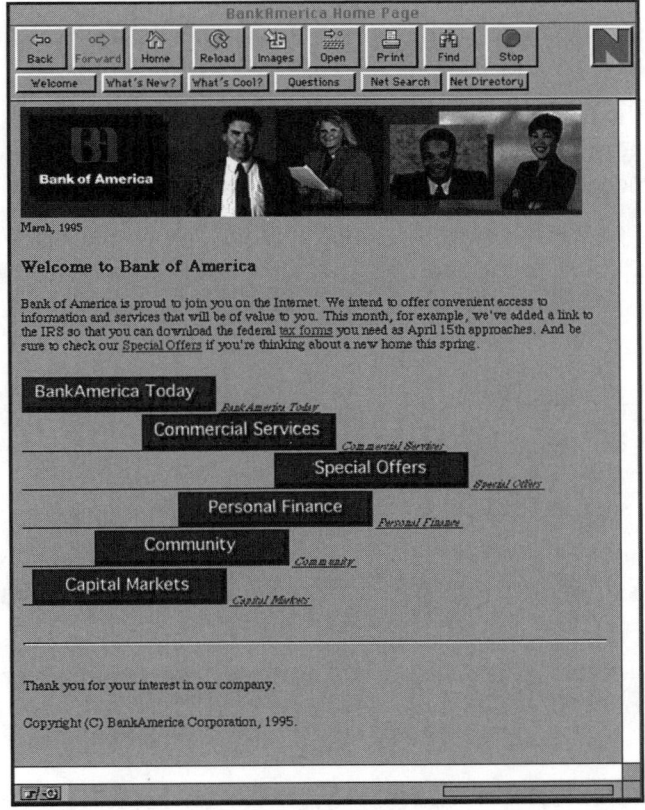

Figure 9.6 Bank of America home page (Copyright Bank America, Corp.).

This page isn't perfect (it could use some better headings), but it does have a nice "human" logo that shows people (presumably) benefiting from the bank and its services (remember the viewer's question: What's in this for me?). More important, though, the page tells you *why you should read it,* and hints at what you will receive when you click to subsequent pages. There's a contest, and there is a link to the IRS where you can download tax forms.

Now go back to the FedEx home page and apply some of the principles you've learned. First, you could create a logo of a friendly person in a FedEx uniform handing a package to a happy customer (which I don't do here). Then you could put a subhead under the main FedEx heading:

Overnight, On Time, and Now, Online!

Then you could hit them between the eyes with exactly why they should read this page:

> Welcome to the FedEx home page, where you can <u>Track Your Package</u> with just a click of your mouse. Enter our <u>Contest</u> to win free overnight delivery, and give us instant <u>Feedback</u> on our service (including our new Web server).

Then, you could create some alternative text next to the buttons and perk up the previous headings:

- <u>Just how does my package get there on a Sunday and 49 other fast facts about FedEx</u>

- <u>Win Free Overnight Delivery!</u>

- <u>Track Your Package With Quick Clicks</u>

The result can be seen in Figure 9.7.

Note that I also took out some of the whitespace that made the page look so empty, moved the images down to break up the row of buttons, and shortened the captions under those images.

Now that you've looked at the elements that lead the Web surfer into your site, you need to provide something good to read: the actual text.

Good Leads Make Web Surfers Read

A "lead" is the traditional term for the opening of a news story. A good lead tells the reader what the story is about in as few words as possible, and gets the reader interested enough to read further.

Painless Writing for the Web:
Style and Content

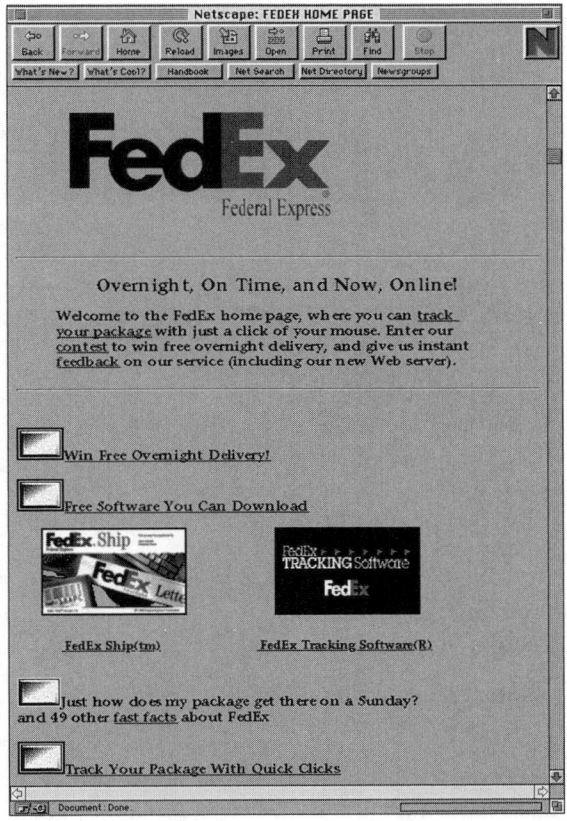

Figure 9.7 Redesigned FedEx home page (copyright FedEx, Inc.).

On the Web, a lead isn't necessarily the opening of a substantial bit of prose. It can also be a summary that a search engine like InfoSeek or a Web directory like Yahoo uses to describe your site. It can also be a short introduction to your home page like the passage added to the previous FedEx page, which guides the reader to a button or link to look at the rest of your Web.

Some of the great leads in newspapers are as simple as:

Lindbergh did it. [2]

"Four days in hell" would be the most fitting way to describe the siege and capture of Nanking.[3]

311

The following lead is especially relevant to Web writing because the writer, Leland Stowe, promotes his own story even as he presents information. He tells you what is special about it and why you should read on:

> Here is the first and only eyewitness report on the opening chapter of the British expeditionary troops' advance in Norway north of Trondheim. It is a bitterly disillusioning and almost unbelievable story.[4]

Even though you aren't describing a battlefield scene for your readers or telling them about a murder, the lead for your Web story should be short and to the point. It should make someone want to find out more about your product, service, or organization.

You don't have to provide every bit of detail in your lead. A common problem (which can be seen in the leads of many newspaper stories today) occurs when the writer tries to put everything into the lead, resulting in a long, rambling sentence that seems to go on and on, rolling through several clauses, and comma after comma— even including dashes—before it grinds to a halt.

In fact, it's better to hold something back. The promise of further information "hooks" people into reading more. The trick is to know what not to say, and what to highlight. Here's a famous example:

> John Dillinger, ace bad man of the world, got his last night—two slugs through his heart and one through his head.[5]

That's certainly good enough to keep you wanting more information, but the reporter, Jack Lait, closed that first paragraph with a dynamite hook that would make anyone read on:

> He was tough and he was shrewd, but he wasn't as tough and shrewd as the Federals, who never close a case until the end. It took twenty-seven of them to end Dillinger's career, and their strength came out of his weakness—a woman.[6]

In general, you want to add anything that will convey some bit of information or even just a feeling about the story to get someone to read it all. The types of leads one sees in business and other communications vary widely, but the effective ones go beyond just the facts to get readers emotionally invested so that they care what comes next.

After the lead, you have to pack a punch. You can't be a tease and make the readers wait too long to find out what's going on. They might dump you before reaching the end of your text or, sorry to say, even the bottom of the screen. The payoff is a straightforward statement that contains who, what, where, how, and/or when. ("Why" can be explained in the body of the story.) Again, journalists have already figured out a way to get all the important information up front, called the "inverted pyramid."

The Inverted Pyramid

In traditional journalism, news stories are written like an "inverted pyramid." The top of the pyramid is broad because most of the factual information is presented in the beginning (the assumption usually being that the further the fickle readers move through your story, the greater the chances that they will stop reading it and move on to something else).

This technique is also useful for lazy editors who can cut the story when the space in the page layout is filled, because they know that each paragraph is less important than the one preceding it.

Here are a few Web examples of leads and following text as they can be applied to various home pages:

Information Center

The Library & Information Center is the first point of contact for thousands of calls to NAB Headquarters each year. It is a vital resource for both broadcasters and others outside the industry who seek information.

Advertiser

Want to advertise your Web Walking Ways?

Want to show everyone you love to Surf the 'Net?

Do both with a shirt from Mighty Dog Designs!

Bookstore

Softpro Books OnLine is an extension of Softpro Books, a retail computer bookstore. We've been in the Boston area for ten years and opened a second store in Denver in September of 1992. Our goal is to be the best computer bookstore anywhere.

Club

When it comes to wine clubs, nobody knows Napa like A Taste of Ambrosia. That's because unlike other "out-of-town" clubs, we're right here, in the heart of California's wine country.

Small Business

Welcome to a place where Entrepreneurs the world over can find useful business information and offer their goods and services to other Entrepreneurs.

College or University

Discover the world and your place in it.

At Trinity College, we'll teach you the classics and chemistry, cubism and impressionism, existentialism and social contract, Kafka and Kerouac. But what we can't teach you is what you'll teach yourself: the insight that comes from everyday conversations with the poets, scientists, mathematicians and historians who are the students and faculty of Trinity.

Press Release

Bolt Beranek and Newman Inc. (BBN) today announced an agreement under which it will build, maintain, and operate a limited portion of the America Online (AOL) nationwide, high-speed, dial-in network.

Topic Paragraphs

Sometimes one paragraph isn't enough to cover a more complex topic. You then have to explain the subject in two or three topic paragraphs. On the Web, each topic should have its own document. After covering a topic, provide a link to the next one.

Within each document, try to be aware of the following general rules:

- Make sure there is a *topic sentence* at the end of the first (sometimes second) sentence of the paragraph.

- Put conclusions, latest developments, or summaries in the last sentence of a paragraph.

Painless Writing for the Web: Style and Content

Where to Find It

National Association of Broadcasters (NAB) Library & Information Center: http://nab.org/www/userguid/libhome.html
Mighty Dog Designs: http://sashimi.wwa.com:80/~notime/Mighty_Dog_Designs.

Softpro Books: http://plaza.xor.com/softpro/index.html.

A Taste of Ambrosia Wine Club: http://www.shopping2000.com/shopping2000/ambrosia/.

Entrepreneurs on the Web: http://sashimi.wwa.com/~notime/eotw/EOTW.html.

Trinity College online viewbook: http://rytter.com/rytter/trinity/.

BBN: http://www.near.net/doc/news.html.

- "News" or material that should be emphasized should be moved right, toward the end of a sentence. Transitions or less important information, move left.

- Organize your subject either chronologically or by cause-and-effect arguments in the middle of a paragraph.

- Boring or extraneous material should be cut. If you can't cut it, bury it in mid-paragraph.

Keep Your Web Documents Short

It's a good idea to break a longer document into several sections that each discuss a discrete topic or aspect of your overall subject. Often you'll see, either on the Web or in books about it, admonitions about keeping your documents to a specific length, such as one and a half or two "screens" in length. I prefer the commonsense advice of Tim Berners-Lee, the creator the Web, who suggests that rather than meeting an arbitrary quota, each document represent a coherent thought and end when another subject begins.

Here's one way to do this. Say you have a single ten-page document, "My Life Story." Take it and save it as five or six separate documents arranged like so:

I Am Born (.5 pp.)

My Childhood (1 pp.)

School Years (1.5 pp.)

The Starving Artist (2 pp.)

Marriage and Respectability (1.5 pp.)

Life Begins at Forty (1.5 pp.)

Convert each document to HTML format using one of the methods described in Part II. At the end of "I Am Born," for instance, skip a line, and include the following two links:

Back to <u>My Life Story</u>, on to <u>My Childhood</u>.

Do this for each one of the documents. (See Chapter 10 for more on organizing a group of documents.)

Leading the Reader On

At the end of each document, you should write a transitional "hook" that gives the reader a glimpse of what's coming and entices the reader to click to the next link in your page rather than escaping to the next site.

In the previous example, you might end the document "My Childhood" as follows:

But the traumas of my childhood were nothing compared with what was to follow.

On to <u>School Years</u>, back to <u>I Am Born</u>

You can do this also when there is no narrative involved and you are simply presenting information, as in a set of instructions about organizing a Web site:

The next step is to name your Web site and tell people who you are.

On to <u>Identification</u>, back to <u>home page</u>.

Writing Captions for Photos and Graphics

Is this writing? You bet your sweet ASCII file it is. Everybody knows what a caption is. It's a short bit of text describing what's in a photo or graphic. With the new capability of HTML 3.0 or Netscape's extensions to HTML to arrange text and graphics, a caption can become a practical part of a Web document. A caption doesn't have to be a simple listing of who's in a photo ("Standing, left to right, are Mayor Jones, his wife," and so on).

Here are some ways to use captions to spice up your Web site:

- A caption can be another graphic element for your page. Put a subhead above the caption, bold, in H5 or H6 style, to draw attention to it. Example:

Hard-Workin' Dad

Prolific author Greg Holden steals a moment from a smoking keyboard to face the media with his daughter, Lucy.

- The shorter the caption, the better. 'Nuf said.

- Start your caption with a humorous phrase ending in a colon. Example:

Riding the Wave: A new breed of cybersurfers are marketing their services on the Web.

- Don't rely on complete sentences. A phrase that captures drama or emotion is better than a complete sentence that produces a "So what?".

Observing Rules of Style in Your Web Document

When you are preparing the content of your Web site, make sure that what you are writing doesn't clash with either the style of your organization or with generally accepted rules of grammar and word usage.

Style, in this context, doesn't refer to writing style or the elements of a home page; it refers to the rules editors and writers follow when deciding how to capitalize, abbreviate, or spell out references to people, places, and things.

Why Should You Bother?

Style is important not only for you but for your company. It's important for you because, as the viewer clicks through the various documents you publish on your Web site, reading them will be easier if they have a consistent appearance and writing style. It will also make your work look more professional, and thus more believable.

Adding style can be as simple as

- Using the same styles of heading from page to page.

- Starting each document with a common banner or logo.

- Adding links to a home page or other elements common to every document in the same place on every document.

Where to Find It

The University of Illinois online writers' handbook contains information on constructing bibliographies, and promises to contain more information about punctuation, grammar, and style: gopher://gopher.uiuc.edu/11/ Libraries/Writers.

In terms of writing, it means capitalizing the same business titles like "president" the same way and punctuating consistently from document to document. It means writing simply and clearly, without explaining too much or overwriting; it means deciding on a design for your work and sticking to it.

If you are fuzzy on rules of punctuation and usage, use the style manual published by your university or company, or use a generally accepted authority such as *The Chicago Manual of Style* or *The Elements of Style* by Strunk and White.

What's a Style Manual?

A style manual can be several things:

- A place where someone has, in writing, the answers to the various questions that come up again and again in written text. Used so that all the material your organization publishes is consistent.

- A place where all the information pertinent to usage and copyediting is compiled, such as *The Chicago Manual of Style*.

- A set of conventions adopted by your organization in order to achieve an appropriate institutional look for your publication.

The widely recognized authority in matters stylistic is *The Chicago Manual of Style*. I'm not just saying that because I work at the University where it's produced. This book has been put out by the U of C Press since 1906, and the latest edition, the 14th, has new information on the role of computers in publishing and in copyright law.

In case you can't get a copy or are in a hurry, the following section contains my own list of the ten most common questions about punctuation and capitalization that I tend to come across in my work. After each is the reference in *The Chicago Manual of Style* that discusses the subject in greater detail.

Ten Common Rules of Style

Without further ado, here are the ten most common guidelines. Remember that these are only guidelines; you can use whichever styles you are comfortable with. The key is to be consistent.

1. At the end of a series of three or more items, put a comma before the "and" that introduces the last item. (5.26)

   Remember to use anchors, links, and tags properly.

2. Capitalize a person's title when it's used before the name, but not after. (7.18-22)

   Chief Executive Officer Vinton G. Cerf; Vinton Cerf, chief executive officer; the chief executive officer

3. Spell out whole numbers from one through ninety-nine and any of these followed by hundred, thousand, and so on; use figures for all others. (8.3)

   The three new Web sites attracted 5,020 users the first week.

4. Italicize titles of books, movies, magazines, newspapers, plays, long poems, paintings, and other works of art, and long musical compositions. Put quotation marks around titles of short stories, short poems, songs, newspaper or magazine articles, and television shows. (7.129-148)

   Fictional visions of computers range from *HAL 9000 in 2001: A Space Odyssey* to the benign voice in the original "Star Trek" series.

5. If a parenthetical item is a full sentence, the period goes inside the parenthesis. If it is a phrase within a sentence, the period goes outside. (5.10)

   It's best to have at least 4 MB of memory to run Netscape or Mosaic (8 MB would be better). (Of course, part of this can be virtual memory.)

6. Double quotation marks go outside a period. Single quotation marks go inside a period. (5.10)

    "I can't believe what my computer just said." He said this to me with a demented smile. "It said, 'You have new mail'."

7. Add apostrophe-s to make a possessive of a proper name ending in "s" or another sibilant except for the names *Jesus* and *Moses* and most names ending with the *-eez* sound. (6.12-21)

    Steve Jobs' s new company; in Jesus' name; R. S. Surtees' novels

8. Use three dots for an ellipsis within a sentence. Four dots are used for the omission of the beginning or end of a sentence, a whole sentence, or a paragraph. *The Chicago Manual of Style* specifies putting blank spaces between the periods, but this won't work online. (10.36-44)

    The attached document describes in more detail a Hypertext project....The project has two phases...we make use of existing software and hardware...we extend the application area....Phase One should take three months....

9. Use a semicolon between two parts of a compound sentence and don't use it with *and* or *but* (unless the sentences are very long). (5.68-73)

    Scotty stared anxiously at the computer screen; he couldn't hold it together much longer.

10. *That* is used to define*; which* is used for special emphasis. (See Strunk and White, *The Elements of Style, p.47.*)

    I wanted to access the mail that was held by my Internet provider.

    I bought this modem, which was once the fastest, but it is already obsolete.

Where to Find It

A list of online writing laboratories, writing consultants, and other resources for writers can be found at http://owl.trc.purdue.edu/writing-labs.html. If you want to discuss fine points of grammar and syntax, check out the Usenet newsgroup misc.writing.

A Large Organization's Web Style

A consistent style is important for a large organization such as a university because many different offices within it may be creating home pages. Ideally, those Web sites should be coordinated in some way, either by a common graphic element such as a logo or by writing style, so they don't sound like they're coming from 25 separate organizations with 25 disparate messages.

Carnegie Mellon University, for instance, is making an effort to achieve a consistent identity among the home pages created by its many departments. It created two sizes of masthead and specified its style and look (these apply to the masthead, not to the HTML text):

- Helvetica compressed type.

- Default Photoshop kerning.

- 42 pt. type for large mastheads.

- 32 pt. type for small mastheads.

Where to Find It

See http://www.cmu.edu/ cmufront/style-guide/ style.guide.html for more on the Carnegie Mellon style guide.

Where to Find It

The main University of Chicago "welcome" page can be found at http://www.uchicago.edu/. The complete list of servers is at http://www.uchicago.edu/ Servers.html.

The University of Chicago, in contrast, is rather decentralized, and is not attempting to achieve a single "look and feel" for its home pages. Rather, it is concentrating on organizing its general "welcome" page so people can easily find its various departments' home pages.

Netscape, for instance, often uses the same style of heading for its home page and related pages. All headings are in caps, but the first letter of each word is slightly larger than the rest.

A large corporation should have an easier time imposing a consistent identity to materials published on the Web. Come up with a logo that complements your official publications or stationery (remember to keep the file size small so it can open quickly over the Internet or via its internal network; see Chapter 12, "Designing Pages for the Web"), and make that logo available to others either on the Web or through file sharing.

[1] Rowsome, Frank Jr., *The Verse By the Side of the Road,* (Lexington, MA: The Stephen Greene Press, 1965), 50-51.

[2] *The New York Times,* May 23, 1927, quoted in *A Treasury of Great Reporting*, ed. Louis L. Snyder and Richard B. Morris (New York: Simon and Schuster, 1949), 447.

[3] *Chicago Daily News*, December 15, 1937, quoted in *A Treasury of Great Reporting,* ed. Louis L. Snyder and Richard B. Morris (New York: Simon and Schuster, 1949), 520.

[4] *Chicago Daily News*, April 25, 1940, quoted in *A Treasury of Great Reporting,* 555.

[5] International News Service, July 23, 1934, quoted in *A Treasury of Great Reporting,* 506.

[6] International News Service, July 23, 1934, quoted in *A Treasury of Great Reporting,* 506.

Copyediting, Proofreading, and Presenting Your Web Documents

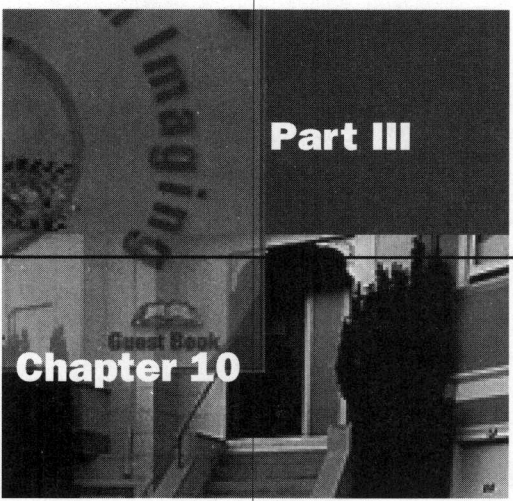

Part III

Chapter 10

Publishing your Web documents without carefully copyediting and proofreading them for errors is like walking around with your zipper open in front of 13.5 million people.

Yet, that's what a surprising number of Web publishers choose to do. Don't be the one getting strange instead of admiring looks at the party because there is spinach between your teeth.

After spending time and effort to create the perfect copy for your Web site, you owe it to yourself to check it over thoroughly both before and after it goes online—or to help out your colleagues in your organization by editing or proofreading what they are preparing to put out on the Web.

You don't have to look far to see evidence of the problem. I am continually amazed by the number and variety of typographical errors and grammatical blunders I see on the Web. Click Yahoo's "A Random Link" feature and I will bet that within five home pages you will find a document with typos. Some of my favorites follow.

Top Ten Typos Found on the Web

1. This counts as five typos in one ("You're," not "Your"; "half way," not "half-way"; semicolon after "there"; just underline the word or phrase, not the space before or after it; and lowercase "To"):

   Your half-way there click <u>Cyteria Plaza </u>To finish your journey.

2. The actual type, including the typo in "Government," was much bigger onscreen:

   ASUC
   STUDENT GOVERMENT

3. I've highlighted the typos in bold. Only one year is being discussed, so it should be singular, not plural:

   The CBD is now available on the Internet. This means that from your own PC you can search the CBD before it's published. You can search it daily or whenever you want because the entire **years'** worth of issues **are** available on-line

   Yet what makes the CBD on Internet so unique is its ability to isolate, in seconds, precisely what you're looking for—whether **its** all the bids and awards...

4. The correct spelling is "Aviation":

   About the DOE Avaiation Gopher

5. Should be "Computer," not "Computers":

Welcome To The Acadia University
Computers Science Club Server

6. "Century," not "centrury":

ECO-MOTION
ELECTRIC CARS
The 21st centrury just can't wait.

7. Can you find the typo? Remember, one space after a period at the end of a sentence.

CRAY COMPUTER CORPORATION REPORTS 1994 FINANCIAL RESULTS

Seymour R Cray, Chairman and CEO, stated that, "We are getting close to the point where our new product, the CRAY-4 supercomputer, can be manufactured...we engaged Marleau, Lemire Securities, Inc., in January 1995, to assist the Company with an equity financing to institutional investors. S Marleau, Lemire, Securities, Inc., is a public-traded full service investment dealer, primarily engaged..."

8. A missing apostrophe (Internets) in a subhead in an otherwise well-written and thoughtful essay by Vinton G. Cerf, "Origins and Evolution in Cyberspace":

Internets Legal, Social, and Economic Side-effects

9. Two "e"s, not three:

ACC - Computer Application
Committeee

10. Sometimes, typos show up not in an HTML document but in software computer code. This isn't something that you, the reader/publisher, can prevent directly. But it shows that anyone can make a mistake. This came up in a Netscape dialog box while downloading a file (it should be "has run," not "has ran."):

Load has been interrupted because Netscape has ran out of memory.

In case you're thinking, "Loosen up, it's *just* the Web," or "it's *just* the online version," consider this: When was the last time you put your business, your organization, or yourself before a potential audience of 13.5 million people? If your Web page looks bad, *you* look bad. In the print world, a typo or other mistake will result in a reprint. One of the advantages of publishing on the Web is that you don't have to pay extra to fix a mistake—all the more reason to fix it. The first way to fix a mistake is by copyediting it.

Copyediting Your Web Document

The same procedures involved in copyediting print publications apply to copyediting online publications. The difference is that Web documents don't always exist in print. They may exist only electronically. There is a temptation to simply scan the text onscreen and pronounce it OK.

Call me old-fashioned, but I believe it's easier to copyedit on paper than onscreen. It's also an easier way for someone else to do the editing, especially if that someone else is not comfortable with computers. Therefore, I suggest that you print out your document in order to edit it.

Copyediting refers to the process of closely reading and correcting text to free it of spelling and grammatical errors and improve its readability. If the author didn't refer to a style manual (or to the previous chapter of this book) during the actual composition, this is the stage in which rules of style are implemented. What I do with any document is compile a style sheet (see the section entitled "Make a Style Sheet").

Where to Find It

A good source for general information about copyediting can be found in Chapter 2 of *The Chicago Manual of Style*. There's a good Web-related style guide at http://info.med.yale.edu/caim/Manual_Intro.HTML, and a list of guides to writing HTML documents at http://www.muw.edu/general/guides.html.

What follows are rules I use and recommend to avoid the sheer sloppiness of what I see on the Web. Perhaps there is something in the Web's nature that makes people hurry along with production and skip over essential stages they would never ignore in print. Anyway, here's some brief information about copyediting.

Some General Rules

The following five rules apply to proofreading as well as copyediting. The first rule bears some explanation. The others are pretty self-explanatory:

Rule 1: Find another pair of eyes.

The best way to copyedit or proofread is to find someone else to do it. This is not a way of passing the buck. If you have done the writing, chances are you are too close to the job and know it too well to check it carefully. In the old days, one person read the proofs out loud while another person scanned the original to see whether there were any mistakes. Few of us can afford the time to do that these days, but it's still probably the most reliable technique.

Besides, there may be someone in your office who has a gift for finding mistakes. Usually this is someone who is looking at your text for the first time. This can happen even after many pairs of eyes have gone over the copy. A few years ago, as we were doing the final printout of our college's course catalog, I found the words "Social Asian Studies" in the section on South Asian Studies. It's the kind of mistake a spell-check program won't pick up.

Rule 2: Print your text so it can be edited or proofread on paper.

Rule 3: Don't edit or proofread when you're tired. Take breaks frequently.

Rule 4: Try to find Hemingway's proverbial clean, well-lighted place. To avoid distraction, it often helps to be somewhere other than your office or usual work area.

Rule 5: Keep track of your place with a ruler or straightedge as you go down the page, so you are looking only at one line of type at a time and can find your way back easily.

Things to Look For

When you do read, make sure your document:

- Says what you want it to say;
- Doesn't use redundant or unnecessary words or phrases, dangling modifiers, or split infinitives;
- Is consistent in tone, punctuation, and spelling with other documents on your page;

327

- Uses character entity substitutes for special characters such as accent marks or ampersands that won't show up on other computers or on all Web browsers (see the following section); and

- Doesn't make references that an international audience won't recognize.

How to Handle Special Characters

Most of the characters you see on your computer keyboard will be recognized and displayed correctly when your document is translated into HTML. However, special characters such as those with accents (à, ü, ç) don't translate and have to be handled in a special way.

Don't be fooled by the fact that your own Web browser seems to display curly quotes or apostrophes correctly on your own screen. That doesn't mean they will show up on a UNIX or Windows computer. Each computer manufacturer has its own idea about how to do accents, and none of them match.

The problem is that HTML recognizes any characters you type that are included in the standard (7-bit) ASCII character set but not the "upper" (8-bit) characters.

What the heck does that mean? Every character that you type has to be recognized by a computer by a series of binary numbers (zeros and ones). ASCII (American Standard Code for Information Interchange) was agreed upon years ago as a standard set of these binary equivalents for characters. The ASCII set of 7-bit characters includes 128 possible characters. These are the set HTML recognizes. There is another set of 128 characters coded with 8 bits of information that may not be accessible from your keyboard or that some computers may not be equipped to deal with.

The way to handle these "special" characters is to substitute a special set of codes called *character entities*. Most Web browsers support the Latin-1 character entity accents defined by the International Standards Organization (ISO). They have to be typed in a special form.

> **Tip:** If, like me, you're not all that comfortable with computer code, let a software program do the work for you. Web Weaver is one HTML editor that will automatically insert character entity references for the more common special characters.

Where to Find It

Web Weaver is discussed further in Chapter 7, "HTML Authoring Assistants." You can find out more about it at http://www.potsdam.edu/Web.Weaver/About.html.

The form to follow is a mnemonic for the name of the accent enclosed between the two characters "&" and "; " (ampersand and semicolon) like this: **´**. To get the word Résumé, you type

Résumé

A complete list of character entities appears in Appendix F. The character entities allow you to include special characters that aren't part of the standard ASCII character set. However, you must also provide entities for the characters that have special meaning in HTML. Here's a list of special characters to watch out for.

You should realize, though, that just because an HTML character entity exists doesn't mean that the correct character will appear. Not all browsers support all characters (try **þ** for the Icelandic thorn, for example).

- **&** produces an ampersand (&)
- **<** produces the less-than (<) sign
- **>** produces the greater-than (>) sign
- ** ** produces a non-breaking en space
- ** ** produces a non-breaking em space
- **"** produces the double-quotation sign

Note: Non-breaking spaces aren't recognized by all Web browsers, and to be on the safe side, you should probably avoid them. But watch out for any that may be lurking in your original word processing or page layout document if you're converting the contents to HTML.

Where to Find It

A list of ISO Latin 1 character entities can be found at http://www.w3.org./hypertext/WWW/MarkUp/ISO1at1.html.

Don't Make Obscure References

On the Web, you are writing for a potential worldwide audience, so be sure to explain any acronyms or obscure local references—especially acronyms—that a foreign browser won't understand. If you're making a local reference, people outside your own city might not even know what you're talking about, either. For example:

"One can reach UIC either by CTA, I-90, or Harrison Avenue."

should be:

"One can reach the University of Illinois at Chicago either by Chicago Transit Authority bus or train, the Eisenhower Expressway (I-90), or by walking west on Harrison Avenue from downtown."

Make a Style Sheet

To help achieve consistency between documents, compile a style sheet. A style sheet helps an editor keep track of special words with distinctive spellings, compound words with or without hyphens, and the like. In Web terms, a style sheet helps you to check the correct forms of links, anchors, and even a correct URL address. Figure 10.1 shows an example of what might go on a style sheet.

How to Mark Up Copy

Whether someone is editing your text, or vice versa, it will help to have at least a passing familiarity with copyeditors' marks. In general, it's better to make the marks directly above the item to be changed, between lines of type, rather than in the margin.

Copyediting, Proofreading, and
Presenting Your Web Documents

ABCD à = & agrave A HREF = cgi-bin checkbox database	MNOP network news group online Perl script
EFGH gif Hyper Card hypertext hypertextual	QRST SLIP connection "source/cgi-bin/ images/(name),html" subfolder
IJKL IMG SRC = JPEG 800 K	UVWXYZ UNIX URL

Figure 10.1 A Web document's style sheet.

Here's a handy reference to the most common marks:

- The caret (^) to insert a new letter or word

- The dot (.) or circled "x" (ⓧ) to add a period

- The close-up marks (⌒) to join separated words or letters

- "Let it stand" or, "never mind the marks I just made!" (ⓢⓣⓔⓣ)

- Insert comma (⌄)

- Insert apostrophe (⌄)

- Insert quotation marks (⁇ ⁇)

- The delete mark (◡)

But you may not have seen all of these marks:

- Spell out the whole word ((SP))

- Insert a colon or semicolon (:|), (;|)

- Transpose letters or words ((tr))

- Insert a hyphen (|=|)

- <u>CAPS and SMALL CAPS</u> (useful when you want to specify that the first letter of a word should be a point size larger than those following it, a style sometimes seen on Netscape-enhanced sites)

SpellCheckers: What They Can and Cannot Do

Where to Find It

If you want to save time doing a spell-check, you can copy this list and add it to your spellchecker's dictionary. To save retyping, I've provided a more comprehensive list and posted it on the home page for this book: http://www.mcp.com/hayden/webmacpublishing. You can copy it there.

Let's face it: There's nothing glamorous about doing a spell-check. You've written your document, you've copyedited it, now what? You have to do a spell-check too? It can be tedious and time-consuming, but think about it. How long are your materials going to reside on the Web. Months? Years? If that's the case, isn't 10 or 15 minutes of spell-checking going to pay off in the long run?

A spellchecker is a great tool, but it can't be expected to keep up with the changing language of Cyberspace. A spellchecker can be made more powerful if you customize it. The standard dictionary that came with my copy of Microsoft Word version 5.1, for instance, didn't recognize most of the following terms:

What I Checked	*SpellChecker's Suggestion*
online	on-line
Netsite	Netsuke
Cyberspace	(no suggestion)
URL	URN
HTML	HT ML
Internet	Interment
imagemap	image map
ftp	ft
http	ht.
login	logic

However, you can add all these words to your custom spellchecker to have it ignore them from now until eternity.

The Importance of Proofreading

"Let's run with it!"

Wait a minute. So you've finished your golden prose, copyedited it, scanned your photos or drawn your graphics, and are ready to put it all online. What do you do first?

1. Take a deep breath.

2. Don't put it on the Web.

3. What to do: Open it in Netscape and at least one other Web browser as a "local" file visible only to you, and proofread it.

One popular rock group's home page includes the sentence: "This is taken more or less verbatim from our OCR scanner software, so pardon any typos you see." Sorry, guys, but to my mind this is just another way of saying, "We're in too much of a hurry to bother making this easy for you to read and you're not that important, anyway." Don't skip this important step: proffread—I mean, *proofread*!

How to Proofread Text for the Web

The five rules listed previously apply to proofreading, with one addition and one difference.

Rule 6: Adjust your editing and proofreading to the document in question.

You have to do a somewhat different kind of proofreading if you are taking text from a previously published brochure or booklet or press release and putting it on the Web, or if you are writing something totally new and off-the-cuff (an introduction to the online version of your catalog, for instance). In the case of the latter, you should follow the previous steps and run your word processing program's spellchecker through it.

Do your proofreading onscreen, after you have opened your document in a Web browser. Compare the output to the original text and check for any discrepancies. In other words, make sure everything works.

> **Note:** A *proof* is a test or preliminary impression from which corrections or additions can be made. (The term applies not only to words set in type but to newly minted coins.) It has its origin in the days when type was set in lead and composed in a flat metal tray called a galley; *galley proofs* were a trial impression taken on a long slip of paper that would be compared or *proofread* against the original manuscript for errors.

In the case of the already printed publication, you can pretty much overlook typos, because presumably the text has already been edited heavily. You should watch out for the following:

- Special characters like accents, ampersands, umlauts, and less common editorial marks like daggers or pilcrows that HTML won't be able to translate.

- Soft hyphens inserted into the typeset publication to make a particular line break, but that will show up on the Web as a hard hyphen (for example, *hyphen*) in the middle of a word.

- Any "hidden" text, such as Microsoft Word's indexing and Table of Contents commands, that appears when you save in ASCII format.

> **Note:** When you proofread your document, be on the lookout for any punctuation marks that are separated from adjacent words by an HTML tag, such as <EM>acrobat</EM>. This will make it appear as though there's a blank space between the *t* and the period (acrobat .).

The Right Presentation for Your Web Document

Congratulations! Your documents are ready to go on the Web. Your text is readable, well organized, and perfectly edited and proofread, and you are beginning to get plenty of visitors. But as you enjoy the thrill of dialing into the Web from a remote computer and checking out your own home page, it seems something is missing. It doesn't really look as good as you had hoped. It needs to be spiced up and organized.

Using Subheads and Other Text Organizers

Because you are writing a document that is intended to be read primarily on a computer screen rather than on paper, you need to include more formatting elements than you do in print. The longer your text, the more "organizers" you need.

Keep in mind that your words might appear not only on a 6-1/2" tall Powerbook or MacPlus screen but on an 11" tall one-page display or even a 12" tall two-page monitor like the one that takes up much of my desk.

Try to break up a long block of text so that you never have a screen full of type, as shown in Figure 10.2.

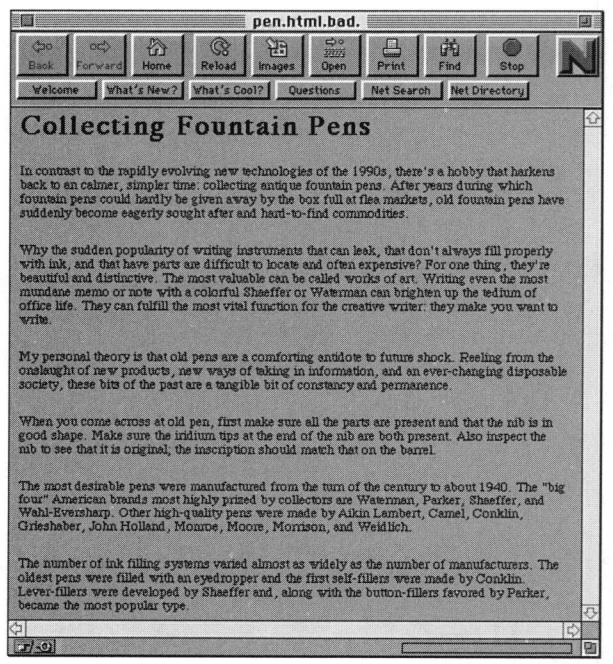

Figure 10.2 The wrong presentation for your text.

Instead, use subheads—perhaps one heading every three to four paragraphs—as well
as callouts, lists, bold, and italic, to break up the layout and make it easier to read, as
illustrated in Figure 10.3.

Subheads

Headings summarize not a whole chapter, but the subject being addressed in the
following two or three paragraphs. Use one of the smaller heading styles in HTML,
Heading 3, 4, or 5. Try them out on one or two browser screens; don't feel tied to
using Heading 3 just because the title above it is Heading 2. Pick the one that looks
best to you. The important point is to be consistent. Headings with the same level of
importance should use the same heading number.

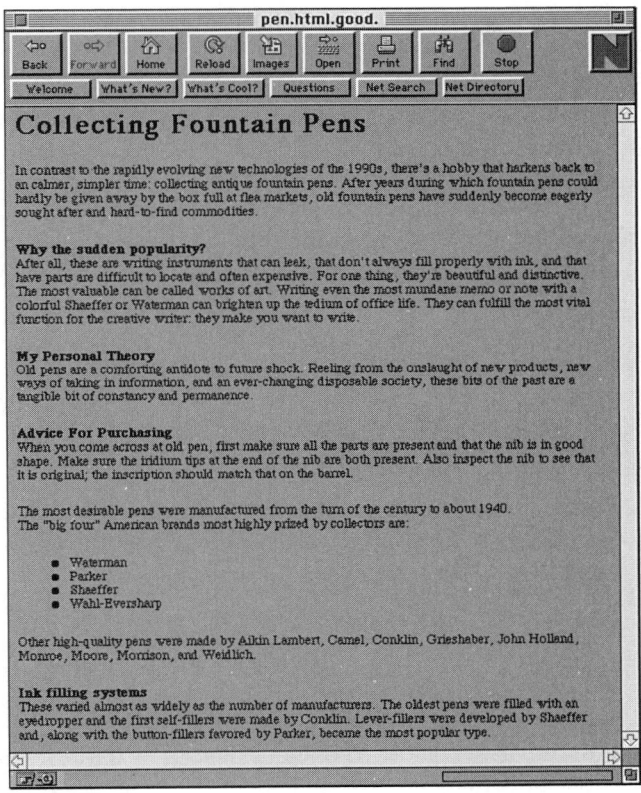

Figure 10.3 A better presentation for your text.

Lists

Lists are a great way to break up text and make it look less imposing. A list is a great way to call attention to essential items that might otherwise get buried in a paragraph. As stated in Chapter 4, "Basic HTML for Web Publishers," you can create a number of different lists: numbered lists, unordered lists, menu and directory lists, and glossary lists.

Rules

Large blocks of text can be divided into logical subgroups using horizontal rules. The <HR> or horizontal line rule tag will, of course, draw a rule across the width of your document.

Callout Quotations

Callout quotations are commonly used in newspapers to break up long stories that don't have a lot of photos or other graphics. Take an important sentence close to your central idea, and do the following.

At the end of the last paragraph before the callout quotation, add the line break tag <BR>, followed by:

```
<HR>
<H3><I><B>"There are plenty of high school students out there who love
to surf the Net, and we're going to reach out to them."</B></I>
</H3><BR>
<center>- -Joe Recruiter, dean of admissions, Online University</center>
<HR>
```

Note that I am using the <CENTER> tag, which (as of this writing, at least) is supported on Netscape, but not by all browsers. The result looks like Figure 10.4.

A more elegant alternative is permitted in one of Netscape's extensions to HTML (see Chapter 4 for more information). You can add a short, centered rule drawn as follows:

```
<HR ALIGN="center" WIDTH=35%>
<H3><I><B>"There are plenty of young professionals with disposable
change out there who love to surf the Net, and we're going to reach into
their pockets."</B></I></H3><BR>
<center>- -Frank Greedly, president, Online Shopping Network</center>
<HR ALIGN="center" WIDTH=35%>
```

The result is shown in Figure 10.5.

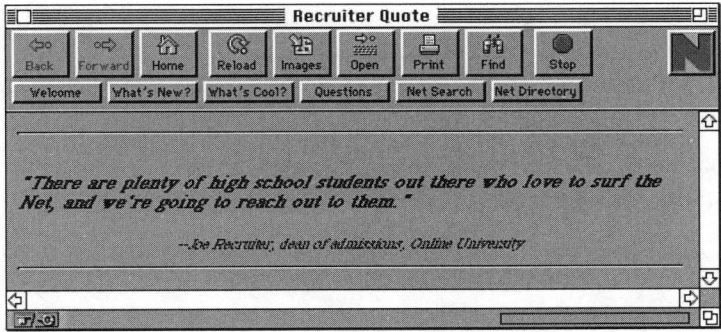

Figure 10.4 A callout quotation with horizontal rules.

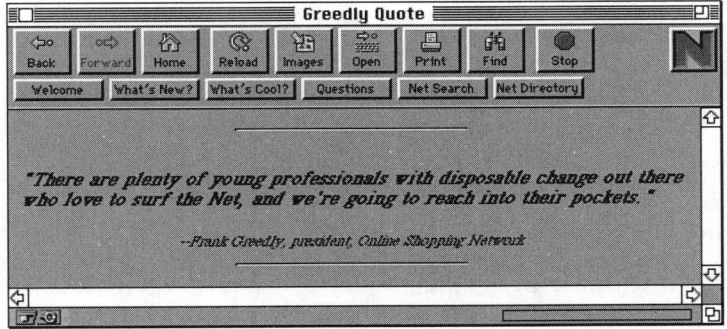

Figure 10.5 A callout quotation with 35% horizontal rules.

Caps and Small Caps

Here are two ways to achieve the effect of caps and small caps. Both of them use
Netscape's extensions. If you don't use Netscape, this section won't mean much to
you. However, I wanted to present this because caps and small caps are used very
often in publishing, and I think you should make use of any tools that allow you to
make a document look the way you want, such as the Netscape extensions, even if
the effect won't be achieved on all browsers.

Warning: Both of these tags are covered by Netscape's <FONT SIZE> extension to HTML and will probably not be displayed on any other browsers (see Chapter 4 for more information about Netscape's extensions).

First version:

```
<FONT SIZE=+2>C</FONT>APS AND
<FONT SIZE=+2>S</FONT>SMALL
<FONT SIZE=+2>C</FONT>APS
```

Second version:

```
C<FONT SIZE=-1>APS AND</FONT>
S<FONT SIZE=-1>MALL</FONT>
C<FONT SIZE=-1>APS</FONT>
```

In both cases, the result looks like so:

CAPS and SMALL CAPS

Proofreading/Copyediting Checklist

- Be consistent with use of % or percent.

- Be consistent with use of capitals or small capitals, and realize that not all browsers will display small caps.

- Use one space after colons and between sentences. Most browsers won't notice if you use one space or two, but it's better to be safe than sorry.

- Don't use lowercase "l" for the number 1.

- Don't use letter "o" for zero.

- Use character entities for accents and other special characters.

- Find alternatives such as <BLOCKQUOTE> to formatting you just can't do in HTML, such as hanging indents or nesting of a paragraph.

Proofreading, spell-checking, and double-checking are tedious but important aspects of publishing, either online or on paper. The real fun begins when you finally put it all together and begin to see the results of your work on the Web, as described in the next chapter.

Organizing Your Web Site

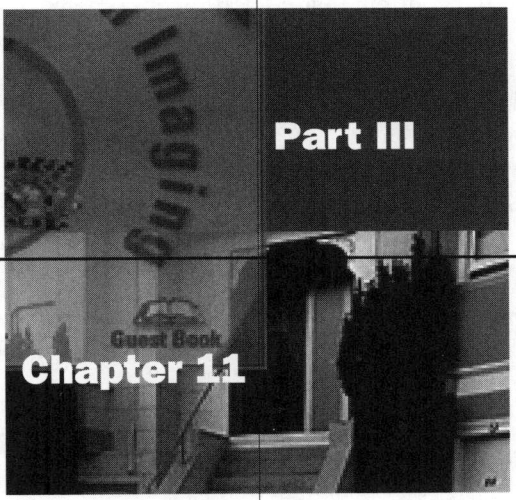

Part III

Chapter 11

Your business or organization might have a tangible product, such as a World Wide Wicket or a Spacely Sprocket, that it wants to sell on the World Wide Web. But the real commerce of the Web is information: not only the information you publish before the eyes of the online community, but access to that information.

The astounding volume of data being put forth electronically—whether it is meant to be informational, educational, or blatantly commercial—makes the Web a buyer's market. A premium is put on how well data is presented, how readable it is, and, generally, how user-friendly it is. The better your information is organized, the more "hits" your Web site will receive, and the longer your visitors will stay.

Look at Yahoo (http://www.yahoo.com). Everybody else is. This index of online resources, started by two college students at Stanford, has become an incredibly popular and lucrative commercial site. Why? Because it organizes the contents of the Web with clear lists of general categories and easy-to-follow paths to specific nuggets of information. Yahoo is proving that organization sells.

On the other end of the continuum are wallflower home pages. What makes them unpopular? They probably take several minutes to load, for one thing. But the real kiss of death is likely to be that the content is not immediately apparent, because they don't state what their purpose is or what they have to offer in a blink or two of an eye. Always remember that you are vying for the attention of an impatient Web surfer who might visit a hundred or more other locations in a typical lunchtime or 4 p.m. browsing session.

> **Note:** A *home page,* often called a welcome page, is the opening document of a Web site. It is the "front door" from which the reader can follow links that will lead to all of the contents of a site.
>
> A Web *document* is a general term for a single file's worth of information published on the Web.
>
> A Web *site* can be either a server that serves up documents on the Web or, for the purposes of this chapter, a set of documents produced by a single publisher. Also referred to as an information "web" or a Web *presentation.*

Let's assume that you either haven't produced information electronically, or that you possess a large portfolio of print or video information but have never set up a Web site. How should you organize and present your stuff to give your online publishing effort maximum impact?

Getting Started

Before you go any further, do some thinking and planning. Take out a low-tech pencil and paper. Write down your initial thoughts and draw out a sketch or outline of how you want the parts of your site to be organized.

Decide What You Want to Say

That is, analyze your content. You probably have a general idea of why you want to publish on the Web. Have you tried to boil your message or your goal down to one or two sentences or main points?

Decide on Your Goals

Decide, for instance, whether your goal is personal gratification or corporate promotion. Do you want more business in the form of orders? More attention to what you think or feel? More educated consumers? Who, exactly, do you want to reach?

Assemble Your Contents

Then, get all your ducks into one row. Make a list so you know how many documents you have and begin to organize them or get an idea of what you want to do with them. Are you going to put all your company brochures online, or just a selected few? Now, before you actually touch the keyboard, is the time to decide.

If you are using already-published documents, convert them to HTML (using one of the methods described in Chapter 7) and put them in a folder so you can begin to distribute them.

Decide on the Type of Site You Want

Think about what kind of site you want to have. Think about the examples in Chapter 2 of this book. Look around the Web and get some ideas from what others have done. Perhaps your site will fall into one of the following categories:

- **Personal:** Who you are, what you do, why people might want to know about you.

- **Recreational:** News about a club or group you belong to.

- **Institutional:** An online "front door" or welcome page for a business or large corporation.

- **Educational:** Teaching tools or information published by a school, university, or organization.

- **Informational:** Writing, documentation, news, museum holdings.

- **Commercial:** A shopping mall, a store, a service, merchandise, anything you have to sell.

- **Marketing:** Surveys, polls, opinion seeking.

- **Creative:** Short stories, poetry, art.

- **Societal:** Political concerns, social causes, special interests.

Decide Who Will Maintain Your Site

Is there someone on your staff who is qualified to set up and maintain a Web site? If not, are you prepared to train someone to do the upkeep? If there is no one on staff, are you prepared to hire someone to do it? Now is the time to decide.

Know Your Budget

If you are setting up your own server, the hardware costs can run from nothing (if you happen to have a good computer on hand in your office that you can spare as a server) to $10,000; and up to $100,000 if you are buying equipment from scratch.

If you are getting an Internet connection with a provider, the costs are minimal, $20 to $50 per month, for a basic SLIP or PPP account that lets you browse the Web. But to be an information provider, you have a server connected to the Internet all the time.

If your organization already has a direct connection, you have a big advantage. Otherwise, you have to pay your Internet provider for such a connection. This can run to several hundred dollars a month or more. Some providers even charge a per-hit fee as well. It pays to shop around (see Appendix C for more information on choosing an Internet provider).

Of course, if photos need to be taken or writers need to be hired, you have to budget for that just as you do with any traditional print publication.

Know Where the Page Fits in Your Communications Program

Your Web site should not exist in isolation but should be part of an overall communications plan for your organization. Do you have such a plan? If so, where does your Web publishing effort fit into it?

If you already put out a periodical whose contents might be duplicated on the Web, you have to ask yourself some hard questions.

Will your latest information go on your Web site, or will you put out the latest information in your print publication and delay your Web offerings until the magazine has sold for a while? Or perhaps your Web publication will be a miniversion of a magazine or newspaper. Now is the time to come up with a plan, especially if you are making a budget request for your online project.

Categorize Your Information

The cans of soup and vegetables in my pantry are not alphabetized, but I do think information published on the Web should be categorized. You will have a better chance of accomplishing your communications goals. Some folks are partial to top ten categories. Others assign numbers. Many even use Dewey's category names.

Your choice depends on your material and your personality. As a general practice, however, it is a good idea to structure your information into several primary categories, as Dave Micko did when he set up the Web site for the Illinois Power Company in Decatur, Illinois. These main divisions are, in turn, broken into subcategories. The welcome page of the Illinois Power site appears in Figure 11.1.

Where to Find It

Get connected to Illinois Power's Web site at http://www.prairienet.org/business/power/ipmain.html.

Figure 11.1 Illinois Power home page.

Where to Find It

If you'd like to check out how
librarians have organized their
Web sites, there's a list of Web
servers based in libraries at
http://www.lib.washington.
edu/~tdowling/libweb.html.

Consult Professional Organizers

Web publishers don't have to look far when
seeking models for classifying information.
There are, after all, people who do this for a
living: librarians. They, too, are jumping on
the World Wide bandwagon and setting up
Web sites from which the rest of us can learn.
(Dave Micko, who was mentioned previously
and who set up the Illinois Power Web site, is
a librarian.)

Don't Be Sidetracked by "Coolness"

After looking around the Web for only a short while, you will be able to discern which information providers have considered their presentation in a reasoned, sensible way and which ones have not.

On the day I spoke to Dave, for instance (this was in May 1995), he pointed out that the Cool Site of the Day was an example of the latter (see Figure 11.2).

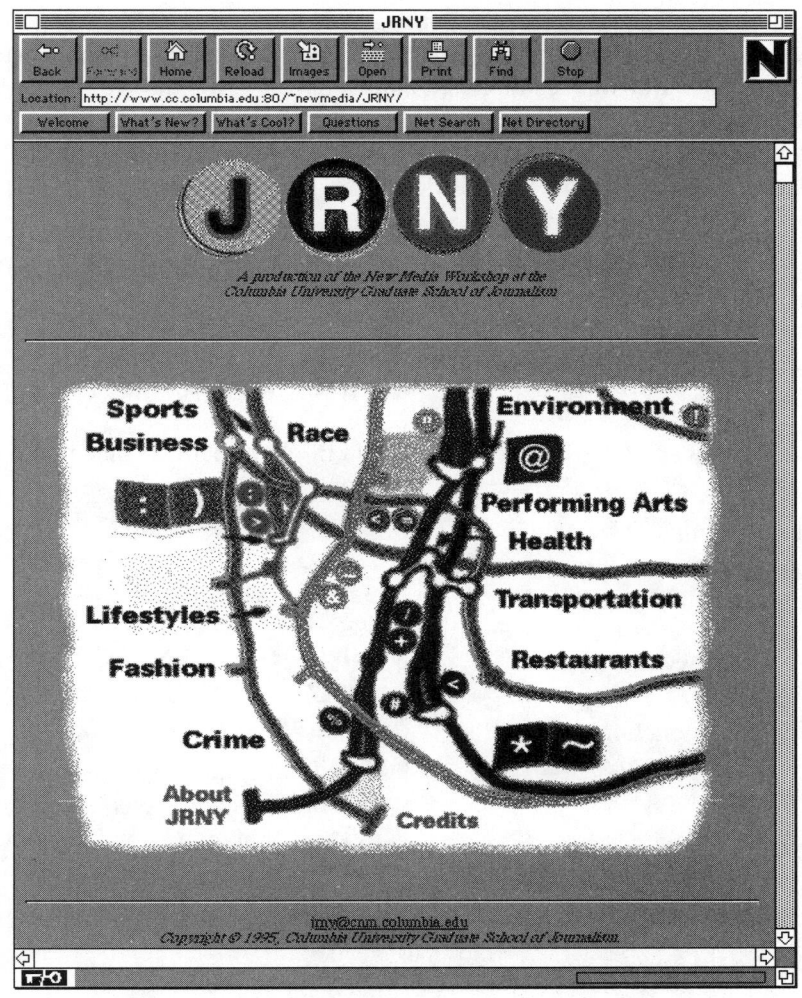

Figure 11.2 JRNY home page.

Where to Find It

The Cool Site of the Day is at http://www.infi.net/cool.html. The JRNY Home Page is at http://www.columbia.edu/~newmedia/JRNY.

Can you tell at a glance who is putting out this information and its purpose (other than supposedly being "killer")? Can you quickly determine what sorts of things you might learn or discover here, or why you should delve deeper into this Web site? At the risk of revealing that I'm out of it, I must confess that I couldn't.

I'm not saying you shouldn't do something cool or eye-catching with your home page. I don't want to give the impression that I think a dull-looking but well-organized site is better than a visually exciting one that happens to be, shall we say, somewhat haphazard. To market yourself in the increasingly crowded online world (see Chapter 14), you do have to grab a Web reader's attention quickly.

However, the more complex or wild your visuals are, the more important it is to provide some basic content to complement your design. To learn how to do that, it's time for a crash course in library science.

Where to Find It

Just to prove that Dave Micko and I aren't the only ones promoting the Dewey Decimal System on the Web, take a look at Patrick's Front Page, http://www.slac.stanford.edu/~clancey/dewey.html, which includes a catalog of Internet resources organized by the DDS.

Mr. Dewey's System

You might remember that a man named Dewey was mistakenly declared president in the famous newspaper headline "Dewey Defeats Truman." That was Thomas Dewey and he's not the Dewey who can help organize a home page. Melvil Dewey (1851–1931) created the Dewey Decimal System for library cataloguing.

Melvil did something that some find more amazing than being elected president: he divided all human knowledge into only ten general categories. He assigned each category a hundred numbers to denote more specific subdivisions:

000	General knowledge
100	Philosophy and psychology
200	Religion
300	Social sciences
400	Language and linguistics
500	Sciences (biology, physics, mathematics, and so on)
600	Technology
700	Arts and recreation
800	Literature
900	Historical studies

You can apply Dewey's idea of dividing knowledge by putting the contents of your home page into categories, such as:

- General information
- Financial information
- What we (or I) do and why we (or I) do it
- People who work for me
- How to get in touch with me

Essential Home Page Contents

What does a well-organized and interesting home page look like? Figure 11.3 shows a home page for The Nine Planets, published by the Lunar and Planetary Laboratory at the University of Tucson. It includes many (although not all) of the elements of a good home page.

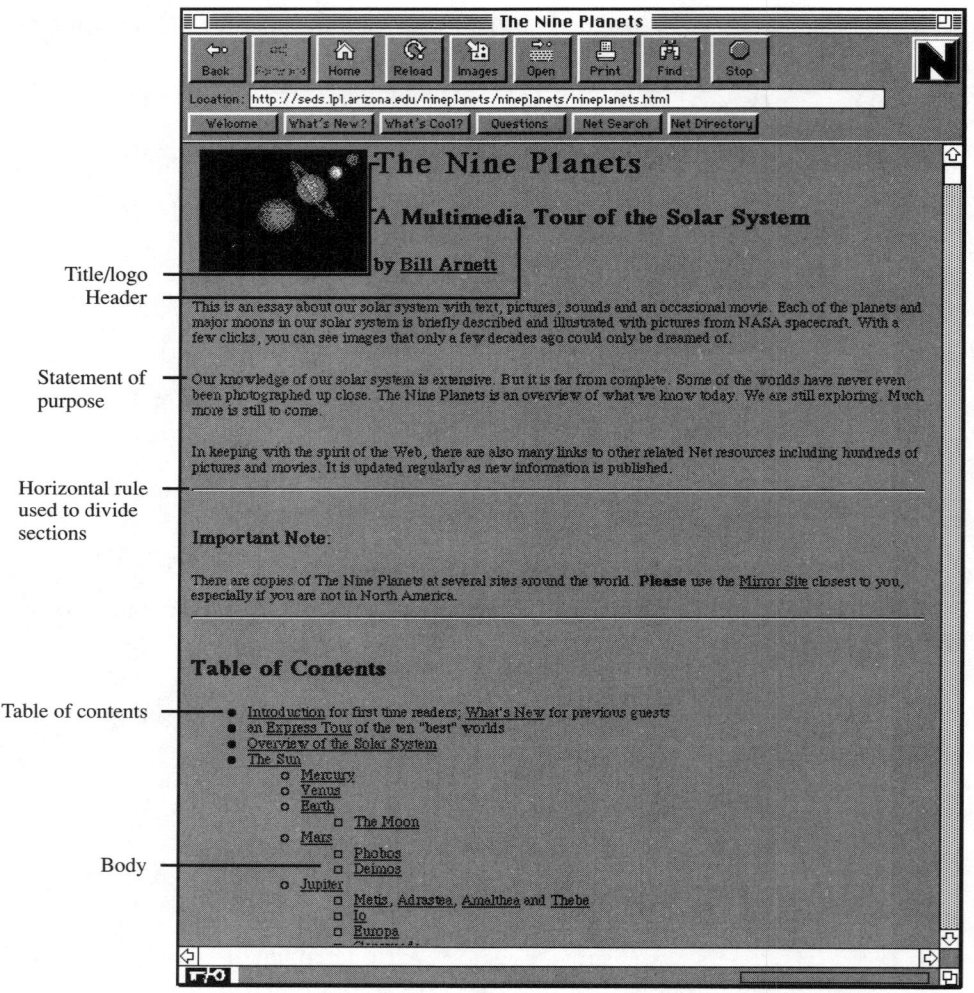

Figure 11.3 Top half of The Nine Planets home page.

Despite its subject, this page is far from spacey. My only quibble is that the lengthy table of contents might have been included as a separate link to make the page less crowded. On the other hand, you don't have to know your Big Dipper from your Orion to find pointers to plenty of text and images about the solar system.

Rules are made to be broken, of course. But in a medium where anything goes, there is something to be said for consistency. What follows are some general principles many people have followed in setting up their home pages. Take a look and decide

Where to Find It

The Nine Planets has a very long URL, but it's worth the effort to type it: http://seds.lpl.arizona.edu/nineplanets/nineplanets/nineplanets.html.

Where to Find It

Carnegie Mellon University has specified a standard logo and other design rules for all home pages set up on its campus to foster a standard look and tone. It's a good example of an organization trying to achieve consistency, while at the same time taking into account that its departments have individual purposes. Find out more at http://www.cmu.edu/cmufront/style-guide/style.guide.html.

what you like and don't like. When you decide what rules you want to follow, stick with them consistently. And make sure your home page does not vary widely or otherwise conflict with other home pages in your organization.

First, The Nine Planets home page illustrates the basic divisions of a home page into a *header*, a *body*, and a *footer*.

- The **header** includes such general information as a banner or logo, a title, an introductory GIF image or imagemap, or a series of buttons or links to various locations on an individual site. It also contains a statement of purpose.

- The **body** of the home page is often set off from the header by a horizontal rule. The body contains some introductory links or a table of contents, and the basic text.

- The **footer** can contain a surprising amount of important information and should not be overlooked. It can contain a copyright notice; an indication of when the site was last updated; an email address or name of the person who set up and maintains the site; and links to other parts of the site.

Header Elements

Usually the first elements in a home page that attract the Web reader's attention are the ones that go at the top, so it's essential to be as clear and concise as possible with them.

Logo or Banner

The top of a Web page is the common spot for the page title, or a logo or graphic banner announcing the office, club, individual, or organization offering this information.

If you are publishing a lot of documents on the same Web site, you may decide to put the same logo or banner at the top of each one to achieve consistency from document to document.

In that case, HTML 3.0 will help by providing a space for a banner at the top of a document so that any image(s) can reside in a separate file external to the main document, which will help the page load faster. See Chapter 6 for information on HTML 3.0.

Statement of Purpose

This is a one- or two-sentence description of the publisher (either you or your organization): what it is, what its goals are, and what the purpose of this site is.

Where to Find It

An excellent section of "WWW Page Design" is included in the style manual published by the Yale Center for Advanced Institutional Media. It's at http://info.med.yale.edu/caim/StyleManual_Top.HTML. Also consult CERN's Online Guide to Hypertext, http://www.w3.org/hypertext/WWW/Provider/Style/Overview.html.

Body Elements

A good Web document won't overwhelm you with all of its content at once. Many organizations and individuals recommend limiting the content to one or one and a half pages. I say keep it short and sweet.

Horizontal Rules

It's usually a good idea to insert an <HR> tag (horizontal rule) between the major divisions of your page: between header and body and body and footer, in other words. A rule also helps to break up and delineate major sections of text.

Table of Contents

Often, when the document is long, the table of contents will contain <A HREF> and <A NAME> links to places later in the same document. In the case of a set of documents for a Web site, each list item is a link to a separate document. This method is preferred because it promotes short, self-contained documents that are easily navigable online.

These items are of vital importance; they should reveal the contents to your readers and suggest to them in a glance what they might find and where they might find it. Each one of these initial links should lead to a point of information that someone will find vital.

The way to come up with this list is to:

- Assess what exactly you have to communicate.

- Break that list of "most important things" into six or seven distinct yet primary categories of information.

- Keep in mind the goals of your organization in general, and of your Web site in particular.

- Take your readers into account. Put yourself in their place, and imagine what they will be looking for and what it is you want them to find.

Because you are selling yourself and promoting yourself on the Web as a commercial site, the table of contents will not necessarily be the perfect taxonomic distribution of information that a librarian might compose. You have to take into account any pet projects the executive level wants to promote, or play up any commercial considerations your organization has that will attract someone's attention.

Dave Micko and the executives of Illinois Power discussed what they wanted to do with their Web site. Together they agreed upon a list of seven topics. Then Dave drew up a "tree" of information with paths leading to various "atomic" bits of information (see the upcoming section, "The Information Tree").

In-Line Graphics

Graphics are great ways to break up the body of a home page, but be sure to use them wisely. Don't overdo it with too many images at once; one good image is worth more than five mediocre, crowded ones.

Graphics almost always make a page slower to load, so use them intelligently. If the image is large, put a cropped thumbnail linked to the full-size image, and tell people how much room the file consumes.

Any image that serves as a link should have a textual link accompanying it.

Note: A *thumbnail* is a small version of a larger, more detailed image. It gives a hint of what the full image contains. The advantage is that a thumbnail takes up less memory so a Web browser can more quickly display both the image and the page on which it resides. To create a thumbnail of an image, simply scan it at a low resolution. You might crop a portion of the image in the graphics program you are using so that the final image is small—only one by two inches, for instance.

Icons and Buttons

If you use icons or buttons on your home page, don't use a lot of different styles. Pick one button style, for instance, and stick with it. And make sure your button actually does something when someone clicks it. Decoration is fine for Christmas trees but somewhat annoying on the Web.

Footer Elements

The footer of a Web document is no afterthought, but contains a great deal of useful information. The essential elements are listed next.

Most Recent Update or Time Stamp

This tells the reader when the site was last updated; in other words, it tells them whether or not it's a "cobweb site," one that hasn't been updated in a while.

Webmaster/Company Address

This tells the reader who created or authored the site, or where to send mail to get more information about the site. It may also give the name of the organization to which the site belongs, in case someone gets access to the page directly without following a path to it leading from the main home page.

Identify your company name clearly, especially if yours is a single office or department within a larger group. For instance, a return address of

Webmaster@The Institute for Learning Sciences

might leave people wondering to what larger entity the Institute for Learning Sciences is attached. Tell visitors what university or organization your office belongs to. A good example of footer information is shown in Figure 11.4.

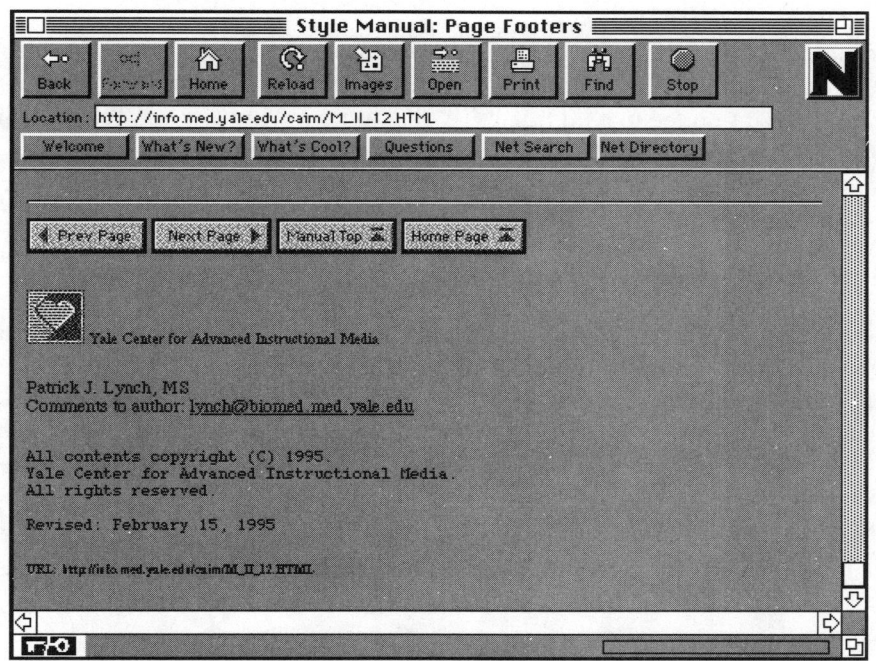

Figure 11.4 Yale C/AIM WWW Style Manual footer information.

Copyright Notice

Technically, you don't have to include a copyright notice to protect your copyright
(see Chapter 15 for more explanation). However, it's a good idea to put a copyright
notice on anything you put on the Web that you don't want people to steal. The usual
form is

Copyright 1995 by Hayden Books. All
rights reserved.

Where to Find It

NewsPage is another example of a
way organization sells. It collects
computer-related articles from
current publications in one place.
Users can view headlines but must
pay a subscription fee to read full
stories. To get the whole story
about NewsPage, go to http://
www.newspage.com.

Navigational Links

Remember that because of the Web's nonlinear hypertextual nature, visitors may
come to your company's Web site through
the "side door" rather than its official
home page. It's useful to provide your
readers with a quick link to that home page
in case they want to find out more about
your organization.

The best organized Web sites provide buttons or links at the bottom of a page that
lead back to the top of the page, back to the home page, back to an upper level folder
or to an index, and (most importantly) on to the next document in sequence. A
typical set of links is shown here:

Index   Previous   Next   Home

The IBM Home Page uses three sorts of navigational tools: a graphical imagemap,
buttons, and textual links. I'm not recommending you do all of this, necessarily, but
it does show the various options together (see Figure 11.5).

Note: Notice the important and useful link to a text-only version at the
bottom of the IBM Home Page (see Figure 11.5). It's a good idea to
include an alternate version of your home page for non-graphical browsers,
especially if the "graphical" version of your page includes complex graphics or imagemaps.

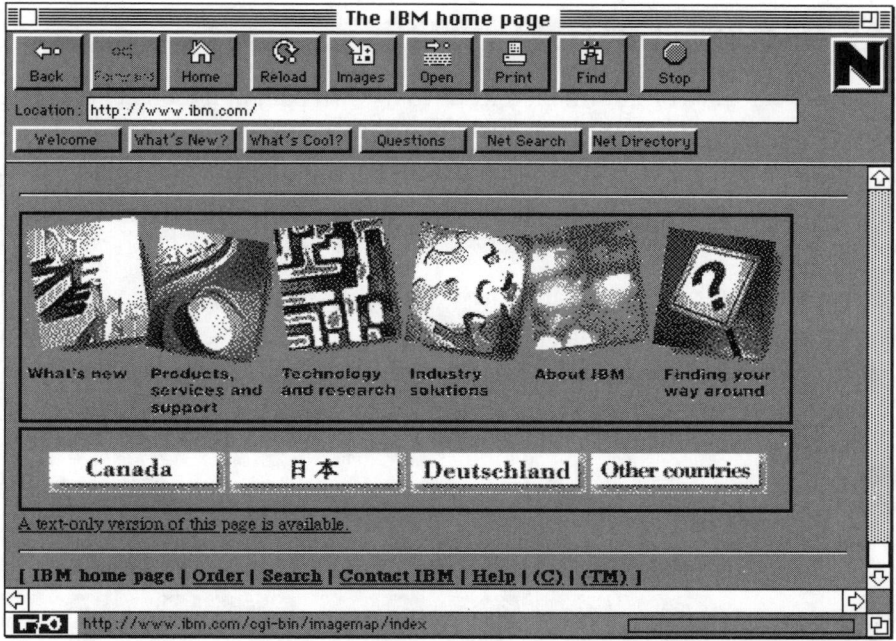

Figure 11.5 Buttons at the bottom of the IBM home page. (This page property of IBM.)

Other Optional Footer Items

You might also include the following optional items here:

- A list of "things to do" that people will see when they visit in the future

- A general policy statement

- The company logo

- The URL of the site

The Information Tree

Each primary category of information leads to its own path of documents. The links that lead the reader through the path, taken together, make a "tree" of information.

How you organize the tree depends on the way you think best. Usually, though, it's a good idea to draw out on paper the things you want to do and draw paths leading to the bottom levels of information.

Figure 11.6 illustrates the information tree of one half of the Illinois Power site.

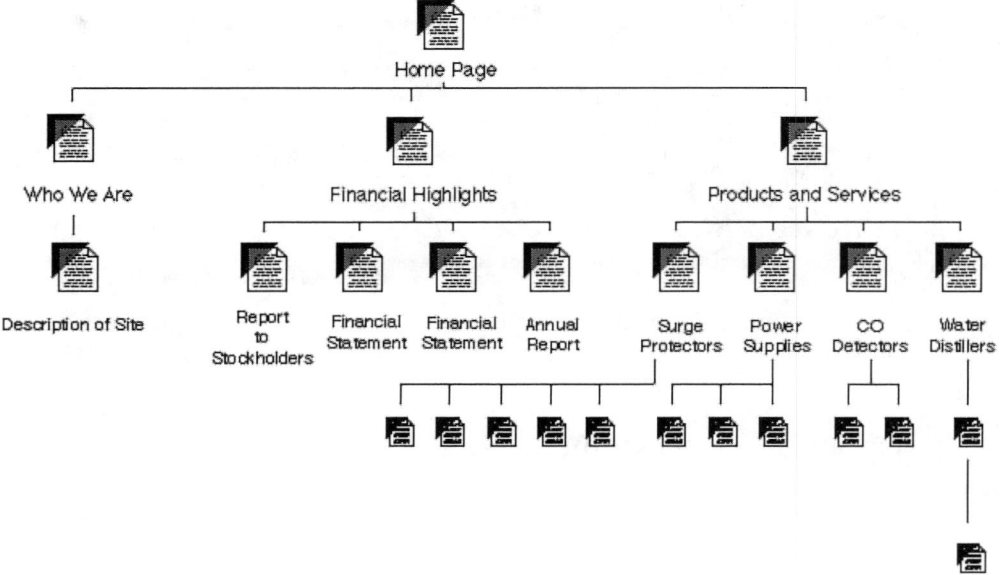

Figure 11.6 Organization of the Illinois Power site.

Another site constructed around elaborate paths of information is NewsPage, an online news service. The NewsPage index map shown in Figure 11.7 illustrates the arrangement of information.

If I wanted to find a list of current news stories about online publishing, I would follow this path: NewsPage/Interactive Media & Multimedia/Consumer Applications/Electronic Publishing.

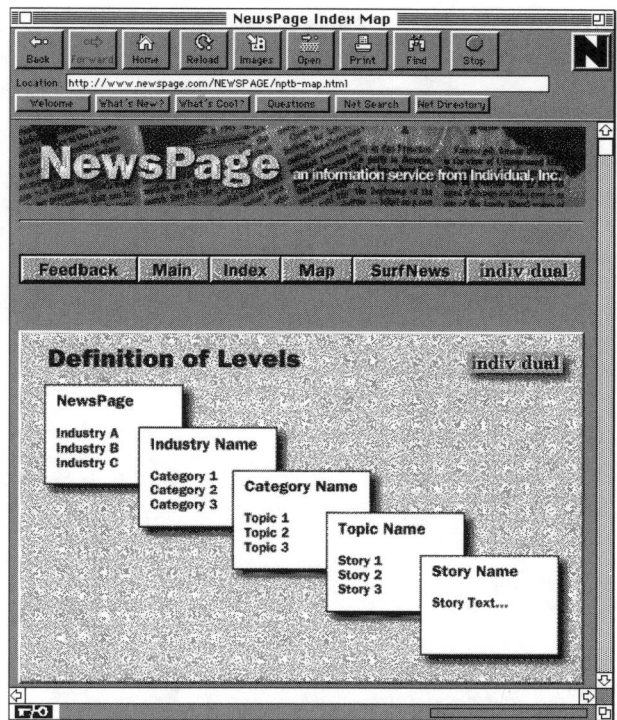

Figure 11.7 NewsPage index map.

Keep Your Links Clear and Specific

The better organized the middle levels of information on your site, the easier it is to navigate, and the more useful the site is.

For instance, how many people actually check out a link that simply says "What's New?" More people might, if you keep the names of your links as brief and specific as possible. Rather than "People," for instance, say, "Company Editorial Department".

Keep Information Paths Simple

Too many links means readers have to click only once to get anywhere; but if, as a result, they end up with a ton of possible places to go and no real guidance, they will be totally confused (see Figure 11.8).

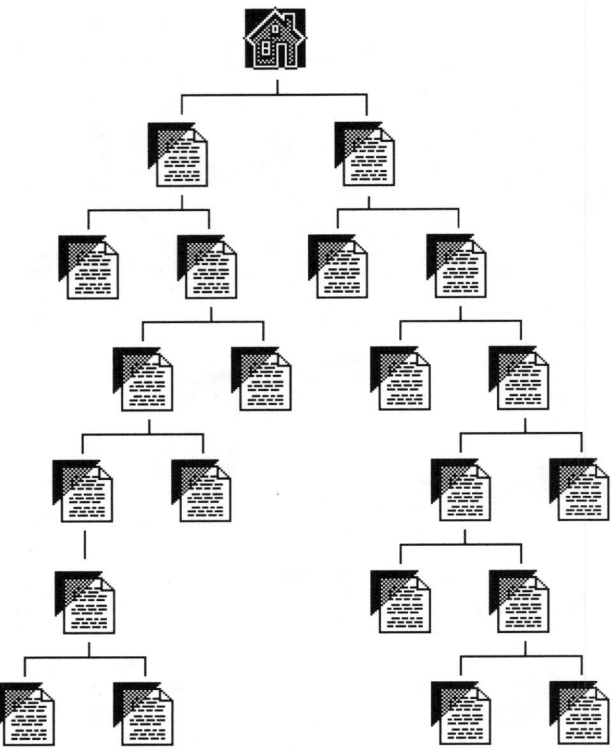

Figure 11.8 Too many links.

On the other hand, having only a few general categories in the beginning means that
someone will have to make link after link before getting to a specific bit of information (see Figure 11.9).

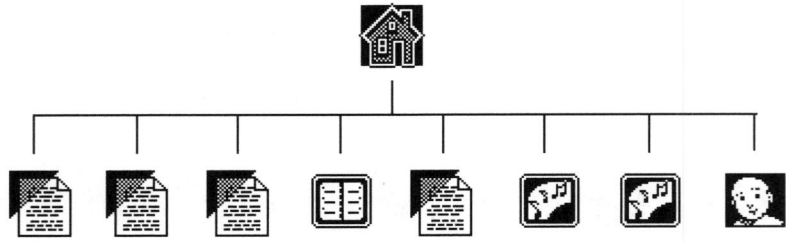

Figure 11.9 Too few links.

It seems to me that people should be able to get to the "bottom level" of a Web site in three to five clicks. Of course, that will vary depending on the amount of information your site contains (see Figure 11.10).

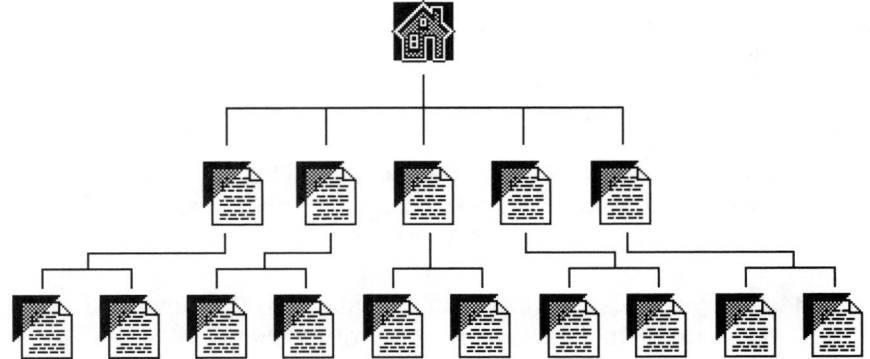

Figure 11.10 Three to five links: just right.

Here's an example of an information path that is comfortable for me. Let's say you want to know what kind of business courses the University of Chicago offers. The easy way, of course, would be to enter the URL someone gave you and go directly to it. But what if you don't have the URL and only know that it's somewhere at the University of Chicago's various Web offerings. How would you find it? See Figure 11.11.

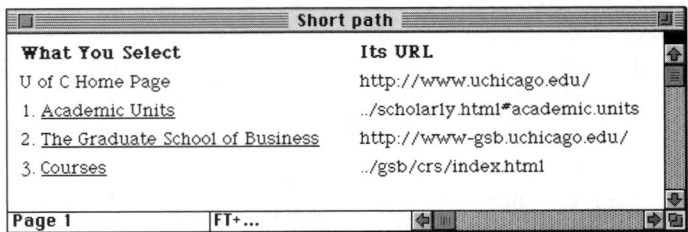

What You Select	Its URL
U of C Home Page	http://www.uchicago.edu/
1. Academic Units	../scholarly.html#academic.units
2. The Graduate School of Business	http://www-gsb.uchicago.edu/
3. Courses	../gsb/crs/index.html

Figure 11.11 Path to course offerings.

Six Rules for a Well-Organized Site

Here are some basic principles you need to follow when you are organizing your Web site.

Organize for a Specific Audience

While it's true that the potential audience of Web readers is huge and nebulous, it's also true that you should identify and target key segments you want to reach.

A university might want to reach prospective students at one site and alumni at another. A media organization might want to reach opinion leaders, such as journalists. An organization might want to lure new customers at one site and provide customer and product assistance at another.

Whatever your audience, tailor your information to it. Don't flood that audience with data. If I'm a prospective student, for instance, I don't want to spend a sizable amount of Internet access time searching for the tuition figures and application dates that I need. Provide a link on your welcome page to the most important information. If you don't know what the most important information is that your audience wants, conduct a focus group. Better yet, use the power of the Internet and have your audience fill out a survey form on your Web site.

Where to Find It

For the most part, I tried to present my home page "rules" in a positive way, but if you want to read the "Top 20 Things Not to Do On a Web Page" go to http://ee.stanford.edu/eecns/www/donts.html. (Actually, when I first visited the site the heading read "Top 10 things..." and 20 items were listed. Accuracy, I suppose, would be the 21st item.) Another site listing some "Dos and Don'ts of Web Design" is at http://millkern.com/do-dont.html.

Focus Your Message

This is another way of saying: Don't lard up your Web site with every bit of printed information your organization creates. Is it really necessary to put on the Web every press release your company has cranked out? If so, take a hint from newspapers and include a one-sentence summary, called a teaser, of each one next to its link rather than simply listing the date.

One way to accomplish this is to identify the "core" content that communicates your message. If your organization or university has a mission statement, distill it into a few sentences and put that right on your home page.

If you can't bear to condense your mission statement, create a link to it and include it as a separate document. But don't call it "Our Mission Statement" or "Statement of Purpose." Use an attention-getting headline that follows the principles outlined in

362

Chapter 9. "What We're Trying to Accomplish" might be better, or even "What Are We Doing on the Web, Anyway?"

Whenever possible, scale down the content of your Web publications. Profiling six students might be good for a university's printed viewbook, but if you're online it makes more sense to restrict yourself to one or two. Don't try to provide the entire history of your organization. A capsule summary will do, along with a sound bite or two from your president as an audio file.

Don't be a Cobweb Site

I saw this term in *Wired* magazine and loved it so much I borrowed it. It perfectly describes a site whose content has been static for so long that it talks about President Nixon or gives directions on using a rotary phone. The worst are "Last Updated" headings that give a date that's several months old. Out-of-date references rob the rest of your content of its credibility.

Maintenance

This is where being a Web publisher gets difficult: follow-up and maintenance. After you complete your site, you have to make a commitment to update it on a regular basis, and stick to the timetable you've set. Stale information makes you look so bad, it's almost better to be putting out nothing at all.

"Last Updated..."

When you do update, tell people with a line that reads "Last updated on (date)." A very recent date, such as a few weeks old or less, will convey a really positive message to people, telling them that this publisher is really committed to providing the best and most timely information. It's the kind of message that will get you the ultimate compliment: the reader will create a bookmark of your home page.

Be Accurate

Sure, any out-of-date information you publish will damage your credibility, but if you really want to look bad, put out something totally inaccurate or misspell the name of someone important and well known. Spellcheck and proofread, proofread, proofread (and take another look at Chapter 10 of this book while you're at it).

Check Your Links

Make sure any HREFs you list actually take someone where you want them to go. If you make links to other sites, check those links from time to time to make sure they are still accurate. Web sites have a way of moving around and changing addresses. Always include the current ones in your HREFs.

Avoid Deadend Links

A deadend link is a link to a document that doesn't lead anywhere else; there are no links to a subsequent document or back to the home page. An interrelated web of information should always include links on every page.

Track Your Visitors

Don't just drop your information on a server and disappear. Keep track of how many people visit you and who they are. This sort of data can be essential when budget cutbacks are announced and your vice-president asks, "Just how useful is our Web site, anyway?" If that occurs, you'd darn well better have an answer.

At the very least, install software on your site that records how many visitors you've had. Better yet, create a form so people can tell you something about themselves and a CGI script that processes the data. And if you are using space on someone else's server, ask the server administrator how best you can get hit statistics for your own pages. (See Chapter 14 for more information on Web site "hit counters.")

Where to Find It

Here are a few suggestions of well-designed Web sites you can visit.
Yahoo: http://www.yahoo.com/
IBM home page: http://www.ibm.com/
Fermilab home page: http://www.fnal.gov/fermilab_intro.html
Library of Congress Web server: http://lcweb.loc.gov/.

Test, Test, Test

I've said it before, but it always bears repeating: test your Web pages (preferably on more than one browser program) after you write the HTML to see how they look onscreen. Make sure all the links work. Scan the text for any errant international characters, soft hyphens, or "curly" quotes that HTML didn't recognize.

Now that you've organized and identified the contents of your Web site, you're ready to go on to the next step: making it look good onscreen.

A Review: Essential Web Page Elements

The standard Web page contains a header, body, and footer.

Header elements include:

1. Logo or banner
2. Statement of purpose

Body elements include:

1. Horizontal rules to divide sections
2. Table of contents or list of primary topics leading to linked "paths" of information
3. In-line graphics
4. Icons and buttons

Footer elements include:

1. Time stamp
2. Webmaster/company address
3. Copyright notice
4. Navigational links
5. "Things to Do," or future improvements to this site
6. General policy statement
7. Company logo
8. The URL of this Web site

Designing Pages for the Web

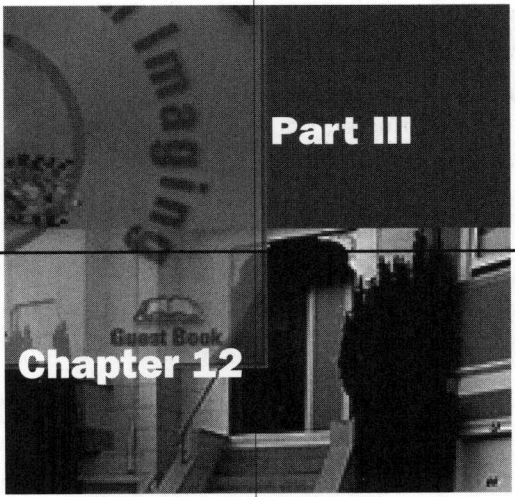

Part III

Chapter 12

Once you have written your Web documents, marked them up using HTML, and organized them, you want to package and present them with the same level of attention by designing Web pages that readers find attractive and easy to read.

Creating a well designed presentation for your publishing effort is an essential part of accomplishing your communications goals and of projecting the image you want for yourself or your organization.

Everybody's a Designer

Any time a new technology comes along that makes it possible for untrained people to accomplish some aspect of producing publications, some ugliness is bound to happen. I know because I was responsible for some poor-looking publications in the mid-80s when desktop publishing tools, such as the Macintosh and Apple LaserWriter, first appeared.

So I encourage you to learn from my mistakes. The hints included in this chapter provide some of the basic principles of making a publication look good. Whether you are on the Web or in other computer environments using programs such as PageMaker or QuarkXPress, you can easily get yourself set up to do design. The challenge is to do *good* design. Knowledge and practice are what you need to learn effective design.

In a nutshell, though, what I'm going to teach you can be summed up in three words, which I'll explain shortly:

Less Is More

The Problem

There's a significant problem facing anyone designing a page on the Web: HTML is not intended for page design. It is a *markup language* that specifies standard page elements so they can be displayed on a wide variety of browsers and computers.

Although some of the new features in HTML 3.0 and Netscape's extensions allow you to include some design elements, they're not going to replace a real page layout program. There's only so much designing that can be done with the available technology.

What You Can't Do

Just think about all the things you can't yet do with HTML:

- You can't divide text into two or three columns and vary column width at will.

- You can't pick any typeface you want, including the ones you use for other publications you produce.

- You can't vary the width and type of rules (unless you use Netscape) or draw boxes, circles, or other shapes.

- You can't use spot color except as a background (even then, you can use only one background color).

I could go on, but I don't want to depress you any further. Sure, HTML 3.0 will take a step forward. And as software becomes more sophisticated, you'll be able to do more and more with Web pages. But you don't want to wait for that to happen; you want to get online now. By breaking this chapter into two sections, I've addressed both what is possible to do right now and what I imagine will be possible in the future.

Two Levels of Design

"So what?" many Web publishers will say when they read this. "HTML is simple to learn and it's good enough for me. It would be crazy to pay a designer when I can make a perfectly fine home page all by myself."

Fair enough. I can be realistic and dream at the same time. What I see, then, are two kinds of design relevant to the Web.

Basic Design

Without giving the subject further thought, most people can come up with a practical, everyday sort of page layout. If your purposes are well served with something closer to a newspaper layout than to a booklet or poster design, there are a few rules you can use to put together a decent-looking home page. Here are some guidelines:

- Don't crowd your page by filling every little bit of space. White space helps make a page easier to read and can direct the reader's eye to the most important elements of the page.

- Don't get so carried away with your ability to use Netscape's extensions that you center every single thing. Center only the elements that you want to stand out from the rest of what's on the page.

- For that matter, don't rely solely on any of Netscape's extensions. Take into account that a large proportion of your audience may be using other browsers such as Mosaic and MacWeb.

- One good photo is far better than four or five bad ones.

- Think about how to align elements so they fit into some organized plan rather than splashing them around a space without any apparent rhyme or reason.

- Don't use too many different headings or heading sizes on a page. Don't put a larger heading size beneath a smaller one. Don't use the <H6> heading for anything except a minor disclaimer or copyright notice. Better yet, don't use it at all.

Ideal Design

In the near future, designers will be able to practice the best of their craft without the limitations that now exist because of what Web software can't do.

It will be a whole new world when a program such as PageMaker can output not only text to HTML but also to page layout elements like columns and graphics, or when Acrobat pages are accessed from Netscape and vice versa. (I'm betting that the connection between Netscape and Acrobat will grow closer, because Adobe has purchased a part interest in Netscape.) There's also a program called HotJava lurking in the wings that promises to blow the Web community's collective mind. Its language is being integrated into Netscape, too.

As new technology brings the worlds of traditional and electronic design closer, the techniques used in creating a Web page with HTML are less important than the basic principles of designing *any* page, whether it appears in print or onscreen. With that in mind, I'd like to remind you what makes publications look good: using white space to direct the eye, developing a page grid and knowing when to conform to it or diverge from it, creating sidebars, and varying linespacing.

Note: There's a very good book about desktop design that presents information about graphics, page layout, and typography that I recommend highly: *Desktop Design and Layout,* by David Collier and Bob Cotton (Cincinnati: North Light Books, 1989).

You Have the Tools

It's useful to remember that the best tool is not contained in computer hardware or software but is located between your two ears. You'll achieve a well designed page if you know what you want to do, plan your design, and are consistent. Don't be afraid to give it a try. Remember that when you are on the Web, there is no reprinting charge for improving a page if you aren't satisfied with your first (or second) edition.

Greg's Soapbox

I have to give credit to Chris Pearce, creator of the "Enhanced For Netscape Hall of Shame," for some of the examples cited in this chapter. The title is a little misleading because his site lists some great-looking pages as well as real duds that blatantly overuse Netscape's extensions to HTML. Chris deserves an award for asking the question: "Must we <BLINK> and <CENTER> everything?" The page is at http://www.europa.com/~yyz/netbin/netscape_hos.html.

Practical Design Principles

Most Web publishers aren't going to be designing a home page for a major corporation or large governmental agency. Maybe your only goal is to put your own home page on your Internet provider's server. You won't go wrong if you keep this one motto in mind. *Less Is More.*

Less Is More!

The main problem with many, many Web pages is that they are too crowded and too complicated. It's as though (IMHO) the designer is endeavoring to achieve the look of a comic book or an Arnold Schwarzenegger action movie.

If the only thing you want your visitor to get out of your page is that there is something exciting going on (whether there is or not), a design like what is shown in Figure 12.1 will do it.

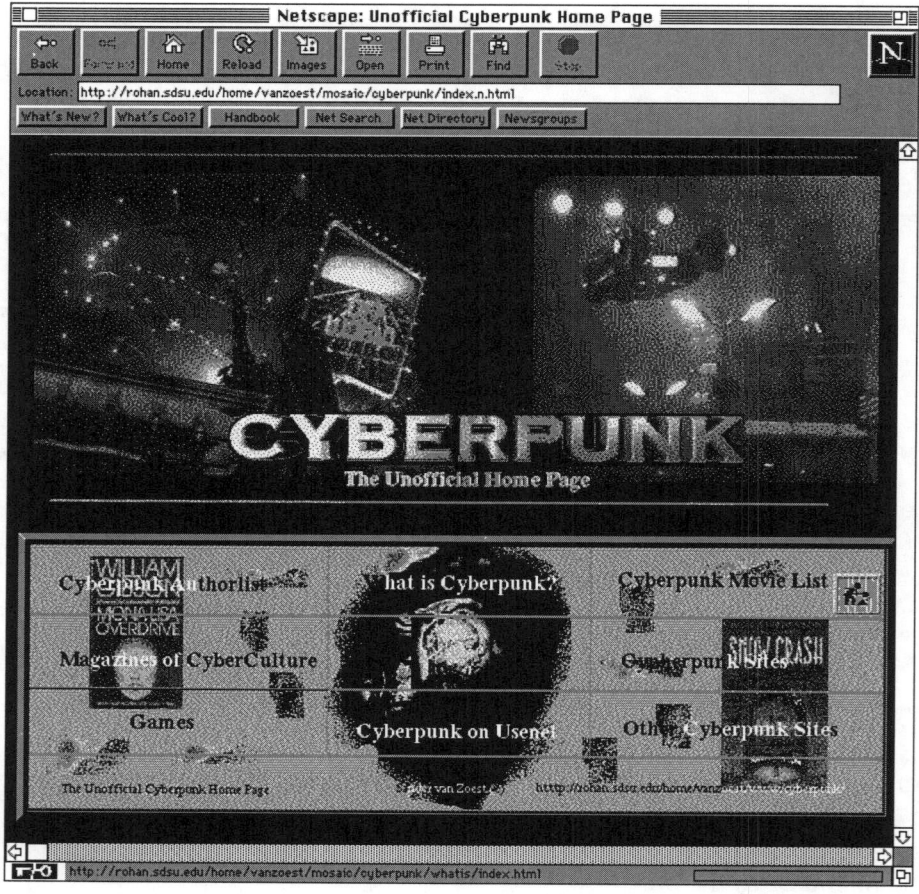

Figure 12.1 Cyberpunk home page.

If, however, you actually want to communicate something and get people to read what you write, go for order instead of chaos. Don't place your words atop a complicated background.

In contrast, the page in Figure 12.2 is unusual because it does not try to fill up every pixel of space. By including only one image and one batch of text, those few items get the reader's attention. Besides that, holding back some information on the first screen arouses curiosity: the reader is likely to wonder what's inside, and will probably take a look.

Figure 12.2 London Calling Internet home page.

Where to Find It

The Unofficial Cyberpunk home page is at http://rohan.sdsu.edu/home/vanzoest/mosaic/cyberpunk/index.html. The Mauritius home page is at http:/www.herts.ac.uk/~cs4bw/. A close second in the "Slowest Page" contest was the Buena Vista Movie Plex Marquee (one minute flat to load): http://www.disney.com/BVPM/MooVPlex.html.

Keep Your Files Small

Many large organizations with flashy graphics software, powerful workstations, and very high-speed connections to the Internet seem to delight in loading pages with inline graphics or imagemaps that take a long time to load on other computers even if they have a fast (56K or T1) connection to the Internet.

Remember, much of your audience is connecting to the Web on a 14,400 baud modem (or slower). No matter how well a page is put together, if it takes too long to appear on a reader's screen, they'll eventually get disgusted, interrupt downloading your page, and move on to another site— or they might disable image loading altogether.

Be nice to your audience by:

- Telling people how big an image is before they download it.

- Providing a text-only alternative to your page.

The Cyberpunk page (Figure 12.1) took about forty-five seconds to load on my office Mac IIcx, which has a direct connection to the Internet. The one shown in Figure 12.3 is my current runner-up for the "Slowest Page to Load" contest at just over a minute (1:02 to be exact—another consideration is that a page like this may be accessed from overseas and will be even slower to load). The Imagex Design page shown in Figure 12.13 is the winner so far, taking 1:27 to load.

Greg's Soapbox

Do you know of another agonizingly slow Web page? Send it to me via email to enter it in my "Slowest Web Page" contest. Sure, this isn't scientific. My computer isn't terribly fast, and conditions on the Net vary from

---

day to day. But I just want to point out in a slightly humorous (not malicious) way the danger of overloading a page with complicated graphics. For more information on this and the "Worst Web Typo" contest, see the Web site for this book.

Figure 12.3 Mauritius home page (copyright University of Hertfordshire).

Conform to a Grid: "Before" and "After"

Here's an example of a home page that I originally noted as an example of poor design, but when I checked on it several weeks later it had been substantially redesigned and improved. Looking at the "before" and "after" versions of the redesign process illustrates the importance of:

- Making page elements conform to a grid.

- Planning as much as is possible when a deadline is looming.

- Having a clear sense of what is most important to emphasize on a page.

- Not trying to make your page do everything at once.

Figure 12.4 shows the original Harvard University page.

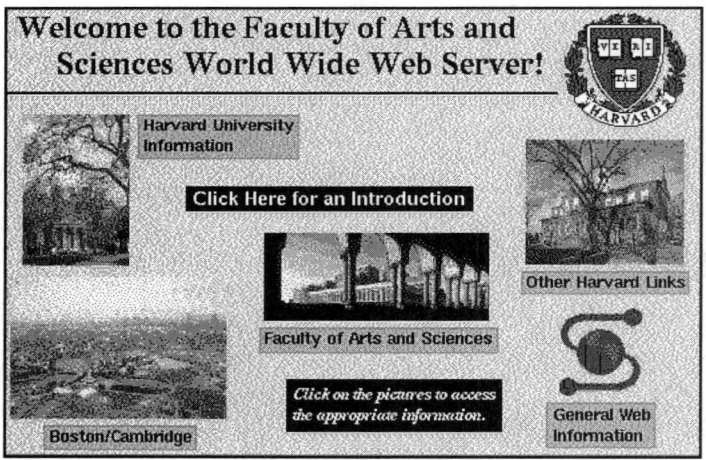

Figure 12.4 Original Harvard University Faculty of Arts and Sciences page.

Figure 12.5 shows the new and improved Harvard University page.

Eugene Eric Kim, the page's creator, explains that he was initially given a very tight deadline and didn't have a clear enough idea of the purpose of the site. At the time he made the first page, there was no Harvard-wide home page. So, because this was the home page that every student would see when they first loaded a Web browser, it was important to include both Harvard-wide information and introductory Web information.

Figure 12.5 New Harvard University Faculty of Arts and Sciences page.

Where to Find It

Harvard University's Faculty of Arts and Sciences Home Page is at http://fas-www.harvard.edu/.

He was also asked to provide an imagemap. With no previous graphic design experience, he decided that he would find scanned images to represent each subtopic on the home page.

Later, Eugene realized that there were several flaws in the design. He reorganized the page so that the most important element—FAS—was at the top. The other buttons are top-down in order of importance. He restructured the page as a whole, and got rid of imagemap buttons, which he describes as "network intensive, too small, and overall, useless."

"We didn't get a 'real designer' to redesign the pages for us," Eugene adds, "It was basically a lot of common sense and experiment."

Where to Find It

Harpreet's home page is at http://www.csua.berkeley.edu/~harpreet/.

Put Your Personality into the Page

If you want to be seen as an individual, put a bit of your unique style into your personal home page. The one shown in Figure 12.6 is a lot of fun. The photo is clear and

377

engaging, the type is playful, and the contents convey something about the author's
personality. Just be careful that the result is pleasing without making the layout
hokey or overcrowded. Keep working until you're happy with it and then ask a
friend for an objective opinion on how it comes across.

Figure 12.6 Harpreet Ahluwalia's personal home page.

Practical Design FAQs

When I first began working on the Web, I figured out a lot through trial and error. What follows are some of the questions I asked myself and the answers that I developed.

Where's the Best Place to Put a Photo?

On a newspaper, the best photos are usually in the upper-right corner of the front page. The theory is that peoples' eyes jump to the right side of the page rather than the left when they're scanning a page to find something of interest.

Web pages, however, aren't as big or as complicated as most newspapers. I don't think it makes much difference whether the photo is on the right or the left. But at the top is definitely better than at the bottom. And most of the time, you'll have to align the photo on the left, because right-aligned elements are possible only with HTML 3.0 or Netscape.

Where's the Best Place to Put a Heading?

They work best either across from an image or under it. Headings tend to get lost above a photo or graphic.

What Size Should Headings Be?

I don't think you automatically have to put an H1 heading at the top of a page. It's more important to have the biggest head at the top of the page and arrange smaller subheads below it.

Where to Find It

The Electronic News home page is at http://www.interport.net/enews/.

How Should Text Interact with Images?

Be sure to leave about an eighth of an inch between photos and text when text is adjacent to images or runs around images. Don't do something on the Web that you

379

would never do in your printed newspaper, such as putting text up against a graphic, or putting a graphic adjacent to ragged-right or ragged-left text (again, you can't achieve this without HTML 3.0 or Netscape). A perfect example of ragged text is shown in Figure 12.7.

Figure 12.7 Electronic News home page.

Where to Find It

Peterson's Education Center home page is at http://www.petersons.com/. The URL for the Interport Communications Home Page is http://www.interport.net/.

How Many Buttons Should I Have?

A better question is: Do you need any buttons at all? I don't know who came up with the notion that rows or grids of buttons are almost a mandatory way to organize the main topics contained in a Web site. They work only when on graphics-capable browsers. And in many cases, too many buttons make a page very slow to load and clutter up the contents, as in Figure 12.8.

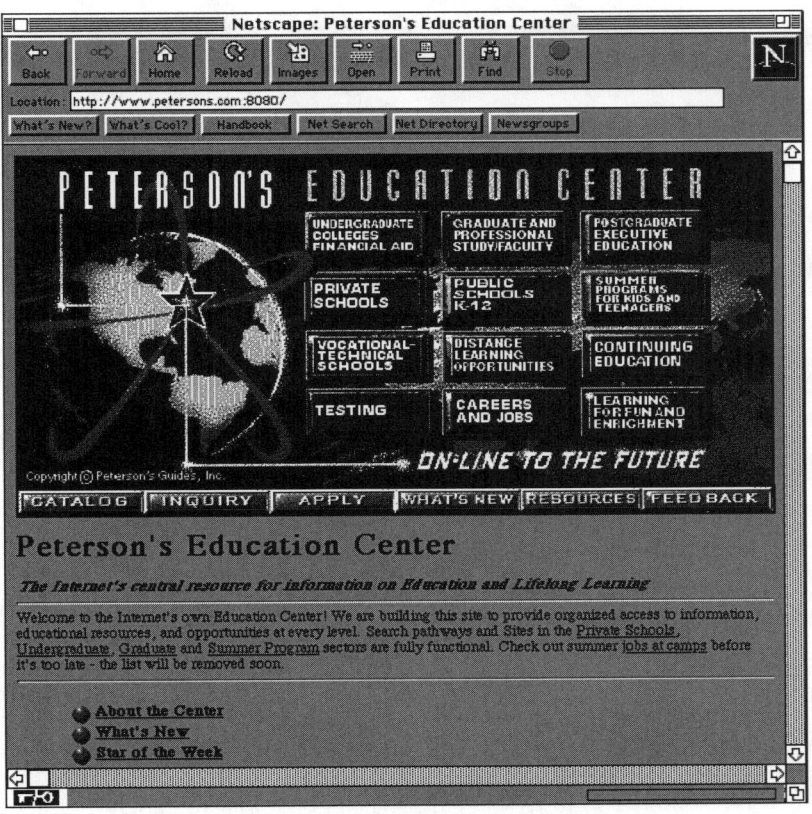

Figure 12.8 Too many buttons: Peterson's Education Center home page.

A home page that's not cluttered and uses only a few textual links might seem
comparatively dull, but it will be read. That's your goal, isn't it? The page in Figure
12.9 loaded up in a matter of seconds. It's clean and uses "empty" space, and at least
seems welcoming, though it's certainly not electrifying.

Figure 12.9 No buttons: Interport Communications home page.

What Makes a Good Logo?

Logos are very common on the Web. A logo is a good way to "anchor" the contents
of a page, direct the eye, make a page more lively, and convey something about the

character of a company. The best logos are simple, yet represent a business through type, images, and typeface. Try to come up with a visual metaphor for the name of a company and incorporate it into the design.

What Image Format Should I Use: GIF or JPEG?

There are two basic types of image files that can be displayed as inline images: GIF (Graphic Interchange Format) and JPEG (Joint Photographic Experts Group). There are two common special cases of GIF files: interlaced GIFs, and GIF89s.

It's important to note that GIFs are the only inline images that are supported by all graphical browsers. JPEGs are supported by Netscape and Mosaic only, as of this writing.

Both GIFs and JPEGs are bitmaps. A bitmap image is broken into tiny squares, called *pixels,* and each pixel is assigned a number value representing the pixel's color. The number of pixels in a square inch is called the image's *resolution.* Although both GIFs and JPEGs may be of any resolution, a typical computer monitor can only display 72 DPI (dots per inch); higher resolution is wasted on an HTML picture and takes longer to download.

GIF files define a palette of colors—usually 256 colors. I recommend that you use less than 256 colors on images you intend to put online, especially if you will have more than one image on a page.

If a color in the image is not part of the GIF's palette, the software you use to create the image can fool the eye by *dithering*—placing small patches of different colors next to each other to appear as a blend of the colors. Because GIFs use a relatively small palette, GIF files are smaller than many other kinds of color files (such as JPEGs).

Interlaced GIF Files

An ordinary GIF file has its pixels arranged from left to right, top to bottom. *Interlaced* GIF files are simply GIFs whose pixels are arranged differently so that they seem to appear quickly as fuzzy shapes and gradually come into focus. It's as if, rather than sending a sentence letter-by-letter, you sent the first letters of each word first, and then the second letters of each word next, and so on, so that the receiver can guess the whole sentence before all the letters are transmitted.

GIF89 Files

A GIF89 is a GIF that supports transparent pixels. It allows one color in the GIF's palette (color number 89) to be rendered as "transparent." GIF89s are most useful for silhouetting your image against the browser's background.

JPEG Files

JPEG files are also bitmaps. Each pixel is defined as a combination of red, green, and blue; or as cyan, magenta, yellow, and black. Each of these component colors (called *channels* in Photoshop) can have as many as 256 levels of brightness, so a full-color image can draw on a range of thousands or millions of colors, rather than the 256 available to a GIF file. As a result, such files are usually substantially larger than GIF's—three or four times as large.

However, JPEG files are significantly compressed. (In fact, JPEG is really the name of the compression technique, rather than the file format.) JPEG actually throws away information, and when it displays files, replaces the lost information with averaged-based guesses. As a result, JPEG compression can create a slight loss in image quality, but in most cases the effect is acceptable or unnoticeable.

When you create a JPEG file, you choose the balance between image size and image quality—the smaller the file becomes, the more the image deteriorates. JPEG files require decompression on the user end, which can take a while, especially on older CPUs. The compression is performed automatically, but it must happen before the file can be opened, so it takes substantially longer to open a JPEG file. Many applications make use of the QuickTime extension to decompress JPEGS, and can't open them if it's not installed.

What Kind of Conversion Programs Can I Use?

Most professional picture-editing programs, such as Photoshop, can save programs in GIF and JPEG formats. Photoshop does *not* create interlaced GIFs or GIF89s, although it is likely that plug-in modules to support these formats will be developed as the Web becomes more and more widely used.

Where to Find It

GIFConverter 2.3.7 can be found at ftp://ftp.utexas.edu/pub/mac/graphics/ and at many other locations on the Web.

GIFConverter

GIFConverter 2.3.7 is a shareware application from Kevin A. Mitchell that can convert files from most common graphics formats to GIFs, interlaced GIFs, and JPEG.

To save a file as an interlaced GIF with GIFConverter, first open the file. (It supports drag-and-drop, so you can simply drag your file onto the GIFConverter icon.) Choose **File Settings...** from the **Special** menu. Choose **GIF** from the popup menu at the top of the window, and check the **Interlaced** box. Choose **Save As...** from the **File** Menu. (You can find the "File Settings" dialog box if you click the **Options** button in the "Save As..." dialog box.)

Transparency

Transparency 1.0 is a freeware application from Aaron Giles that converts GIF files into GIF89 format, allowing you to select one particular color in your image to be displayed transparently.

To use it, first set up your image in GIF format. Transparency doesn't allow you to retouch your image—you must remove the background or other area in an image-editing program, and replace the area in question with a solid color not used in the part of the image you wish to display. (It's likely that the software you used to scan your image will allow you to edit the image, too.)

Save your image as a GIF—if your editing software doesn't support GIFs, save it as a PICT or TIFF image and use the GIFConverter software described previously. Open your image with Transparency by dragging the document's icon onto the Transparency icon. Your image will appear in Transparency's window. Click the color you wish to make transparent, and hold down the mouse button. A palette that contains all the colors in your GIF appears under your cursor, and the color that you have clicked is selected. If the palette hasn't changed your mind about which color you'd like to be transparent, release the mouse button.

Where to Find It

Transparency 1.0 is available at
ftp://ftp.med.cornell.edu/pub/
aarong/transparency/.

If you'd like to try removing a different color from the one you clicked, drag the cursor across the palette to the new color and release the mouse button. In either case, Transparency displays a preview of the converted image. You can keep clicking and previewing until you're happy with the results. Choose **Save as GIF89...** from the **File** menu when you're through.

How Do I Color-Correct Images?

Color correction is a truly gnomic science whose secrets are guarded by prepress professionals. Knowing when an image needs to be color-corrected in the first place is a matter of experience that involves comparing an original transparency or photographic print against the scanned version and evaluating whether some area is too yellow, not red enough, and so on. Then, when a color that's not one of the CYMK group doesn't seem right (notably, green), it takes a lot of experience to know how to make the green look greener, bluer, or yellower.

Fortunately, it's much simpler to prepare images for the Web because you don't have to take into account the many variables involved in printing on paper. Besides, you can spend a considerable amount of time getting the color just right on your particular monitor, only to have it look substantially different on someone else's screen.

Here are some basic color correction principles:

- **Don't scan in halftone mode.** Halftones are used to create the illusion of gray from one ink or the illusion of many colors from four inks. Many scanning software packages have a halftone setting: ignore them. You have many more colors at your disposal than a printer does.

- **Scan at the correct resolution.** Remember, a resolution greater than 72 DPI will not display onscreen. However, this doesn't mean that you should scan everything at 72 DPI. If you plan to enlarge the image, scan at a higher resolution so that when you resize your picture, the *final* resolution will be 72 DPI. Refer to your scanning software document software for instructions on resizing and *resampling* (changing the resolution of) your image.

- **Use the RGB model.** Many image-editing software packages allow you to view your image in one of several color modes: RGB (Red-Green-Blue), CMYK (Cyan-Magenta-Yellow-Key (Black)), and HSB (Hue-Saturation-Brightness) are the most common. Your screen, and all screens, are RGB, and changing modes will not change that. The other modes are conceptual tools for editing the image for particular printing applications, such as removing yellowish casts from a scan for a four color process illustration. Because your work will be displayed on an RGB device, there's no advantage to other modes unless you're a specialist.

- **Edit individual channels, when possible.** Very often, a strange cast in an image's color indicates a problem with a single channel. If your image software allows you to look at the R, G, and B channels individually, make sure that one of these channels isn't "underexposed" or "overexposed." It's much easier to correct strange color problems by fixing the channel with brightness and contrast controls than by adjusting the colors of the whole image with simple color sliders.

Where to Find It

Remember how I told you home pages can come and go without warning? The IceMacHTTP home page is at http://wonga.eecs. uic.edu.

Is Line Art a Good Choice?

Sometimes, the best pages use line art rather than memory-intensive photos. Line art is much simpler and less memory-intensive than a photo because it is composed primarily of solid lines (that's where the term "line art" comes from) as opposed to the many thousands of pixels of color that make up a complex photo (called a "halftone" in printing).

Because there is less information to scan, when the computerized version of the image is created, it takes up less disk space than a photo. Your computer and browser don't have to work nearly as hard to display line art. The disadvantage, of course, is that line art isn't as dazzling visually as a good color photo. But good line art can have style, and can get your message across quicker than big scanned images. A good example is shown in Figure 12.10 (the background is a mild ice-blue color).

Figure 12.10 IceMacHTTP home page.

Where to Find It

An audio file format FAQ file
is available at http://
tjev.tel.etf.hr/josip/DSP/
AudioFile1.html.

How Do I Put Sound on a Web Page?

There are many incompatible sound file
formats. Unlike images, which have
resolved to a few standards supported on
almost all platforms, there are many kinds

A very nice shareware application for recording sounds and saving them in AIFF is SoundEffects by Alberto Ricci, available at ftp:// ftp.alpcom.it/software/mac/ Ricci/. This well-documented program allows you to edit your sounds once you have recorded them, and to apply special-effects filters. You may record from a microphone or from music CDs if you have a CD player. SoundEffects does not, alas, support Undo. Save before you experiment.

One useful freeware converter program for the Mac is SoundApp by Norman Franke, available at ftp://ftp.utexas.edu//pub/ mac/sound/. It allows you to convert your sound files to virtually all of the common sound file formats, including .au.

Where to Find It

FlattenMoov is available at http://www.astro.nwu.edu/ lentz/mac/qt/.

The video file format with which QuickTime competes is MPEG.

continued

of sound files, and many are platform-specific. The AIFF (Audio Interchange File Format) is shared by Macs and other machines; it is probably the best *single* format for Web publishing, but not everyone on every platform can play them.

Another very common format is Sun's .au, also known as Ulaw and Sun audio. Several sites serve sounds in both AIFF and .au formats side by side.

How Do I Add Video to My Web Page?

The standard video format for Macintosh is Apple's QuickTime. Apple has developed QuickTime as a cross-platform tool, so you can use QuickTime movies with the expectation that many users will be able to view them.

If you have the hardware to record movies onto your Mac, it almost certainly came with bundled software, and that software probably saves files in QuickTime format. To make your QuickTime movie compatible with other platforms, you must first "flatten" it with Robert Hennessy's "FlattenMoov."

"Flattening" is simply the removal of Mac-specific code from the QuickTime file. QuickTime works by creating a pointer to your original movie document as an alternative to saving every revision or addition you make to it, which would use up large amounts of memory. When you "flatten" the document you are removing the Mac-specific code, including the pointers, and selecting or "grabbing" the movie itself.

To offer your QuickTime movies to users with MPEG, you can use Sparkle, at ftp://ftp.hawaii.edu/mirrors/info-mac/_Graphic_%26_Sound_Tool/mov/.

To use FlattenMoov, you must first start it up; it doesn't support drag-and-drop. You are presented with a File dialog box. Navigate to the QuickTime movie you wish to flatten. If you cancel at this point, QuickMoov will quit. QuickMoov opens a window that shows the movie. Nothing appears in the menubar, including the application menu—it's a little scary. You can play the movie by pressing the **Play** button in the movie's window. When you click the movie's Close box, QuickMoov presents another File dialog box asking you where you'd like to save the flattened movie.

Where to Find It

Sparkle is available at: ftp://sumex-aim.stanford.edu/info-mac/grf/util.

MPEG

QuickTime's main competitor as a movie file format is MPEG, common in the UNIX world. MPEG files take a fair amount of CPU horsepower (or added proprietary hardware) to decompress. It's much faster for a machine that supports QuickTime to play a QuickTime movie, but users with SGIs or Sun workstations at their disposal can play your movies only if you serve them in MPEG format.

To convert your saved QuickTime movies as MPEGs, use Maynard Handley's Sparkle, which requires System 7.5.

How Do I Use Backgrounds Effectively?

Warning: Backgrounds are an extension to Netscape 1.1. Remember that a user with a browser that does not support Netscape extensions, such as Mosaic, MacWeb, or Netscape 1.0 (or lower) cannot see your background onscreen…they'll just see gray, white, or whatever color you specify.

Also remember that color-matching on computer monitors is still not a perfect science. Different monitors can display the same color differently, and even the display of a single monitor can change as its temperature changes. Even if you take steps to calibrate your monitor and view your screen under controlled lighting conditions, it's unlikely that your readers will view your page under the same conditions. The color will be in the same ballpark, but it will not match exactly.

To set the background color of your document, use the Netscape-specific attribute of the body tag:

```
<BODY BGCOLOR = "#RRGGBB">
```

where RR, GG, and BB stand for the amount of red, green, and blue, respectively. This system of color definition, the RGB model, specifies the levels of these base colors as a number from 1 to 256. To squeeze 256 levels into a two-digit number, Netscape uses hexadecimal, or base 16, notation.

In hexadecimal, the numbers 10 to 15 are represented by the letters A to F. Thus 2A in hexidecimal is $((2\times16) + 12) = 44$ in decimal (base 10) notation. FF is the highest two-digit number in hex notation, so to specify a pure red page, you use the sequence:

```
<BODY BGCOLOR = "#FF0000">
```

For a white page, use

```
<BODY BGCOLOR = "#000000">
```

and for a black page, use

```
<BODY BGCOLOR = "#FFFFFF">
```

RGB numbers are hardly intuitive. If you have Photoshop, you can check a color's RGB value by opening the information palette and holding the cursor over the color you like. (You may have to change the preferences in the information palette first.) Convert each decimal value to hexadecimal as follows: Divide by 16. Put the result in the first digit (using A..F in place of 10..15) and the remainder in the second digit, also using A..F in place of 10..15.

You can specify the color of your type in exactly the same way, using:

```
<BODY TEXT = "#RRGGBB">
```

There's a reason we use black ink on white paper: it's legible. Keep in mind that the screen is a low-resolution device, and that the type is going to be difficult to read anyway. Very light type reversed on a very dark background is really the only safe alternative, and it's still not as readable as black on white.

You may also tile a GIF image in the background. Netscape 1.1 also allows you to use a GIF file as a background for your Web page. Of course, as with all images on your Web pages, the color of your background varies from monitor to monitor.

Backgrounds are specified with an extension to the body tag, like so:

```
<BODY BACKGROUND = "picture.gif">
```

 **Warning:** Netscape loads and displays background GIFs before it loads text or other images. Because Netscape usually loads text first, specifying a large, slow-to-load image may make it seem as if Netscape has slowed to an excruciating crawl. And if image-loading is off, background images don't load either.

Netscape tiles the background GIF, so that if the Netscape browser window is larger than the GIF, the GIF is repeated to the edges of the browser's window. Of course, it's possible to use a background tile that consists of a huge image that will almost certainly be larger than any browser's window. However, such a large image will take forever to load, and it's not unlikely that the user will cancel your page. Don't put an important image in the background; non-Netscape users and those with non-graphical browsers will never see it anyway.

Tiling has been used for novel (and usually ugly) effects at some Web sites—for example, tiles like the one in Figure 12.11 are used to create a sort of wallpaper background.

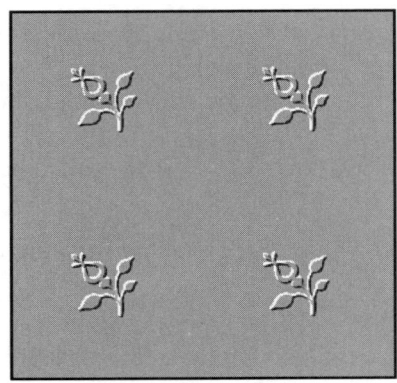

Figure 12.11 Tiles used to create backgrounds on pages.

Where to Find It

Kai's Power Tips and Tricks for Photoshop page is a great place to find out more about creating patterns in Photoshop and a source of Netscape-ready patterns. It's at http://the-tech.mit.edu/KPT/. This site contains notes on Photoshop techniques by legendary 'shop maestro Kai Krause, and an archive of textures. A similar archive can be found at the aforementioned Netscape Hall of Shame.

You probably don't come across too many "real" publications printed on wallpaper, because it just doesn't work very well. The background competes with the type for the reader's attention, and as with the excrescent <BLINK> Netscape extension, there's no way for the reader to turn the background off. If you insist on using this technique on your Web page, please don't tell anyone you learned it from me.

A more eye-friendly technique is to use a tile for textural effects. I created the left tile shown in Figure 12.12 in Photoshop, with the **Filter > Noise > Create** command (set at about 500) and **Filter > Stylize > Emboss**.

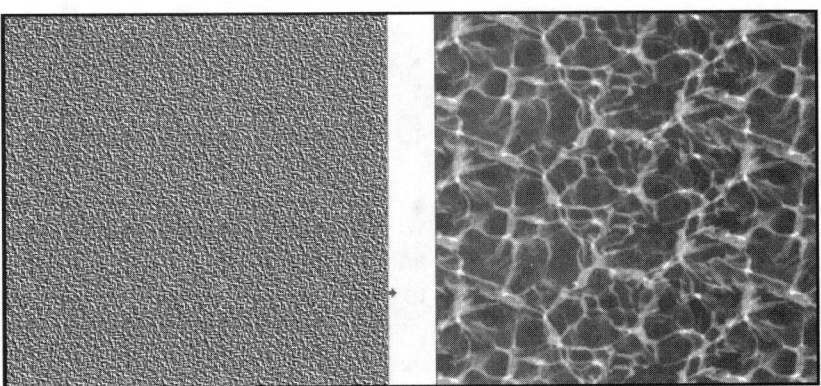

Figure 12.12 Tiles used for textural effects.

The seams don't show because this tile has no concentrations of light or dark areas or recognizable shapes, but does consist of tints of single color. Under the right circumstances and used sparingly, this sort of technique can be effective.

Some digital stock photography is available in ready-to-tile format. Here's an example taken from Wraptures, Disk One (from Form and Function, 1595 17th Ave., San Francisco, CA 94122, phone (415) 664–4010, fax (415) 664–4010).

Remember to boil something like this down to a reasonable size before including it on your Web page and, as always, make sure that your software license agreement allows use of the stock photo. The results of such tiles can be impressive, as shown in Figure 12.13.

I still have no idea how they manage to make these tiles appear to merge seamlessly. Some things are best left to the pros.

Other Unusual Effects

Just because you're on a diet doesn't mean you can't look at the menu. I'm not recommending that you attempt unusual effects that many Web readers will not be able to see. However, I want you to have a comprehensive overview of publishing options so I'm going to briefly describe how some unusual effects are achieved. That way your decision not to use them will be well informed.

Where to Find It

The Sunset Kahili home page is at http://planet-hawaii.com/~sunset/.

Making the Letters Dance

I dislike Netscape's <BLINK> command when it's used to make text blink. There's another use, though. <BLINK> can be used to make the title of your document unroll gradually on the menu bar at the top of the user's screen. The letters can even be made to spread out and then move back. One example is the Sunset Kahili, Kauai home page. The source code makes the title appear gradually:

```
<HEAD>
<BLINK>
<TITLE>S</TITLE>
<TITLE>Su</TITLE>
<TITLE>Sun</TITLE>
<TITLE>Suns</TITLE>
<TITLE>Sunse</TITLE>
<TITLE>Sunset</TITLE>
```

...and so on, until you get the full title:

```
<TITLE>Sunset Kahili, Kauai — The Best View in Poipu!</TITLE>
</BLINK>
</HEAD>
```

It's worth noting that this effect is lost on users of Mosaic, MacWeb, or other browsers.

Server Push Animation

There's a way to achieve a neat animation effect using the server push/client pull feature of Netscape 1.1. This uses the <META> head element in HTML 3.0, the tag that covers general instructions for a document. Of course, there's always a danger that overuse may make it as obnoxious as <BLINK>.

I wouldn't recommend this, necessarily, but I thought it was an interesting sort of "movie" feature achieved through the <META> command. When I connected to the home page of a student at Dartmouth, Phillip Cheung, a series of pages flashed across the screen (I was using Netscape, of course; other browsers won't support this).

The HTML that achieves this home page movie goes at the head of the document:

```
<META HTTP-EQUIV="REFRESH" CONTENT="1;
URL="http://coos.dartmouth.edu/~bizarre/biz_html/cat/(variable).html">
```

The URL specifies what document ("variable," in previous code) should appear when the user's screen is refreshed in one second. Each page specifies a different document until the "movie" is complete.

If you want to see a bald guy sitting in a chair spinning around and around several times as a result of a CGI application, check out the "Pilgarlic Animation" at

Where to Find It

Keep your eyes open when you connect to http://coos.dartmouth.edu/~bizarre. To find more about server push in Netscape 1.1, go to http://www.netscape.com/home/demo/1.1b1/pushpull.html.

Where to Find It

Jason R. Heimbaugh's Home Page is at http://www.cathouse.org/CathousePeople/JasonHeimbaugh/.

Jason R. Heimbaugh's home page. It might seem silly, but I can imagine a practical use for this, as a way of displaying an item for sale (such as jewelry) in an online store.

A Capsule Summary: Two Design Approaches

After all the criticism I've leveled at various Web pages, you may be wondering if there is any good design on the Web. Of course there is. The best design complements the contents of a page and effectively conveys the author's message.

Where to Find It

The Imagex Design welcome page is at http:// sandpiper.rtd.com/~imagex/ newindex.html. The Body home page is at http:// www.thebody.com/.

Personally, I prefer a more orderly, "classy" design. (I also admire *HotWired,* by the way.) But there are a lot of Web surfers who go for something much more energetic and frenetic. The page shown in Figure 12.13 is exciting, and anyone wanting to reach an audience on the Web should be aware that this is considered extremely cool. The intent, obviously, is to impress potential clients with eye-catching graphics.

Although I don't think the page illustrated in Figure 12.14 is perfect (there's almost too much empty space), the design and content complement each other. The page requires the reader's eye to focus only on a few important elements. It doesn't try to do everything all at once. It's classy and restrained. It doesn't tie up my computer with complicated photos or imagemaps. And the buttons don't look like buttons but are graphics in their own right. In other words, I like it!

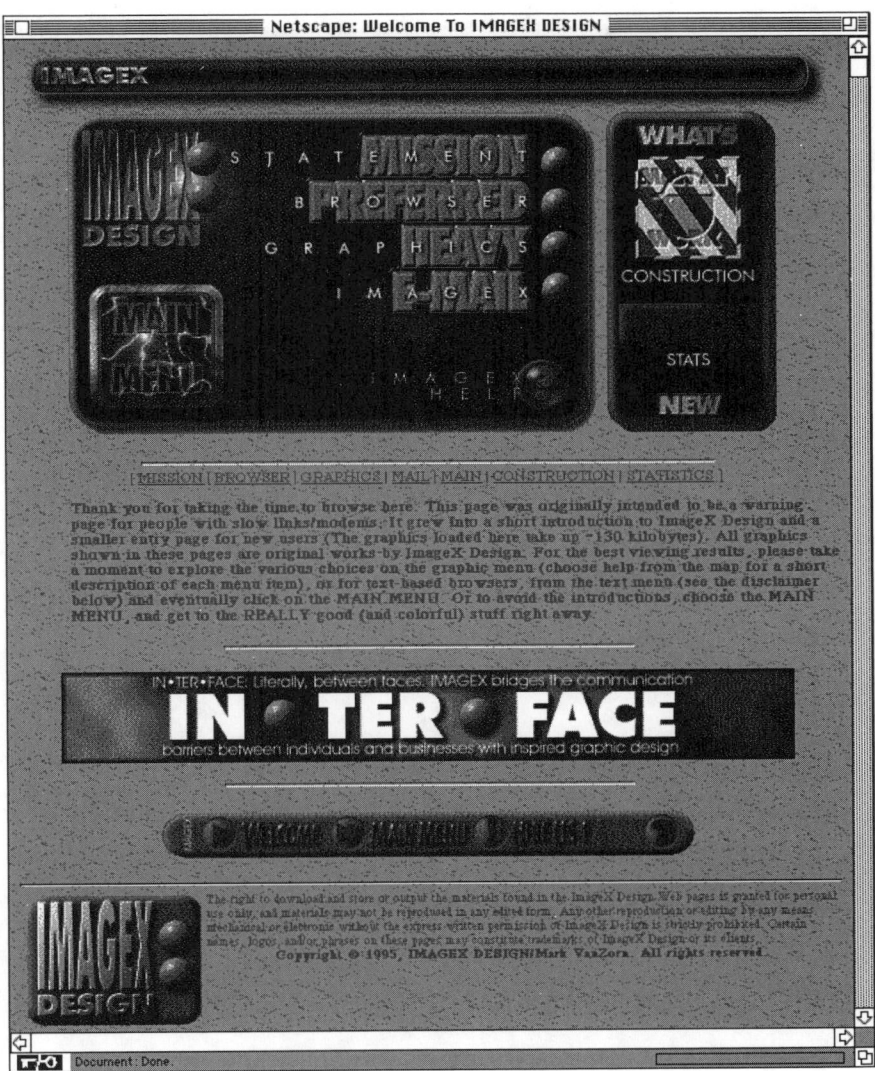

Figure 12.13 Imagex Design main menu page.

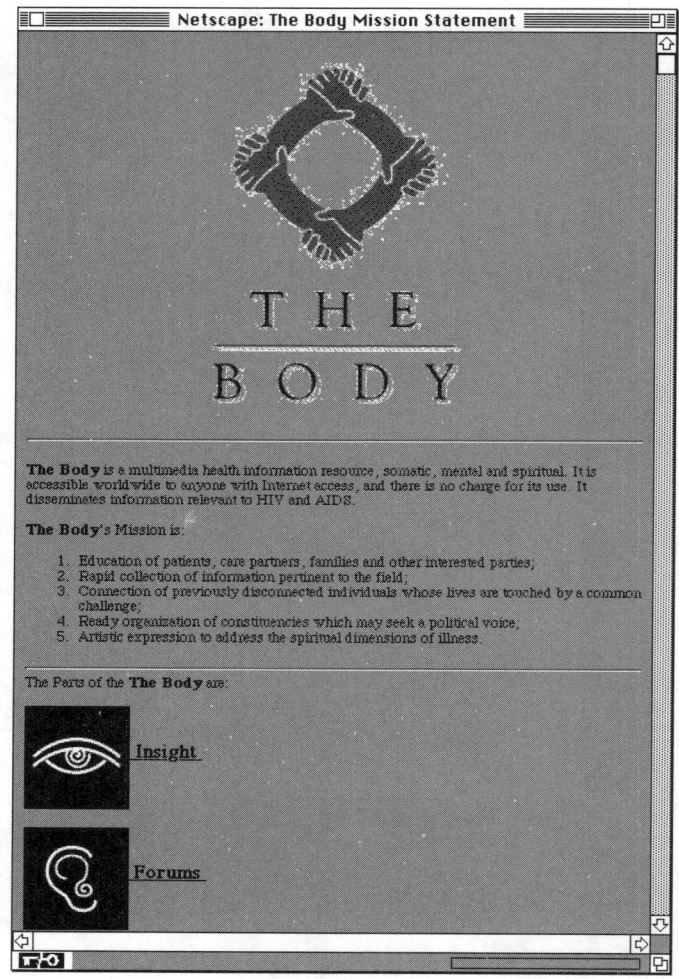

Figure 12.14 The Body mission statement page.

Ideal Design: A Wish List

As new technology brings the worlds of traditional and electronic design closer
together, it becomes less important to think about how to use HTML to design a Web

page, and more important to know the basic principles of designing *any* page, whether it appears in print or onscreen.

Here is a brief wish list of design functions that Web publishers will probably be able to accomplish in the near future, as HTML gets more powerful and complex, or as portable document programs such as Acrobat become easier to access from within Web browsers.

Linespacing

The usual linespacing for desktop publishing documents is about 120 percent of the type size—for example, 10-point type with 12-point leading.

Sometimes, a more elegant effect can be achieved by increasing leading—for example, 10-point type with 15 or more points of leading.

Columns

Usually, publishers try to avoid any block of text that is more than about six inches wide. On the Web, this is pretty much irrelevant; the text is as wide as the browser window.

In the future, if and when HTML allows creation of columns, consider dividing lengthy text into two or even three columns to make it easier to read. (The problem, of course, is that many monitors are too narrow to display several columns anyway.)

It would also be nice to have the option of making a mixed grid, as many newspapers do—a grid that varies from page to page depending on the content. Many newspapers use narrow columns for news items, and wider columns for editorials and features.

Text Wrap

Sometimes an interesting layout can be achieved by making text wrap around an image, as shown in Figure 12.15.

Figure 12.15 Text wrap example.

Drop Caps

Drop caps are a good way to direct the eye toward the beginning of an article and to break up the "sea of words" effect on a page full of type (see Figure 12.16).

Designing a good home page is important for anyone who wants to get a message across. It's essential, though, for advertisers who want to see commercial or other benefits from Web publishing. That's the subject of the next chapter, "Advertising on the Web."

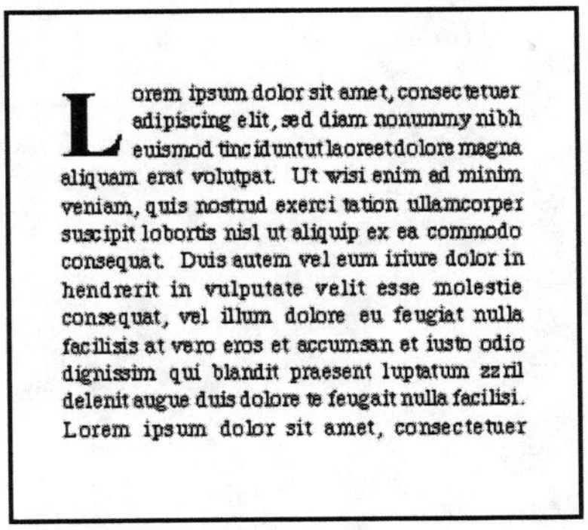

Lorem ipsum dolor sit amet, consectetuer adipiscing elit, sed diam nonummy nibh euismod tincidunt ut laoreet dolore magna aliquam erat volutpat. Ut wisi enim ad minim veniam, quis nostrud exerci tation ullamcorper suscipit lobortis nisl ut aliquip ex ea commodo consequat. Duis autem vel eum iriure dolor in hendrerit in vulputate velit esse molestie consequat, vel illum dolore eu feugiat nulla facilisis at vero eros et accumsan et iusto odio dignissim qui blandit praesent luptatum zzril delenit augue duis dolore te feugait nulla facilisi. Lorem ipsum dolor sit amet, consectetuer

Figure 12.16 Drop cap example.

Part IV

Things to Consider
When Going Online

Advertising on the Web

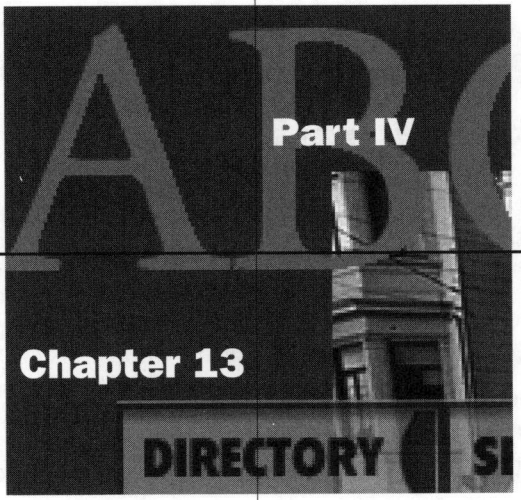

Part IV

Chapter 13

DIRECTORY SI

In short, we are looking for content, communication, and ultimately, some form of community. Advertising has never addressed these requirements in any substantive way. Which is precisely why advertising—in the forms we have known it to date—is deader than the proverbial doorbell.

—Christopher Locke, "Storytime," an essay on Internet Advertising published on MCI's Web site, http://www.mci.com/, 1995

The subject of advertising on the World Wide Web is a thorny one that gets a lot of Internet users worked into a froth. The purpose of this book is not to debate the subject of whether there *should* be advertising on the Internet. In the first place, that question is irrelevant, because advertising is already there.

As an information provider, I realize that advertising is essential to the survival of many businesses. Even when I was an objective newspaper reporter, I knew who buttered my bread. As long as ads don't get in the way of my looking through lists of links or reading text onscreen, I tend to tune them out without any feelings one way or the other.

What You Should Know about Internet Advertising

As a Web publisher, though, you should know that a lot of your readers hate the idea of advertising on the Web in any form. Yet if you need to advertise to stay in business, what are your options?

Established methods of advertising in print or on video aren't effective on the Web because of what I just confessed about my short attention span a few paragraphs ago:

- The Web is an active—not a passive—medium; the users are in control and can switch you off if they are not interested or, for that matter, can ignore you altogether.

- The users are accustomed to advertising and can spot an ad immediately.

So what do you do? You have to get people interested. How do you accomplish that goal? Businesses and organizations have to adopt a totally new approach to advertising on the Web. They need to include some activities that seem unrelated to advertising but that add value to a product, such as storytelling and community building. But, before I get into that, let me give you a wrap-up of some of the other ways advertisers are using the Web.

Where to Find It

Netscape's Internet Search Screen is at http://home.mcom.com/home/internet-search.html. My current favorite search engine is InfoSeek (which also uses advertising), at http://www.infoseek.com/Home. The EDS home page doesn't say what EDS stands for (Electronic Data Systems) until the small type in the copyright line: http://www.eds.com/.

The Conservative Approach

An attempt at translating traditional advertising to the Web is shown in Figure 13.1 (copyright Netscape). It shows Netscape's list of search engines, which uses display advertisements.

But on the Web, nothing is traditional. You can do something with a display ad that you could never do in a newspaper. The ad itself is a clickable link. Click it to go to the advertiser's home page, where you can find out more information about the product (see Figure 13.2).

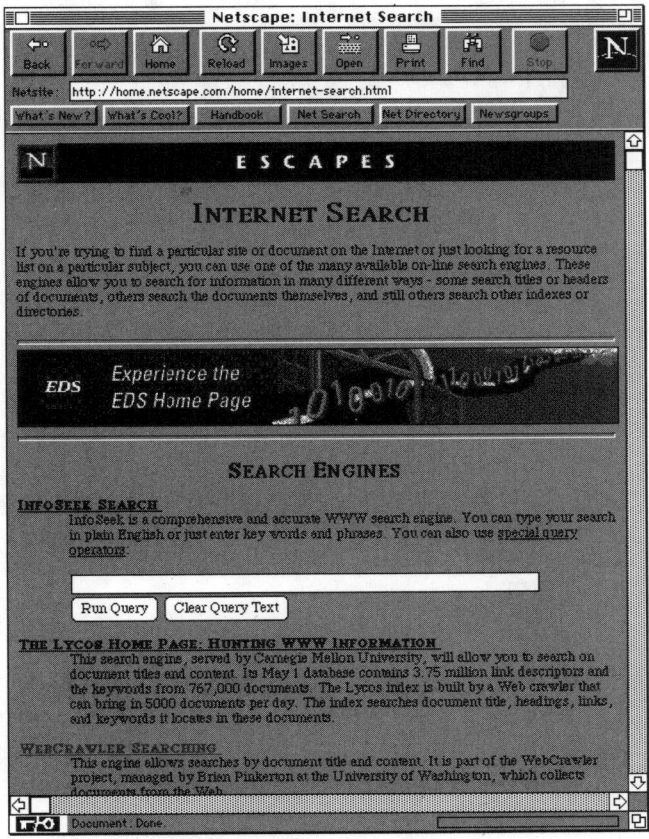

Figure 13.1 An ad on the Internet Search screen.

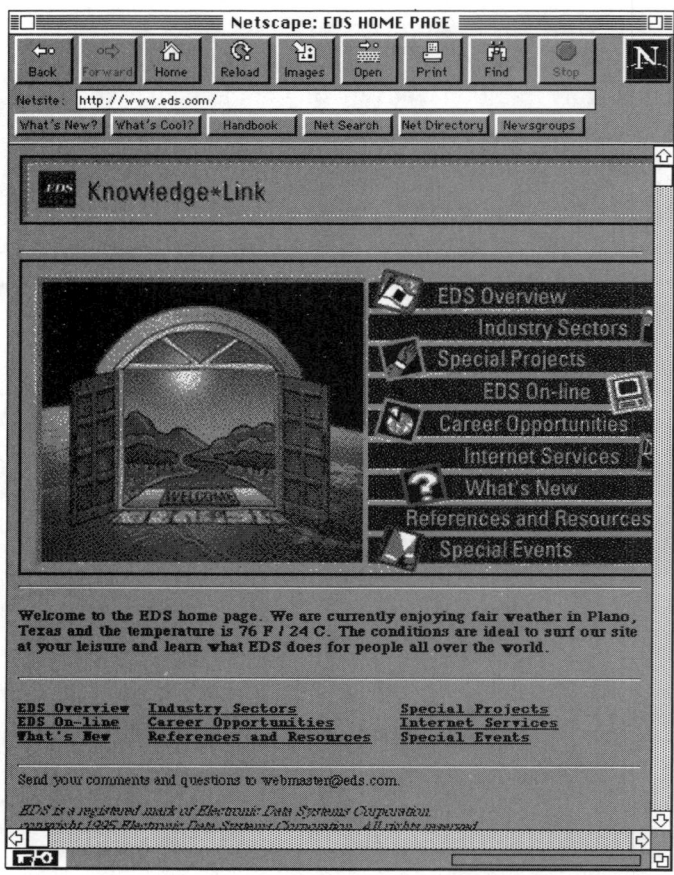

Figure 13.2 Experiencing the EDS home page (copyright Electronic
Data Systems).

The Benefits

The conservative approach can have substantial benefits for a traditional publishing
concern—such as a newspaper or magazine—that wants to have a presence on the
Web.

The publisher now has a new market to offer to advertisers: not only will they appear
in your magazine (so you may tell the advertiser), but they will be on your Web site,
too (or a bulletin board service, if you have one).

It should interest advertisers to know that their products and services can appear before a potential audience of millions. You can give them more concrete information if you keep track of visits to your Web page or gather some demographic information on your visitors.

Location, Location, Location

Once you begin to get advertisers to commit to placing ads in your publication, you have to decide whether you will help them create the ad. You may end up helping them create a home page if they don't already have one.

There's another question, though: once the advertiser has a home page, will that page reside on your server or on the advertiser's?

If it resides on your server, you have to run CGI scripts to process forms, and perform maintenance, which involves updating files, receiving email, compiling statistics of "hits," and so on. (Hint: You can charge the advertiser extra for this service.)

On the other hand, if it resides on a remote site, you run the risk of having the readers leave your site and your publication completely when they follow a link to an advertiser's site.

Most large advertisers will probably choose the latter option because they have their own Web sites already. Smaller concerns, such as local businesses, might leave it up to you.

The question is moot, however, unless a Web reader actually clicks an advertisement. That brings up the bottom-line question: Does anybody actually click these links? Not many will do so unless you give them an incentive. Advertisers have to provide motivation in entirely new ways. You, the publisher, can help in the process.

> **Note:** Who's the publisher here? If you put out a magazine, you're a Web publisher, without a doubt. But if your advertisers put out home pages that contain information about a product or service, they are also information providers. In this chapter, I address both kinds of publishers.

Other Traditional Approaches

A number of tried-and-true advertising techniques have been attempted on the Web, including cybermalls, downloadable ads and TV spots, classified ads, and trade directories.

Cybermalls

I dislike electronic shopping centers on the Web almost as much as I hate malls in real life, but they are an alternative way of business promotion.

Some cybermalls do allow secure electronic commerce transactions for purchases, which can be a real benefit. It can also be less expensive and time-consuming to sign on with a shopping mall on the Web than to start up your own site. But, personally, they wouldn't be my first choice. There are so many malls that your home page might get lost in the crowd.

Where to Find It

A list of shopping malls on the Web is at http://www.yahoo.com/Business/Corporations/Shopping_Centers. The Online Ad Agency's site is http://www.nyweb.com/toaa/.

Downloadable Ads and TV Spots

The Online Ad agency created a site called the New York Web. If you desire to watch commercials, it provides a portfolio of the ads and TV spots that can be seen online and downloaded. After the novelty factor wears off, however, I don't think you are likely to spend the time and disk space downloading a ten-second spot for suntan lotion.

Classified Ads

The classifieds, if presented as a searchable index in an online newspaper, for instance, can work wonderfully on the Web. (If cybermalls had their contents also arranged as "searchable," I'd probably like them better.) The index isn't easy to set up, however. It requires that all of the ads be downloaded to an HTML file on a daily, weekly, or monthly basis, depending on how often the publication is produced. Another way involves a user making a query; the query goes to a CGI on the server, which runs a database search, gathers the results, and returns them back to the viewer in HTML form "on the fly." Either way requires a good deal of CGI scripting.

Then, when users log onto the ads and search them, it consumes a good deal of your server's processor time. In other words, you need a powerful server and the cable leading into your Internet provider's facility must be able to accommodate a lot of simultaneous traffic.

The publisher who can do all that, however, provides the reader with an invaluable resource: a searchable database of ads. One of the best examples is provided by the Mercury Center, the Web publication of the San Jose Mercury News. For example, I did a search for computers, and got 150 ads. I refined the ads to search for Macintosh PowerBooks listed in that day's paper, and came up with seven listings. This took all of two minutes (see Figure 13.3). Figure 13.3 has been reprinted with permission of Mercury Center, http://www.sjmercury.com.

Where to Find It

The Mercury Center classifieds are at http://www.sjmercury.com/searchcl.html. The Mac/Chicago Trade Directory is at http://www.macchicago.com/home/TD/Categories.html.

Trade Directories

Another way to give advertisers coverage is to include their home page or display ad in a directory of advertisers that you can post on your Web site. These may or may not be advertisers you give coverage to elsewhere in your publications.

Like the classifieds, this set of ads is searchable and can be downloaded. Together with your printed publications and other services you provide, a trade directory can be part of an attractive package for advertisers.

In June 1995, for instance, Mac/Chicago magazine was offering coverage in its printed publication, its online trade directory (Figure 13.4), and its bulletin board service for $30 a month.

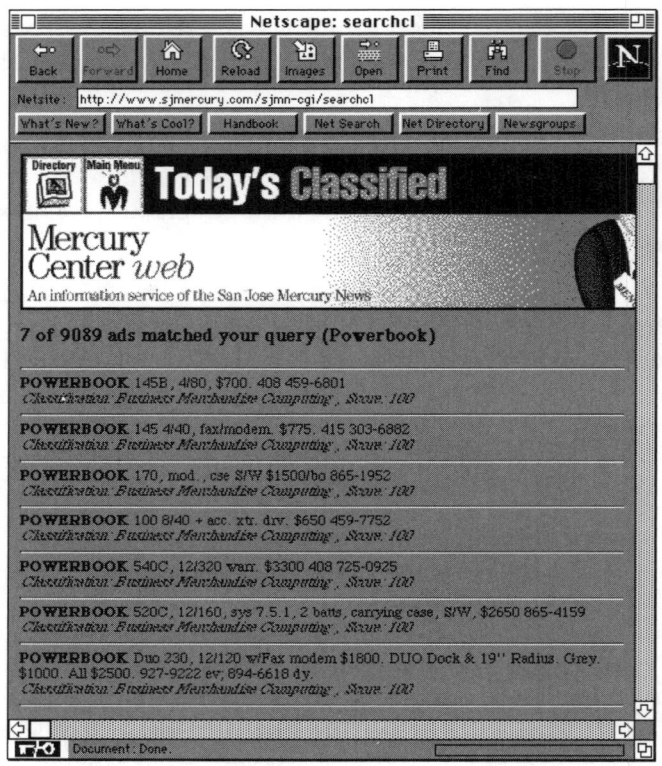

Figure 13.3 Classified ads search results.

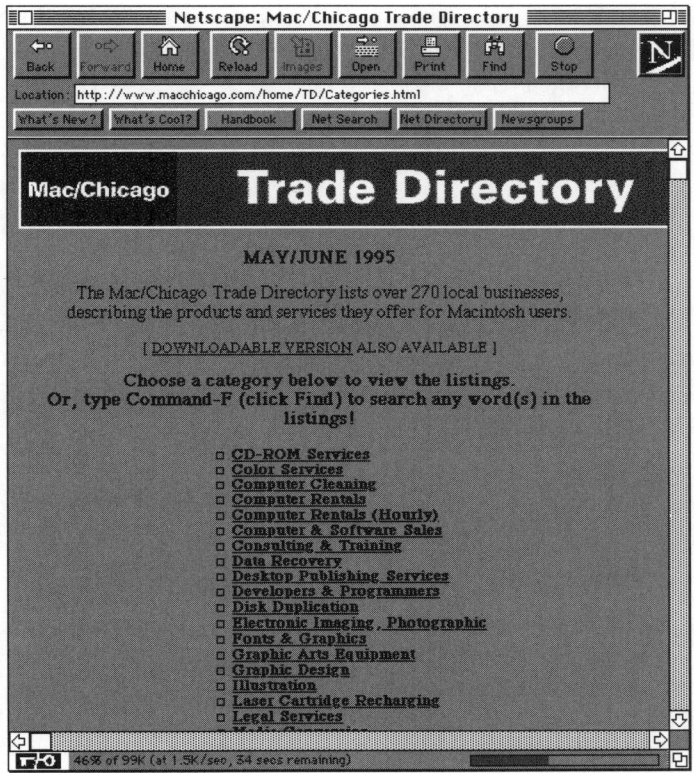

Figure 13.4 Part of Mac/Chicago Trade Directory.

Creating Ads that Interest Web Surfers

Is there such a thing as an advertisement that grabs the readers' attention and actually entices them to find out more, or even to add a bookmark to the site (the ultimate compliment)?

I believe there is. The key is to find out about your potential audience's wants and interests. To do that, examine some of the most popular sites on the Web. What do they have that attracts visitors?

At the time this book was being completed, these were the five most popular categories on the Yahoo index (at least, the ones that didn't focus on sex):

1. Entertainment

2. Computers

3. Society and Culture

4. Art

5. Business

An ideal offering for an advertiser, then, would bring together several of these areas. It would be entertaining; somehow use computer technology; and have something to do with society, culture, art, or business.

At this writing, because of technological limitations such as the bandwidth of the cable delivering data to individual Web surfers and the speed of the modem accessing that data, the Web doesn't entertain in the sense of providing a lot of music or video the way a radio, television, or VCR does. Similar elements are available on the Web, to be sure, but they they require a lot of memory, a lot of bandwidth, and a lot of patience: things many Web surfers lack.

What the Web *does* provide are words and images. People might not go to the Web to be entertained directly, but they will go to find out something about their favorite entertainers—or about computers, or society and culture, or art, or business.

Presentation and Content

Presentation and content drive the effectiveness of advertising on the Web. I'd suggest that you call it "Infotising," but I hate those sorts of hybrid words.

If you want to see quickly what kinds of information a large organization with a lot of resources can put on the Web to attract readers, do a search on Yahoo for "AT&T." When I did this, I came up with a list of 35 different Web pages related to AT&T. They included:

- AT&T Stories (http://www.att.com/stories/), described as "A slightly skewed retelling by AT&T's friendly Wizard of stories you grew up with";

- A contest to "experience the first totally interactive simulator adventure ride on the planet" (http://youwill.com/);

- A directory of 800 numbers (http://att.net/dir800);

- A clickable imagemap that "lets you explore the electrical power system at all levels through text and colorful graphics." This includes a course with animation, video, and audio (http://www.att.com/talkingpower/);

- Information about a security-enhanced HTTP protocol (http://hecatomb.research.att.com:8001/jsac/charge/demo.html); and

- Coverage of the forty-eighth annual Pebble Beach Pro-Am golf tournament (http://www.best.com/~abcnet/).

Where to Find It

As stated in the list of AT&T sites, the AT&T Stories page is at http://www.att.com/stories/. The MasterCard International stories site is at http://www.mastercard.com/.

I'm not eager to give AT&T free advertising, but I wanted to give you an example of a business with considerable resources that's trying just about anything and everything to market itself on the Web. Not one of these offerings resembles a traditional TV or newspaper ad spot.

The site offering information about a security-enhanced HTTP protocol is notable because it offers a useful service and can make AT&T appear to be a helpful member of the Web community.

See Figure 13.5. Does this look like an ad? Not until you get to the annoying mentions of AT&T's name after every story title. To my mind, the site would be better off without them.

The most effective ads on the Web are sites, rather than single images. These sites don't look like ads at all, but offer some information or entertainment. The advertiser stays in the background while providing the service or event, and contributes something to the Web community. The effect is to add value to the advertiser's name.

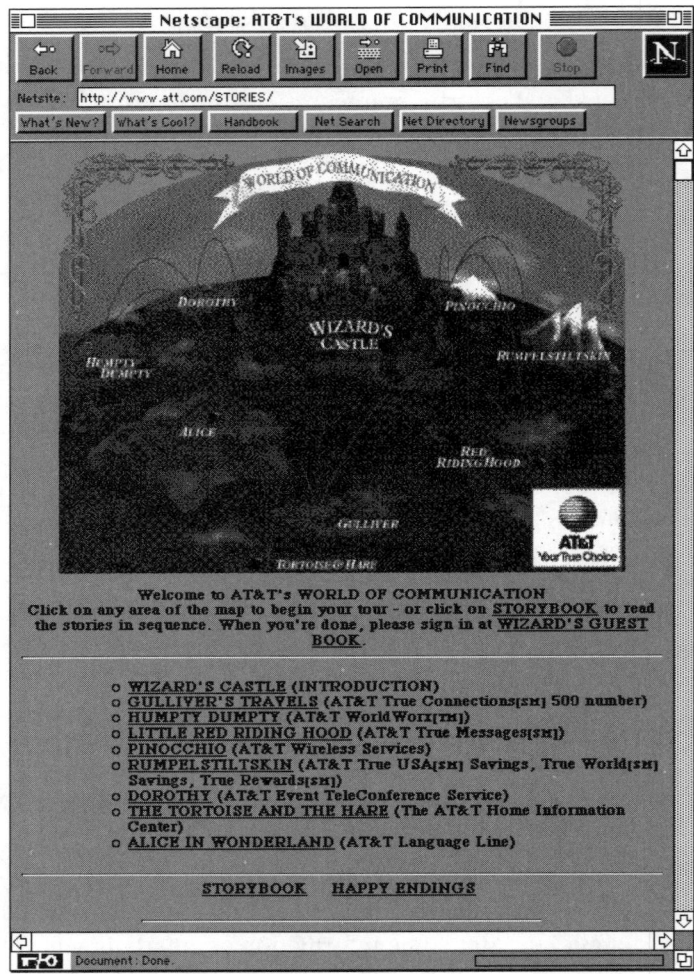

Figure 13.5 AT&T stories page (copyright AT&T).

The Radical Approach

The best ads take advantage of one of the most positive and exciting qualities of the Internet: the way the Net brings people together from all over the world in new electronic communities.

If advertisers can play a role in actually helping to build those communities, they will be "cutting edge." They will also be positive influences in much the same way that Ben and Jerry's is perceived by those concerned about the environment.

An example of one of these "adversites" (sorry, I couldn't resist that) is shown in Figure 13.6 (site copyright MasterCard International).

Figure 13.6 MasterCard International stories site.

417

I already mentioned this site in Chapter 9 to get free content for Web documents. The point here is that the content of the site is in accord with the strength of the medium on which it is presented.

You see, another wonderful aspect of the Web is the way it can be used to tell stories. That's the reason I got interested in it in the first place: it seemed like the perfect place to publish my own poems and short stories.

The most effective advertising on the Web will do what this one attempts to do:

- Entertains

- Uses computer technology

- Is about culture, society, and community

- Promotes the arts

Where to Find It

To get more ideas on promoting culture and community on the Web, visit the WELL's Web site, http://www.well.com/, or the Culture section of the WWW Virtual Library: http://hirsch.cosy.sbg.ac.at/www-virtual-library_culture.html.

My advice to Web advertisers is to promote themselves indirectly and provide content that adds value to their goods and services. Large corporations will thereby counteract the impression among Web users that they are "invading" a previously non-commercial territory by becoming active participants in the Web community.

An advertiser will create a good impression, for instance, by creating the kinds of sites that bring people together, just as the Web does:

- A site where artists with access to the Web can publish their work.

- Chat groups where people can discuss issues related to their own product.

- Libraries of software available for downloading.

- Online service centers where customers can complain, ask questions about how to operate a device, or find information about repairs.

Any ad that gets people involved or promotes the culture of the Web will benefit advertisers and publishers alike. It's all part of using the Web as a marketing tool, which is explored further in the next chapter.

The Web as a
Marketing Tool

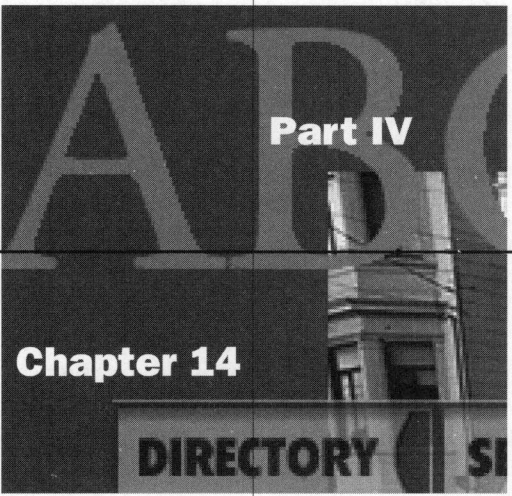

Part IV

Chapter 14

Beauty may be only skin deep, but if your site on the Web is not attractive enough to provoke your electronic "blind dates" to take second looks, they are not likely to discover your great personality.

In publishing, as in dating, the difference between success and failure often boils down to how well your product has been marketed. You don't need a Ph.D. in business to promote yourself online and get the attention you deserve. The marketing-oriented Web writer or publisher will stand out from the growing crowd by following these simple steps:

- Defining the product to be marketed.

- Determining the need or demand for the product.

- Identifying the potential audience.

- Strategizing communication and follow-up.

Where to Find It

Marketing On the Internet is a Web site for a marketing service that practices what it preaches: instead of a straight sales pitch, it gives you a lot of good information about Web marketing practices. After building up some initial goodwill, the sales pitch comes after you have gone several documents into its site. Check it out at http://www.netresource.com/itp/reptoc.html.

New Web sites are likely to be flooded with hits immediately after they are announced on a "What's New" or "Cool Site of the Day" list. But after receiving a deluge of visitors the first few days, interest often slows to a trickle. The reason? Faulty marketing, or no marketing at all, may be to blame for drying things up.

The field of marketing used to be just for large corporations and advertisers. But now the sophistication of the consumer and the high level of competition in all areas, including my niche in higher education, means that none of us can ignore these skills. If you have something to communicate (and don't we all), you have to do some sort of marketing to reach your audience.

Why Market on the World Wide Web?

If you have decided to become an information provider on the Web, you probably think you have an answer to this question already. But, especially if you haven't consciously done marketing before, a closer examination of the following points will help you come up with a good plan.

Immediacy

The Web not only provides you with a sizable new group of potential customers, but it lets you convey information about your goods and services instantly. What's more, your online audience can respond with the same immediacy.

Your Audience Is in Control

How many evenings have been lost forever because you couch potatoed yourself in front of the television and watched whatever came on next? The Web isn't as passive a medium as television. The viewer controls the flow of information by doing searches, following links, and deciding what sites to visit or what articles to read. Visitors who follow a link to your company or organization have (in most cases) made a conscious decision to do so and want to know more.

The Reader Can Keep a Record

Because it's so easy to save or print information accessed through the Web, it's no extra trouble for a potential customer/reader to make a printout of your site's content or save the file to disk to record your email address or URL.

It's "Cool"

There's that word again. You hear it over and over with regard to the Web. For someone marketing goods and services, that's a great thing. Because the Web is relatively new and "cool," what you put forth will allow the name dropper to brag to the crowd around the office water cooler (as in the phrase "I bought it on the Internet," or "I downloaded it from the Internet").

It Uses Multimedia

Words, pictures, sounds, video, color… the Web puts it all together along with immediacy and viewer control. True, it's hard to get fast access to all this multimedia potential with a modem connection. But as faster bandwidths become more affordable, multimedia will become more practical.

It's Inexpensive

Starting up a rudimentary Web site is far less expensive than buying an ad on a popular television show—and once it's out there, as long as you pay your Internet provider's fee, you have a lot longer than 30 seconds to strut your stuff. People can access your publishing effort around the clock, so if insomniacs want to do some surfing or online shopping late at night, your message isn't asleep even if you are.

The Web Evens the Playing Field

It's a free country and the Web is a great believer in the average citizen. Companies with big names will naturally get some initial attention because of their reputations. But reputation is only worth so much on the Internet. After that, it's up to the ingenuity of the author to entice a reader or potential customer. A multinational conglomerate with a dull site won't get as many "hits" online as a local company with a "killer" Web site.

What Can You Expect to Gain?

Cyberspace abounds with grandiose pronouncements about how the Internet is "open for business" and is a "competitive business tool."

The hype goes like this: The Internet has as many as 40 million users. In the next five years, the revenue from goods and services purchased on the Net will reach as high as $600 billion. Everybody is going to be jumping on the Information Superhighway bandwagon.

The real answer is: No one knows for sure how many people are "on the Net" right now. No one knows how many new customers you will get from a Web presence.

All indications are that Internet use is growing by leaps and bounds and will continue to do so. The initial investment is relatively low, and because it's very likely that your competitors are going online, you'd better get with the program too, or you'll be left in the dust.

Greg's Soapbox

Am I telling you to be a lemming, one of those creatures who follows the crowd blindly? Of course not. I'm encouraging you to be realistic and not to get caught up in the hype. I believe the Web has the potential to change the way much of the world gets information and does its commerce. It's definitely worth the investment in time and money, but like making any business decision, advance planning is essential. In fact, it is because being online is so essential to your survival that it is even more vital that you take the time to establish your identity and present it effectively.

Where to Find It

Plenty of attempts have been made to figure out how many people are on the Internet and what sorts of people use it. But there's no central Internet governing body, so no one (happily) can make a user fill out a form or register. That doesn't stop people from trying. The GVU WWW Survey Home Page is an oft-cited source of information. It's at http://www.cc.gatech.edu/ gvu/user_surveys/ User_Survey_Home.html. A list of sites with Internet-related statistics and demographics can

continued

Who Can You Expect to Reach?

In a nutshell, someone like myself, only not necessarily a writer, and with a bit more money to spend. However, I'm including this list only as a historical artifact. As I said before, the Web is a great equalizer. Segments of our world-wide audience that may have been under-represented when this information was gathered and are increasing in numbers even as we speak.

The GVU Center's third annual WWW survey compiled data from 13,000 of the supposed 13.5 million Web users, so take the results for what you will. The survey reports that the typical Web user:

be found at http://
www.yahoo.com/Computers/
Internet/
Statistics_and_Demographics.

- is male;

- is 35 years old (okay, I haven't seen 35 for a few years now, but who's counting?);

- earns $50K to $60K per year;

- lives in the U.S.;

- has a college degree; and

- has a computer, professional, or educational job.

How Can You Expect to Benefit?

You may see direct benefits from credit card or other purchases of the goods and services you're marketing. But don't count on it. You *can* count on indirect benefits brought about by increased exposure on the Web or positive "vibes" produced in the Web surfer.

You will get bonus points for being graphically exciting or using the newest technology—as long as you don't make a page too slow to display for those with modems. (Update your site to support HTML 3.0 tags, for instance, as AT&T did, or offer extras such as animation or video.) If it's consistent with your message, go for it.

So How Do You Do It?

That's what the rest of the chapter is about. But if you're looking for a quick answer, it's as follows:

- Induce the Web readers to come to you by promising to offer them something—information, ideally. In other words, become an Internet resource.

- Make your publication interactive. Get your readers involved by inviting comments, subscriptions, a place to request more information, or any way to get them to tell you something about themselves.

- Process the data you receive and follow up on it with prompt personal contacts.

Although the Web is a new medium, the principles of marketing are the same as they have always been in print, or television, or radio.

What's also the same is the way those principles are being misused. You see the same unattractive marketing techniques now that you've always seen. In fact, there is the potential to go from bad to worse because the Web is so new and because it has been dominated by people who know a lot about computers but are clueless about business or communication.

Of course I'm not talking about you, because you are reading this book. This chapter discusses some simple, practical techniques that all Web publishers can apply to better market their product or information.

Four Basic Marketing Techniques

The traditional definition of marketing calls for four factors to converge:

- Product
- Price
- Place
- Promotion

Product: The Importance of Presentation and Content

Why do people go surfing on the Web? Most often, I think, because they want to find information. Someday, when real-time video becomes more prevalent and cables get faster, the Web may turn into as vast an entertainment wasteland as television (I hope not). For all we know, the Web may turn *into* television (I can't even bear to think about it).

Shopping, of course, is becoming a more established and more popular activity on the Web. Even I, who avoid malls like the plague, have enjoyed online shopping.

But, the Web wouldn't exist if researchers and educators didn't need to exchange information and communicate with one another. For now, the primary product on the

425

Web is *information*. Your online audience can't reach into your computer and pull out a can of your product. They want to have facts and ideas they can *read* and *use* and think about.

The knowledge and the goodwill visitors receive from your Web site might introduce them to your product, encourage them to think about it more positively, and give them easy ways to use or purchase it later on.

Web surfers don't just want to glance at cool things for an instant (well, not all of the time). They want programs and utilities they can download and useful information they can read onscreen. Give them whatever you can. Don't hold back your best content. Put it right out there and then, when people do respond to you, offer them some more. The Web is not all or nothing. It's not now or never.

Price: Packaging Yourself Well

I have a coworker whose favorite sentence is, "Presentation is everything." Her motto applies to putting goods and services on the Web because it is more a matter of packaging than of actually setting the right "price" for a specific product.

Of course, there are those who do charge a fee for access to information and that's a different matter.

But usually, in a literal sense, the "price" your customer pays to go through your Web site is the time they have to spend locating you and the effort required to search for information on that site. It's to your advantage to keep the price low by identifying yourself clearly and making your site easy to navigate.

Identify Yourself Clearly: Your URL

URL addresses weren't invented with marketing purposes in mind. They were created so a remote computer could contact a host computer and locate a file on it.

That's no reason why your URL has to be hard to remember, however. Save your creativity for later. If you have a chance to name your own URL, keep your address as short and obvious as possible. You want your potential reader or customer to remember your address or even to find you without knowing exactly what it is ahead of time.

It's becoming a convention to put the prefix "www" in front of any URL address that denotes a World Wide Web server. So, play follow the leader, as in

http://www.*yourname.suf*

where "*suf*" is a suffix for .com, .edu., net, and so on.

An address such as the URL for the Advil Home Page keeps people who can't remember the address off the site:

http://199.97.97.11/advil/index.html

Instead, make it as easy as falling off a log. If your Internet provider or system administrator allows you to set up an alias for your site, do it. Or, if you can, set up your own domain name by registering it with the InterNIC Registration Authority:

http://www.advil.com/

Clear Links, Short Paths, Good Benefits

No question about it. Easy does it. Just as you make it easy for visitors to find you on the Web, also make it easy for them to find something on your site as soon as they arrive. Present as much information as you can right on your home page without making it too crowded—or, hint at what people can find if they follow the links you give them.

Where to Find It

Hot Wired has one of those URLs that is so simple you can guess it: http://www.hotwired.com/. By the way, information on registering your domain name can be found at http://www.catalog.com/catalog/domains.html.

Design Ideas that Excite and Entice

Hot Wired, the Web version of *Wired* magazine, is a good example of a publication that makes readers pay a small price and, in return, gives them some good benefits.

Hot Wired doesn't charge people money to gain access to its contents. The "price" they charge is to have each reader fill out a form providing some essential marketing information about themselves. The reader then gets a password. After that they can read as much as they want, although they'll have to renew their registration from time to time so that *Hot Wired* has updated data.

What does the reader get in return? A glimpse at what a lot of technology and a large staff can publish, an entré into Web culture, some good articles to read, and great graphics to view.

Whether or not you go for its design, from a marketing standpoint, *Hot Wired* and its parent magazine, *Wired*, are among the best places to work on your third marketing objective, knowing your audience.

Place: Know Your Audience

Look before you leap. If you want to publish on the Web, you should know what you're getting into. Not only do you have to know what the competition is putting out, but it's good to get an idea of the culture of the Web. Like a foreign country, it has its own language and its own virtual communities.

In other words, you have to get to know your audience so that you can communicate to them. Communicate without the proper "Netiquette," and you can pay a big price and get "flamed." A disgruntled Net user can send out a nasty letter about you to thousands of people in a newsgroup consisting of the very people you want to reach.

Your Internal Audience

Your Web publication may be intended for an external audience, such as prospective students or prospective purchasers. But there's an internal audience as well that includes your peers, both within your institution and at other similar institutions around the country.

Familiarizing yourself with this audience can prevent you from copying something someone else has done. If you are putting out a newsletter, for instance, and you've come up with the title "Widgets," you should make sure there aren't any other publications already on the Internet that are using this term.

Get to Know Usenet

Usenet and its newsgroups can help you learn something about both your internal and external audiences.

Usenet is a worldwide discussion system. Newsgroups are formed around a particular subject and articles are posted to the groups. Usenet consists of people who exchange "articles."

Where to Find It

A source of information on netiquette, net.acceptable, is at http://arganet.tenagra.com/net-acceptable.html. A list of acceptable use policies is at ftp://nis.nsf.net/acceptable.use.policies/.

Newsgroups are a huge and important means of electronic communication. They are far more popular than the Web (it's estimated that there are more than 11,000)—and they've been around longer, too.

A good marketer will unearth the right newsgroups and then approach them tactfully so as not to get "flamed," or in other words, ridiculed and vilified online so as to lose virtually all credibility.

Remember that many of the networks that comprise the Internet have "Acceptable Use Policies" that govern the kinds of traffic permitted on them.

How to Approach a Newsgroup

1. Find a newsgroup that includes the audience to which you want to market your Web publication. If necessary, subscribe to it.

2. "Lurk" in the background, reading messages and getting a feel for the current issues and concerns of the group as a whole, as well as its jargon.

3. Look for the FAQ files for the newsgroup.

4. If an article appears online in which a user asks a question that you can answer or make some observations on, do so. That's the least intrusive way to get into a newsgroup—in other words, become a participating member of the group and help your fellow members. Let people get to know you.

5. After a while, you can take a risk and announce yourself with a short, polite posting, offering some information about your product or services in return to anyone who makes an initial contact with you.

6. Whatever you do, DON'T commit a "spam" by simply making an unsolicited offer of your services that amounts to an advertisement. (To find out more about the term "spam," see the glossary in Appendix G.)

Where to Find It

The Usenet Info Center Launch Pad contains general information about Usenet, a browsable list of newsgroups, and a way to search for a group of interest. You can see how many readers there are in each group and how frequently messages are sent. It's at http://sunsite.unc.edu/usenet-b/home.html.

Where to Find It

A Web site that acts as a "clearinghouse for cyberart and culture" is at http://www.earthcom.com/cyberculture.html. A good introduction to "Hacker Culture and the Politics of Cyberpunk" is in Great Britain, at http://www.york.ac.uk/~jjrk1/hackult.html.

Where to Find It

To find out more about virtual communities, take a virtual trip to

The Art of Netiquette: Reaching Your External Audience

You can't just create a home page and then run away. You have to go out and find your audience. A good way to start is to get to know the culture of the Web.

Virtual Communities

Virtual communities, to my mind, are some of the most fascinating and creative aspects of online life. Far-flung Internet users collaborate to build virtual towns, neighborhoods, or worlds. Take a virtual trip to one and you'll get an idea for how well people can work together online—often, I'm sorry to say, better than they work together in the real world.

Web Jargon

Hans de Wolf and his collaborators have been publishing the Jargon File since 1975. It collects slang used by computer hackers and provides information on email conventions.

Emoticons and TLAs

Emoticons, also called "smileys," originated long before the Web and stem from email and Usenet. They are a set of keyboard symbols used to portray emotions in email messages and thus avoid misunderstandings. They should be used sparingly, but can help in communicating with

http://www.well.com/user/hlr/vircom/. Take a virtual trip to France and see the AJL Cyberculture Web pages (http://eerie.eerie.fr/~alquier/cyber.html), where you'll find links to virtual communities, virtual reality, and cybersex.

Where to Find It

The Jargon File is at http://www.ccil.org/jargon/jarginfo.html. A list of emoticons can be found at On Line Emoticon, http://www.emoticon.com/emoticon/smiley.html.

Where to Find It

Axcess magazine is at http://www.internex.net/axcess. Internet World is at http://www.mecklerweb.com/mags/iw/iwhome.htm. "Off the Net" is at http://home.netscape.com/assist/net_sites/off_the_net.html. The Internet Underground Music Archive is at http://sunsite.unc.edu/ianc/index.html.

newsgroup audiences who can't read your body language or tune into your tone of voice. Emoticons are becoming a subculture within the culture of the Web. You can buy emoticon T-shirts, for instance.

Examples of Three-Letter Acronyms (TLAs) are the relatively common BTW (by the way), IMHO (in my humble opinion), as well as the humorous ROFL (rolling on the floor, laughing) and RTFM (read the (bleeping) manual).

Read Web-Savvy Publications

Besides *Hot Wired,* there's *Axcess* magazine, which covers "Art, Cyberculture, Music, and Style." Internet World is a good place to check out, as is Netscape's site "Off the Net," or the Internet Underground Music Archive.

Promotion: Communicating and Getting Feedback

Publishing isn't a one-way street. After you put your message out, you need to give your readers a way to respond to you. The Web is ideally suited for getting feedback from your audience.

Plan Your Response

The time to figure out what sort of response you want to get from your Web publication is now, before you've put

431

anything online. Surprises are fine for birthday parties, but you have a lot at stake here.

What sort of emotions do you want your publication to evoke? What reactions do you want your words, images, and sounds to produce? Do you want to shock or amuse people? Is your primary goal to inform? Try to visualize the feeling you want to produce in your audience, and then strategize ways to create the desired effect.

Where to Find It

The newsgroup for announcing new Web sites is comp.info.systems.www.announce (you can view archives of past articles at http://www.cs.rochester.edu/u/ferguson/announce.www/). What's New With NCSA Mosaic is at http://www.ncsa.uiuc.edu/SDG/Software/Mosaic/Docs/whats-new.html. Be sure you read the instructions on how to announce in these resources.

Where to Find It

Carleton University's Web site is at http://www.carleton.ca/.

Announcing Your Web Site

After you have gone through all the effort of planning, writing, and assembling a Web site, don't hide your light under a bushel. Broadcast your accomplishment to as many outlets as possible.

Forms

You've seen a number of forms in this book already. Most of them ask a respondent for information, or provide a place where someone can search for information on your site.

Figure 14.1 shows different sort of form: a class schedule form offered as a service by Carleton University in Canada. Carleton has one of the best sites of any university I've seen.

This doesn't ask for the inquirer's personal information, but it does get a visitor to interact with the site and provide them with information to make the site more useful. (They also offer a telephone book form.)

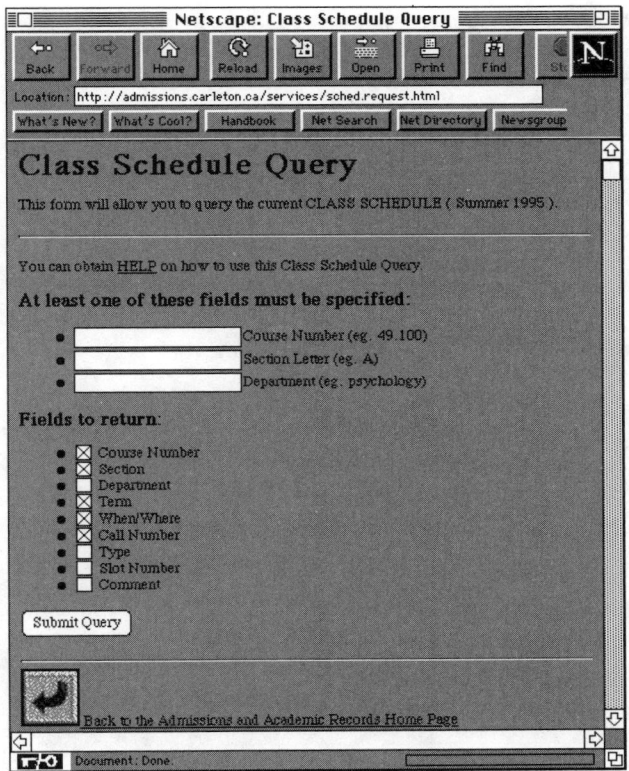

Figure 14.1 Carleton College class schedule form.

Pseudo-Surveys

One subtle way to get information is to invite the reader to ask *you* for information. Carleton has an extensive form in which a prospective student can request further information (see Figure 14.2).

Finally, Carleton also offers a place for anyone to email comments or questions (see Figure 14.3).

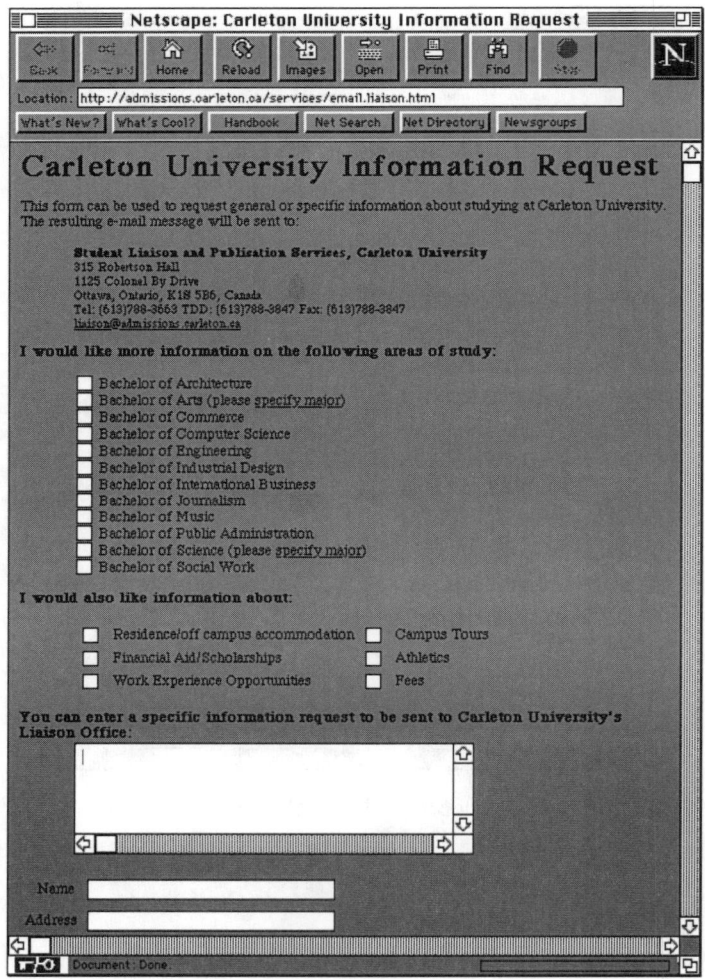

Figure 14.2 Carleton College information form.

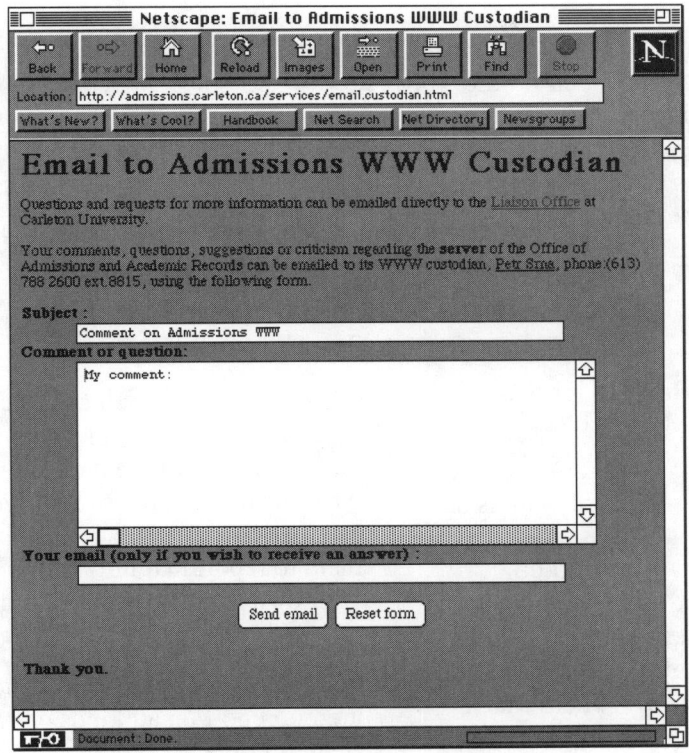

Figure 14.3 Carleton College comment form.

Surveys and Questionnaires

Contests and Giveaways

A contest can be as effective a means of establishing contact with potential customers on the Web as it is off the Web. On the Web, though, there's a big advantage: entering a contest can be done in a matter of seconds. The most effective contests give something away that people want, and are well publicized.

Note: I did a search for the word "survey" on Yahoo and came up with 113
different references. Plenty of people are either doing surveys or offering to
help. Personally, the ones I found the most interesting were those that
related to the Internet or the Web and that offered information on browsers
or Internet usage.

Track Your Visitors

Where to Find It

A version of WebStat for use with
MacHTTP server software is at
http://
snodaq.phy.queensu.ca/
WebStat.html. For a summary of
utilities, check http://
arpp1.carleton.ca/machttp/
doc/util/stats/. There *was* a
good counter program at http://
www.ualberta.ca/GEO/
CounterFull.html. Visit the site to
find out why it had to be taken off
the Web.

It's essential that you keep track of such
essential information as how many people
visit your site, where they are from, or
what the busiest times are. If you use an
Internet provider, you can probably get
them to report that information. If you have
your own server, you need to do it yourself.

WebStat is a good piece of software for
tracking the server usage. It can be configured to report on all kinds of variables,
such as usage per day or per week. It
generates HTML files that you can then
link to in order to review the data.

There are also CGI scripts called "hit
counters" that tell each visitor how many
previous visitors have been to your site,
and what number they are in your "guestbook." There's an example of one at the
Home Page of InterAccess, an Internet Provider: http://www.interaccess.com.
Ask your system administrator if such CGIs are available.

Be a Great Communicator

After you have researched your Web readers by locating them in the Internet, either
on the Web or in Usenet, what do you do? Communicate with them. Develop as
personal an online style as possible—often, it seems, communication online can be
more personal and frank than face-to-face conversation.

You could do worse than to follow the example of Bob Topor. Bob has been marketing in higher education for the past 35 years. Bob brought himself to my attention again recently through the PUBS-L newsgroup for publications professionals in higher education. Bob sent a message to Pubscrawlers, as we are called, announcing one of his "Seminars By the Sea" on Web-related issues.

Where to Find It

There's a mailing list for marketers called htmarcom. A mailing list consists of a group of subscribers who communicate by email. To subscribe, send an email message to: listserv@cscns.com. In the body of the message, type: "subscribe htmarcom *fname lname*". ("fname lname" means you should type your first and last name. Don't use periods or quotation marks.)

Bob followed up a few weeks later by offering some information on marketing on the Web; anyone who sends email back to him would get a pamphlet on the subject. Response seemed to be pretty good, although he neglected to remind people to respond to him directly in a separate email message rather than clicking the "reply" button on their mail program. Because his original message was coming from America Online through PUBS-L central, a lot of people sent their responses to everyone on the PUBS-L list. Nobody's perfect.

One morning, while I was feeding my kids breakfast, I sent Bob Topor an email message asking for some input on my book. Less than two hours later (at around 8 a.m. California time) he called me on the phone. Later that day he sent me publications I could read and use for background material. Now I'm mentioning him in my book. The moral, I guess, is when someone from your audience approaches you, be as helpful and quick in your response as you can. You might be pleasantly surprised with the results.

Copyright and Security

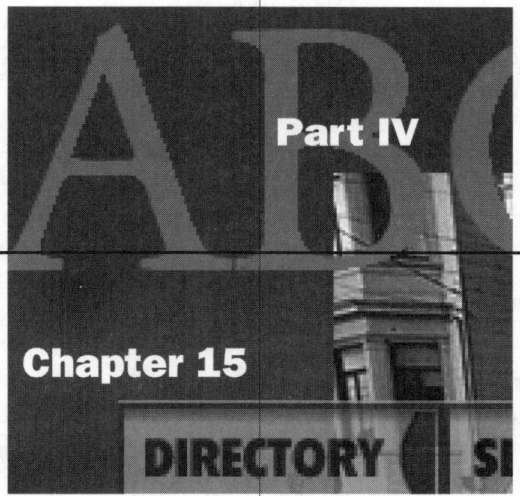

Part IV

Chapter 15

DIRECTORY

You are creating a home page about farm animals and decide that the perfect illustration for the cover of your online magazine would be Bart Simpson shouting, "Don't have a cow, man." Would you be breaking the law? Could you be sued?

You are publishing a Web version of your magazine that includes an article written by a freelancer. The fee that you paid was for one-time rights to the article in the paper version of your publication. Could you be taken to court?

Where to Find It

John Perry Barlow, co-founder of
the Electronic Frontier Foundation,
wrote an influential article called
"The Economy of Ideas" for *Wired*
magazine that proposed a radical
rethinking of conventional notions
of intellectual property, copyrights,
and patents in the age of
Cyberspace. A copy has been
posted on the Web; you can read it
at http://sunsite.unc.eduwxyc/
economy.ideas.html.

Where to Find It

The U.S. Copyright Office now
has a home page at http://
lcweb.loc.gov/copyright/. It
includes links to copyright basics,
registration, and the office's online
database. The Berne Convention
text is at gopher://wiretap.spies
.com/00/Gov/Copyright/
US.Berne.Convention.txt. The
Copyright Act as amended in 1976
is at http://www.law.cornell
.edu/usc/17/overview.html.

The answer to both questions is yes. If you
flunked this test, reading this chapter is a
prerequisite to putting your publication on
the Web. In fact, even if you think you
know a lot already about copyright law and
Web security, I recommend that you take a
refresher—nothing ruins a day like a trip to
court.

If you publish on the Internet, you need
some background on copyright law to
protect your work. Just because this
chapter comes at the end of this book
doesn't mean that it's an afterthought. In
fact, dear reader, I suspect that you have
interests on both sides of the law. In the
first place, you value your work and want
to make sure that your rights are well
protected. Equally important, you want to
make sure you are not sued for inadvert-
ently infringing on the rights of someone
else. So read on.

A New Way of Copying

As long as there has been creative work,
securing and protecting its ownership has
been a primary concern. Charles Dickens,
for example, repeatedly appealed for an
international copyright law that would
prevent bootleg American publishers from
stealing his work. When recorded music
began to be mass-produced, artists formed groups such as ASCAP to make sure they
would be compensated every time their work was played or sold. The Web
represents a new medium for mass-reproduction, and history is likely to repeat itself
with writers banding together to secure their online rights.

> **Note:** A famous turn-of-the-century legal dispute also brought into question new technology and copyright law. A music publisher who owned the rights to two songs, "Little Cotton Dolly" and "Kentucky Babe," sued a maker of player piano rolls for copyright violations. The case went to the U.S. Supreme Court, which found that because a machine is required to read the rolls, the piano role maker did not violate copyright in the same way that someone copying the sheet music would.

In fact, the need for publishers to know how to protect the information they provide has never been greater. After all, readers on the Web can print, copy, alter, and reuse information with a few clicks of a mouse.

Because of the way computer technology works, simply emailing a publication to a friend means you have made a copy of it. "If I have a Star Trek logo [on paper] and I give it to you, I haven't made a copy of it. If I upload a picture [on a computer] and send it to you, I've made a copy of it," says Larry Lessig, a University of Chicago associate law professor who specializes in constitutional and Cyberspace law.[1]

But does uploading a copyrighted publication and emailing it to a friend violate copyright law? The answer is not clear—like most things in the copyright world, it would depend on a number of factors, including whether the act constituted "fair use."

Lawmakers, publishers, and others with an interest in copyright are currently debating where to draw the line on this issue. As of this writing, no cases have appeared in court in which an individual was sued for sending someone a copyrighted picture. However, a federal judge in Florida held in 1993 that a bulletin board infringed a copyright by carrying images scanned from *Playboy* magazine.

The proliferation of information being distributed electronically also means that writers, graphic designers, photographers, and other artists increasingly are unpleasantly surprised to discover that their work has been duplicated without compensation or even credit. They are beginning to stand up for their rights.

This chapter suggests prudent, sensible ways for both groups of people to protect themselves. It will not keep people from stealing your work. It *will* quote chapter and verse about existing electronic copyright law, because most copyright lawyers and other authorities believe that even though it's easy to copy and reuse material taken from the Internet, precedents have been set in other media. Not that I have personal knowledge of such a thing, but I've heard that it's possible to use a tape recorder to take songs from the radio and to duplicate movies that have been rented. There are existing laws that cover electronic distribution of intellectual properties.

Note: Intellectual property is the type of property protected by copyright law—original work such as plays, cartoons, television shows, personal letters, software, and so on. Intellectual properties are the children of the brain. Web pages, too, are intellectual property.

Tip: As this book was going to press, for instance, the U.S. Copyright Office was developing an electronic copyright registration system. Web publishers will be able to send copyright registration applications and deposit their works with the Copyright Office over the Internet. Also in the works is a tracking system on the Internet that would track every time stories written by members of the Writers Guild were reproduced, so those writers could be paid royalties.

Copyright FAQs

Once again, I've borrowed the familiar Internet convention of frequently asked questions (FAQs) to present some basic facts about copyright as it pertains to electronic publishing.

Why Do Web Publishers Need to Care about Copyright?

Under current law, the online world is no different than the print world. It is subject to copyright law. If you were to take copyrighted material and distribute it through the Internet or World Wide Web without getting permission from the author, you would violate copyright just as you would if you sold photocopies of a book. Whether you make one or a hundred copies, if you use something in a way that is found to be illegal or that violates the concept of "fair use," you can get sued. Likewise, the original work you produce on the computer is protected by copyright, and you can sue someone who violates your rights.

Where to Find It

Check the Library of Congress server or Copyright Office home page (http://lcweb.loc.gov/ copyright/) for more information on recent copyright law discussions. For more information, you can also check out http:// www.benedict.com/ or gopher:/ /wiretap.spies.com/11/Gov/ Copyright.

An ongoing task force in Washington made up of representatives from the U.S. Patent and Copyright offices, the library world, and the publishing business has been discussing the subject of copyright violations on the Internet. A conference, held in Washington in the spring of 1995 and co-sponsored by the Library of Congress, discussed how and if copyright law should be changed to accommodate this new technology.

So, new laws and procedures are evolving but, in the meantime, there are existing laws that will make anyone who violates copyright in Cyberspace liable for damages.

What Is Copyright?

Copyright is a right of intellectual property that gives authors the exclusive rights to their work for a limited time (see the following section "How Long Does Copyright Last?" for a definition of a limited time).

The U.S. Constitution (Article 1, Section 1, Clause 8) gives Congress the authority to "promote the Progress of Science and useful Arts, by securing for Limited Times to Authors and Inventors the exclusive Right to their respective Writings and Discoveries." In other words, through copyright law, Uncle Sam is trying to help out creative types by protecting original works.

But this protection covers only an author's original expression. It does not protect any ideas, facts, short phrases, or preexisting material the author has used in the work.

Where to Find It

A good deal of general information on copyright can be found on the Web. One source is ILTWeb: A Guide to Copyright, at http://www.ilt.columbia.edu/gen/ref/ILTcopy.html. Another source for general Internet information that includes crytpography, citizenship, and your rights in Cyberspace is at http://www.law.indiana.edu/lawlib/iclu.html.

In other words, if Karl Marx were writing "The Communist Manifesto" today, the exact wording he chose to use in the Manifesto itself would be copyrighted, but the general ideas expressed would not be. How is the law implemented? Copyrighted work can't be distributed, sold, or used in any way inconsistent with the owner's rights. The owner can sue a copyright violator for damages and it is possible to have a court of law issue an injunction to stop the illegal use. Federal penalties against copyright violations include fines and jail time.

So, we can all agree that direct plagiarism is a no no. It's obvious that you can't reproduce an image of Bart Simpson saying, "Don't have a cow, man." But neither can you rip off an image of the little imp saying, "Don't have a horse, lady." The United States recognizes the reproductive, adaptive, distributive, performance, display, attribution, and integrity rights to original work. The "integrity right" refers to the author's right to prevent the use of his or her name as the author of a distorted version of the work, and to prevent intentional distortion or destruction of the work.

The application of these rights depends on the medium. For example, there's no need to protect the performance right of a work of architecture, but the play you are so proud of writing is another matter. Nobody can legally perform it, claim authorship of it, distribute it, make copies of it, adapt it, or display it publicly unless you give the green light.

If William Shakespeare were somehow resurrected, he would make a bundle. No one could perform his plays without his permission. He'd also get a cut of the action for a production of "West Side Story" (adapted from "Romeo and Juliet") or when Giuseppe Verdi (also brought back to life) made an operatic version of "Othello."

How Do I Get Copyright for What I Put on the Web?

You don't have to do anything. You automatically have the copyright for everything you publish. The Copyright Act of 1989 brought the U.S. practice into accord with the Berne Convention, and does not require that a work contain a copyright notice to obtain protection. So your poem is copyrighted whether it's tucked away in a forgotten folder on your hard drive or scribbled illegibly in a spiral notebook.

You may be wondering if you are protected when your work is distributed overseas. For instance, you distribute your work from a computer in the U.S., but your graphics are distributed from a server in Turkey, and someone in Brazil copies some or all of this material.

Most likely, you are covered, because the U.S. belongs to both the Universal Copyright Convention (UCC) and the Berne Convention for the Protection of Literary and Artistic Works. The UCC came into effect on September 16, 1955. A work created by a citizen or resident of a country that is a member of the UCC, or a work first published in a UCC member country, may claim protection under the UCC.

By joining the Berne Convention on March 1, 1989, the U.S. gained protection for all its authors in all member nations of the Berne Convention. A work first published in the U.S. or another Berne country is eligible for protection in all member countries.

There are, as usual, some gray areas. For instance, what if you distribute some information through a machine in the U.S. but you were actually located in Israel the whole time? What if you live in Brazil, but use a machine in Turkey, and someone else in the U.S. mirrors your site? Cyberspace can create some pretty complex relationships, and judges and lawyers would have to wrangle over any such complex international copyright disputes.

However, if you want to make sure that people do not use your work illegally, I recommend that you actively take these precautions:

- You should put a copyright statement on a document, "Copyright 1995 Your Name. All rights reserved." When you give notice that you have an interest in your work, usurpers can't claim in court that they infringed it unknowingly and thus try to escape liability.

- If someone does violate your copyright and you want to sue, you first must formally register the copyright as explained in the next section. (Soon, you'll be able to do this electronically, as previously noted.) Also, before you think about suing, you might go about contacting the violator to tell him or her to either cease and desist or give you a cut. Who wants to go to court?

Tip: Netscape recognizes two nonstandard character entities that come in handy when making a copyright notice on an HTML document (but remember, they show up only on Netscape):

® = Registered Trademark = ®
© = Copyright = ©

How Do I Register Copyright?

To register your work, get an application from the Copyright Office, fill it out, pay $20 for each, and send one or more copies of the work to:

The Copyright Office
Information and Publication Section LM0455
Library of Congress
Washington, D.C. 20559

For more information, you can write to the Copyright Office or call 202-707-3000. You can register after someone steals your stuff, but you must register before you actually sue.

How Long Does Copyright Last?

The federal Copyright Act has been rewritten many times, but 1976 was an important year. That's when the time was changed that a copyright lasts and when it became easier to get a copyright.

To simplify a lot of legalese, for works created after 1977, a copyright lasts for 50 years after the author's death. After that, it becomes public domain. Copyright time limits for work created before 1978 vary considerably. For example, for works published between 1904 and 1963, copyright lasted for 28 years from the date of publication, unless it was renewed for another 28 years.

In general, all copyrights secured before 1920 lapsed at the latest in 1995 and are now in public domain. So if you want to include in your Web document an illustration from the early twentieth century, it's probably okay. But if you want to make a computer online comic strip using characters from Walt Disney's "Aladdin," you'd better think twice.

There are even exceptions to the pre-1920 rule. For instance, the rights to publish letters and other writings of certain famous people may be retained by their respective family estates. Even if the copyright has lapsed, give credit to the original artist if you know who it is—you don't want to be haunted by angry creative ghosts.

Does It Make a Difference if I Have a Long or Short Copyright Notice?

Adding "Copyright 1995 Your Name" to your document is sufficient to protect your work, and will protect you from someone claiming innocent infringement and thereby trying to escape certain kinds of liability in court. Adding "All rights reserved" also covers you in some Latin American countries.

Some people put a very long copyright notice on their work—stating impressively that all rights are reserved, no portion of this work may be copied without express permission from the author, and so on. Does the long version work better? According to Brad Lyerla, a Chicago intellectual property rights lawyer, it depends on what it is you are trying to protect. A lot of people don't know what copyright notice is, Lyerla said, so a "fuller admonishment" is sometimes a good idea.

Whichever version you choose, Lyerla said he believes some kind of notice helps deter violators. "I'm not a cynical person. I think 99 percent of the public when given a legal notice will honor that. That's the value of it for people who are essentially honest but might not know any better." Lyerla added that he believes many people do not copy movies off videocassette strictly because of the FBI warning telling them not to.

What Is Fair Use?

What if you are a teacher who wants to use a portion of a copyrighted work to illustrate a point to a class? What if you are a movie reviewer who wants to quote some dialogue to demonstrate why it was lousy? These uses are okay under the doctrine of "fair use." They don't violate copyright and you don't need permission.

447

Like other portions of copyright law, however, there is a large gray area in "fair use."
"But my copying was just fair use!" is often given is an excuse by copyright violators trying to get around the law.

According to prior court precedent, fair use includes such diverse activities as
quotation of excerpts in a review, reproduction by a library of a portion of a work to
replace part of a damaged copy, or copying by a teacher or student of a small part of
a work to illustrate a lesson.

> **Note:** To decide what's naughty and what's nice, the courts look at the
> purpose and character of the use, the nature of the copyrighted work, the
> amount and substantiality of the portion used, and the economic effect on
> the author.

In the nice category, there may be a high school student writing an essay on *The
Catcher in the Rye* who quotes a sentence or two to make a point. The extract is
small, it is for a noncommercial purpose, probably no one will see it except the
teacher, and author J. D. Salinger won't lose any royalties from book sales because
of it—chances are, it is fair use.

What Is Not Fair Use?

In the naughty category, I once saw an ad in a magazine for a hunting hat like the
one worn by Holden Caulfield, the main character of Salinger's novel. Holden's
unique way of speaking was used to get angry young people to buy the hat. As
Holden might have said, it was a pretty phony ad. Was it fair use? Probably not.
Unless they got Mr. Salinger's permission and gave him a licensing fee, the
hatmakers might have been liable for damages.

But, back to the Web, what if you download a photo of a forest, grab a portion that
shows a tree, rearrange it using a fancy graphics program such as Photoshop, and
publish it on your site. Resourceful? Maybe. Improper? Yes.

Agreements with Freelancers

One thing that's tricky for Web publishers is when you have already produced a
printed pamphlet with photographs and other original work you have paid for the

right to use. Do you then need to ask permission (and pay more money) when you publish the same pamphlet with the same photos on your Web site? It depends on your agreement with your photographer. If the agreement does not address electronic rights to the freelancer's work, you should discuss it.

Lyerla says that when you are making future arrangements with a contracted author or writer, it is important to make it clear what you are entitled to do with this work once it is in your hands. "The key is to make it clear and avoid the potential for disagreements and avoid potential for litigation."

You may need to draw up a formal agreement for the artist whose work you want to reproduce. An example is shown in Figure 15.1. This is an agreement form Hayden Books uses when reprinting an author's work.

Greg's Soapbox

I'm not a lawyer and each situation is different, so don't take what I say as the definitive word on drawing up a contract. When preparing agreements, it's always best to get help from an attorney with experience in this area.

This is where it becomes essential to have clear agreements with freelance graphic artists, photographers, and writers you employ.

Keep a file of signed contracts that clearly spells out exactly what rights you are buying from your freelance contributors. If you plan to reproduce their work on the Web, make sure the words "electronic rights" are included.

There are many different kinds of rights and uses that can be specified on a contract. Generally, the more rights a publisher specifies as belonging to it, the less rights the artist has to compensation for future reproduction. So, it's only logical that the artist should charge a higher fee for the work up front in these cases.

Note: Every contract should be adapted to its specific use but, as a starting point, I recommend the examples of standard contracts included in the *Graphic Artists Guild Handbook, Pricing and Ethical Guidelines, 7th Edition* (Cincinnati: North Light Books, 1991).

HAYDEN ARTIST'S REPRINT AGREEMENT

This reprint Agreement ("AGREEMENT") is made this ____day of ___, ____ between Hayden Books, an imprint of Macmillan Computer Publishing, having a place of business at 201 W. 103rd Street, Indianapolis, IN 46290, hereinafter referred to as "Hayden" and «address», hereinafter referred to as "CONTRIBUTOR" concerning the book tentatively title _____ hereinafter referred to as the "WORK."

1. GRANT OF RIGHTS

The CONTRIBUTOR grants to Hayden non-exclusive, worldwide right to reprint with the WORK, according to the terms set out in the AGREEMENT, any artwork that CONTRIBUTOR has provided to HAYDEN for use in _____ hereinafter referred to as "ARTWORK." This permission includes the rights to reproduce and publish the ARTWORK, but only in conjunction with the WORK as set forth in this AGREEMENT. This agreement shall be in effect during the full term that HAYDEN determines to sell the WORK, including any revised editions of the WORK.

Hayden shall include an acknowledgment of the CONTRIBUTOR in the WORK.

      REPRINTED BY PERMISSION OF:

      _____

      _____

2. WARRANTY AND INDEMNITY

The CONTRIBUTOR represents and warrants that it has, or has licensed, sufficient right and title in the ARTWORK and associated trademarks or copyrights to grant the reprint permission of HAYDEN set forth in this AGREEMENT, and that the CONTRIBUTOR has the right and authority to grant the reprint permission to HAYDEN under this AGREEMENT, and that the person whose signature appears below is duly authorized to enter into this AGREEMENT on behalf of CONTRIBUTOR. HAYDEN represents and warrants that it has full corporate power and corporate authority to execute and deliver this AGREE-MENT and is duly authorized to enter into this AGREEMENT on behalf of HAYDEN.

3. CHANGES

This agreement and endorsements hereto shall not be subject to change, modification or discharge in whole or in part except by written instrument signed by the CONTRIBUTOR and HAYDEN.

4. WAIVER

No waiver of any terms of this agreement will be effective unless in writing signed by the party making such waiver, and no waiver of any breach hereunder shall be deemed a waiver of any subsequent breach.

5. CONSTRUCTION

This agreement shall be deemed to have been entered into in the State of New York and shall be interpreted and construed in accordance with the laws of the State of New York applicable to agreements executed and to be fully performed therein. Each party hereby agrees to submit to the exclusive in personam jurisdiction of the courts of the State of New York, New York County, for the resolution of all disputes between them, or, if jurisdictional prerequisites exist at that time, to the sole and exclusive in personam jurisdiction of the Federal Courts of New York with venue to be in the Southern District of New York.

IN WITNESS WHEREOF, the parties hereto have executed this reprint AGREEMENT as of the dates signed below.

Signed: _____   _____
          CONTRIBUTOR   DATE

Signed: _____   _____
          David Rogelberg (HAYDEN)   DATE

Figure 15.1 Sample artist's reprint contract.

Some other rights include:

- "All Rights" cover any use you want to make of a contributor's work. This is likely to be expensive at the beginning, because it leaves the artist with virtually no way to make more money later.

- "Electronic, including CD-I, CD-ROM, electronic books, floppy disk, and other forms which may be developed," an elaboration on the shorter "Electronic Rights."

Releases

The "advertising or trade" use of a living person's name or likeness without permission is an invasion of privacy and can be a very costly mistake.

The best protection is to obtain a signed release from the person whose image you want to use. It might seem unlikely that a celebrity or agent would want to challenge your use of a photo in court. But just because it hasn't happened doesn't mean it won't. Find another way to get attention for your Web site other than being sued!

Security Issues

The focus of this book is to encourage as many people as possible to visit your home page. The basic means of getting information on the Web involves a computer running client software downloading data from a server and interpreting it. In essence, the client is going into a server (possibly yours) and getting something every time a connection is made. The scary question is how much farther would they have to go to find something, such as credit card numbers and other financial information, that you don't want them to see?

Note: In general, material held on a Macintosh Web server is much more secure than it is on, say, a UNIX or other server, because the Mac operating system is difficult to penetrate and acts as its own "firewall."

Eavesdropping is presently the biggest barrier to commerce on the Web and several companies are working on a standard security system.

Where to Find It

An introductory explanation of security on the Web is given by Terisa Systems at http://www.terisa.com/faq.html. To find out more about SSL, go to http://www.netscape.com/newsref/std/SSL.html. To find out more about S-HTTP, go to http://www.eit.com/.

Where to Find It

CommerceNet, a consortium of companies and organizations seeking to create an electronic marketplace, was planning to implement S-HTTP and a special version of Mosaic, Secure Mosaic, in autumn 1995, to allow secure transactions for its members. This version requires a "secure server," which they're also working on. Check at http://www.commerce.net/ to see what's going on.

At the time this book was being written, Terisa Systems was developing a universal World Wide Web transaction security strategy that integrates the two major security protocols available on the Web: S-HTTP, a security-enhanced version of HyperText Transfer Protocol developed by Enterprise Integration Technologies (EIT), and SSL (Secure Sockets Layer), developed by Netscape Communications.

Secure HTTP is considered a "higher level" protocol than SSL. It provides security for individual documents being transmitted over the Web by allowing each document to be marked as private and/or signed by the sender.

It uses an encryption system that combines a "public key" that can be widely disseminated with a "private" or "secret key" known only to one user. The party sending information uses the recipient's public key to encrypt text; the recipient uses the secret key to make it readable.

SSL concentrates on the link between servers and clients. The SSL protocol allows client/server applications to communicate over the Internet in a way that prevents eavesdropping. Data in SSL is transmitted within a record, which consists of a header and data.

Information Sources

Where to Find It

The Baltimore *Sun* has tried to address security problems by putting its Web page in the same place where its email account resides. That way, in theory at least, subscribers' numbers stay in one location once they get to the *Sun's* server. However, they also very wisely suggest that people telephone or mail their orders. For more information, go to http://www.clark.net/pub/baltsun/security.html.

Graphic Artists Guild Handbook, Pricing & Ethical Guidelines, 7th Edition (Cincinnati: North Light Books, 1991), 1-800-543-4644.

Barlow, John Perry, "The Economy of Ideas: A framework for rethinking patents and copyrights in the Digital Age," an article in *Wired* 2.06 (March 1994).

Branscomb, Anne Wells, *Who Owns Information? From Privacy to Public Access* (New York: Basic Books, 1994).

Carroll, Terry, "Frequently Asked Questions About Copyright" (v. 1.1.3), Part 2 - Copyright Basics, Copyright 1994 by Terry Carroll, available at http://www.eff.org/pub/Intellectual_property/copyright.faq.

Cavazos, Edward A. and Gavino Morin, *Cyberspace and the Law: Your Rights and Duties in the On-line World* (The MIT Press, 1994).

Fishman, Stephen, *Software Development: A Legal Guide* (Berkeley: Nolo Press, 1994), Chapter 13.

Martin, James A., "Are You Breaking the Law? A Guide to Copyright Do's and Don'ts," *Macworld* vol. 11, no. 5 (May 1994).

Security Resources

Electronic Frontier Foundation (EFF): http://www.eff.org/

Electronic Privacy Information Center (EPIC): http://epic.org/

The WELL: http://www.well.com/

[1] Larry Lessig, quoted by Mary Holden, in "Intellectual-property disputes flare on the electronic frontier," *Chicago Daily Law Bulletin*, April 22, 1995.

Visions of the Future

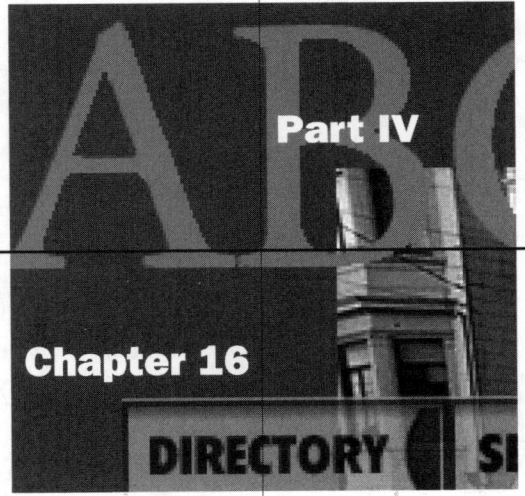

Part IV

Chapter 16

DIRECTORY

To get a glimpse of what the future might be, it's sometimes illuminating to ask the viewpoints of those who will *be* the future. Nine separate visions of the future as it relates to the Internet were posed to students at Desert View High School in Arizona. In keeping with the information revolution, they posted their responses on the Web.

The topic most pertinent to publishers was covered in Vision Three: "Magazines will become entirely electronic and no paper will be used for them."

While the prospect of saving trees received positive responses, not having any paper magazines to tote around also met some skepticism. While one special education student said, "You won't have to worry about your little brother tearing your mag's," another one, M. Parra, nicely summarized the mixed benefits of online publishing:

Where to Find It

The Desert View students' "Visions of the Future" page, part of their magazine "The Desert Web," is at http:// wacky.ccit.arizona.edu/~susd/ fut.html.

Where to Find It

Want to get a more random view of the future? Flip the coins or turn the cards at the Tarot, I-Ching, and Biorhythm pages listed at: http://cad.ucla.edu/ repository/useful/useful.html.

"Magazines should not be entirely electronic because people want to take a magazine to travel or just read, but then again, it would be good, because people could get smarter and people all over the world could go over to a computer and read the newest magazines on the shelf."

The problem with electronic publications are portability, readability, and difficult access for those who don't have a computer or who have a slow Internet connection.

Some of the benefits are immediacy, distribution around the world, easier updating, and possible printing savings (economic and environmental).

While it's difficult to imagine the extinction of paper magazines and books, the rapid growth of the Web indicates that "virtually" anything is possible—provided that the hardware and transmission infrastructure of the Internet keep up with that growth.

Better Infrastructure

Think about how you connect to the Web. If you dial up from home using a modem, you probably connect to an Internet service provider. The provider might have one of a number of connections to the Internet—perhaps a bunch of fast modems, a 56K dedicated line, or a T1, multiple T1s, or a T3 cable.

If, like me, you connect from a university campus, your office either has a LocalTalk or Ethernet network connection. The campus Ethernet is connected to a regional Wide Area Network.

All of these different kinds of connections are linked in elaborate chains, and the number of nodes and chains is growing amazingly fast. Already, there are signs that the existing networks are inadequate to the demands being placed on them.

Every Web surfer is familiar with the slowdowns that occur around lunch hour or just after dinnertime when, it seems, everyone wants to get on the Net. Traffic volume is still limited by the amount of information that can be pushed along analog telephone lines.

The structure of the Internet itself has to get better, or the Web will become a sloth. The cabling needs to grow in bandwidth, and the slowest connections on the Net need to be eliminated.

That could happen in a couple of ways: Modems will probably get faster very soon, so that people will be able to reach a 56.6K baud rate, or ISDN lines will become more widely used.

ISDN Lines

ISDN stands for Integrated Services Digital Networks. It is a digital data transmission system that integrates video, audio, voice, and data services in a single cable (hence the name). ISDN is an inexpensive way to get faster data transmission than an analog modem connection. It is being enthusiastically promoted by telephone companies. It allows video conferencing and digital audio transmission, as well as traditional voice telephone service, and without the noise of traditional telephone lines.

Where to Find It

A set of FAQs about ISDN is at http://www.crimson.com/isdn/isdnFAQ.txt. Ameritech is at http://www.ameritech.com/.

Telephone companies are already beginning to make ISDN lines available to consumers. One Chicago-area company, Ameritech, has an ISDN Direct program that offers data transmission rates of up to 64Kbps for modems, using the same lines for voice and data.

In order to get all this speed, you not only have to have the telephone company run the new digital cable to your house, but you also need to purchase a piece of hardware called a terminal adapter to convert the ISDN signal into something your computer can recognize. Also, your Internet provider must have the hardware to support ISDN. Right now, the hardware isn't cheap—about $700, in my area—but the price will surely go down as the technology becomes more widespread.

ATM

ATM (Asynchronous Transfer Mode) is another high-speed networking technology that has a lot of people excited. (It has nothing to do with Automatic Teller Machines, by the way.) It might be described as a broadband version of ISDN ("broadband" meaning it has a much higher capacity to transmit data). It uses cell relay as a way of transporting small, fixed-sized, information-bearing units of data. The speed of data transfer can vary from megabits through gigabits.

Where to Find It

A set of reference information about ATM is at http://www.whitetree.com/. Also see the ATM Forum Home Page, http://www.atmforum.com/atmforum/atm_introduction.html.

A very rough description is that in ATM, you don't send all your data in a continuous stream, but only when some part of the data changes. This allows transmissions that are three to ten times as fast as other methods.

ATM isn't yet available for the general public, but is being used by large research institutions and corporations.

More Powerful HTML

HTML will either evolve or be swept aside by something else. My guess is that there will always be something called HTML, but it will be replaced by some code-transparent application that provides more powerful ways of marking up documents.

HTML is presently too crude to allow a lot of document formatting. It needs to become richer, like the SGML of which it is a subset. Some of those needs may be accomplished before too long, when you can create HTML from within applications like PageMaker and Word.

HTML doesn't allow a lot of programming functions; people wanting to process forms have to write separate CGI programs. It would be much better to be able to write the programs inside HTML, which I hope will be possible soon.

Competition and Consolidation

For the next few years, the Web will be the prize over which a steadily smaller number of communications companies fight. Corporations will continue to form alliances, some will purchase others, and others will fall by the wayside. It's sure to be exciting.

Some small, local Internet providers are likely to get squeezed out by telephone and cable companies as they begin offering faster connections—other providers will align with the big companies and continue to thrive.

Virtual Reality

This is one of those things that is tantalizing and exciting to think about, until you realize that the equipment needed to enjoy a virtual reality experience on the Web is going to be very expensive, and the technology itself won't take off until faster means of data transmission become more widely available.

Where to Find It

David Raggett's paper on VR is at http://r703a.chem.nthu.edu.tw/~ks/docs/www/htmlplus/hpwww94.html. There's a Virtual Reality Tech Form at http://www.hyperreal.com/~mpesce/vrml/vrml.tech/.

Virtual reality is a technology that tries to fully immerse the user in a computer-generated environment. The VR user interacts with the environment by sensors, data gloves, headsets, and even full body suits that sense the way the participant is moving and orienting in that environment.

Once the Net itself gets faster, VR will be a big deal. A paper by David Raggett, author of HTML 3.0, in 1994 speculated on virtual reality environments that would allow users to "walk" around and push through doors to follow hyperlinks to other parts of the Web.

Where to Find It

Information on VR and the Web can be found at http://zaphod.ncsa.uiuc.edu/VR/mason/CAVEview.paper.html. In particular, take a look at "CAVEview: Mosaic-based Virtual Reality," which allows virtual reality applications to be inserted into hypertext documents.

Instead of searching for a file in a group of folders on the Macintosh desktop and pointing at it with a mouse, VR would allow you to walk around the file and seem to literally pick up the file you need.

VR could be used to show the interiors of rooms and buildings as a way for architects to present their work and potential buyers to review a structure.

It could also act as a showroom for carpets, windows, and furniture. It could show outdoor scenes complete with buildings, water, roads, sky, and different weather conditions. Museums could allow virtual tours.

Although the potential of VR for cybersexual experiences is obvious, when adventurers realize that the virtual experience is no match for the real thing, they will probably turn to more wholesome uses for VR, such as virtual teleconferencing. Family members separated by hundreds or thousands of miles can "get together" virtually.

VRML

Virtual Reality Modeling Language (VRML; sometimes pronounced "vur-mole") has been proposed as a standard way of describing virtual reality experiences accessed via the Internet and integrated with the hypertextual power of the Web.

In VRML's 1.0 version, the user can select an object with a hyperlink, and a viewer application is launched that allows VR viewing of the object. VRML specifies if the object appears to be illuminated with a directional light, for instance.

If the user selects a VRML document, a VRML viewer is launched. The aim is to place the user in the middle of the Internet, with the power to "order" the electronic universe.

WebSpace

WebSpace (Figure 16.1) is billed as the first commercially available 3-D viewer for the Web. It is a browser that reads VRML files and lets you "travel" through 3-D environments, where you can manipulate 3-D objects. A useful feature allows you to automatically choose the right level of detail for your operating system. The Macintosh PowerPC version hadn't been released as this book was being written.

Figure 16.1 The WebSpace home page. (Image courtesy of Silicon Graphics, Inc.)

461

HotJava

HotJava gets my vote for best name for a new product. It's also a very exciting piece of software. HotJava promises to make the World Wide Web even more dynamic and interactive.

Where to Find It

Find out more about WebSpace at http://www.sgi.com/ Products/WebFORCE/ WebSpace/.

HotJava is a Web browser that supports programs written in the Java programming language (which are referred to as "applets"). Java is an object-oriented programming language designed to create executable applications that can be sent over the Internet. Figure16.2 shows the home page.

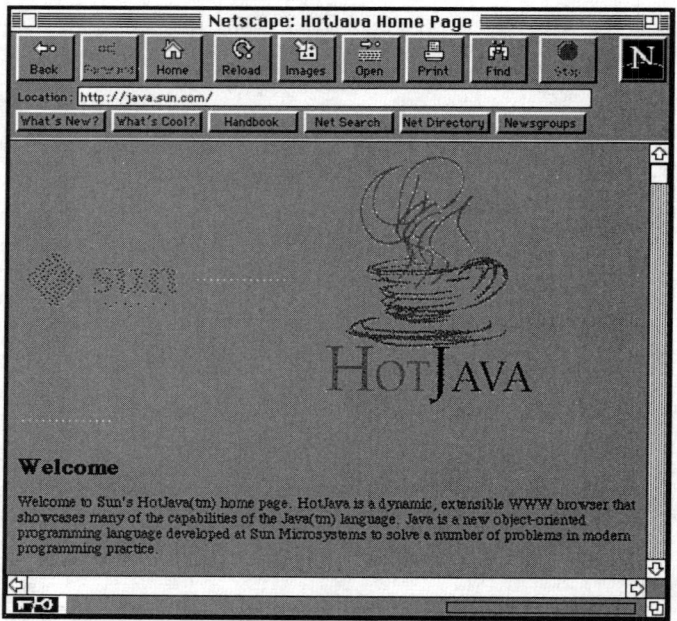

Figure 16.2 The HotJava home page (copyright Sun Microsystems).

When you connect to a page that contains one of the applets with the HotJava browser, the applet's computer code is sent to your system and executed. Using Java, text can move onscreen, fireworks can explode, and 3-D models can be manipulated with a mouse. Interactive advertising and real-time stock portfolio management are only two of the many possible applications.

Unfortunately, as this book was being written, a version of HotJava for Macintosh was still under development. Netscape, however, had announced an agreement with Sun Microsystems, the developer of HotJava, that would enable Netscape to support the Java language.

Note: Many of HotJava's functions can already be performed by Aretha, a shareware release of the Frontier scripting language, which is available for the Macintosh. See the next page for info on where to find Aretha and Hot-Java.

More, More, More

All indications are that the World Wide Web is not going to vanish or be replaced by some newer way of retrieving and exchanging information, but will continue to grow in size and popularity.

In his "Growth of the World Wide Web" page, Matthew Gray, who has been keeping track of Web use since its early days (not so long ago), attempts to quantify its explosive growth:

Dates	Sites
June, 1993	130 sites
December, 1993	623 sites
June, 1994	1,265 sites
December, 1994	11,576 sites

Obviously, in the near future, the Web will continue to grow, and it's likely that commercial sites will continue to be a dominant presence.

Final Observations

What is the reason for all this popularity? What need does the Web fulfill?

The Web is unquestionably the easiest and friendliest way to access the Internet. What need, then, does the Internet fulfill? I think it has to do with the basic human need for communication and connection in a world that is increasingly disjointed, alienating, and marked by constant change.

Where to Find It

Keep an eye on the HotJava home page, http://java.sun.com/, for news on the Macintosh version of the HotJava browser. Aretha can be found at http:/www.hotwired.com/staff/userland/aretha/.

The growth of technology as a tool of commerce and industry in the 20th century has given people some great ways to amuse themselves, such as movies and television, and some new ways to communicate, such as radio and telecommunications, but it hasn't done much that's new for what I still stubbornly regard as the highest and most profound form of expression and education: reading the written word.

The Web combines the speed and immediacy of twentieth-century technology with the need for human beings to communicate through reading, writing, and illustration.

Where to Find It

The Growth of the World Wide Web page is at http://www.netgen.com/info/growth.html.

When you take the tools you've learned in this book and become a Web publisher, you're not just adding another home page to the infinitely expanding Internet encyclopedia of facts and figures. You're joining a community of human beings—a community whose bounds haven't been fully tapped. You're making a connection with millions of people around the world, all of whom are connected all the time despite language, distance, background, age, gender, skin color, and countless other seeming differences.

The Web and the Internet itself are metaphors for the connection and dependence we, by the nature of our common humanity, have with one another. When you add your voice to those already on the Web, you affirm that you aren't alone. You touch people. I encourage you find your publisher's voice and look forward to your joining me as part of the community. Good luck!

Part V

Appendixes

An Extremely Abbreviated History of the Internet

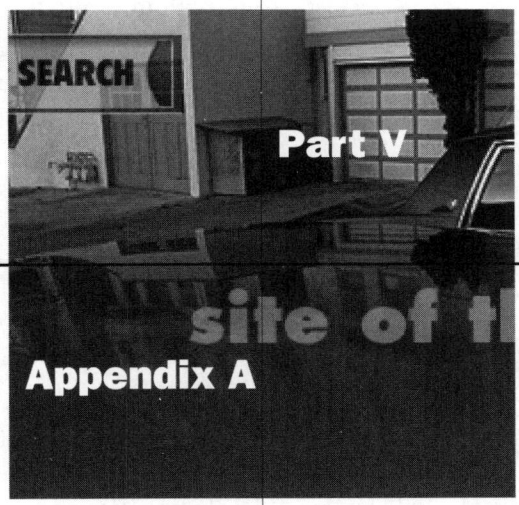

SEARCH

Part V

site of t

Appendix A

When you sit down at your computer and check your electronic mail, you probably don't ask yourself, "How does all of this mail get to me? What is this thing called the Internet?" This is a question that you and I, the end users, don't have to think about, thanks to the people that establish the structure and protocols for the Internet.

Who Runs the Internet?

Before I began to do research for this book, I did wonder from time to time who "runs" the Internet. Who allows me to send a mail message to a colleague in Connecticut or my publisher in Indiana? Who pays for this? My attack of inquisitiveness tended to vanish when the day's first email message or news flash came across my computer screen and sent my mind spinning off in other directions.

Where to Find It

Zen and the Art of the Internet, an electronic book: http://www.cs.indiana.edu/docproject/zen/zen-1.0_toc.html.

But, what I have discovered is an enlightening insight into a new kind of organization and distribution of information in the computer age.

In a nutshell, no single organization now "runs" the entire Internet. In the beginning, before it got so big and complex, the Department of Defense ran it, and after that, the National Science Foundation. Today, commercial interests have more and more influence over what goes on the Internet.

What Is the Internet?

Because I am an editor by trade I can't resist beginning by examining the word itself: "Inter-Net." My first guess was that it was an abbreviation for "International Network" or "Interconnected Networks." Actually, it comes from an Internetting Project in the early 1970s that studied how to link networks together. A *network* can be defined a number of ways. It can be:

- Two or more computers connected directly by cables, or indirectly, by phone lines.

- The users of those computers.

- The shared or commonly available information accessible to the connected users.

- As is the case with the Internet, all of the above.

The international aspect of the Internet is obvious: recent estimates are that the Internet includes more than 40 million users in nearly 100 different countries. But the notion of interconnected networks is the essential one because the Internet is not a single entity but a "network of networks." The original network, which was called ARPANet, was developed in 1969 for the Advanced Research Projects Agency of the U.S. Department of Defense (ARPA).

ARPANet

ARPANet connected university, military, and defense contractors; its original intent was to assist researchers in sharing information. Much of that information centered on how to develop a communications network that could still operate if part of it was destroyed by nuclear attack.

The idea was that every computer could talk to every other computer on the network by sending a packet of information using an Internet Protocol (IP). A *protocol* is a set of conventions that determines how data is relayed between different programs. After the user "addressed" the packet correctly, the computers themselves—not the users—had the responsibility of transmitting the information.

Where to Find It

Eff's (Extended) Guide to the Internet (formerly known as Big Dummy's Guide to the Internet), written by Adam Gaffin for the Electronic Frontier Foundation, includes a thoughtful introduction by Mitch Kapor: http://www.eff.org/papers/bdgtti/eegtti.html.

The Internet Companion, another electronic book: ftp://ftp.std.com/OBS/The.Internet.Companion/internet.companion.

Because the system was decentralized, if one part of the network was disconnected (presumably by a bomb), packets of information would still be sent along the rest of the network by the remaining computers.

Eventually, much of ARPANet's functions were taken over by the National Science Foundation Network (NSFNET), which linked researchers with five high-speed supercomputer centers. A standard protocol of choice was developed, TCP/IP, or Transmission Control Protocol/Internet Protocol. Because it was now possible for all sorts of computers to talk to each other, the Internet grew by leaps and bounds.

A Decentralized System

Although the Internet has become complex with many different networks connecting, the notion of decentralization remains central. This characteristic distinguishes it from commercial online services managed from the top by a single business.

A university administrator such as myself doesn't have to pay for being on the Internet, but the university does. Who runs the Internet? A governing board called the Internet Society (http://www.isoc.org/) appoints the Internet Architecture Board (IAB). We pay Advanced Network and Services, Inc. (now owned by America Online), which was created in 1990 to give structure to the NSFNet operation. Our campus computer department makes sure the university is connected.

Today the Internet includes standalone computers, local area networks in single offices, and large-scale regional networks connected to high-speed network backbones. For example, there's CERFnet, a commercial service; ESnet, run by the Department of Energy; and NSInet, run by the National Aeronautics and Space Administration. BITNET, FidoNet, and UUCP networks aren't "on" the Internet, but act as mail and file gateways to it.

The important thing for an online publisher to remember is that although it is simple to learn how to put our material "out there," we need to invest a little more time to understand the workings of the Internet. Because we are all interconnected, and because the system is so decentralized, we all depend on each other to be responsible about self-policing.

Where to Find It

For a timeline of some of the key events in Internet history, go to http://info.isoc.org/guest/zakon/Internet/History/HIT.html.

Where to Find It

CMC (Computer-Mediated Communication) Information Sources includes a list of pointers to resources about the Internet: http://www.rpi.edu/Internet/Guides/decemj/icmc/toc3.html.

Internet Services FAQ: ftp://rtfm.mit.edu/pub/usenet/news.answers/internet-services/faq.

A Brief History of the World Wide Web

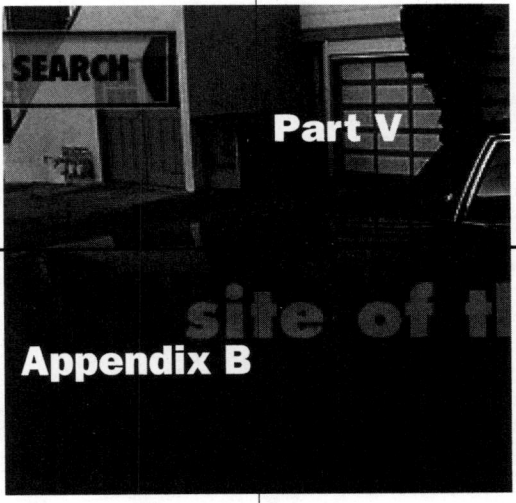

Whenever I'm exploring a new product or resource that I find particularly interesting, I find myself asking, "Who came up with the idea for this?" or, "What were they thinking of when they created this?" Despite the Internet's capability to distribute authorship among far-flung groups of people, I still find it comforting to think that one or two individuals "made" something, and that it has an identifiable "birthplace."

Where to Find It

A concise and clear explanation of the subject of online publishing by Tim Berners-Lee is available at http://www.w3.org/hypertext/WWW/Talks/OnlinePublishing93/Overview.html.

In contrast to the Internet, the "history" of the World Wide Web is relatively brief and straightforward. The Web has creators and it has a "home," and what's more, much of its development has been documented online. And for our purposes, electronic publishing was recognized early on by the Web's primary creator, Tim Berners-Lee, as one of its most important benefits.

What Is the World Wide Web?

The Web is

- A format, such as HTTP, HyperText Transfer Protocol, used to access information on the Internet.

- A way of presenting information with type, graphics, color, sound, and hypertextual links.

- A subset of the Internet that consists of files linked together by computers.

The Web was proposed in 1989 by Berners-Lee at CERN, the European Laboratory for Particle Physics in Switzerland. A more advanced proposal was put forth in 1990 by Berners-Lee and R. Cailliau.

Where to Find It

The official timeline for the development of the Web is at http://www.w3.org/hypertext/WWW/History.html.

The Web was originally envisioned as a tool to allow researchers access to information that resided in many different computers, each with its own distinct operating system and programming language. One computer might contain a database, another an address list, another a series of reports, and so on.

To get at the data without access to the Web, a researcher had to use a different search routine and be familiar with a different interface for each machine. Once the information was found, it was difficult to make a note or leave a "marker" to quickly retrace steps later.

474

Berners-Lee and Cailliau proposed a way of gaining access to all the information at the same time, with the capability to jump at will between one set of data to another. They decided to use hypertext.

Spinning the Web with Hypertext

Hypertext is a method for navigating through information in a nonlinear way. Information is joined by highlighted references known as "links." Clicking a link with a mouse or selecting it from a keyboard allows you to move from one place to another in a document, or from one document to another.

Once you've made a jump, you can either move back to your starting point or on to another link as specified by the programmer. (Another feature of hypertext, one which is implemented in the HyperCard presentation environment as developed by Bill Atkinson for the Macintosh in the 1980s, is that the programming language is easy to use and closely resembles written English.)

Hypertext provides a single user interface between many different types of information—text, graphics, databases, and so on. The networking of this information joined by hypertextual links was dubbed a "web" by Berners-Lee and Cailliau. This Web is not hierarchical; you don't have to move up to a root or top-level folder to climb down and move somewhere else. A small number of jumps enables you to get from the beginning to the end, or anywhere else in the document. It allows keyword searches, includes online help, and is available free of charge.

Navigating the Web with Browsers

All of these features were incorporated into the Web during its development, and the browser programs for navigating the Web include them as well. Development was rapid.

The first browser, known as "www," was completed at CERN in 1991 and released that May. The first demonstration was held at the Hypertext 1991 conference in San Antonio. More presentations, browsers, and development continued in 1992.

In 1993, the first alpha version of Mosaic was released by Marc Andreesen of the National Center for Supercomputing Applications (NCSA) at the University of Illinois.

In September 1993, NCSA released working versions of Mosaic for Macintosh, PC/ Windows, and X computers. In December, *The New York Times* included a one-and-one-half page article about Mosaic in its business section.

Between June 1993 and June 1994, Web traffic grew an astounding 2,500 percent. In July 1994, an agreement between MIT and CERN to start a W3 Organization received attention on the AP wire and other media. At that time there were 81 countries on the Internet and approximately 10,000 Web servers.

One example of the Web's growing importance took place in November 1994. During a strike blocking deliveries of both the *San Francisco Chronicle* and *San Francisco Examiner,* groups from both labor and management created electronic news reports and made them available on the Web.

A Web of Changes

As this book is being written, both the character and content of the Web are continuing to change rapidly. In particular, commercial concerns continue to grab a greater percentage of sites, and commercial online services are beginning to recognize the Web's growing importance by building their own Web browsers. America Online, in fact, announced that it would offer a standalone Internet service along with its commercial operation.

Three separate international conferences were scheduled to be held on the World Wide Web alone. And the way of displaying information on the Web was beginning to get more complex, as browsers began to support more HTML 3.0 elements, and some browsers began to display examples of VRML—Virtual Reality Markup Language.

How to Choose an
Internet Provider

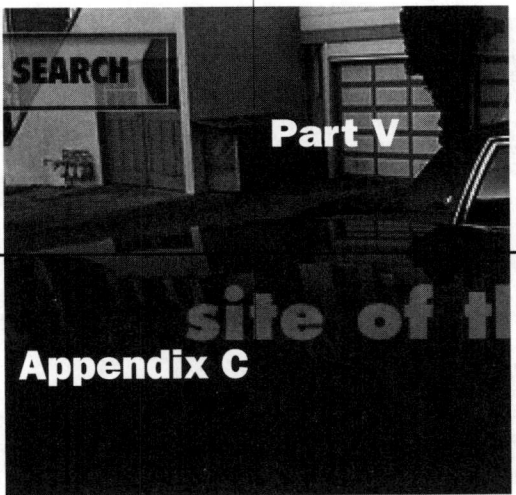

SEARCH

Part V

site of tl

Appendix C

The explosive growth of the Internet has attracted all kinds of companies interested in making profits by offering people a way to get on the Internet. Some of these are small businesses that had to borrow heavily to get started and that may face a financial crisis before too long, when their bank loans come due.

The emergence of telephone and cable companies offering faster connections than many of these providers means that some of the weaker concerns will not be around very long, however.

These are just a few reasons why you should choose an Internet provider carefully. Internet access is becoming an indispensable tool for many businesses, and being able to count on long-term, high-quality service is increasingly important to their financial health.

What Do You Need?

The criteria used to choose an Internet provider differs, depending on your needs. Those who want to dial up to the Net for personal or family use won't have requirements as elaborate as those who need to establish a business online.

The most important thing is to find a provider that's either close to home or that offers toll-free access, so you won't spend a fortune on telephone bills.

For personal use, a shell, SLIP, or PPP connection is adequate, but if you are starting up a commercial site or expect to have a heavy load of visitors, consider a leased line or 56kbps link. If you might have up to a hundred visitors at once, you might have to get one or more T1 lines or a much more expensive T3 link.

Types of Connections

Shell: The basic bare-bones connection to the Net running on top of a host's operating system, usually UNIX: for example, Lynx. It allows you access to Usenet, and allows you to send and receive email, FTP, telnet, gopher, and so on. However users of a shell account are not directly connected to the Internet and can't use applications (like Netscape) that require a direct Internet connection.

TIA (The Internet Adapter) and SLIP: TIA is an inexpensive commercial product that allows clients of an Internet provider's Web server to run a shell account as a SLIP account.

SLIP/PPP: If you're dialing up with a modem, SLIP (serial-line Internet protocol) or PPP (point-to-point protocol) access is the basic way for an individual to get connected to the Net. PPP is considered the better protocol. Both protocols provide a temporary direct Internet connection for the duration of the call.

Typically, basic service is about $20 per month for a limited number of hours, with $2 or so for each additional hour, with unlimited access costing around $30 per month.

Providers may charge more for 24-hour technical support seven days a week, but it will come in handy, especially in the beginning.

FTP: Offers you anonymous FTP space. FTP stands for File Transfer Protocol, a means of transmitting information on the Internet. Usually, users of FTP are prompted to enter a password. Anonymous FTP space on an Internet provider's server offers software or documentation to users who can connect as guests anonymously—without having to use a name or password.

LAN: Lets you connect a local area network to the Internet.

Where to Find It

A good essay on choosing an Internet provider is at http://www.tlg.org/how-to-select-ISP.html. Also check out http://www.man.net/Astra/provider.html.

WWW: Provides space and a server for publishing and maintaining Web pages.

ISDN: High-speed network connections that provide access to the Net via dial-up digital modems.

Leased lines: 56K, T1 through T3 lines that have high speed and high bandwidth. The price can run from $285 for the 56kbps line to over $800 for the faster links.

Technical Questions to Ask

Following are good questions to ask your potential provider:

1. How good is the network? How often does service go out? How susceptible is it to power outages, for instance? Ask to see a diagram that illustrates its *network topology*.

2. How fast is their connection to the network? Perhaps there is a T-3 connection at one place, but another 56kbps link between you and the site. That would make the T3 connection meaningless to you because your connection is only as fast as the lowest link in your path.

3. Do they have only one connection to the Internet? Several direct connections to other Internet providers serve as backups in case of trouble.

4. Are all of the connections in operation now, or are they promising something they plan to be capable of in the future?

5. Are they using the best equipment to bring you their service? Is it new or surplus?

6. How many people do they have on staff? Do they have several people who have experience running TCP/IP networks in case of trouble or if backups are needed?

7. Are staff people available nights, weekends, or holidays in case the system goes down?

8. How long have they been in the business? Try to gauge if they are in this for the long haul or are a fly-by-night operation.

9. Do they have an "Appropriate Use Policy" that users must observe?

10. Do they provide a full range of services, from low end to high end, in case you want to upgrade some day?

11. How many customers do they have? How many of those are actually connected?

Where to Find Commercial Internet Providers

The best places to start:

Primus Consulting's provider list: http://www.primus.com/staff/peggy/provider.html

Colossus's THE LIST™, sorted by area code: http://thelist.com/

POCIA (Providers of Commercial Internet Access): http://www2.celestin.com/pocia/

Yahoo's list: http://www.yahoo.com/Business/Corporations/Internet_Access_Providers/

General information:

http://gnn.com/gnn/helpdesk/access/index.html
http://www.rpi.edu/Internet/Guides/decemj/icmc/organizations-commercial-providers.html
http://helpdesk-www.cit.cornell.edu/IAP/INAccess.html

"Panel" page of major commercial providers: http://www.ncsa.uiuc.edu/SDG/IT94/Proceedings/Pub/hoffman/hoffman.html

Commercial networks (including CompuServe-like services):

http://sunsite.unc.edu/~masha/Commer2.html

Complete list of world servers:

ftp://nis.nsf.net/internet/providers/providers.around.the.world

Web Browsers for the Macintosh

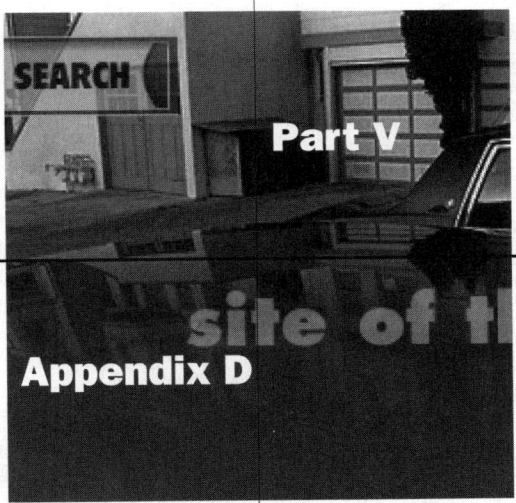

SEARCH

Part V

Appendix D

site of t

The list of browsers for the Macintosh doesn't look very long, but as long as you have Netscape, you don't need a lot of other options, IMHO :-).

All of the browsers in the "soon to be released" category had not yet come out with Macintosh versions as this book went to press. Be sure to check their home pages to get their status, because when they are available, they'll make the Web an even more exciting environment for Web publishers and readers alike.

Available Web Browsers

Enhanced Mosaic (Spyglass)

Address: http://www.spyglass.com/mos_home.html

(You can't really buy Enhanced Mosaic on its own; it comes bundled with other products. It runs faster than NCSA Mosaic.)

MacWeb (ElNet)

Address: http://www.einet.net/ElNet/MacWeb/MacWebHome.html

(A straightforward, reliable browser that doesn't take up quite as much disk space as the other programs.)

NCSA Mosaic for Macintosh

Address: http://www.ncsa.uiuc.edu/SDG/Software/MacMosaic/ MacMosaicHome.html

(The program that started all the excitement about the Web in spring 1994. An astonishingly innovative piece of work. It's slow, but unlike the other browsers, an early version actually runs on my PowerBook 100, the one with the old 68000 processor.)

Netscape Navigator

Address: http://www.netscape.com/info/how-to-get-it.html

(What's impressive, aside from the program itself, is the rate at which Netscape Communications continues to make new alliances and come out with new products. If you work at an educational institution, you can download Netscape free of charge.)

TCP/Connect II for Macintosh

Address: http://www.intercon.com/

TCP/Connect II for Macintosh, a fast and reliable Web browser is offered by InterCon Systems, and is the basis for America Online's Web browser. An upgraded version, WebShark, had not yet been released as this book went to press.

Samba

Address: http://www.w3.org/hypertext/WWW/Macintosh/Status.html

(An early and primitive Web browser created by CERN.)

Soon to be Released for the Mac

Where to Find It

Get the latest news about browsers, including latest releases and statistics, at Browser Watch: http://www.ski.mskcc.org/browserwatch/index.html.

HotJava (Sun Microsystems): http://java.sun.com/

WebSpace (Silicon Graphics): http://www.sgi.com/Products/WebFORCE/WebSpace/

HTML Elements

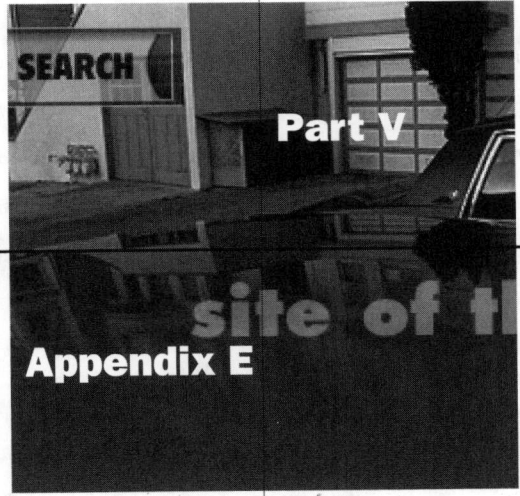

SEARCH

Part V

Appendix E

site of t

It's getting difficult to keep track of all the things you can do with HTML, whether they are elements included in HTML version 1.0 or 2.0, Netscape extensions, or proposed HTML 3.0 tags.

The table that follows attempts to bring together all of these categories of HTML elements. I've attempted to indicate, in the right column, which elements are either Netscape version 1.0N or 1.1N extensions (and thus, only recognized by Netscape and not Mosaic or other browsers), and which are included in HTML 3.0.

The HTML 3.0 elements are taken from the March 28, 1995 Internet draft. Because HTML 3.0 is still in the proposal stage, many of its elements are not yet supported by browsers, and their names may change.

Element	Description	Version
<!- - *TEXT* - ->	Comment (is not displayed by the browser)	2.0
<A HREF="URL">anchor text</A>	Link to URL	2.0
<A HREF="URL#identifier">anchor text</A>	Link to destination (in another document)	2.0
<A HREF="#identifier">anchor text</A>	Link to destination (in current document)	2.0
<A NAME="identifier">destination</A>	Identifies a named link destination	2.0
<A HREF="URL?*searchtext*"></A>	Send search (use a real question mark)	2.0
<ABBREV></ABBREV>	Used to mark up an abbreviation	3.0
<ACRONYM></ACRONYM>	Used to mark up an acronym	3.0
<ADDRESS></ADDRESS>	Return or email address	2.0
<AU></AU>	Author's name	3.0
<B></B>	Bold	2.0
<BANNER></BANNER>	Link to an external banner, masthead, or logo	3.0
<BASEFONT SIZE=*n*>	Specify base font size (*n* is from 1–7; default is 3)	N1.0
<BASE HREF="*URL*">	Specify base URL of this document (must be in header)	2.0
<BIG></BIG>	Bigger than normal text	3.0
<BLINK></BLINK>	Blinking	N1.0
<BLOCKQUOTE></BLOCKQUOTE>	Block indent	2.0
<BODY></BODY>	Specifies body of document	2.0
<BODY BGCOLOR="#*RRGGBB*">	Background color (order is red/green/blue)	N1.1
<BODY BACKGROUND="*URL*">	Background texture	N1.1
<BODY TEXT="#*RRGGBB*">	Text Color	N1.1
<BODY LINK="#*RRGGBB*">	Link Color	N1.1

Element	Description	Version
<BODY VLINK="#*RRGGBB*">	Visited Link Color	N1.1
<BODY ALINK="#*RRGGBB*">	Active Link Color	N1.1
 	Line break (a single carriage return)	2.0
<BR CLEAR=LEFTIRIGHTIALL>	Breaks line; text continues in clear margin	N1.0
<CAPTION></CAPTION>	Table Caption	3.0
<CAPTION ALIGN=TOPIBOTTOM>	Alignment (above or below table)	3.0
<CENTER></CENTER>	Center (for both text and images)	N1.0
<CITE></CITE>	Citation (usually italic)	2.0
<CODE></CODE>	Text to be displayed in computer code (usually monospace)	2.0
<DEL></DEL>	Denotes deleted text, as in legal documents	3.0
<DFN></DFN>	Definition	3.0
<DIR><LI></DIR>	Directory list	2.0
<DIV>	Division of a document	3.0
<DL><DT><DD></DL>	Definition List (<DT>=term, <DD>=definition)	2.0
<DD>	Definition	2.0
<DT>	Definition term	2.0
<EM></EM>	Emphasis (usually italic)	2.0
<FIG>	Specifies a figure	3.0
<FN>	Footnote	3.0
<FONT SIZE=*n*></FONT>	Font Size (*n* ranges from 1–7; default is 3)	N1.0
<FORM ACTION="URL" METHOD=GETIPOST></FORM>	Define form	2.0
<H*n*></H*n*>	Heading (*n* ranges from 1–6)	2.0
<H*n* ALIGN=LEFTICENTERIRIGHTINOWRAPICLEAR></H*n*>	Align heading	3.0
<HEAD></HEAD>	Head of HTML document	2.0
<HR>	Horizontal rule	2.0
<HR ALIGN=LEFTIRIGHTICENTER>	Aligns horizontal rule	N1.0

Element	Description	Version
<HR SIZE=*n*>	Thickness of horizontal rule (in pixels)	N1.0
<HR WIDTH=*n*>	Width of horizontal rule (in pixels)	N1.0
<HR WIDTH=%>	Width of horizontal rule (as a percentage of page width)	N1.0
<HR NOSHADE>	Draws solid black rule (without the 3-D shading)	N1.0
<HTML></HTML>	Document type (encloses an HTML document)	2.0
<HTML VERSION="*n*"></HTML>	*n* specifies HTML 3.0 or other version	3.0
<HTML URN= "*docname*"></HTML>	Specifies Universal Resource Name for document	3.0
<HTML ROLE= "*rolename*"></HTML>	Defines role of document (table of contents, and so on)	3.0
<I></I>	Italic	2.0
<IMG SRC="URL">	Displays image with this URL	2.0
<IMG SRC="URL" ALIGN=TOPI BOTTOMIMIDDLE>	Aligns image relative to text baseline	2.0
<IMG SRC="URL" ALIGN=LEFTIRIGHT>	Aligns image with text relative to page	N1.0, 3.0
<IMG SRC="URL" ALIGN=TEXTTOPI ABSMIDDLEIBASELINEIABSBOTTOM>	Aligns image relative to text	N1.0
<IMG SRC="URL" ALT="*alttext*">	Textual alternative (if image not displayed)	2.0
<IMG SRC="URL" ISMAP>	Image is a clickable imagemap	2.0
<IMG SRC="URL" WIDTH="*n*" HEIGHT="*n*">	Image dimensions (in pixels)	N1.0
<IMG SRC="URL" BORDER=*n*>	Image border (in pixels)	N1.0
<IMG SRC="URL" HSPACE=*n* VSPACE=*n*>	Text runaround space (in pixels)	N1.0
<IMG SRC="URL" LOWSRC="URL">	Specifies low-res version of image	N1.0
<INS></INS>	Denotes inserted text, as in legal documents	3.0
<ISINDEX>	Indicates a searchable index	2.0
<ISINDEX PROMPT="*inputtext*">	Specifies text to accompany input field	N1.0

Element	Description	Version
<INPUT TYPE="TEXT|PASSWORD|CHECKBOX|RADIO|SUBMIT|RESET">	Input field for HTML form	2.0 (for forms)
<INPUT NAME="*fieldname*">	Field name	2.0 (for forms)
<INPUT CHECKED>	Checked? (checkboxes and radio boxes)	2.0 (for forms)
<INPUT SIZE=*n*>	Field size (in characters)	2.0 (for forms)
<INPUT MAXLENGTH=*n*>	Max Length (in characters)	2.0 (for forms)
<KBD></KBD>	Keyboard style text	2.0
<LANG></LANG>	Changes language context	3.0
<LI>	List item	2.0
<LI TYPE=DISC|CIRCLE|SQUARE>	Defines bullet style for list items	N1.0
<LINK REV="*reldoc*" REL="*reldoc*" HREF="URL">	Relationship between current document and other documents or elements (must be in head section)	2.0
$$	Specifies mathematical equation	3.0
<MENU></MENU>	Menu list	2.0
<META>	Meta-info about document (must be in head)	2.0
<META HTTP=EQUIV="*name*">	Binds element to HTTP response header	3.0
<META HTTP=EQUIV="Refresh" CONTENT=*n*>	Refreshes content every *n* seconds	N1.1
<NEXTID>	Specifies numeric identifier (must be in head)	2.0
<NOBR>	Prevents line break	N1.0
<OL><LI></OL>	Ordered List (<LI> before each list item)	2.0
<OL COMPACT></OL>	Compact ordered list	3.0
<OL CONTINUE></OL>	Prevents renumbering of ordered list	3.0
<OL INHERIT></OL>	Inherits numbering from parent list	3.0
<OL SKIP></OL>	Skips a missing number in list	3.0

Element	Description	Version
<OL START></OL>	Starts numbering at specific number list	3.0
<OL TYPE=A|a|I|i|1>	Format of list items (caps, small, numerical, roman, or default)	N1.0
<LI TYPE=A|a|I|i|1>	Controls format of list item	N1.0
<OPTION>	Option (items that can be selected)	2.0 (for forms)
<OPTION SELECTED>	Default option	2.0 (for forms)
<P>	Paragraph return	2.0
<P></P>	Paragraph	3.0
<P ALIGN=LEFT|CENTER|RIGHT|NOWRAP|CLEAR></P>	Aligns text	3.0
<PERSON></PERSON>	Specifies proper name for indexing program	3.0
<PRE></PRE>	Preformatted (display text as-is)	2.0
<PRE WIDTH=n></PRE>	Width of preformatted text (in characters)	2.0
<Q></Q>	In-line quotation	3.0
<RANGE>	Marks a range of the document (for searching)	3.0
	Subscript text	3.0
	Superscript text	3.0
<STRIKE></STRIKE>	Strikethrough text	3.0
<SAMP></SAMP>	Sample text	2.0
<SELECT></SELECT>	Selection list	2.0 (for forms)
<SELECT NAME="*listname*"></SELECT>	Name of list	2.0 (for forms)
<SELECT SIZE=n></SELECT>	n=number of options	2.0 (for forms)
<SELECT MULTIPLE>	Multiple choice (can select more than one)	2.0 (for forms)
<SMALL></SMALL>	Smaller than normal text	3.0

Element	Description	Version
<STRONG></STRONG>	Strong emphasis (usually displayed as bold)	2.0
<STYLE></STYLE>	Overrides standard style sheet	3.0
<TAB ID=*name*>	Establishes tab stop (and specifies tab stop name)	3.0
<TAB TO=*name*>	Designates tab stop (and refers to tab stop name)	3.0
<TABLE></TABLE>	Defines table	3.0
<TABLE BORDER></TABLE>	Table border (on or off)	3.0
<TABLE BORDER=*n*></TABLE>	Table border (width of table border)	N1.1
<TABLE CELLSPACING=*n*>	Cell spacing	N1.1
<TABLE CELLPADDING=*n*>	Cell padding	N1.1
<TABLE WIDTH=*n*>	Desired width (in pixels)	N1.1
<TABLE WIDTH=%>	Width percent (percentage of page)	N1.1
<TD></TD>	Table cell (must appear within table rows)	3.0
<TD ALIGN=LEFT|RIGHT|CENTER VALIGN=TOP|MIDDLE|BOTTOM>	Alignment	3.0
<TD NOWRAP>	No linebreaks	3.0
<TD COLSPAN=*n*>	Columns to span	3.0
<TD ROWSPAN=*n*>	Rows to span	3.0
<TD WIDTH=*n*>	Desired width (in pixels)	N1.1
<TD WIDTH=%>	Width percent (percentage of table)	N1.1
<TEXTAREA ROWS=*n* COLS=*n*></TEXTAREA>	Input box size	2.0 (for forms)
<TEXTAREA NAME="*boxname*"></TEXTAREA>	Name of box	2.0 (for forms)
<TH></TH>	Table header	3.0 (for tables)
<TH ALIGN=LEFT|RIGHT|CENTER VALIGN=TOP|MIDDLE|BOTTOM>	Alignment	3.0 (for tables)
<TH NOWRAP>	No linebreaks	3.0 (for tables)

Element	Description	Version
<TH COLSPAN=*n*>	Columns to span	3.0 (for tables)
<TH ROWSPAN=*n*>	Rows to span	3.0 (for tables)
<TH WIDTH=*n*>	Desired width (in pixels)	N1.1 (for tables)
<TH WIDTH=%>	Width percent (percentage of table)	N1.1 (for tables)
<TITLE></TITLE>	Title (document name; must be in header)	2.0

The following TR tags are related to creating HTML tables:

Element	Description	Version
<TR></TR>	Table row	3.0 (for tables)
<TR ALIGN=LEFT|RIGHT|CENTER VALIGN=TOP|MIDDLE|BOTTOM>	Alignment	3.0 (for tables)
<TT></TT>	Typewriter (display in a monospaced font)	2.0
<U></U>	Underline (not widely implemented yet)	3.0
<UL><LI></UL>	Unordered List (<LI> before each list item)	2.0
<UL COMPACT></UL>	Compact version of unordered list	3.0
<UL TYPE=DISC|CIRCLE|SQUARE>	Specifies bullet style	N1.0
<VAR></VAR>	Variable text	2.0
<WBR>	Forces word break within <NOBR> element	N1.0

The Bare Bones Guide to HTML, maintained by Kevin Werbach, presents HTML elements arranged by function rather than in alphabetical order. It's at http://www. access.digex.net/~werbach/barebone.html.

ISO-Latin 1

Character Entities

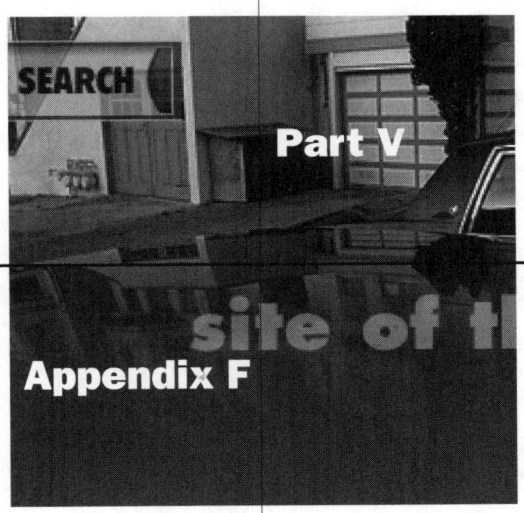

HTML allows you to display special characters in a Web document by typing a *character entity reference* for each one. The characters supported by HTML correspond to the ISO-Latin 1 character set, which appears in the following table. The characters themselves are shown, when possible.

Character entity references do not exist for all valid characters. As an alternative, there are numerical references. The numerical reference of any ISO-Latin 1 character is &***; where *** is the decimal code of the character. But because the numerical references are translated as ASCII values, the way the character is displayed may vary widely depending on the computer or browser. For that reason, it's best to use character entities whenever possible.

> **Note:** All browsers cannot display all characters. In some cases, special fonts may be required. Try them out on several browsers before putting your page on the Web.

Alphabetical by Character

Character	Character Entity	Description
Æ	&AElig;	Capital AE dipthong (ligature)
Á	&Aacute;	Capital A, acute accent
Â	&Acirc;	Capital A, circumflex accent
À	&Agrave;	Capital A, grave accent
Å	&Aring;	Capital A, ring
Ã	&Atilde;	Capital A, tilde
Ä	&Auml;	Capital A, dieresis or umlaut mark
Ç	&Ccedil;	Capital C, cedilla
É	&Eacute;	Capital E, acute accent
Ê	&Ecirc;	Capital E, circumflex accent
È	&Egrave;	Capital E, grave accent
Ë	&Euml;	Capital E, dieresis or umlaut mark
Í	&Iacute;	Capital I, acute accent
Î	&Icirc;	Capital I, circumflex accent
Ì	&Igrave;	Capital I, grave accent

ISO-Latin 1 Character Entities

Ï	&Iuml;	Capital I, dieresis or umlaut mark
Ñ	&Ntilde;	Capital N, tilde
Ó	&Oacute;	Capital O, acute accent
Ô	&Ocirc;	Capital O, circumflex accent
Ò	&Ograve;	Capital O, grave accent
Ø	&Oslash;	Capital O, slash
Õ	&Otilde;	Capital O, tilde
Ö	&Ouml;	Capital O, dieresis or umlaut mark
Ú	&Uacute;	Capital U, acute accent
Û	&Ucirc;	Capital U, circumflex accent
Ù	&Ugrave;	Capital U, grave accent
Ü	&Uuml;	Capital U, dieresis or umlaut mark
á	&aacute;	Small a, acute accent
â	&acirc;	Small a, circumflex accent
æ	&aelig;	Small ae dipthong (ligature)
à	&agrave;	Small a, grave accent
å	&aring;	Small a, ring
ã	&atilde;	Small a, tilde
ä	&aauml;	Small a, dieresis or umlaut mark
ç	&ccedil;	Small c, cedilla
é	&eacute;	Small e, acute accent
ê	&ecirc;	Small e, circumflex accent
è	&egrave;	Small e, grave accent
ë	&euml;	Small e, dieresis or umlaut mark
í	&iacute;	Small i, acute accent
î	&icirc;	Small i, circumflex accent

Character	Character Entity	Description
ì	&igrave;	Small i, grave accent
ï	&iuml;	Small i, dieresis or umlaut mark
ñ	&ntilde;	Small n, tilde
ó	&oacute;	Small o, acute accent
ô	&ocirc;	Small o, circumflex accent
ò	&ograve;	Small o, grave accent
ø	&oslash;	Small o, slash
õ	&otilde;	Small o, tilde
ö	&ouml;	Small o, dieresis or umlaut mark
ß	&szlig;	Small sharp s, German (sz ligature)
ú	&uacute;	Small u, acute accent
û	&ucirc;	Small u, circumflex accent
ù	&ugrave;	Small u, grave accent
ü	&uuml;	Small u, dieresis or umlaut mark
ÿ	&yuml;	Small y, dieresis or umlaut mark

Numerical Entities

Character	Numerical Entity	Description
	&#00;–&#08;	Unused
	&#09;	Horizontal tab
	&#10;	Line feed
	&#11;–&#31;	Unused
	&#32;	Space
!	&#33;	Exclamation mark
"	&#34;	Quotation mark

#	#	Number sign
$	$	Dollar sign
%	%	Percent sign
&	&	Ampersand
'	'	Apostrophe
(	(	Left parenthesis
)	)	Right parenthesis
*	*	Asterisk
+	+	Plus sign
,	,	Comma
-	-	Hyphen
.	.	Period (fullstop)
/	/	Solidus (slash)
0–9	0–9	Digits 0–9
:	:	Colon
;	;	Semicolon
<	<	Less than
=	=	Equal sign
>	>	Greater than
?	?	Question mark
@	@	Commercial at
A–Z	#65;–Z	Letters A–Z
[	[	Left square bracket
\	\	Reverse solidus (backslash)
]	]	Right square bracket
^	^	Caret

Character	Numerical Entity	Description
_	&#95;	Horizontal bar (underscore)
`	&#96;	Grave accent
a–z	a–z	Letters a–z
{	&#123;	Left curly brace
|	|	Vertical bar
	&#125;	Right curly brace
~	&#126;	Tilde

 **Warning:** Be careful if you use any of the following numerical entities, as the display can vary widely depending on the browsers and computers being used. Be sure to test them thoroughly before going online.

Character	Numerical Entity	Description
	&#127;–	Unused
¡	&#161;	Inverted exclamation
¢	&#162;	Cent sign
£	&#163;	Pound sterling
¤	&#164;	General currency sign
¥	&#165;	Yen sign
¦	&#166;	Broken vertical bar
§	&#167;	Section sign
¨	&#168;	Umlaut (dieresis)
©	&#169;	Copyright
ª	&#170;	Feminine ordinal
«	&#171;	Left angle quote
¬	&#172;	Not sign
–	&#173;	Soft hyphen
®	&#174;	Registered trademark

ISO-Latin 1 Character Entities

‾	&#175;	Macron accent
°	&#176;	Degree sign
±	&#177;	Plus or minus
²	&#178;	Superscript two
³	&#179;	Superscript three
´	&#180;	Acute accent
µ	&#181;	Micro sign
¶	&#182;	Paragraph sign
·	&#183;	Middle dot
¸	&#184;	Cedilla
¹	&#185;	Superscript one
º	&#186;	Masculine ordinal
»	&#187;	Right angle quote
¼	&#188;	Fraction one-fourth
½	&#189;	Fraction one-half
¾	&#190;	Fraction three-fourths
¿	&#191;	Inverted question mark
À	&#192;	Capital A, grave accent
Á	&#193;	Capital A, acute accent
Â	&#194;	Capital A, circumflex accent
Ã	&#195;	Capital A, tilde
Ä	&#196;	Capital A, dieresis or umlaut mark
Å	&#197;	Capital A, ring
Æ	&#198;	Capital AE dipthong (ligature)
Ç	&#199;	Capital C, cedilla
È	&#200;	Capital E, grave accent

Character	Numerical Entity	Description
É	&#201;	Capital E, acute accent
Ê	&#202;	Capital E, circumflex accent
Ë	&#203;	Capital E, dieresis or umlaut mark
Ì	&#204;	Capital I, grave accent
Í	&#205;	Capital I, acute accent
Î	&#206;	Capital I, circumflex accent
Ï	&#207;	Capital I, dieresis or umlaut mark
Ñ	&#209;	Capital N, tilde
Ò	&#210;	Capital O, grave accent
Ó	&#211;	Capital O, acute accent
Ô	&#212;	Capital O, circumflex accent
Õ	&#213;	Capital O, tilde
Ö	&#214;	Capital O, dieresis or umlaut mark
×	&#215;	Multiply sign
Ø	&#216;	Capital O, slash
Ù	&#217;	Capital U, grave accent
Ú	&#218;	Capital U, acute accent
Û	&#219;	Capital U, circumflex accent
Ü	&#220;	Capital U, dieresis or umlaut mark
ß	&#223;	Small sharp s, German (sz ligature)
à	&#224;	Small a, grave accent
á	&#225;	Small a, acute accent
â	&#226;	Small a, circumflex accent
ã	&#227;	Small a, tilde

ISO-Latin 1 Character Entities

ä	&#228;	Small a, dieresis or umlaut mark
å	&#229;	Small a, ring
æ	&#230;	Small ae dipthong (ligature)
ç	&#231;	Small c, cedilla
è	&#232;	Small e, grave accent
é	&#233;	Small e, acute accent
ê	&#234;	Small e, circumflex accent
ë	&#235;	Small e, dieresis or umlaut mark
ì	&#236;	Small i, grave accent
í	&#237;	Small i, acute accent
î	&#238;	Small i, circumflex accent
ï	&#239;	Small i, dieresis or umlaut mark
ñ	&#241;	Small n, tilde
ò	&#242;	Small o, grave accent
ó	&#243;	Small o, acute accent
ô	&#244;	Small o, circumflex accent
õ	&#245;	Small o, tilde
ï	&#246;	Small o, dieresis or umlaut mark
÷	&#247;	Division sign
ø	&#248;	Small o, slash
ù	&#249;	Small u, grave accent
ú	&#250;	Small u, acute accent
û	&#251;	Small u, circumflex accent
ü	&#252;	Small u, dieresis or umlaut mark
ÿ	&#255;	Small y, dieresis or umlaut mark

In addition to those listed previously, HTML 3.0 proposes recognition of character entities for new symbols, including:

** ** for an em space

** ** for an en space

— for an em dash

– for an en dash

** ** for a non-breaking space

­ for a soft hyphen

Note: Netscape recognizes two nonstandard character entities that come in handy when making a copyright notice on an HTML document:

® = Registered Trademark = ®
© = Copyright = ©

Glossary

SEARCH

Part V

site of t

Appendix G

A

Absolute path name: A detailed and explicit way of locating a file or device on a network by starting with the name of the computer on which the object or file resides, and then listing any intermediate folders or directories, thus ending with the name of the file or object. For example, <http://upubs-71.uchicago.edu/wwwbook/appendixes/glossary.html>.

Acrobat: Portable document software developed by Adobe Systems, Inc. It allows a user to save a file as read-only and to allow any number of users to view the file with the free reader utility. Users cannot change text.

Address: The location of a computer, file, or other object on a network (as in FTP address).

Aiff: A type of sound file format.

America Online: Commercial online service.

Anchor: A hyperlink created in an HTML document. For example: <A HREF="http://www.mycomputer.com/files/doc.html">Clickable text goes here</A>. (See *Hyperlink*.)

Andreessen, Marc: Vice president of technology for Netscape Communications. He came up with the idea for the NCSA Mosaic graphical browser interface for the World Wide Web while a student at the University of Illinois in 1992.

Anonymous FTP: FTP (File Transfer Protocol) is a common way to connect to a network, access directories, or obtain files. It uses TCP/IP commands, and usually requires a username and a password. Anonymous FTP allows users to use FTP as a "guest" and without a password, i.e., anonymously.

Arachnid: An HTML authoring program developed at the University of Iowa that operates in a WYSIWYG (What You See Is What You Get) environment.

ASCII: American Standard Code for Information Interchange. Pronounced "ask-ee." Computers don't know what letters or numbers are; they recognize only bits of information—zeros and ones. ASCII is binary code that represents characters. It allows computers to display, transmit, and print textual information.

ATM: Asynchronous Transfer Mode. One of the fastest ways of transferring information, using high-speed cell switching network technology. Works for both LANs and WANs. Fast enough to handle real-time voice and video. Not yet widely used.

AU: A type of sound file format used frequently on the Web.

B

Bandwidth: The capacity of a computer channel or data transmission cable, often expressed in bits or bytes per second.

Bin: Abbreviation for binary. Binary means "made up of two parts." All input to a computer is binary, made up of combinations of 0 and 1 data bits. Binary is also a techie term for a computer program. "Bin" is often used in "cgi-bin," a commonly used name for a folder/directory where binary files such as CGIs are stored.

Binhex: A method of encoding files from 8-bit to 7-bit format while preserving file attributes.

Bitmap: A binary representation of a graphic object created by translating the object into "pixels." Pixels are computerized "dots," each of which represents a binary bit of information. In a black-and-white bitmap, for instance, white is "on" and black is "off."

Bookmark: A marked address for a location on the Internet that many browsers allow the user to record and save on a list or pull-down menu. Allows quick access to the site.

Browser: A program designed to read HTML files and retrieve and display information on the World Wide Web. Also called a client. *Graphical browsers* have the capacity to display images, colors, and other graphic elements. *Non-graphical browsers* display textual information but not graphics. (See *Netscape Navigator* and *Mosaic*.)

BTW: By the way, an acronym commonly used in email and on the Internet.

C

CERN: The European Laboratory for Particle Physics, where the World Wide Web was created.

CGI: Common Gateway Interface. A standard interface between a Web server and an external (or "gateway") program such as a Web browser. A program that handles a request for information and returns information or performs a search or other routine. Can be written in a number of programs—on the Mac, most CGIs are written in MacPerl or AppleScript.

Character styles: HTML tags used to add emphasis to specific words, rather than paragraphs, such as <B> </B> for bold, <I> </I> for italic, and so on.

Client: A synonym for browser. A program that reads and navigates through the Web and retrieves files. (See *browser*.)

Cobweb site: A Web site that has not been updated for a substantial length of time and whose contents are obviously out of date. It is considered bad form to let your site become a "cobweb site."

Codaphobe: Someone who isn't comfortable with writing, reading, or otherwise dealing directly with computer code (also called a techno-phobe).

Common Ground: Portable document software developed by Common Ground Software. It allows a user to save a file as read-only and to allow any number of users to view the file with the free reader utility. Users cannot change text.

CompuServe: One of the bigger commercial online systems.

Copyright: The right of authors to control, for a limited time, the reproduction, adaptation, distribution, and other treatment of their work(s) of intellectual property.

Cyberspace: A term originally used in the novel *Neuromancer* by William Gibson to describe a computer network of the future that can be connected directly to peoples' minds. Now represents the Internet and/or the Web.

D

DNS: Can stand for 1) Domain Name System, 2) Domain Name Service, 3) Domain Name Server. (See *domain name system or service* and *domain name*.)

Domain name: A textual alias for an IP address based on the domain name system. Components of a domain name are separated by a period. For example, an IP address for a computer might be 197.99.87.99; it might then have several aliases, one of which is www.mycomputer.com.

Domain name server: A computer that keeps track of addresses in a given organization or domain and routes requests to specific addresses.

Domain name system or service: A way of distributing information worldwide across the Internet so that no one computer, person, or organization has to keep track of everyone in the world. Instead, computers are assigned standard types of names

depending on their domain, and domain name servers share information about their specific area with other computers. Computers in educational institutions are given names ending in the suffix .EDU, governmental offices have the suffix .GOV, commercial ones end in .COM, and so on.

E

External image: An image that is not an inline image and thus part of an HTML document, but that resides in a separate file and is accessed by means of a hypertext link.

F

Fair use: A legal doctrine by which courts can avoid rigid application of copyright law when a work is reproduced for purposes of comment, criticism, news reporting, teaching, scholarship, or research.

FAQ: Frequently Asked Questions. FAQs are often seen as sections of Web sites or as updated files posted to newsgroups or servers. They answer the most common questions on a certain topic. It's considered poor form to ask a question that's covered in a FAQ.

Flame: A "heated" message from a fellow surfer in regards to a breach of "nettiquette" on your part.

Font: A set of characters that, together, makes up a typeface such as Times or Helvetica.

Frame relay: High-speed packet switching protocol suited for data image transfer. Used with WANs (Wide Area Networks). Not the most efficient way of transmitting real-time voice and video. (See *ATM*.)

Freeware: Software created by independent technoids and available to users free of charge by downloading it from the Internet or from local areas. (See *shareware*.)

FTP: File Transfer Protocol, a method for transferring files to and from remote computers on the Internet. (See *Anonymous FTP*.)

G

GIF: Graphics Interchange Format, a file format commonly used with graphics or photos displayed on Web documents.

Gopher: A text-only, menu-driven Internet information system developed at the University of Minnesota that preceded the Web. It's still very common, and most Web browsers can connect to gopher servers.

Grep: 1) A UNIX search command; 2) a search utility; 3) a verb referring to scanning or searching anything for information.

H

Hit counter: A script on a Web server that calculates each "hit" or visit to a Web page every time a connection is made, and displays the current total on the page to the current user.

Home page: The welcome page of a Web site, the place where visitors are supposed to start when finding out about an organization or personal Web.

HotJava: Dynamic Web browser developed by Sun Microsystems, Inc. that uses Sun's Java programming language. HotJava can execute "applets" or programs written in Java that can be included in HTML documents.

HREF link: See *anchor* or *hyperlink*.

HTML: HyperText Markup Language, the set of commands used to mark up documents with standard elements so they can be displayed and read on the World Wide Web by different browsers on different computers. A subset of SGML, Standard Generalized Markup Language.

HTML cookie: (Also called the HTML tag.) The tag "set" that makes up a complete HTML markup command. For example, in <B>Attention!</B>, the <B> </B> is the cookie.

HTTP: HyperText Transport Protocol, the protocol used by Web servers to communicate with Web clients.

HyperCard: A multimedia presentation environment that has hypertext capability, allows scripting or coding of applications, interprets data, and has a number of other characteristics that make it hard to define. Created by Bill Atkinson in the 1980s.

Hyperlink: Also called an anchor. A link in an HTML document, usually distinguished by underlined or highlighted text that, when selected, takes the user to another file or Web page. The hypertext link is added to the document by using the HTML tag, <A HREF> </A>.

I

IETF: Internet Engineering Task Force, the community of Internet users that determines how the Internet will evolve and operate. Most of its technical operations are conducted in workgroups. Maintains two types of Internet documents, Internet-Drafts and Requests for Comments (RFCs).

IMHO: In My Humble Opinion, an acronym commonly used in email and on the Internet.

IMO: In My Opinion, an acronym commonly used in email and on the Internet.

Inline image: A photo or graphic image that can be displayed in the window of a Web browser along with HTML text (as opposed to an external image, which must be downloaded and viewed with a separate program).

Interlaced GIF: An extra step in the information process that allows you in three or more passes to display increasing amounts of information, in quantum leaps, instead of just one line or another. Displays a low-resolution version first, a better version next, and then a full-blown version

Internet: An international network of networks, originally started for military purposes, that connects about 40 million higher education, government, military, and commercial users.

IP: Internet Protocol. The set of standards by which information is transmitted on the Internet.

ISDN: Integrated Services Digital Network. A set of standards for transmitting voice, data, and video data simultaneously. A reasonably inexpensive way of getting higher bandwidth through a digital connection.

ISO: International Standards Organization. A group that defines computing and communications standards.

J

JPEG: Joint Photographic Experts Group, a graphic image compression format.

Where to Find It

A fascinating summary of the cult of Kibo can be found at http://www.shadow.net/~proub/net.legends/kibo.html.

K

Kibo: An Internet deity. The word itself is the middle name of James "Kibo" Parry, who "greps" or searches the entire Usenet community for any messages containing the word Kibo. He is revered as a god by his own newsgroup, alt. religion.kibology.

L

LAN: Local Area Network. A network usually associated with a single office, building, or organization.

M

MacTCP: Apple Computer software that allows a Macintosh to interact with other computers via TCP/IP.

MIME: Multiple Internet Mail Extensions. A way of identifying files in which the initial packet of information received by a client contains information about the file that the server sent.

Modem: Short for MOdulator/DEModulator. A device that connects a computer to a phone line. It converts the computer's digital signals to analog audio frequencies so they can be transmitted over phone lines.

Mosaic: A graphical information browser for the World Wide Web developed at NCSA (See *NCSA*). Its user-friendly interface was instrumental in the Web's popularity.

MPEG: Moving Pictures Experts Group, a movie file format commonly used on the Web.

N

NCSA: National Center for Supercomputing Applications at the University of Illinois at Urbana-Champaign. An interdisciplinary group consisting of scientists, artists, engineers, educators, and others involved in computational science. The place where NCSA Mosaic was born.

Netscape Navigator: A fast, easy-to-use graphical information browser for the World Wide Web that was developed by some of the same people who created Mosaic. Created by Netscape Communications Corporation.

Newbie: A newcomer, someone just getting started on the Internet.

NSFNet: National Science Foundation Network, which linked researchers with high-speed supercomputer centers. For a while, this was the "backbone" of the Internet.

P

Parser: A module or routine within a program that reads or "parses" computer code and processes it to make it usable or readable.

PDF: Page Description Format in which documents created with Adobe Acrobat portable document software are presented. Acrobat documents end with the suffix .PDF.

Photoshop: Common parlance for Adobe Photoshop, image-editing software that allows a number of sophisticated graphics functions such as retouching and editing of images on personal computers.

PostScript: A page description/programming language developed by Adobe Systems Inc. It describes a page in a way that is device independent, so that the quality of the output depends on the resolution of the device on which it is printed.

Protocol: A specific method of communication or "conversation" for exchanging information on the Internet. SMTP, FTP, HTTP, and NNTP are all protocols.

Q–R

QuickTime: A method developed by Apple Computer for storing movie and audio files in digital format.

RFC: Request for Comments, the agreed-upon designation by which all methods of communicating over the Internet, such as the various versions of HTML, are developed and defined.

Robot: A program such as InfoSeek or Aliweb that searches huge numbers of files automatically when given search criteria (also called a worm).

S

SGML: Standard Generalized Markup Language, an agreed-upon international standard for specifying and marking up documents. HTML is a subset of SGML.

Shareware: Software created by independent technoids and available for downloading to anyone for a trial time. At the end of that time, users are asked to pay a fee if they decide to keep the software. (See *freeware*.)

Silicon Graphics (SGI): Silicon Graphics, Inc., a manufacturer of computer hardware and software, including the Indy workstation. Actively exploring virtual reality applications on the Web. (See *VRML*.)

SLIP: Serial Line Internet Protocol. A way of using TCP/IP over a serial line, such as a dialup modem. A very common way of connecting to the Internet from home. Often referred to as a point-to-point connection. Also lovingly referred to as "slirp."

Spam: 1) A tinned pork product whose letters are an acronym for Spiced Pork and Ham. Spam was immortalized in a routine by the British comedy troupe Monty Python in which the word "Spam" was repeated over and over by a waitress reading off a menu. On the Internet, Spam has come to mean a particular repetitious or bandwidth-consuming act of absolutely no redeeming value. 2) To send an unsolicited advertising message across the Internet to huge numbers of newsgroups. The most famous practitioners are Laurence A. Canter and Martha S. Siegel, who were bombarded by complaints for an ad for their "Green Card Lottery."

Spork: A plastic knife and fork set. For some reason, these are a source of fascination on the Internet.

Sun: Sun Microsystems, Inc., a company that makes high-performance workstations and servers using its SPARC architecture. Its Solaris operating system is based on UNIX.

T

TCP/IP: Transmission Control Protocol/Internet Protocol, a packet-based communication protocol that forms the foundation of the Internet.

TIA: Stands for The Internet Adapter, not Thanks In Advance. An inexpensive commercial product offered by Cyberspace Development, Inc. for an Internet service provider's UNIX Web server that allows a user of that server to run a basic shell account as if it were a more powerful SLIP account.

TIFF: Tagged Image File Format, a format for storing computerized image files.

Transparent GIF: A GIF image that appears to float directly atop a Web page without its own background or border. A specific number in the GIF color palette (#89) is assigned to be the same color as the background of the page, giving the image a transparent appearance.

U–W

UNIX: A multiuser/multitasking operating system developed by AT&T and written in the C programming language (also developed by AT&T). Its TCP/IP protocols are integral to the Internet.

URL: Uniform Resource Locator. A standard address for a file or location on the Internet. URLs always begin with an Internet protocol (FTP, gopher, HTTP), an Internet host name, folders, and the destination file or object.

VRML: Virtual Reality Modeling Language (VRML; sometimes pronounced "vur-mole"). It has been proposed as a standard way of describing virtual reality experiences accessed via the Internet and integrated with the hypertextual power of the Web.

WAIS: Wide Area Information Server, a powerful text retrieval engine that allows full text searches of massive databases via the Internet.

WAN: Wide Area Network. A communications system that spans great distances, as opposed to a LAN.

Web document: A general term for a single file's worth of information published on the Web. (Also called a Web page.)

Web server: A computer set up to exchange information with another computer over the Internet using one or more standard protocols, such as HTTP, FTP, gopher, and so on.

Web site: Either the server that sets up documents on the Web, or a set of documents produced by a single publisher.

World Wide Web, WWW, W3: A subset of the Internet that allows hypertextual navigation and multimedia presentation of information globally.

Index

Symbols

A

J–K–L

M

N

T

Fmpro.acgi, 201

FMProCGI, 201

Gateway Quark to HTML converter, 262

GIFConverter 2.3.7, 385

GIFServ, 201

graphics converters, 384-386

HTML authoring assistants, 254-261

NetCloak, 202

PageMaker WebSucker HTML converter, 262

Quark to HTML converter (version 1.0 beta), 263

rtftohtml HTML converter, 245-248

rtftoweb HTML converter, 248-249

TR-WWW, 202

Transparency 1.0 graphic converter, 385

see also software

V

validation/checking services (HTML), 263-266

<VALUE> attribute (<INPUT> HTML tag), 192-193

<VAR> (HTML tag), 138

video files, adding to Web pages, 389

virtual communities, 430

virtual reality, 459-461

VRML (Virtual Reality Modeling Language), 460, 515

W

WAIS (Wide Area Information Servers), 515

WANs (wide area networks), 515

<WBR> (line break HTML tag), 129

Web pages, *see* home pages; WWW sites

Web, *see* WWW

Weblink PDF software, 289

Webmasters, 20

WebSpace home page, 461

WebSpace VRML browser, 461

WebSpace Web browser, 485

white space, inserting in HTML documents, 135

windows (Web browsers), 75-76

Wired magazine, 41

word processing files, converting to HTML, 244-249

World Wide Web, *see* WWW

worms (HTML documents), 119

<WRAP> (HTML tag), 232

WWW (World Wide Web), 516

  advertising on, 406-418

  browsers, 475-476, 484-485, 507

    HotJava, 462-463

    lesson windows, 75

    preview windows, 75

    windows, navigating, 76

  future development, 464

  graphics, 96

  hands-on-applications, 25-26

  history, 474-476

  impact on publishing industry, 24-25

  Internet connections, 479

  IRCs, 60

  jargon file, 430

  netiquette, 430-431

  online marketing, 420-425

  resource home page, 63

  servers, 516

    cost, 344

    Internet connections, 22-24

    IP addresses, 24

    Macintosh, 22

    setup, 18-24

    software, 23

  software documentation, 76

  user statistics, 423

  vs. online services, 16

WWW sites, 516

  1-800 number directory, 415

  acronyms, 330

  announcing online, 432

  AT&T Stories, 414

  Bare Bones Guide to HTML, 494

Y–Z

PLUG YOURSELF INTO...

THE MACMILLAN INFORMATION SUPERLIBRARY™

Free information and vast computer resources from the world's leading computer book publisher—online!

FIND THE BOOKS THAT ARE RIGHT FOR YOU!

A complete online catalog, plus sample chapters and tables of contents give you an in-depth look at *all* of our books, including hard-to-find titles. It's the best way to find the books you need!

- **STAY INFORMED** with the latest computer industry news through our online newsletter, press releases, and customized Information SuperLibrary Reports.

- **GET FAST ANSWERS** to your questions about MCP books and software.

- **VISIT** our online bookstore for the latest information and editions!

- **COMMUNICATE** with our expert authors through e-mail and conferences.

- **DOWNLOAD SOFTWARE** from the immense MCP library:
  - Source code and files from MCP books
  - The best shareware, freeware, and demos

- **DISCOVER HOT SPOTS** on other parts of the Internet.

- **WIN BOOKS** in ongoing contests and giveaways!

TO PLUG INTO MCP: →

GOPHER: gopher.mcp.com
FTP: ftp.mcp.com

WORLD WIDE WEB: **http://www.mcp.com**

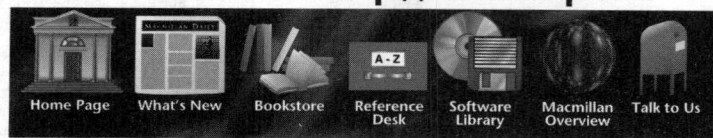